RETURN OF THE FATHERS

by

William Kitchin

Dedication

To Nanny & Daddy

To Rebecca, Jennifer, and Katie

And To Beverly, My Beloved Life Partner

Characters

Peter Randolph Thomas Jefferson; cloned in GeneVision California facility

Joe (Josiah) Folger Benjamin Franklin; cloned in GeneVision St. John facility

Augustine Ball George Washington; cloned in GeneVision Atlanta facility

Jim Fawcett Alexander Hamilton; cloned in GeneVision Ohio facility

Andrew Jacobs Director, GeneVision-CA; Raised Peter Randolph

Phil Security guard at GeneVision-CA

Marina Novokatnaia CEO GeneVision; member of the White House Bioethics Panel

James Durango Director, Special Projects at GeneVision-CA

Marta Norman Security guard at GeneVision-CA

Dave Security Guard at GeneVision-CA

Hans Meier Director GeneVision-Ohio

Troy Meier's driver in Barbados

Jason Dave's brother

Abby Driver for Pete; later acknowledged to be Omi

Dr. Johan Schweers Scientist at the Deep Ecliptic Survey for the Lowell Observatory

Westmoreland Deputy Commissioner of California Highway Patrol

Sue Ellen Chalmers President of GeneVision Board of Directors

Dr. Charles Delna (CD) Tulane linguistics professor; formerly with Procurement Project

Angelina Bajan vendor in St. Lawrence Gap

Van Eaton Turner Director of Caribbean Biologics which is GeneVision of St. John

Rufus (Roof) Security for Charles Delna

Danny Brass Trucker with 18-wheeler

Dreamer Biker with Rugged Cross

Killer Biker with Rugged Cross

Cuffs Biker with Rugged Cross

Timeout Biker with Satan's Gang

Olive Jones CD's wife; formerly with Procurement Project

Omi Works with CD; known earlier as Abby

Mercedes Man Owner of HondaJet; former arms dealer; aka T-Bone

Rebekita Driver; works with Omi

Jenifur Driver; works with Omi

Katerina Driver; works with Omi

T-Bone Aka Mercedes Man

<u>U. S. Government</u>
Ben Strong CIA Director, 30 years ago
John Powell Supreme Court Justice, 30 years ago

John Ray President
Theodore Trentini (TT) Attorney General
Royster Armstrong Vice President under President Ray; becomes President

Joelle Lucado Director of the CIA
Dorothea Smythe CIA agent at Winchester Business Consultants front
Fabian Miles Lucado's Personal Assistant
Michael Habig Security guard for the President
Phyllis President Ray's Administrative Assistant
Douglas Cordero Secretary of State
Pete Garland FBI Agent
Mary CIA agent in Melbourne Beach, FL
Agent 324 CIA agent in Melbourne Beach, FL
Carsten Shulla Secretary of Defense
Jonathan Fogg Director of FBI
Lee Brown President Ray's Chief of Staff
Diana Holk Presidential spokesperson
Kit Tercents Armstrong's Chief of Staff
J. D. Delta Secret Service Agent
Louis Fogarassy Runs G2 for the CIA
Agent Byron CIA Agent at Andrews
Caroline Sullivan Director of CIA after Lucado
Jay Howie Caroline Sullivan's Administrative Investigator
Hulk CIA guard at safe house
Baldy CIA guard at safe house
Agent Gorman CIA Agent
Guy Skipper Caroline Sullivan's pilot
Roberto Esposito Vice President; becomes President

<u>Russia</u>

Afanasii Pakoslav Member of the GeneVision Board
Sergei Verionsky Director of Russian FSB
Oleg Morozov Security Guard at Sheremetyevo
Nikolai Polzinov President of Russia

RETURN OF THE FATHERS

By William Kitchin

PART ONE

Chapter 1

THIRTY YEARS AGO

"This room's been swept today?" Ben Strong looked intently at John Powell who sat opposite him in a comfortable wing chair in Powell's fashionable office.

"Yes, John, it's completely secure, so we can talk freely." Since the Nixon years, everyone in the nation's capital was jumpy about being watched, taped, or bugged. Both men wanted to be certain that the room had been swept for eavesdropping devices.

Free talk was always dangerous, but between these two men, there were few secrets anyway. John Powell and Ben Strong, both elderly, wealthy, and well connected, no longer feared reprisals from politically powerful people, and both were true believers in creating a cleaner, more honest government. And more than anything else, they yearned for what they described as "a return of government to the design our founding fathers laid out."

"OK, and we're still sure that the President knows nothing about it, right?" Ben Strong, the Director of Central Intelligence, was suitably cautious and lived by the doctrine of "plausible deniability."

"Right, Ben. He knows nothing. I gave him the regular briefing today about the same old stuff, and he's out to lunch as usual. He doesn't care about anything but getting more money from the trial lawyers lobby. I don't know who's screwing whom. Is he screwing them, or are they screwing him?"

"Every lawyer I've ever known can screw and get screwed at the same time. That's why they always come in pairs. As long as the President caters to that parasitic lobby, they'll pay him whatever they have to." Both men laughed, though both silently acknowledged a sad truth in their joke. Both had been in politics a long time. John Powell, 72, had worked in law enforcement and been a Senator for three terms before accepting the appointment to the Supreme Court as the second Powell. Ben, at 74, was the oldest Director of Central Intelligence in the country's history after having been in the House of Representatives for what some considered to have been too long.

"It's not just the lawyers, Ben. It's the insurance companies, the banks, the entertainers, the media, everybody. You know it and I know it. You and I couldn't have ever stayed in for as long as we did without shaking 'em down every year." Justice Powell paused and sighed. "Anyway, that's why we're here. Is everything in place?"

"Yeah. California had some problem with state licensing until last week, but it's all ironed out now. The facility is state of the art, and young Dr. Jacobs is tops. I was there last month, and it is outfitted with everything, even stuff my boys in Tech-Sys don't know about." The CIA's super-secret Technical Systems unit, Tech-Sys's preoccupation was hardware gimmickry. Its latest experimental toy was a drone the size and shape of a wasp that could be dispatched into a room to fly around silently and transmit high quality video back to a central station. Knowledgeable people claimed such a device was far away in the future. Little did they know. Such searches were clearly illegal, like much of what the CIA and NSA were involved in, but no one would ever know about these searches, at least not until a leak put everyone on notice. Edward Snowden in 2013 would put everyone on notice after Ben and John were long gone, but Snowden's revelations only touched the exposed tip of the technological iceberg. Tech-Sys was way out in front even of what science fiction writers imagined.

"I know the facilities are ready. Ohio's ready, and so is St. John. Why did we pick a place like Ohio anyway? If I were one of them, I'd surely hope I got St. John. I'd take the Caribbean any day over Ohio."

"We picked Findlay, Ohio, because the university there paved the way for us to put an off-limits facility on their campus, but I agree. Who'd want to be in Ohio? Anyway, that's where Dr. Meier wanted it, and he's running that center."

Both men sat. Neither felt the need or ability to utter appropriate words. Both fully knew that the plan they had put into effect would have an impact beyond what either could even begin to guess. They both truly loved America's constitutional system, and they both bemoaned what they saw as a deterioration of that system. Having been part of the Washington scene for decades, both trusted their own daring plan more than they trusted the system to correct itself. Though they both felt they were doing the right thing, a heavy silence hung over the room.

Ben broke the silence, voicing a fear that the two men shared. "I just hope down the road that the right wingers don't kill the plan."

"Or the extreme left. They are just as short-sighted and much more prone, they think, to know what's good for the rest of us." John stood and walked slowly over to the small wine cooler and pulled out a bottle of Krug champagne. He looked at the bottle with admiration, then loudly popped the cork.

"This is the best. At least that's what Franz claims." John spent an inordinate amount of time going through the *Washington Post* wine columns. He poured champagne for each man. After a long two minutes with neither speaking, they lifted their glasses, and John toasted a future that both knew they would not be around to see. "To a bright future, to genetic salvation" he said solemnly.

"Yes, the future." Ben said softly. After a pause, he added, "I wonder. Do clones even have souls?" The question hung in the air. Finally Ben continued, "God bless and save this nation."

"What are the words? 'If my people will humble themselves and pray and turn from their wicked ways, I will heal their land.' I think that's a pretty close paraphrase," John responded.

Ben sighed. "Yeah, and when it needs it, I pray that God will intervene in this project."

Chapter 2

CALIFORNIA, THIRTY YEARS LATER

All was quiet on the sprawling GeneVision campus. GeneVision was a private company carrying on various types of genetics research, and though most people knew very little about the company, its general reputation was favorable, albeit fuzzy. At 5:38 A.M., Pacific Time, Sunday morning, the comforting silence of the predawn hours was shattered as a catastrophic earthquake struck with deafening violence. Most of GeneVision's facilities were immediately destroyed. At a Richter force of 11.4, the quake was far too much for most of the thirty-year-old buildings. After the violent shaking stopped, Peter Randolph stayed perfectly still in his small condo, terrified that any movement would further bury him in falling debris and concrete. After waiting for a tortuous ten minutes, Pete cautiously pushed aside wood, concrete, and insulation and emerged from what remained of his condominium building. The scene of destruction spread out before him triggered memories of pictures he had seen from Normandy villages of World War II and from Russia did in Chechnya and Ukraine. There was only rubble, angry piles of concrete, wood, plastic, furniture, and here and there, dead bodies. The once modern GeneVision campus simply did not exist any longer. Only one building remained standing among the piles of concrete and steel rubble, the new Information Citadel Building — everyone called it ICB — which housed most of the computers and information processing technology of the facility. Everything else was destroyed, but ICB, built according to California's revised "Destruct-Proof" codes, looked surprisingly intact.

Pete was miraculously not seriously injured. He stumbled and clawed his way through the residences, or what used to be the residences, looking for any survivors. He called out but got no responses. Everyone he found was dead, and then he heard a faint moan. Pulling back some sections of what must have been parts of a wall, Pete was horrified to see a bloodied Dr. Jacobs. The old geneticist's body was hopelessly contorted, and part of his chest was under a crushing slab of concrete.

How can he even be alive? Pete loved Andrew Jacobs. Dr. Jacobs had been Pete's teacher - - - and a father-—for almost all of Pete's life.

"My God!" Pete exclaimed and strained mightily to move the concrete. It would not budge. Pete tried from another angle but could not move the huge piece of concrete.

"Pete, you can't stay here." Jacobs gasped, spitting blood. "Get your file! Get out now before anyone finds you!" Jacobs weakly coughed blood, then managed in a whisper, "Pete, go through the top!"

"You're hurt! I can help you! You —"

"Pete, use my chip." Jacobs' words were now so soft that Pete had to lean in closely to hear the dying man. " My billfold. Use it to get in."

"Get in where? Doc, please don't die! Please don't die." Pete was becoming frantic.

"Go!!! Run!!! Listen to me!!!" Andrew Jacobs coughed more blood and seemed to lie back though he could actually not move at all under the weight of the concrete.

"Why? Dad, what's going on? I'll get some help and get this thing off you. You'll be OK!"

" No! Pete! Dammit, listen to me! You're in danger." Dr. Jacobs paused, seeking some final vestige of energy. "They'll be after you. ICB. Data Suite. File forty." Andrew Jacobs had no more effort in him. "Use my chip," he whispered.

Pete felt helpless and just stared into Jacobs' eyes. "Please, no!" Pete pleaded.

Jacobs locked onto Pete's eyes. "I'm so sorry," Jacobs gasped, then gave a spasm, then another spasm, and released what little air his crushed lungs had held, and then Pete was holding his friend's lifeless head in his hands.

Through his tears, Pete prayed, "Lord, take this good man into your kingdom."

What did he mean, before anyone finds you? They'll be after you. What was Doc talking about? The dear old man had sounded so panicked, not because he was literally crushed and dying but because he thought that somehow Pete was in danger. He'd told Pete to go before anyone found him. What was that all about? And go where?

Though he was just short of thirty years old, Pete really did not know how to *go*. Pete had lived on the campus for all of his life, and except for outings with Dr. Jacobs and the other residents he had seldom left the GeneVision campus. He knew virtually nothing about the outside world. Dr. Jacobs had long ago explained to Pete how when Pete was only days old, Doc and his wife, Sienna, had adopted Pete after Pete's own parents and siblings had been killed by Islamic extremists in a terrorist bombing. Dr. Jacobs had explained that he had known Pete's biological parents and had willingly taken Pete in since there were no other relatives. Pete's father and mother -—that's the way he thought of Andrew and Sienna Jacobs — were wonderful parents. Though the family had not traveled much, everything they needed for a comfortable life was on this campus. Pete had really not seen much of the USA except when the family had gone to a remote vacation spot on the Hawaiian island of

Molokai for summer vacations. His schooling and entire social life had all been centered on the campus.

He had even fallen in love when he was 25. Kylla, a GeneVision employee, was tall, brunette, lively, and seemed to always have a smile or a smirk on her face. Pete spent two years in bliss before Kylla gradually seemed to become withdrawn and preoccupied. Then, one day she told him that her mother back in Maryland was terminal with cancer, and Kylla had to go take care of her. Kylla wrote and called a few times, but the bliss was over. After Kylla, Pete withdrew socially and had little desire to leave the campus.

Pete laid Dr. Jacobs's head softly down on the ground. Heeding the man's desperate warning, Pete reached into Dr. Jacob's pocket and found the dead man's wallet. Through his tears, Pete whispered, "Dad, I love you. Goodbye forever." But Pete's immense sense of loss was suddenly transformed into fear as a dark shadow fell across Dr. Jacob's body.

"Not so fast there, cowboy. Just turn around very slowly." The man's voice was gravelly and commanding.

Pete turned around slowly and stared into the barrel of a laser rifle held by a man in a security guard uniform. "It's OK. I didn't kill him. I was trying to help him." Pete pocketed the wallet with one hand as he motioned with the other to the lifeless Dr. Jacobs. *Had Jacobs been warning me of this man?* "You can put the gun down. I live here. I'm Pete —"

"I know who the fuck you are. You're Peter Randolph, the old man's little project. Let's just put these on." The man pulled out of his left front pocket a set of electrified, stainless steel handcuffs. The crackle of the man's two-way radio erupted, "Phil? Where are you? Have you seen him yet?"

"I've got him. I'm going to cuff him and bring him in. Jacobs is dead."

Bring me in where? What the hell is going on? What project? Pete was fast creating a plan of action. There was no way he would allow himself to be cuffed.

"Give me your twenty," the voice on the two-way radio asked.

"We're across from the —" Before the guard could finish the sentence, Pete threw his body at the security guard, knocking the laser rifle into the concrete rubble. The man went down, and Pete was on top of him, but Pete's assailant was built like a professional wrestler. He easily flipped Pete off, leaped on top of Pete, and started to choke him.

"Maybe it'll be easier if you're dead, you fucking freak," the man shouted, and his fingers dug into Pete's throat. Pete struggled, but the guard was too heavy and too strong. Pete felt things begin to go fuzzy. He wildly grasped for something, anything, on the littered ground. His hand found a concrete chunk in the rubble. He clutched the concrete with his right hand and with all the effort he could manage, he crashed it into the side of the man's skull.

The man fell off of Pete and grabbed his head, blood running through his hands. He staggered, but he did not go down. He yelled, "You shithead! I'll kill you for that!" He lunged for Pete.

"Not too smart," Pete growled as he smashed the concrete slab into the guard's head as hard as he could and then again and again crashed the concrete into the guard's bloody head. The security guard collapsed, unconscious. Now bleeding profusely from the head, if he were not yet dead, he soon would be. Pete turned and threw up. His stomach heaved. He felt dizzy, but he also felt charged. *That must be the testosterone and adrenaline,* he thought as he strangely recalled his biopolitics class from Dr. Schubert. *How detached I am. I just killed a man,* Pete thought in a strange moment of introspection. Pete had never killed anyone before and had never even been in a serious fight since his middle school years. He felt both emotionally energized and also objectively detached at the same time.

"Phil? What's going on? Answer me, damn it!" The radio must have been blaring all this time.

Pete now knew there were hunters on the GeneVision campus, and he was their prey. He ran and stumbled through the debris across the wide lawn toward ICB, the still-standing computer building. On one side of the lawn was the rubble of the Rotunda and residential housing, modeled on Jefferson's architectural masterpieces on the campus of the University of Virginia, except the traditional brick fireplaces had been replaced by air conditioners. On the other side of the lawn, the Biological Laboratories Center was completely destroyed, and smoke was coming from the rubble. Next to it, ICB was standing and appeared to be relatively undamaged.

Pete entered ICB. The emergency lighting was working. Pete had only been in this building a few times and did not know the layout. The directory next to the elevators listed the Operations Data Suite as being on the second floor and had the notation, "Appointments Only". Pete took the stairs two at a time. The second-floor hallway was dark. The emergency lights had been knocked to the floor along with large parts of the ceiling and walls. The double door to the Data Suite was still standing and was locked. A red light glowed, and the digital display below the light read, "Data Suite Secure." The door to the Data Suite was like no other door that Pete had ever seen. It appeared to be a metal-type material and had no visible door handle or locking mechanism. Pete put his shoulder against the door, but quickly realized that there would be no forcing of this door. And there was no obvious way to open it, no locks, and no electronic panel. And Jacobs seemed to have said that Pete had to get inside.

Pete then spotted a damaged door down the dark hallway. He entered that office hoping to find an alternate way to get into the Data Suite. This office must have been some kind of monitoring station because there were more than a dozen computer monitors, but most had apparently been damaged by the quake though two were still lit up. No one was in the room. Pete heard no noises at all in the building. It had apparently been empty in the early morning hours when the quake had struck. Pete walked quickly into the back of the office and looked through another door which led into a small workroom with a table and several chairs and a small end table with a lamp. There was a large hole in the ceiling of this room, and the panels that had once been that part of the ceiling had fallen in several large pieces amidst the dust and clutter that the earthquake had created.

The door to this room still swung true. Pete now knew for certain GeneVision's security would not hesitate to kill him. He also knew that he could possibly get inside the impenetrable Data Suite. He quickly entered the workroom, shut the door, and locked it from the inside. Now he was alone in the inner room with only the dim light coming through the broken ceiling. Pete brushed the torn ceiling board from a wooden desk and dragged the desk directly below the large hole in the ceiling above. He then lifted an intact side chair onto the desk. Next, he ripped the electrical cord from the table lamp and tied it to the top of the chair back. The other end he tied to his own ankle. Then Pete climbed up on the chair, grabbed the metal ceiling support beams, and hoisted himself into the hole in the ceiling and lay astride the thin structural ceiling beams. He then pulled the chair through the opening, untied the cord from his ankle, and carefully put the chair out of sight from below.

The space in which Pete found himself was only about four feet high. Pete could see a hole about twenty feet away where another part of the ceiling had collapsed, and if his reckoning was accurate, that hole would be above the Data Suite itself. He crawled sloth-like along the thin metal beams, finally reaching the gap in the ceiling. Pete was stunned by what he saw as he stared down into the heart of the Data Suite below him.

Chapter 3

The Data Suite was unlike anything Pete had ever seen or even imagined. The room below him was filled completely by a translucent dome that was bordered all the way around by a narrow walkway. The dome itself emitted a soft greenish glow, and a catwalk crossed over the top of the dome and descended out of sight down the far side. The floor on which the large dome rested was apparently a good ten feet lower than the floors of any adjoining rooms so that the domed container itself was larger than an ordinary room. There was nothing outside of the dome other than the catwalk.

A room housing a dome! This is the Data Suite, but the dome has no opening. How do I get inside?

Pete hung from the ceiling joist and then dropped down onto the catwalk. *Go through the top. That is what Dr. Jacobs had said.* Then Pete saw it. Right before him at the very apex of the catwalk was a circular indentation labeled "Emergency Portal." A small digital control panel glowed softly. The panel had no numbers, only a small, sharply angled, concave screen. The screen itself had in its center a tiny pyramidal indentation which glowed a soft red. With no way to activate the control panel, the dome looked impenetrable. Pete tentatively reached out, hesitated, then tentatively touched the dome. It had the temperature of cold glass but felt like textured plastic. He hit the dome with his fist, but as he fully expected, it was resoundingly solid. Pete had nothing other than the chair with which to batter the dome, but he doubted that the material could be so easily cracked. But then he remembered. *Use my chip.* Those were his dad's final words. Pete reached into his pocket and pulled out Dr. Jacob's wallet. He looked in the currency section. Nothing. He opened the card compartments, and found only the ordinary identification cards and credit cards. There was no chip! Increasingly despondent, Pete now pealed back each leather slot in the wallet, and then he saw it. In the bottom corner of one of the slots was a tiny, oddly shaped, plastic container. Pete opened the container, and found an incredibly small, bluish, multi-sided object unlike anything he had seen before. *If this thing is a chip, then what do I do with it?* Each side of the strange item looked different. Pete turned the item over in his hands and then recognized that it was an incredibly small pyramid. He slowly inserted the tiny pyramid into the panel slot, and at the last second, the chip fairly leaped into the awaiting slot, as if drawn into it by some invisible force. The control panel lit up, and then the circular indentation of the dome itself silently spiraled open, and Pete stared down into the Data Suite itself. A soft beep sounded, and Pete read the flashing message on the digital panel as a soothing voice intoned, "Retrieve Chip." Pete pulled the chip from the panel and pocketed it.

Pete's eyes opened wide in surprise as he stared into a room with a dimly lit floor and what looked like four separate, glass-enclosed computer workstations. Pete could see that there was no one in the Data Suite. He slowly descended into the Data Suite on the translucent steps leading from the emergency entryway. He then saw that interlacing laser beams protected each workstation. There was no way to approach a workstation without triggering some type of laser-activated alarm. The workstations themselves looked totally undamaged from the quake. When the quake struck, anyone in the Data Suite at that early morning hour had apparently been evacuated, but, Pete knew, inevitably they would return. Dr. Jacobs had said to find *file forty* and flee. Pete realized that he had little time to find "file forty." What could *file forty* be? It was obviously a computer file, but was guarded by the laser system so that Pete could not even approach the computer stations without alerting whoever might be monitoring the Data Suite, *if* anyone was still doing that after the quake.

Pete stepped as close as he dared to the laser pattern bordering the first workstation. He dug into Dr. Jacob's wallet, and pulled out a credit card. As he was about to toss it into the laser pattern, he heard muffled voices approaching. Pete frantically looked around but saw no place to hide. The domed room had only the laser-guarded workstations. He instinctively crouched but was, nevertheless, completely exposed should anyone enter the Data Suite. He heard two men's voices.

"Well, he's not in there because it's still armed. If he gets in there without a chip, it'll sound the general alarm."

"The emergency generators are working for this part of the building so he's not around here. I think we'd better get to the Cycle Pad. The only way he can escape is to use a Motorbike."

"He killed Phil, so there's no way I'm letting him get away."

"One clear shot is all I need to waste that little shit."

The voices became fainter.

Pete remained motionless for several full minutes before he dared move. As he slowly stood, he saw several small, rectangular electronic devices lying ten feet from him across the floor. Pete picked up the nearest device and saw that it had a red, blinking diode and blank screen. Beside the screen was a small, sharply angled, concave indentation in the panel. The arrangement was identical to the pyramidal panel above in the catwalk.

Hoping for a miracle, Pete pulled the pyramidal chip from his pocket and cautiously inserted it into the indentation, and the laser beams on each of the workstations immediately vanished, and a green light glowed in a holographic panel beside each workstation. Pete then could discern that each workstation was itself inside of its own protective, glass dome. *Four domes within a dome.* The glass had to be a special composite because none of the glass enclosures in the entire room had been damaged at all by the powerful earthquake. The floor itself was apparently a suspended, shock-absorbing floor. The building around the room might be severely damaged, but the Data Suite was apparently a cocoon-like module, designed to survive even the destruction of the building itself. Obviously the computer files this room contained was considered by someone to be incredibly valuable.

Pete tried the composite-glass door to the first station, logically labeled "Operations Station One." It opened smoothly and quietly. He entered the computer station and sat at the computer console. "Computer," he intoned, in the ordinary manner by which the other computers he had used on the campus were "awakened." The screen read, "Protocol Twenty" and intoned in English and simultaneously displayed on the screen a menu with five options — Profiles, Targets, History, Projection, Archive. Pete voiced "Profiles" to the voice-controlled computer and was presented with another Menu. This menu was both more cryptic and also more informative — Composite, Psychological, Genetic, Educational, Developmental, Biological-Other, Social, Spiritual, Linguistic, Physical, Cognitive, Neurological, Mental-Other, and Executive Summary. Obviously this was a profile breakdown of some program or some*one.*

Pete said "Educational." The screen went green, and then a one-paragraph narrative appeared:

> This is the summary educational update for Project
> Twenty and was entered on April 25 by Harold
> Lucent, PH.D. M.D. Twenty remains on schedule in
> his educational development. This is especially

remarkable given the lack of resources and outlets in the geographic area. He shows startling similarity to the target profile and has as of this date completed graduate studies in sociology, military strategy, and political science. My recommendation is that formal schooling be continued only through the current academic year.

He shows startling similarity to the target profile. Who is 'He'? Who is Project Twenty? Is it me? No. Pete had never taken even a single course in Military Strategy. But who was this, and why was an entire, super-protected computer station apparently devoted to *Twenty*?

Pete then commanded, "Executive Summary." The soft voice of the computer intoned, "Executive Summary of Project Twenty, Josiah Folger" and those words immediately appeared on the screen. The first sentence of the short summary stunned him:

This report summarizes the progress to date in the production and post-production processing of Project Twenty, Josiah Folger, GeneVision's human clone of Benjamin Franklin. All components of the protocol have been successfully manipulated at the Caribbean GeneVision facility in St. John. The recommendation is that the Initiation Stage be prepared for revealing the existence of Benjamin Franklin and that Josiah Folger be brought completely up to speed on his genetic identity and his status as a genetic clone.

Pete sat motionless, paralyzed. He read no further. His thoughts raced. *Benjamin Franklin? Benjamin Franklin! This whole thing is one huge cloning project, and somehow I am part of it! St. John?* Then Pete recalled the words of Dr. Jacobs. He had said, "File Forty." Pete needed the file numbered forty, not twenty. Stunned by the short paragraph he had just read, Pete nevertheless felt his time was limited so he hurried to the next computer station. He now knew that file forty was his file!

The next computer station, Operations Station Two, was identical to the first one. Pete voiced, "Executive Summary," and the screen went green and then gave a brief paragraph:

> The subject not yet been informed that he is a derivative of Alexander Hamilton's DNA. All genetic parameters of the subject have been tested at GeneVision of Ohio, and all of the tests have yielded high positive scores.

The summary continued, but Pete was still in too much of a state of shock to read further. *A clone of Alexander Hamilton! GeneVision is not just cloning humans. They are cloning some of America's founding fathers!* Pete was now in a mixed state of shock, fear, and anticipation. *Where do I figure into this? Who am I a clone of?* Pete was now literally trembling. His hands were shaking, and his legs felt weak. He also was feeling betrayed as the fleeting thought hit him that Dr. Jacobs knew all of this all along and never let on one damn thing. And then words from millennia ago flashed in his mind, "Work out your salvation with fear and trembling."

If it's my salvation, then I'd better work it out fast," Pete thought.

Pete quickly went to the next computer station, accessed the data, and immediately requested the Executive Summary. *Gosh! If I'm a clone, I hope it's somebody good,* Pete thought in his own private moment of black humor. *I hope I'm not Benedict Arnold!* He read:

> Project Seventeen represents the successful human cloning of the first President of the United States, George Washington. To date, genetic parameters have tested positive with the exception of G-H-K. The results for G-H-K have been indeterminate. The protocol in Atlanta is to test all genetic parameters until the subject is 21 years old.

Pete was incredulous. *Benjamin Franklin! Alexander Hamilton! George Washington! They are alive. At least their clones are. And who am I?*

There was only one computer station remaining. Pete's heart beat heavily as he entered the final computer workstation. He stood silently for a moment as the thought flashed through his head that if this was not file forty, he might never know for sure that he was a clone himself. Pete mused that he could easily be satisfied with being a clone so long as it was someone good. Pete hesitated, and then in a strong voice addressed the computer. "Executive Summary," he said, and the screen jumped to life and immediately contained the following words on the now familiar green background:

> Executive Summary: Project Forty.

Pete then began reading from the screen. He was jolted as if from a stun gun by the very first sentence. But before he could recover and continue reading, he heard the voices. The men had returned. Pete immediately plugged in the small holographic virtual disc (HVD) that he always carried with him for data storage and pressed "Download." The screen responded,

"Downloading File Forty," but then said, "Download Incomplete."

Chapter 4

The White House Press Secretary strode into the pressroom at 10 A. M., Eastern Daylight Time. The White House press corps had assembled more than an hour earlier, waiting for some word about the earthquake disaster in California. This particular White House had a very strained relationship with the press, and those waiting for a statement did not have high expectations. Those expectations were met by the President's Press Secretary's relatively empty statement:

> At 4 A.M. Eastern Daylight Time, the President was awakened and informed of the California earthquake. He was in immediate contact with Governor Susan Dee of California and the heads of various federal agencies, which will supply relief and assistance. Governor Dee has requested that the President declare a major disaster, and the President has granted the request. This will release federal aid to the state of California. The President has already been informed that no American defense facilities in the quake area sustained major damage, but, of course, that is a preliminary assessment. The White House is sending a team of experts to California to assess the situation, and that team should arrive in California later today. The President is particularly concerned about the inevitable loss of life in the quake area. That loss could be quite large, but we have no numbers at this time. That's all I have for you currently. We simply don't know anything more so I can't yet take your questions.

With those words, the White House spokesperson quickly left the pressroom, ignoring the shouted questions.

A more complete White House press release went out at 10:30 A.M. It attempted to demonstrate that the President admirably combined calmness with power, control with compassion. The statement did not hint at the panic among the President's closest advisors. Initial reports flowing into the White House confirmed that the damage to defense facilities and other government installations was apparently quite serious, and California television coverage was beginning to give visuals of the extensive destruction.

The President had called several of his advisors to the Oval Office. At precisely 11 A.M., President John Ray walked in and said, "Please sit down. Let's get started. TT, what do we know?"

Theodore Trentini, or TT as his friends and enemies called him, was the bulldog-like Attorney General and the President's closest personal confidant. Stocky, crew cut, and with a dominant Italian air and complexion, TT had been a well-known criminal trial lawyer in Minneapolis when he hitched a ride on John Ray's obviously rising star. He had been with President Ray since the President was Mayor of Minneapolis, and most Washingtonians believed that TT had single handedly engineered the President's unexpected rise to the top of America's national political scene. TT's loyalty was beyond question, and his public image was one of toughness and honesty. He had also been a federal prosecutor for five years. Having skillfully played both sides of the fence, TT was well connected and even mentioned by some as a possible Supreme Court nominee.

Others joining the President and the Attorney General in the Oval Office were the patrician, articulate Vice President Royster Armstrong, and only the second woman Director of the

Central Intelligence Agency, Joelle Lucado. Lucado had made her reputation as a federal district judge presiding over the insider trading trials of two prominent Democratic Senators. The two Senators were charged with using information that they had gained in closed committee meetings to buy stock. For some years Congress had legalized this sub rosa, corrupt practice for members of Congress, though for anyone else in America such insider trading was a federal crime. Political luminaries such as Nancy Pelosi and John Kerry had allegedly profited handsomely from this practice, but because of the exposure of the practice by Peter Schweizer in *Throw Them All Out*, the passage of the STOCK Act of 2012 finally eliminated this perk of the American political parasites. The STOCK Act made a number of those practices illegal but carefully left a few hidden loopholes.

The two Senators in the trial Judge Lucado presided over had used some of the remaining legal loopholes but in the process had gotten greedy and careless. Lucado was known as a no-nonsense judge, and she validated that reputation in the trial of the first Senator. When the Senator shouted in open court that he was being railroaded, Lucado immediately gagged him. What was noteworthy about the gagging was that Lucado herself literally leaped over the bench, screaming "Not in my court, you shithead!" and personally applied the gag to the stunned Senator. President John Ray, impressed with Lucado's aggressive demeanor in those two trials, snatched Lucado from the federal bench as part of his plan to drastically expand the CIA's clandestine activities within American borders.

Lucado and Trentini were frequently in the Oval Office, but, ordinarily, the President would not have included Vice President Armstrong in such a sensitive discussion. President Ray had never liked his Vice President. He thought that Armstrong was too prissy and too weak. However, the President had decided that sooner or later the Vice President should be made somewhat aware of what the President described as "that California bullshit," so he included the Vice President in this morning's meeting. However, President Ray had no intention of fully informing Vice President Armstrong of what was actually at play in California. The Vice President was about to learn that "that California bullshit" was not about the earthquake.

"Mr. President," Trentini began. "As you know, but I'll summarize where we are anyway so we are all on the same page, our electronic surveillance leads us to believe very firmly that a particular biological research company headquartered in California is engaged in secret human cloning experiments and in fact has probably cloned at least one human and maybe several. The company is GeneVision, LLC, and they have offices in several states. The FBI's plan is to coordinate our entries into each GeneVision facility to prevent any destruction of data."

The Attorney General and the President exchanged glances, so quickly that no one other than the most keenly observant would have caught it. But the Vice President was, if nothing else, observant. Sensing that something further was not being disclosed, Armstrong started, "Can you tell me —"

The President curtly cut him off. "I'd like TT to finish his summary before we open it up, if you don't mind, Roy."

"I thought we were here to talk about the earthquake and the damage. What's all this about cloning?" The Vice President's tone was accusatory.

"Mr. Armstrong," the President said formally, "will you just please wait a minute? I have people dealing with the damage stuff, but this cloning thing is a lot more serious."

Roy persisted, "*What* cloning thing?"

"Will you just *please* wait, Mr. Vice President! Will you just please let TT finish what he is trying to tell us?" The President faked a calm tone but his face had already reddened. Everyone knew the President had a short fuse.

"Of course, Mr. President." Armstrong's sarcasm was evident.

"Roy, damn it, this California bullshit is drastic stuff. We can't have human clones out there, loose, spreading their poison." The President was now angry.

"Mr. President, what the hell are you talking about? Poison? What poison? And I've never heard of this whole —"

"Enough! Damn it! Enough!" The President slammed his fist down on the coffee table, spilling the Vice President's English breakfast tea. "TT, keep going, damn it all!" The President stood and began to pace.

As the Vice President mopped up the spilled tea, Attorney General Trentini continued, "In order to penetrate that company, we intensified our surveillance and have monitored GeneVision's cell phone traffic, email and social media transmissions, and all of their internal and external communications. Much of that traffic has been encrypted. That justifies our heightened suspicion, of course. A month ago, you authorized Operation Discovery. This enables the FBI to enter the California facility and seize whatever was needed to understand the scope of GeneVision's activities. Operation Discovery is based on several provisions retained from the old Patriot Act and also some of the surveillance provisions passed during the COVID-19 pandemic. That entry was to occur today, but as a result of the earthquake, Operation Discovery is now in some disarray. As you know, FBI Director Fogg is in San Diego with about 40 special agents, but everything is now on hold."

The Vice President interrupted, "What the hell are you talking about? What the hell are you people talking about?" His tone now showed how completely outraged he was at having been kept in the dark by President Ray. Royster had long accepted that he was not in President Ray's circle of trust.

The President stiffened. The Attorney General continued as if the Vice President had not spoken. "The national security letter was issued several days ago. As you know, we don't have to worry about the courts and search warrants so long as we invoke the Intelligence Authorization Act of 2003. Under that Act, just about anything is a "financial institution," so we don't have to get search warrants. We can just walk in."

"Yes, yes, I know all that," the President snorted. "We no longer have to worry about the Fourth Amendment, thanks to Bush and that empty-headed Obama. Yeah, Trump and Biden too. So clueless. Anyway, that Patriot Act was a stroke of genius! Luckily, Congress did not even read that law before they lined up behind it. What a bunch of sheep!" The President shook his head dismissively.

"Sheep always respond to fear." Joelle Lucado spoke for the first time. "And they will follow obediently. We can get that bunch on the Hill to do anything we want them to. Just use the fear factor. The Tonkin Resolution, the Iranian stuff they passed, the Patriot Act, the Coronavirus stuff, Putin just uttering the word 'nuclear', the list is endless. As long as they can get their reelection money, we won't have to worry about them."

"OK, OK. What else?" The President was getting impatient. Ray had little regard for constitutional niceties, and those in the room quickly perceived that he was very troubled about "that California bullshit."

Attorney General Trentini continued, "I talked to FBI Director Fogg a few minutes ago, and he said that things at the GeneVision facility are chaotic. He has had agents watching the facility for about a week. A drone flyover shows that the destruction there was considerable. Fogg is inclined, however, to go ahead with the entry because with the chaos it will be harder for GeneVision to hide anything. Plus, he is concerned that if he waits, they will start destroying evidence."

Vice President Armstrong, spoke, and this time, his voice, as the President's earlier, was angry. "Mr. President, this is the first I've heard of this contemplated entry or even the whole cloning thing. I feel left out of the loop since I am head of the Administration's Task Force on Medical Technology, and frankly I resent being left out of the loop. And to me, the whole idea of raiding a private company because we think that maybe, just maybe, they could perhaps be doing something that might," the VP paused, then emphasized, "*might*, be illegal. Well, Mr. President, as a policy, that policy stinks."

The President, surprisingly and uncharacteristically calm, responded, "I understand your feelings, Roy, but this operation had to be kept as tight as possible. That's why I asked you here today so I could bring you into the loop. And, yes, I felt like I had somehow misled you by not consulting with you before, and I apologize for that. But I do not at all agree that the entry itself is bad policy. That is what we are here to decide -—whether to go ahead or not."

The Vice President thought that President Ray's words sounded rehearsed. "I appreciate that Mr. President. As a policy, the raid stinks, and we shouldn't do it." The Vice President was hardly mollified. "Besides," he added, "I personally don't see why you all are so scared of a few clones. We could just shut down the operation, pass some stricter anti-cloning laws, make the criminal penalties a lot stiffer, and then other companies would not do it."

"There's more involved - - - a hell of a lot more involved - - - Roy, but I can't go into that yet." The President looked

Roy straight in the eye. "Please accept my word on it. This is a national security situation. I will personally give you a full briefing very soon. Please give me some space on this one, Roy, and please accept my word that the threat that that cloning company is creating is more serious than I can describe. It's more than just several clones - - - much more." The President's tone was dark as he added, "And you have known about this thing for about five minutes, and that is a mighty damn short time for you to suddenly be a fucking expert about how *I* -—*I*, Mr. Armstrong -—*should* handle things."

It was not a request as much as a command. The Vice President clearly saw the worry and fear in the President's face. Royster Armstrong currently had no choice. *Currently*. He nodded consent.

"The fact remains, Mr. President," Trentini joined the conversation again. "We are in place, and we can legally go in if we want to. After all, we are the government, and the law says we can go in if the national security is at stake. These particular genetic experiments on human cloning definitely are not in the national interest."

The Vice President, surprising even himself, shot back, "National security and national interest are not synonymous, TT. The law requires a threat to national security. It says nothing about national interest. With all due respect, Mr. Attorney General, your logic is flawed."

The Attorney General opened his mouth to join battle with the Vice President, but the President, now ignoring the Vice President, said, "Tell me again, TT, what's the legal basis for the entry?"

"Mr. President, if I may," the resonant voice of the Vice President Royster Armstrong sounded more controlled. "After 9/11, President Bush asked Congress for additional search and seizure powers to be administered by the FBI with no interference from the courts. The Congress, in their desire to at least *appear* to be on top of the situation, passed the Intelligence Authorization Act of 2003 and in 2006 amended and extended the Patriot Act. The language of those laws explicitly provides for the Executive Branch to issue national security letters, not national interest letters, under which without having to go to court, we can enter and search any institution dealing in any way with money. Obviously that includes practically every institution in America." The Vice President glared at the Attorney General.

"OK, good, thanks for the history lesson," the President snarked.

Vice President Armstrong responded, "We don't have any proof of anything as I understand it, so on what basis is the national security letter written for this particular entry?"

TT responded, attempting to regain control of the flow of the discussion from the Vice President. "The law requires only that there be what the lawyers call ' reasonable suspicion' that activities incompatible with the nation's security are taking place." TT emphasized the words *reasonable suspicion*. "In other words, we don't need probable cause to enter, only reasonable suspicion. Reasonable suspicion is a pretty low level of proof. But since we can now bypass the courts, we really don't have to get too legalistic about it. Since we can really write our own search warrants now — we just call them national security letters -—as a practical matter we really don't even have to have reasonable suspicion. It's pretty similar to how the Obama Justice Department hoodwinked the FISA Court to allow the FBI to surveil Trump."

"That's not the language of the Act. What we are doing here is making a shambles of the Fourth Amendment," Vice President

Armstrong protested and was about to launch into the legality of the intended entry when the President exploded.

"What-the-fuck-ever! I don't give a damn about the fourth amendment!" The President was almost screaming. "If my intelligence is right, there's a lot more to this cloning thing than just a few human clones running around. This country is in trouble and I don't intend to sit around and have some fucking constitutional debate about the fucking fourth amendment. That antique went out the window with the first Patriot Act. Congress killed the fourth amendment, Mr. Vice President. The fourth amendment is buried! It's obsolete! It's dead! The Constitution is not a death pact! And this country is better off for it!"

Everyone in the room was completely motionless. The silence lasted only a few seconds. The President suddenly returned to a calmer voice, "The question is should we go ahead with the entry?" The President turned to the Attorney General. "TT?"

"Mr. President, I think we should go ahead with it," Attorney General Trentini said. "The chances are good that we'll be able to get all the documents we need to find out what they're doing in that facility. I don't see how the earthquake makes that any more unlikely. It probably helps us since they won't be able to concentrate their efforts on covering up things and keeping us from finding things."

"Mr. President, I strongly disagree," the Vice President's words were forceful. "Even though I might be the only one in this room who believes in the Fourth Amendment, even assuming that we needed to search this company's labs in the name of national security, we will have one shot at this, and we'd better make it our best shot. TT said that GeneVision has branches in several other states, and if they are doing something illegal, they'll circle the wagons, and we'll never be able to find out what's going on. They'll go to court, and the courts won't give us a second look-see. Those other facilities inevitably have security measures that we might not be able to penetrate. I mean on their computers. Or to hide incriminating evidence, they could just destroy them like the IRS did back in 2014 and Hillary did in 2015. And they had to have learned from Trump to get rid of incriminating emails. Even Hunter Biden and "the big guy" knew how damaging emails can be. My guess is that if someone is doing human cloning that their computers will self-destruct if the wrong codes are entered. The chances are too good that the computers in San Diego are disabled, and that given the extraordinary emergency, GeneVision's lawyers will have an injunction within the hour if we go in. You have already declared California a disaster area. You can hardly claim that the disaster somehow bypassed GeneVision's facility. It'll look pretty merciless if you go ahead with this when the quake has brought them to their knees. To go on this fishing trip is bad policy and bad politics."

Trentini responded derisively, "Mercy has nothing to do with it. This is not a church service. This is a national security operation. Anyway, you are forgetting that the Patriot Act makes it illegal for them to go to court to contest our entry. That itself would be a felony punishable by five years incarceration if anyone tells anyone, a judge included, that they have been the target of an entry pursuant to the Patriot Act."

"It doesn't work like that," the Vice President said.

After a few moments of quiet, the President turned to the Director of the CIA, "And Joelle, what say you?"

Joelle had been a field agent with the CIA for about ten years before serving as a federal district judge for twenty years when the President surprised her and everyone else by asking her to be the Director of the CIA. She found time during those years before the President's call to write the controversial book, *Judicial Ideology*, in which she argued persuasively that in the big cases judges simply rule according to their personal ideologies and then cite whatever principles they can find or make up in order to enforce the illusion that their conclusions were dictated by neutral principles. Because she was admitting what most judges try to keep secret, she was roundly criticized by most judges but applauded by the empirical political scientists, who had known all of that for some decades. Lucado had been Director of the CIA for two years now and had earned the respect of politicians on both sides of the aisle. "Mr. President, I agree that this is a one-shot deal. If we take our one shot now, there are too many variables out there that we do not control. It's a long shot, a gamble. The whole thing could be a waste, and it could also be a public relations disaster. I think we should wait. The only disadvantage in waiting is that GeneVision gets wind of what we are up too and they cover their tracks before we can execute a search. I say we wait, in the hope of getting better results later as opposed to taking an unnecessary and huge gamble now. We can in the meantime continue to gather information. " Lucado paused and looked at TT and the President. Her expression clearly communicated that the CIA had other ways of getting the information.

The President if nothing else was decisive. "Thank you, gentlemen and lady. We'll wait. The entry is off. Given the earthquake and the logistical nightmare that the damage presents, there are simply too many uncontrollables in California, and our information is that the California facility is GeneVision's main cloning operation. I agree that there are too many unknowns and too many uncertainties for us to go ahead today. TT, this is a delay, not a cancellation. I remind everyone that you can discuss this with no one on your staff or anyone at all without the OK from TT. This is all Omega level security." This was obviously intended to muzzle the Vice President.

"Yes, Mr. President," Lucado and TT dutifully intoned.

"Yes, Mr. President," the Vice President said in a quiet voice.

"Thank you everyone," President John Ray said, adjourning the meeting. "TT, let me have a word with you before you leave. And, Joelle, please wait outside for a few minutes."

After the Director of the CIA and the Vice President had left the Oval Office, the President's facial expression grew tense. "Do we know anything else about the clones? Who they are? Do we actually have any hard facts? Do we actually *know* anything?" The President's face again betrayed the fear that had surfaced several times in the meeting.

"No, Mr. President. That's what we'll be able to confirm or deny when we break in, or rather, when we enter. The only thing we have is rumors."

"Well, I don't like the rumors." The President was silent for a few moments then said, "I understand that Marina Novokatnaia is the head of GeneVision. Is that right?"

"Right, Mr. President."

"She is on my Bioethics Panel. How the fuck did she get on there?"

"She bought her way on. She has made some large contributions to your recent campaigns."

"Well, I want her off the panel."

"Mr. President, you can't just kick someone off the panel and then raid their company just because of some suspicion that something is going on in their company. She is well respected and knows a lot of powerful people, and to date there is no evidence that she has done anything illegal. Kicking her off the panel could backfire on you."

"I don't like it," the President said. "This is going to hurt us. She has a forum, and by implication, we have endorsed her judgment. Meet with her, and see if you can come up with a way out of this whole bucket of shit."

"OK, Mr. President, but remember that it's our bucket, and we are the ones who filled it up and created this problem to start with."

"And we can unfill it," the President retorted. "And TT, who recommended her for the Bioethics position? Isn't she Russian or something? How the hell did she get past our vetting process?"

"She is Russian by birth but is an American citizen now. The Vice President, Mr. President, recommended her. Roy thought the appointment would send a good signal to the women's organizations. She is sufficiently vague in her public position on most issues, but she does support a woman's right to an abortion, to not have her body become a pregnancy vehicle at the command of the government, but she still opposes abortion as solely a means of birth control. She also contributed heavily to the Vice President's primary efforts when the two of you were vying for the nomination."

"Ahh, so that's it. So she's one of *his*, not one of mine. Get her off that panel, TT, and let me know when she's off. I don't care what the blowback is. Just get her the fuck off my panel."

"I'll try, Mr. President."

"No *try*, TT. You do it!"

"I'll get it done, Mr. President."

Chapter 5

The President buzzed his secretary, "Send Joelle in."

CIA Director Joelle Lucado walked into the room, and before the President said anything, Lucado said, "Mr. President, this clone thing could spin out of control very, very easily."

"Joelle, it's already out of control. I want those clones. Dammit to hell, we don't even know how many clones there are! I want them. Find them and bring them in. I don't care whether you do it legally or illegally."

"Why do you want them so badly? What's so special about these particular clones?" Lucado thought she knew but wanted to hear the President's answer.

The President sat heavily behind his ornate desk. He sighed and then looked up at Joelle Lucado. "Joelle, our information is that they have cloned one of the founding fathers. We don't know which one or how many."

Lucado whispered, "My god!"

They both remained silent. Finally Lucado said quietly, "OK, Mr. President, we'll do what we have to. But I wonder since the agency technically is not supposed to operate within our own borders that maybe we should get the FBI to do it."

"This is a matter of national security and national survival. Besides, as we both know, the CIA has operated inside our borders ever since 9/11. That's no longer such a big deal."

"OK, I'm not so sure that that is true, but, OK. I just wanted to make sure we're on the same page."

"We are. Just get those clones. That's the page we're on. And keep me totally up to date."

Joelle turned to leave, and the President said ominously, "And Joelle, bug every phone of this Marina Novokatia, or whatever her name is. Get whatever info we need, then bring her in too."

"Mr. President, we can't just *bring her in*."

"I'm sure you can figure out a way. I want her silenced, and I don't care how you do it. Just do it, Joelle. That's all."

The conversation was clearly over. Joelle Lucado left the room, knowing she had a blank check to tackle the problems of the clones and the problem of the Russian-born clone-meister. She had never had a blank check before to use the agency's power without limits. She had in the past written about the dangers of such power, but now that she had the power itself, it felt good. She felt energized, just as from a soldier's adrenalin rush. Joelle Lucado was smiling as she exited the White House. She well knew that she would have no hesitation to aggressively -—and ruthlessly -—use the CIA's powers, both legal and illegal.

Chapter 6

Three thousand miles away, outside of San Francisco, the persistent ringing of her telephone awakened Marina Novokatnaia.

"Hello," she said sleepily.

She heard the voice of the Special Projects Director of the San Diego facility, James Durango. Novokatnaia listened without speaking as Durango briefed her on the quake, its damage, and the chaotic state of affairs at the GeneVision facility.

Durango concluded, "The entire campus is pretty much a rubble field. A lot of people have been killed. But the bad part is that we can't find Forty. I know he's alive, but we can't find him."

Marina Novokatnaia bolted upright, fully awake. Her deepest, secret fear was threatening to become reality. The clone's existence simply could not become public knowledge. Not yet anyway. Forty could simply not be allowed off the campus. "If Forty is not found, there will be hell to pay! How do you know he's even alive? Maybe he was killed too."

"Because one of our guards found him, we think, and it looks like Forty killed the guard?"

"Killed the guard!" Novokatnaia was now pacing her bedroom. *Forty was supposed to be anything but a killing machine. Why would he kill a guard?* "What kind of search do you have going? Who's in charge down there?"

"Right now, I'm running things, but Marta Norman is on the scene, too. We can't find any of the corporate officers, and we can't find Forty's tender. We have seven guards searching the buildings, or what's left of them."

"Have you blocked all the exits from the campus?"

"There's no way we can do that because the walls are mostly down, and the gates at the roads are either down or have lost their power."

"Don't we have generators?"

"Yes, we have generators, but the gates are manned so we don't have them on a generator circuit. The problem is that the guardhouses at four of the gates were destroyed, and the guards were either killed or injured."

"So you really can't control who goes in and out of the campus? Is that what you're telling me, Jim?"

"To some extent, yes. We're trying to reestablish the integrity of the campus, but it's slow going. Most of the surveillance cameras are down, but we're putting up temporary cameras at every hole on the campus perimeter. I don't think he can get out, Marina."

Marina thought for several moments, and then said, "Jim, it is critical that Peter Randolph not be allowed to slip through our hands. If he killed a guard, he's either gone berserk or he knows too much. Find him, and find him fast, Jim."

"I'll find him."

"I'm depending on you. It's in your hands." Marina Novokatnaia clicked off the phone and walked to the large picture window overlooking the Pacific. *I'd better do some contingency planning*, Novokatnaia thought and began preparations for what she knew would be a long, difficult day. As she was dressing, her cell phone chirped with a text message. She read the message and then hissed, "Shit!" She read the message again. *You need to secure all projects ASAP. POTUS is looking.*

Novokatnaia now realized that the day was going to be even worse than she had previously thought. Things were beginning to spin out of control. They had to find Peter Randolph. And she had three other matters to attend to.

Chapter 7

Fearing that he would be discovered, Pete stopped the download and pocketed the HVD. He quietly stepped into the reception room and listened. If the men came into this room, he would surely be apprehended. Pete was scared to breathe. He listened.

"This is the only room which our master key won't open," said the first voice. Pete recognized the voice of a man whom he knew only as Dave, a security guard who had always gone out of his way to be considerate and courteous to Pete.

Then Pete heard a woman's authoritative voice that he did not recognize. "That's not a problem. Watch this!"

At that moment, two shots rang out, and splinters flew from the door lock and handle. The lock miraculously still held, and the door stayed closed. But it would not survive another shot. Pete ran back into the Strategic Protocols room, quickly shut the door, and frantically looked for a place to hide. He saw a door labeled Electrical and tried the doorknob. It did not turn. It was locked. With no place to hide, Pete heard another shot.

"OK, that did it. Wait here. I'll turn off the lasers," the woman said. From the sound of her voice, she was at the receptionist's desk. That she had the codes to disarm the lasers meant that she was obviously in charge.

Pete then remembered that he had the key ring. He tried a key in the locked door to the electrical room. It did not fit. He tried another key, then another. Nothing fit!

"OK, come on in, and let's search this place and make sure he's not here somewhere. And be ready to shoot if he tries something." The woman's voice again, this time devoid of compassion. "Looks like the quake knocked out the lasers."

"Ms. Norman, he killed Phil. If he tries something, I'd just as soon kill his ass as not."

Yet another voice that Pete could not identify, but he now knew that the woman was Marta Norman, head of security. By reputation she was tough and cruel. The reputation probably resulted from her serving a total of twelve years for the voluntary manslaughter of the second of her two husbands.

"We don't know that he killed Phil. All we know is that *someone* killed Phil. There's already some looting on campus from outsiders. It could have been one of them," said Dave.

"Whatever," said the first man.

"You two get busy and cut the chatter." Pete could hear Marta Norman asserting her authority.

Pete tried the final key. It fit! Pete quickly opened the door and entered the small electrical closet. When he shut the door, it automatically locked behind him, and the room was pitch black.

He heard the voices of the two men as they entered the Strategic Protocols room. He could hear them walking around. Then Pete heard one of the men trying the door to the electrical closet. Pete said a short prayer of thanksgiving that the door was locked. "He can't be in here," Dave said, "this door has not been opened. You can tell by the dust from the quake."

"Yeah, let's keep going."

For a fleeting moment Pete wondered how could he have gotten into the electrical closet without disturbing the dust and debris from the quake. *A bit of luck*, he thought.

The voices faded as the men apparently went to some other area of the suite.

Pete waited. He would have to wait until the three were long gone. Five minutes passed. Though he could no longer hear them, it would take them a full twenty minutes to search the entire suite. The electrical closet was too small for Pete to risk moving. He might hit something or make some sound. He could see nothing. Though there was a row of shielded LED's, they did not project enough light for him to see his way around the room.

Pete waited motionless. After about fifteen minutes, he heard Marta Norman's voice getting louder as she apparently was walking back into the Strategic Protocols room. "He's not in here, and the computers look like they have not been touched. Let's get out of here and check the other offices."

"I'll make one more check of the computers." Pete heard Dave's voice.

"OK, but make it quick," the woman replied. "We're heading next door to search the labs."

The voices of the woman and the other man faded as they apparently left the Strategic Protocols room. Pete stayed perfectly still and quiet. He could hear Dave in the computer area and thought he could hear the sounds of terminal keys being punched. After a few moments, he heard Dave mutter, "OK, back to work with the bitch of the west." Pete could hear Dave leave the room and heard the door of the computer room shut. *Nothing subtle about a noisy security guard*, Pete thought.

Pete heard the faint voices of the three talking among themselves as they left the suite. Pete forced himself to wait a full thirty minutes. The wait was agonizing. He was still feeling the shock and disbelief from what he had read about himself on the computer screen. Finally, he quietly cracked open the door to the electrical room. No one was in the room. Because Dave had closed the door between the Strategic Protocols room and the reception lobby, Pete could not see into the lobby nor could anyone in the lobby see him. He tiptoed to the lobby door and put his ear to the door. He listened for several minutes and heard nothing. He cracked open the door and peered into the room. No one was there. Pete was alone.

Pete entered the computer station where he had started to read and download his own file. *I've got to download the rest of my file*, Pete thought. He sat in front of the screen and brought the screen to life. The screen was blank! Pete punched the Start icon and then clicked on "All Programs." The screen read, "File Corrupted." He then clicked on the icon for the Recycle Bin. It was empty. He then tried to take a directory of the entire computer, and the message on the screen again read "File Corrupted." He clicked on "Reconstruct Files," and the screen immediately read "File Reconstruction Corrupted."

Pete could not retrieve anything! Everything was gone! *Shit!* The file that sounded like it was all about him was gone! He quickly stepped into the next computer station. He triggered the screen to life and read "Protocol Twenty." Pete then hit the automatic backup icon on the top left portion of the screen and the HVD backup unit adjacent to the computer whirred to life. Within ten seconds, the screen read, "Backup Complete." Pete then ejected the micro HVD and pocketed it. He repeated the same steps at the remaining computer stations.

There was no time to worry about his own data, which had somehow disappeared from the corrupted computer. Pete had had time to read only three sentences before the security guards had entered the Strategic Protocols room, and those three sentences would forever alter the way he saw himself:

> Peter Randolph, clone of Thomas Jefferson, along with the other products of the Fathers Project, represent the most significant breakthrough in genetic history. As the first human clones, they are historic, but because of whom they were cloned from, they will inevitably make, even change, history.

Whoever controls the clones will determine what those historic changes are.

The arrival of the security guards had prevented Pete from reading further, and now the rest of File Forty was lost.

The guards had already talked about killing Pete! One had called him a "freak." And Pete now knew that was indeed what he was - - - a freak! A Thomas Jefferson freak. He smiled to himself. *So I'm Thomas Jefferson. Not Benedict Arnold!* Obviously, if he were some kind of genetic experiment, everyone would be looking for him. He had to find his way off the campus before the security guards figured out where he was. He softly walked into the receptionist area and cracked open the door to the outside hallway. The hallway was empty. Pete quickly and quietly walked to the stairs and listened for noises in the stairwell. There were none. He took the stairs down to the ground floor, and before opening the door to the spacious lobby, he listened for voices. The lobby was quiet. He needed to make his way across the open lobby and get outside where he could conceal himself behind the rubble and trees. The lush landscaping of the campus and the piles of rubble would provide plenty of cover. Even though leaving the building would be risky, Pete also knew that staying in the building was tantamount to being trapped. His only hope for escape and ultimately freedom was to get out of the building and then to get off the campus. Once in the outside world, he could somehow blend into the post-earthquake disorganization of southern California.

Pete stepped into the lobby and immediately, a man's bass voice said, "Pete! Stop!" Don't move!! I've been waiting for you."

Chapter 8

Pete stopped. The voice said, "Just turn around slowly. Don't make any noise, and don't run."

Pete slowly turned around. Dave had his revolver pointed squarely at Pete's chest.

This was the second time in two hours that Pete had faced the business end of a firearm. Strangely he did not feel panicked and was already alert for the first moment when he could disarm Dave. *There is no way I will let him take me in*, Pete thought to himself.

"Don't panic. Just listen," Dave said quietly. "Everyone is looking for you. We have orders to kill if you resist. I am on your side. I'm not going to shoot you. You need to escape. I'll help you, but there's no time to explain now. They'll be back in a few minutes. You've got to trust me, or you have no chance of getting out of here."

"Orders to kill? Why? How are you going to help me?"

"I'm going to help you get off this campus because I know who you are and I know what's going on here. I don't much like it, and I surely don't want them killing you. There's too much at stake for them to kill you. There are others."

"Other clones?"

"Yes, clones. And not just any clones. Pete, there's so much you need to know. There'll be time for all that later. First things first. Let's get you to a safe place."

Pete quietly said, "If you're on my side, then put the gun away."

Dave started to respond but quickly stopped. "Shhhh," he said, with a finger to his lips.

There were voices in the lobby. Marta Norman and the other security guard were back.

Marta Norman's voice called out, "Dave?"

"That's Marta Norman," Dave whispered. "She's as hard as nails and will just as soon shoot you as take you in." Dave checked his revolver. Pete recognized the revolver as a .38 and noted that it was equipped with a silencer.

"Dave? Where the hell are you?" This time, the male security guard was doing the shouting.

Dave shoved the revolver into his back belt, pointed to the stairwell, and said quietly, "Get in the stairwell." With that, Dave walked out of the ICB lobby onto the littered walkway outside, closing the door behind him.

Pete heard Dave's voice. "I was checking the stairs again. I thought I heard something. Did you find anything?"

"No, nothing," Marta Norman answered. "He's hiding. There's no way he could've left campus. We've got all the gates guarded now, and we're getting help in searching the campus. But I'm still not satisfied that he's not in this building, so let's go through it again."

"OK," Dave agreed.

Then Pete heard two quick metallic spits. No voices. Then the door to the stairwell opened, and Dave said urgently, "Help me drag 'em in here." He was pulling the body of the male security guard into the stairwell. The guard had a clean bullet hole right through the middle of his forehead.

"You killed them?" Pete exclaimed, paralyzed.

Dave grabbed Pete and shook him by the shoulders. "You don't have time for that, Pete! The word is out to shoot you on sight. They were heading for this stairwell. I had no choice. And you clearly don't know what's at stake."

"You killed them!" Pete's voice was louder.

"You still don't understand, do you? Help me get her in here." Dave motioned to the prone body of Marta Norman, which was still in the lobby. Blood oozed from a hole in the side of her head.

Pete felt nauseated and could hold it back no longer, staggered to the side, and threw up. *This sucks. Every time somebody gets killed, I throw up!*

Dave dragged Marta Norman's lifeless body into the stairwell. He took Pete by the shoulders again. "Pete, you've got to get your shit together! Stay low and follow me."

With that, Dave cautiously led the way through the lobby. Dave did not head to the main entrance doors, but instead walked quickly to the information desk and pressed a button located out of sight on the underside of the main counter. A concealed door behind the information counter opened. "God must be on our side. That circuit still works. OK, in there." Dave motioned towards a passageway that was dimly lit by emergency lighting.

Pete followed Dave as the two men walked quickly down the passageway. After a sharp right turn, the stairs led down into darkness.

Dave triggered the flashlight on his phone and moved quickly down the stairs. "We'll take the stairs down and then we can make our way underneath the campus to the outside," Dave said. "This is an emergency passageway and connects the ICB with the outside world."

The outside world. Did Dave mean that somehow the campus was intentionally kept isolated from the surrounding area? He was a clone, an illegal experiment, so secret escape tunnels somehow made sense. After several minutes, the two men were deep underneath the campus. The stairs ended at a metal door, which Dave tried to open. The door was locked. Dave said, "Cover your ears and lie down. This might ricochet." Pete did as he was told, and Dave shot one silenced bullet into the door lock. The shot made a clean hole in the lock mechanism, and Dave manipulated the tumblers by hand until the door opened.

Pete saw before him another dimly lit tunnel with curved, opaque walls. Dave led the way through the tunnel, which gently curved, up and to the left. After a full five minutes at a brisk pace, they arrived at another door. This door stood partly ajar and completely off its top hinge. Dave peered around the door and said, "Good. Nobody's here."

The tunnel door opened into an office, which had a conference table and some chairs, all thrown by the quake into a heap on one side of the room. Dave cracked open a side door, peeped through, then opened it fully, and they walked into another conference room, this one also severely damaged by the quake. They proceeded to go through two more rooms until they came to the main outer reception area in which everything was in disarray. The reception area had been outfitted in plush furniture, sleek, contemporary lamps, and the usual array of Californian potted plants, but everything was now in shambles. The glass double doors leading onto the sidewalk were both shattered, allowing Pete and Dave to be seen by anyone passing by. Luckily, Californians did not stroll around much after a 11.4 earthquake, and Pete saw no one outside. As Pete looked around, he could not readily figure out what kind of office complex they had entered, but judging from the damaged pictures, now on the floor, of exotic, distant locales, he guessed. "A travel agency?" he asked Dave.

"No, it's not a travel agency. It the main office for GeoTech." Dave replied. "This is a front for the campus and gives us a secret way of getting in and out of the campus in case we have people who need to get in or out without being seen. We've had some influential people who visited but did not want there to be any record of their presence on the campus. We bring 'em in through here and get 'em out the same way."

"What is GeoTech?" Pete asked.

"GeoTech is a legitimate think tank. It is nonpartisan and produces papers and research on various topics related to the distribution and depletion of the world's resources. It has nothing to do with what goes on at GeneVision other than serving as one of our secret gateways. But enough of that, we need to get you out of California."

That sounded good to Pete, but how would it be done? At that moment, a police motorcycle roared to a stop directly in front of the shattered glass that before the quake had been GeoTech's stylish entry. The rider wore the distinctive uniform of the California Highway Patrol. He was a burly man, roughly the same size as Dave, a few years younger, and looked up and down the street nervously. Then he headed straight towards the GeoTech lobby.

Pete immediately bolted back into the adjacent conference room. To his surprise, Dave stayed put and had not drawn his gun. Dave seemed frozen! Pete hissed, "Dave! Get in here!" Dave stayed perfectly still and seemed to ignore Pete.

At that moment the trooper, with his own gun drawn, stepped cautiously into the GeoTech lobby and faced Dave.

Chapter 9

Jim Durango punched in Marta Norman's cell phone number for the fifth time in ten minutes, and as before it went directly to her voice mail. That either meant that the signal was not adequate or something had happened to Marta. Durango knew that her last communication was when she was getting ready to enter ICB again. She had explained to Jim that she thought the building needed to be searched more thoroughly.

It took Durango only two minutes to get to ICB. He saw no signs of anyone and heard no one. He called out several times but got only an echo in response. He walked into the building and headed to the Operations Suite since that was the area with the most important files and equipment. He noted that the lasers were down and attributed that to the earthquake though for a fleeting second, he thought that the security at the Operations Suite should have been able to withstand the quake. He entered the Suite, and as elsewhere in the building, there were no signs that anyone had been here since the quake happened. He entered the Strategic Protocols room, and immediately saw the computer terminal blinking its message to anyone who would look its way: "File Corrupted." But only one terminal had that message. The other terminals were blank.

Though he was not a computer nerd, Durango had been consulted when the Strategic Protocols Room was set up, and he knew that the computer stations were dedicated to specific human projects. Each station was wired into the central monitoring office that came under Durango's authority. Of course, his central monitoring office was now a pile of debris, and there was no monitoring going on. Durango punched in a cell phone number, and one of the specialists answered immediately.

"This is Durango. Check the directory and verify for me, which project is Operations Station Three dedicated to?

"I don't have to look it up. I remember that——-"

Durango interrupted irritably, "I don't want what you remember. Look it up. There can be no mistake on this."

After a few minutes, the specialist said, "It's Project Forty, Mr. Durango."

"Shit. And what does it mean when the terminal just blinks, 'File Corrupted'?" Though Durango knew the answer, he felt he must double-check.

The specialist responded, "That means someone got into the computer drive without entering the proper passwords. That's just about impossible to do, but no security system is perfect. When that happens, the system is programmed to self-destruct the file."

Durango asked, "Couldn't the message just mean that the quake damaged the computer, like there was a power surge, or something?"

"No. It's a special message indicating that there was an unauthorized entry. Our software generates this message. What color is the screen?"

Durango had wondered about the screen's green color. "Green."

"That distinguishes this message as a security violation and not a hardware failure. Mr. Durango, someone accessed that computer and did not have the passwords."

Durango said, "Thanks. Let me know as soon as you have anything working over there."

"Yes, sir." They both broke the connection.

Durango immediately called Novokatnaia.

She answered with irritation and anxiousness in her voice, "Yes, Jim."

"Marina, we have a problem. It looks like someone got Peter Randolph's file from the dedicated computer station. That's his main file, and that file———-"

"I know what it is, " Marina snapped. "And I know what it means. It changes everything, damn it. You find him and bring him in. If that means you have to kill him, then kill him, damn it! I don't give a shit what happens to him. Just make sure he doesn't get away! Have you got that?"

Novokatnaia abruptly broke the connection without waiting for an answer. Durango knew that more than just Peter Randolph's future was at stake. His own future was now on the line, and probably Marina Novokatnaia's and GeneVision's, too.

Chapter 10

Findlay, Ohio, is a flat, featureless town with a nationally recognized environmental waste disposal curriculum at a local university. About thirty years earlier, a little known program under the title of Environmental Service Systems (ESS) was organizationally attached to the university, but ESS was wholly independent from the university in its operations. In return for sizable cash infusions from GeneVision each year, the university allowed ESS total autonomy and exempted it from any university oversight. ESS was GeneVision's campus in Ohio. The Ohio facility was not connected to the main university campus but was two miles out of town next to the English Equestrian barn, the University's other nationally recognized academic program. Since ESS was in a rural area, its facilities were relatively easy to secure, and GeneVision had artfully blended its sophisticated security arrangements into the surrounding environment. ESS's secluded location virtually guaranteed the secrecy of its human cloning program.

The core of ESS was, as the California operation, a state-of-the art computer facility, housed in Crick Hall, a nondescript, low-slung concrete building unlikely to draw a second glance from any of the English riders from the nearby stables. Those riders were usually in such painful concentration on their equestrian technique that ESS was practically invisible to them anyway. It was in the Director's office in this building where Dr. Hans Meier was seated behind his large oak desk staring at the noble features of his prized pupil, Jim Fawcett. Dr. Meier had always been amazed but was no longer surprised at Jim's easy grasp of the twists and turns of the financial markets. Jim's talents seemed to mirror those of the original Alexander

Hamilton who was after all, America's first Secretary of the Treasury.

"Well then, Jim, should I actually just sit on my REIT or switch into some type of real estate fund?" Though he was serious, Dr. Meier's smile showed that he thoroughly enjoyed talking stocks with Jim.

As Jim started to answer, Dr. Meier's cell phone beeped. He answered it tersely, "Meier." Dr. Meier's smile immediately dissolved into a frown. After listening without talking for a couple of minutes, he said somberly, "I'll have to call you back. Give me a few minutes." He hit the off button on the cell phone. "Jim, some business has come up that I need to take care of right away. Can we continue this a little later?"

"Sure, Doc." Jim always called Dr. Meier "Doc," even though everyone else at ESS treated Dr. Meier more formally, probably out of great respect for Meier's Nobel Prize in genetics which had been awarded him five years ago. "I'll dig up some good funds for you."

"OK, see you later, Jim."

Jim closed the door as he left the office. Dr. Meier then immediately dialed a number. "Meier here. What's going on?"

Marina Novokatnaia spoke. "We might've lost track of Peter Randolph! That earthquake destroyed just about everything, and somehow he must have gone haywire. He killed a security guard, and it looks like he might've gotten hold of his own computer file."

"My God!" Hans Meier exclaimed. "If he can open that file, that means he'll know everything." Meier was silent for a few moments, then spoke again. "Did he get any of the other files or just his own?" Meier was just realizing that his own project might be compromised.

"I don't know, but the files are so comprehensive that sooner or later he'll figure out that you are part of the picture. Therefore, I want you to go into a lockdown. To start with, seal off the facility. I don't want anyone getting to your boy. And don't permit any unmonitored communication between him and anyone on the outside. OK?"

"OK."

"To make the lockdown work, use the Islam Scenario. That's it for now. I'll call if there's anything new." Novokatnaia broke the connection before Meier could acknowledge.

Meier sat perfectly still for a full several minutes and then got up and walked slowly over to the large window looking out onto the sprawling lawn leading to the residences. The Islam Scenario was designed to completely seal off the GeneVision facility from the outside world. Its steps would include the monitoring of all Internet activity and all cellular communications, including voice, text, twitter, and other methods of communicating. It would also disable all VPN's in the geographic area. The monitoring was all handled by ESS's own supercomputers, which used software similar to NSA's older Echelon surveillance network. Known as AACS (Accelerated Analysis of Cognitive Systems), this artificial intelligence software simultaneously utilized word analysis, phrase analysis, topical analysis of conversations, and voice print analysis to discern whether those conversations should be intercepted or cataloged. This was considerably less detectable than a "kill switch." Under the Islam Scenario, Meier knew that the software would automatically shut off any conversation, either on the telephone or over the Internet, which even hinted of a threat to the project. Unlike earlier generations of NSA's Echelon software, the current software had the means of delaying the communication while the filtering was occurring, and if the filtering identified something threatening, the communication links were automatically shut down. The result was that persons using the telephone or computers thought they were using them in real time, but their conversations or communications were actually delayed for between one and twenty seconds for the accelerated monitoring to take place. An actual interruption in communications resembled a "dropped call" for telephones or buffering for Internet traffic.

Meier quickly ordered his own security people to put the Islam Scenario into motion and then began to work on his own plan to further isolate Jim Fawcett from whatever might unfold. Meier fully realized that Fawcett's true identity was now in danger of exposure.

He called his prized project. "Jim, how are you?"

Fawcett answered, "Fine, but it seems like we might be under a terror alert or something. It seems like the buildings have been put into a lockdown."

"Don't worry about that. Things are OK. It's just a precaution because there was a shooting or something over at the university. Anyway, I have just come into a great travel deal, and you know how I've been saying you and I need to get away. Well, I've got tickets to the Caribbean for a week, and my travel agent just called and said if we can leave today, she can get us gratis first class tickets. So with the shooting and all that, it's a great time to get out of town. What about your own tests and schedule and things, can you get away?" Meier knew Jim's schedule in detail and knew the answer to the question before he even asked it.

"I can go. That sounds great! Let's do it! Is it just us or is it the rest of the staff too?"

"It's just us this time, but we'll have some work to do, too. Bring those new economic models you're supposed to be working on, and I do have a meeting or two to go to when I'm there. Pack up and come over to my office in a couple of hours and we'll drive to Columbus this afternoon and catch the 5 PM flight."

"Cool!"

"OK. See you later."

The two hung up. Meier's regular secretary had been out sick for the last few days, and he had used a secretary from GeneVision's list of approved substitutes. She was actually excellent. She was efficient and caught on fast. After he explained his needs to her for air reservations and two rooms at the Southern Palms in Barbados, she called Meier's travel agent and asked her to get him two first class tickets from Columbus connecting at O'Hare to the Air Barbados evening nonstop flight to Barbados. Luckily, the seats were available, and just as Meier had hoped, his secretary was able to reserve the seats and print out boarding passes and also reserve two oceanfront rooms at the Southern Palms in St. Lawrence Gap, Barbados.

She buzzed Meier. "It's all set. You leave at 8 PM from Columbus, connect at O'Hare, and you have two oceanfront suites at the Southern Palms." Meier breathed a sigh of relief. Now he could get Jim out of town and then figure out what to do next.

In the outer office, Meier's secretary placed her own telephone call to California. The phone rang only once and a staccato voice answered, "Yes?"

The substitute secretary spoke softly. "Meier and the subject are departing for Barbados at 8 PM today. They're staying at the Southern Palms Resort at St. Lawrence Gap."

Both parties hung up without saying another word.

Chapter 11

Dave faced the barrel of the trooper's Smith & Wesson. Then to Pete's surprise, the trooper holstered the gun and embraced Dave, "Well, little brother, what hornet's nest have you stirred up this time?"

"My boy's on the run, and we have to get him out of here. Everything inside is in shambles. They're looking for him, and I think they might even kill him if they find him. I don't think he knows everything yet. And Jason, if you are with him, you are in danger too." Pete heard the man addressed as Jason let out a low whistle. "No problem. Where do I take him?" Jason looked to be about the same age as Pete, was over six feet tall, muscular, and exuded an air of confidence. He had the same high cheekbones, black hair, and dark eyes as Dave but seemed to smile more freely.

Dave said, "I think you need to get him to Ohio and then let the two of them work things out."

"I agree. And the sooner the better. Where is he?"

Pete stepped into the room. "What do you mean, 'I don't know everything yet'?"

Jason and Dave glanced at each other. Dave spoke. "Pete, there's a lot about your background that you don't know and stuff that Dr. Jacobs never told you. It's all here." Dave handed Pete a black bag made of some type of resin material. "This is a lead-resin containment bag. It contains an HVD. Your whole file is here, and I think you'll be better off if you just read it for yourself. But keep it in this bag because this bag shields the disk from satellite and GPS detection."

"Dave, I know who I am."

Dave and Jason just stared at Pete. Finally, Dave broke the silence. "Then you know you've got to get out of Dodge."

"Pete, there's a HVD in the bag. It's got all your information on it, but it has a tracking chip embedded in it that allows GeneVision to track it. This bag shields it so that no signals get in and no signals get out, but once you take it out of the bag, they'll be able to locate you."

"Wait a minute," Pete spoke rapidly as he pulled from his pocket the HVD he had brought from the GeneVision computer facility. "I've got this. What do we do with it?"

"Oh shit!" Jason exclaimed. "Now they know exactly where we are!"

"Maybe not," Dave said hopefully. "Just maybe their computers are down. Just maybe they were destroyed by the earthquake."

"I was on the computers. They are not down," Pete said dejectedly.

" No, their security computers, not the one in ICB." Dave opened the bag. "Put it in here." Pete dropped the HVD into the bag which Dave quickly closed.

"Just opening the bag that much might have given them our location, so you two better get moving," Dave said.

Dave looked at Jason and continued, "Whatever. Pete, this is my brother, Jason, and he will get you out of the state. If you stay here, they'll surely find you, and then your life ain't worth shit. Jason can get you headed to Ohio. There's someone there who can help you out and keep you away from these people until everything blows over."

"I'm just a clone, so I'll never be safe. There's no chance in hell that things will just blow over." Pete's tone showed that he was now feeling vulnerable and weak. "I'm basically consigned to a fucked-up life of running and hiding."

Dave and Jason glanced at each other. Neither answered at first, but finally, Dave said, "You are just as human as I am, so don't jump to any conclusions. You just need to read it all and then you'll understand, but right now, you two had better get going."

Jason said, "OK, let's go."

"But, Pete, one more thing." Dave said seriously. "You have a historic destiny in front of you. There are others, and you all have a God-ordained mission. You all can make things right for this country."

Pete looked directly at Dave. "We will. But we will still be running and hiding. We'll never be able to be out in the open."

"OK, enough. Let's bounce," Jason said, moving to the CHP customized Harley-Davidson.

"Won't it look sort of strange, a California trooper riding a Harley to Ohio with a passenger hanging on?" Pete's question sounded like a good one. "And won't that permanently alter my posture?" He paused, then added, "And my ability to have little clones?"

The three had their first moment of laughter.

Dave answered, "That trooper outfit is just to get you out of California. Jason is not a trooper. He's retired CIA. You are in good hands, Pete. Just do what he says, and you'll be OK."

Pete wondered, *What next? I might be a clone. People are trying to kill me, and I'm going to Ohio with a CIA agent who is dressed up as a state trooper!*

"And, Pete, in that bag is a backup I made at ICB, but when I finished it asked for a termination code. I didn't have it so the computer shutdown. That's going to put them on notice that someone got your file without authorization, and that's why you couldn't access the data when you tried. The other files you have on that backup are about other people." Dave, his expression now somber, paused then added, "Pete, I'm sorry. I wish I had done something a lot sooner. I just didn't know what to do."

"Sorry for what? What do you wish you had done sooner?"

It was then that the three heard faint voices coming from the direction of the inside conference rooms. "Time's up!" Dave said with urgency.

Dave and Jason looked at each other. Pete detected an unspoken communication between them. Something profoundly sad passed between the two brothers.

Jason grabbed Pete by the arm, "Let's go," he said softly, and the two ran from the building, mounted the cycle, and Jason fired up the engine. Pete's quick glance at Jason revealed the tears in Jason's eyes. He looked back at the building they had just left and saw Dave standing at the door, shoulders drooped, face drawn. He also saw several men with guns drawn approaching Dave from the interior of the room. Dave rose to his full height and yelled loudly, "Rubber side down, brother!"

Jason pointed to a black helmet behind the seat and yelled over the sound of the engine, "Put that lid on, and then just talk! It's voice activated." Pete grabbed hold of Jason as Jason roared off, not waiting for Pete to get situated, and the cycle sped down the littered street.

Pete got his helmet on and managed at the same time to hold onto Jason who now seemed to be attempting to set a new urban speed record, weaving through the rubble on the streets leading out of town. The advanced, German-made communications system in the helmets would allow Jason and Pete to talk to each other without the interference of motor noise and wind noise.

When Pete got his helmet in place, he heard Jason already talking, " . . . out of California in a couple of hours, but we'll make a short stop first." With those words, Jason took a sharp left turn down an alley and pulled under a garage door which was just finishing its opening cycle. Jason pushed a button on the cycle handle, and the garage door closed behind them.

"You can't ride this bike with those clothes, so put on this uniform." Jason dismounted and grabbed some clothes from a drawer of a workbench. He handed Pete an official California Highway Patrol uniform. "Be quick about it. We need to be out of this state before they launch a statewide search for you. The Arizona border is 170 miles away. We'll avoid tollbooths. We don't want any pictures."

Pete quickly changed clothes, and then Jason handed Pete a standard issue CHP revolver and holster. "Take this, but please, *please*, don't shoot it," Jason said as he looked Pete in the eye. "Let's roll."

Jason took California Highway 94 East, then 125 North for two miles, and then entered the relatively undamaged Interstate 8. Jason opened the bike up, doing close to 100 mph on the straight sections, but soon they were in the mountains, and their speed slowed. After close to an hour, they had still seen no signs of a search and had not even seen another state trooper.

Jason took the exit, which read, "Last Exit in California" and pulled the bike up under a stand of palmetto trees. "Lucky for us, there's nothing unusual about a CHP bike pulled off under the trees, but it would look pretty strange for us to be driving around in Arizona. So here is where we change clothes." Jason tossed a book bag to Pete. "Put these on."

Jason stripped off his CHP uniform and then peeled off the CHP logos from the Harley. So that now it looked like any run-of-the-mill Harley headed to some bike-week.

Chapter 12

Novokatnaia's voice was shrill. "There's no way in hell that they are going to get out of California. You get the state patrol on it and seal off the whole fucking state if you have to. Now get your ass in gear!"

Jim Durango was exasperated at not being on the scene and did not allow many people to talk to him this way, but the head of GeneVision was the most powerful person in Jim's world, so Jim simply said, "Yes, ma'am." Jim was especially irked that it was a woman talking down to him and swearing like a man. Her clipped accent made it even more insulting. He had had about as many telephone calls from her as he could handle in one day.

Jim continued, "I'll call the Commissioner. He's one of ours. He can make sure nobody leaves California."

"You do that!" Marina Novokatnaia slammed the phone down. "Damn, damn, damn!" she exclaimed in English. The she reverted to her native Russian and continued to swear. She had built GeneVision from nothing. It was an international genetics research conglomerate with four ultra-modern campuses and with financing beyond anyone's imagination because of Novokatnaia's connections to the Russian mafia plus her connections to the corrupt public teachers' lobby in Washington. In addition, she was tied into Europe's leading money launderers, especially the Swiss banks, experts at the art of willful blindness as they greedily processed large amounts of money, no questions asked. Novokatnaia had control over the most advanced genetics research in the world, using American technological superiority to achieve unparalleled breakthroughs in designer genetics. When the Americans had passed laws making certain types of research "illegal," she simply shifted that research to GeneVision's labs in Russia, China, India, and other nations where the corrupt politicians were willing to use the Swiss bankers' policy of looking the other way - - - for a price. The money was no barrier to Marina Novokatnaia. And America was the best country in which to carry out the long-range project once the preliminary experiments had been done in the labs of the other countries.

Novokatnaia took several deep breaths, calmed herself, took a slug of pepper vodka which she kept in the lower right-hand drawer of her teak executive desk, and buzzed her secretary. A male voice answered, "Da?" *Yes.*

"otmenitye vse moi proklyatye naznacheneya v techeneye nedeli!" *Cancel all my appointments for the week!*

"Da."

And with that, Marina Novokatnaia had cleared her calendar for the rest of the week. She realized that if this particular project became public, there would be no way to control the fallout. She knew too that the new Commissioner of the California Highway Patrol would seal the borders. After all he was a political appointee, and the donations from GeneVision and its subsidiaries had gotten him the appointment even though he was not at all qualified. Such was the fundamental operative of American politics. It still amazed Novokatnaia that incompetents could rise so high even to the White House itself as at least two recent Presidents had proven. Her interoffice phone buzzed.

"It's Jim Durango," said her secretary.

Novokatnaia picked up the phone, "Yes, Jim," she answered with authority.

"OK, I've got the borders sealed. Commissioner Westmoreland said he would also carry out surveillance at the airports but that he did not have the authority to seal them. He has already put out an "'All Points' for Peter Randolph."

"Good job. Keep me informed." Novokatnaia wanted to convey the impression that she was in control. She well knew that employees and dependents needed praise for them to keep whatever loyalty they might have.

"Thank you, ma'am."

They both hung up without saying "Goodbye."

"I hate that woman," Jim said to himself.

"No balls," Novokatnaia said to herself.

Novokatnaia's fleeting thought was that too many people knew who Peter Randolph actually was, and Jim Durango had now risen to the top of the list of those who were expendable. She buzzed her secretary. "Get me a first-class ticket to Washington, and get me a suite at the Hay-Adams. I need to leave tonight." Marina Novokatnaia knew that she needed to leave California and be in the nation's capital as soon as possible. There were powerful people she needed to brief on the latest problems. And there was another need. Too many people, mainly GeneVision's own Board of Directors, might be aware of the clones' true identities. She had managed to keep the Board in the dark for years, but feared that the recent rumors of clones might have tipped them off to what was really going on in the company the Board was legally responsible for. Novokatnaia, therefore, decided to do some "preemptive damage containment."

Chapter 13

"Jason, why the hell are you doing all of this?" Pete asked.

"Pete, I used to work in intelligence. I know our government. I know the deep state. It that simple. I don't want you or the others falling into the clutches of the government. That would be a disaster. We learned from the corruption in the Obama Administration, especially in the Justice Department, FBI, the State Department's pay-to-play and all that shit that no way could we let the government get hold of you. Same with Trump and the same shit with Biden. Trump's corruption was born out of his narcissism, and Biden's corruption was born out of his greed and his incompetence. The current Administration is no better. I don't know about the other clones, if they are in danger, but you surely were, so that's why we rescued you. So, Pete, we are basically freeing you. There's nothing in it for me, but there's a hell of a lot in it for the country. That's why I'm doing it."

Pete looked skeptical. "Altruism sounds good, but it is usually a camouflage for what's really going on."

"Pete, if I wanted to do you harm, I never would've showed up to get you the hell out of California. I would never have risked my life to save yours!"

Pete remained skeptical. "Yeah, right."

Jason was getting impatient. "Fuck it, Pete. I'm risking my life to do this shit, and so did my brother. As a matter of fact, you can just walk away any time you want to. Better yet, here are the keys to the bike. Take it!" Jason threw the keys to Pete.

Pete caught the keys, stared at them, looked off into the distance, and then tossed them back to Jason. "I don't think I have any choice." Pete's voice rang with sadness.

Jason's voice was hard. "That's true fucking gratitude." After stalking back and forth in frustration, Jason said, "OK, if you're with me, let's go. We rescued you, Pete. I'm taking you into Arizona where a friend will meet us and take you on to Ohio."

"One more thing, Jason. Who is *'we'*?"

"Pete, we are a group that is trying to keep our country from deteriorating. We are committed to preserving the political system and the values which have made America great. That's who we are."

Pete stared off into the heat waves of the California sky. *I still don't really know who 'we' are. I was an experiment, and those bastards kept everything from me for my entire life. How stupid and how fucking naive I've been, but no longer. I may have been GeneVision's little experiment, but no more. I've got to get to Ohio and get Hamilton out of there!*

Pete hesitated as Jason mounted the bike. "OK, I'm with you. Thank you, Jason," Pete said quietly as he got on behind Jason, and the two roared off.

Chapter 14

Earlier in California where Pete and Dave had met Jason, two security guards had entered the lobby where Dave stood looking out into the street as Jason and Pete sped away on Jason's motorcycle. The guards' weapons were drawn. Their eyes showed nothing but anger and cruelty.

"You need to lie face down with your hands stretched out above your head," said one of the guards.

"Why? What's -—" Dave did not have a chance to finish his sentence as one of the guards hit him with 20,000 volts from a stun gun.

Dave collapsed to the floor. When he could get his breath, he gasped, "What's wrong? I thought he had come through the tunnel and I tried to catch him."

"You forgot to pick up your casings," one of the guards said as he tossed two shell casings on the floor beside Dave. "I thought they taught you, don't ever leave any evidence behind."

One of the guards buzzed Durango on his communicator. "We've got Dave. He helped Forty escape and he shot Marta Norman."

"Shot Marta Norman!" Durango's voice barked through the communicator. He considered that to be a most interesting development.

"What do you want us to do with him?" the guard asked.

"Take him, sweat him, find out everything he knows, and then get rid of him," Durango said without emotion. "Update me in an hour." With that, Durango clicked off.

"Normally if you kill two people in cold blood, you'd be tried for murder, but Dave, I don't think you need to worry about a trial." The guard smirked, stepped back from Dave, and delivered a karate-style, vicious kick to Dave's head. Dave blacked out

The two guards bound Dave's hands behind him with nylon cuffs, taped Dave's mouth, wrapped strapping tape around his torso, binding his arms tightly beside his body, and then one guard pulled out a syringe and shot 2 cc. of 3-quinuclidinyl benzilate into Dave's arm. Commonly known as BZ, this chemical would cause Dave to become completely incapacitated and suffer various hallucinations. One guard radioed for a conveyor, and they waited without talking. Though they did not know the stakes, they were religiously obedient to the latest orders they had received from Durango who in turn had gotten his orders directly from Novokatnaia.

Chapter 15

As Marina Novokatnaia waited for her flight to Washington, D.C. to board, her cell phone vibrated. She answered curtly, "Yes, Jim." Immediately after their wild weekend together two years earlier, during which she had enjoyed the sex, Marina had hired him to head up GeneVision's security, but she soon saw him for the lightweight that he was. For his part, Durango liked the job but abhorred his arrogant boss.

"We've had an unexpected development." Durango knew that Novokatnaia did not like long-winded explanations, so he cut to the quick. "One of our guards helped Peter Randolph escape. He also apparently gave Randolph a copy of Randolph's own computer file. It's on a holographic disc, so we can track it. Randolph made his getaway on a trooper's motorcycle. Commissioner Westmoreland has an All-Points bulletin out for him, and his picture on TV as a dangerous fugitive, but so far nothing's turned up."

Shit, Marina thought. "How about the guard, what are you going to do with him?"

"We've already done it. He won't be talking to anyone else."

"OK, good, Jim. Now on tracking that HVD, I know it can be tracked, but exactly how is that done?"

"Every GeneVision micro HVD has a dedicated GPS chip which allows our satellites to track it. We haven't tracked his disc because our tracking hardware was destroyed in the earthquake, but we think we can have something up and running in an hour or two. And once we have it up and running, we will know immediately where he is."

"Well, shit," Novokatnaia used her favorite American expletive again.

"It'll be a matter of hours. We have to have a completely new satellite receiver, and the type we need is proprietary from GeneVision's Research Triangle facility. It should arrive here in about an hour and then it will take an hour or so to get it calibrated and functioning."

"OK, keep me informed."

They broke the connection, and Durango wondered, *how could someone so pretty and so good in bed be so ruthless and so heartless. She didn't even blink when I told her we offed Dave, but I guess it doesn't matter now anyway.*

As they called the first-class passengers to board, Novokatnaia's thoughts turned to her Executive Board (GVXCom). *Except for Jacobs in California, Meier in Ohio, and Turner in St. John, no one outside of GVXCom knows the whole story. I'll have to deal with GVXCom. Meier is trustworthy, but Turner's a loose cannon. At some point, I'll have to deal with him too, but not now. Durango does not know the whole story though he thinks he does. All he knows is that we have cloned some people. That in itself is enough to get everybody tarred and feathered, but that is not the major part of the project. But can I be sure that nobody else knows? How did that security guard find out? There's got to be a leak somewhere.*

After Novokatnaia took her seat and asked for a vodka on ice from the flight attendant, she speed-dialed Durango. When he answered with a hint of irritation in his voice, she spoke crisply, "Jim, we've got to nail down the leak. We need to polygraph absolutely everybody to find out who the leak is. Put California in a complete lockdown, and polygraph them. Polygraph everybody!"

"Yes, ma'am" was Durango's terse response.

With that, Novokatnaia hung up. She doubted that Jim Durango was astute enough to know whom she thought she was quoting, but she knew he would follow her orders, unlike the White House staffer who had received a similar order some decades ago. President Nixon had been delusional to think they could polygraph everybody in the State Department, but polygraphing everybody at GeneVision was totally possible.

Novokatnaia ordered another vodka on ice. She then selected the classic Russian movie that she had pre-requested before leaving her office, "The Councillor of State", and settled in for the long flight to Washington, D.C.

Chapter 16

Pete and Jason rode in silence into Arizona, staying on Interstate 8 and staying within the speed limit. After about three hours through the beige scenery of western Arizona, Jason took the exit marked "Bumble Bee/Crown King." After a short, slow drive on a jarring road through the semi-desert, the SUV pulled up in front of The Trading Post. This dilapidated structure was apparently the one functioning commercial building in Bumble Bee, Arizona. It was nighttime, and since there were only several nearby dwellings, there were almost no lights.

"We wait," Jason said.

As he began to doze, Pete's thoughts raced. *Am I really Thomas Jefferson cloned? Do I have a soul? The way I feel, is that the way other people feel who are normal humans? Can someone tell by looking at me that I am different? So I'll meet Alexander Hamilton in Ohio, but what then?* For the first time in memory, he could see the infinite number of stars in the endless darkness of the heavens. The very immensity of what he was looking at simply awed him. Pete was jerked back to the present by the slamming of a car door. A large SUV had pulled up across the parking lot, with a horse van in tow. It was the only other vehicle in the parking lot. Jason blinked the headlights of his bike two long times.

Pete asked, "So, what now?" Jason did not answer.

After only half a minute, a shapely brunette exited the SUV and looked toward Jason's bike. Jason flashed his headlights once, and the brunette immediately got back in the SUV, started it, and pulled away from the parking lot. After about half a minute, Jason started the Harley and followed the SUV that was already a half mile down the road. With the flat, straight road and no house lights, it was easy to follow the SUV. Pete by now realized that this was all according to some script that Jason and the unknown woman had worked out, a script that he had no alternative but to trust. After a few miles, the two vehicles pulled into the long drive of what appeared to be a defunct horse ranch. After crossing over the cattle guard and then under the arched gate above the driveway, Jason stopped in front of a dark Airstream mobile home sitting just inside the driveway. The woman got out of her car and walked backed to Jason's bike.

"There's not too much buzzing around here," the woman said.

"Abigail, you never did learn how to make a joke. How are you, girl?" Jason jumped off the bike and embraced the woman.

Pete noted to himself that the hug looked a little too tight not to have some history to it. The woman eyed Pete closely. "I think I'll enjoy the trip after all," she said with a smile that carried a message that Pete couldn't quite decipher.

"I'm Abigail," she said as she held out her hand.

Pete gladly shook Abigail's hand. *Yes, I think this trip is going to be a lot of fun,* Pete thought.

Abigail looked to be Pete's age, had an interesting smirk on her face, and carried herself so that her 5'8" height looked imposing. When Pete looked closely, which he had been doing ever since he first saw Abigail, he could see that her skin had weathered a little bit, probably from the Arizona sun, and that she wore very little makeup. He took in all the curves of her good figure, and from her posture he felt that she was pretty proud of her curves. It was then that he noticed that she was very obviously looking him over and saw the hint of a smile on her lips.

"Pete, pay attention" Jason said, "Abby's going to drive you to Ohio. She and I have worked together in the past, she knows completely what to do, and you two will look like a regular couple. By now, they're probably looking for us, and your description has probably gone out to whomever they can send it to. Probably you'll see your picture on TV as a fugitive or something, so don't be surprised."

"Two questions," Pete said in a business-like tone. "First, was Abigail, or whatever her name is, CIA, and second, won't we run into roadblocks?"

Before Jason could reply, Abby answered, "Pete, I wasn't exactly part of the CIA, but I did work as an independent contractor for them. I know the ropes on how to keep you from getting nabbed by whoever is chasing you. And, yes, there could well be roadblocks, but we are going to change the way you look, so no one will be able to recognize you."

"Like giving me a beard?"

"No, that's too easy for them to see through. With computer generation, they can look at you with facial hair, without facial hair, with more head hair, bald, you name it. What we are going to do is turn you and me into a loving Chinese couple for the drive to Ohio. You speak Chinese, don't you?"

Pete recognized the language part as a joke, but he also realized that some of what Abby had said was serious. "So what did you do for the CIA, work on disguises or something?"

"No. I basically did other things for them."

Jason spoke up. "Abby's being modest."

Jason was prepared to go on, but Abby stopped him. "OK, enough," Abby said. "Let's turn you and me into a happy Chinese couple. We'll be second generation Chinese so don't worry about the language. We'll work this little bit of magic in there." Abby motioned to the mobile home.

The three walked toward the mobile home. They mounted the several steps into the Airstream and entered into what looked to be a cross between a laboratory and a beauty salon. Two women, who could have modeled for a French fashion magazine, stood together beside a sophisticated makeup counter, and one of the women said, "Welcome to our world of visual magic. We shall now strive for Chinese bliss."

Chapter 17

The late night Air Barbados flight landed at the modern Grantley Adams International Airport, the only airport in Barbados. Dr. Meier and Jim easily cleared the casual customs procedures and walked outside the baggage claim area to the curbside. A black man in pink flip-flops walked up to them. "Dr. Meier, I am Troy, and I'm your driver. If you have all of your baggage, we can go directly to the Southern Palms."

"Yes, we've got everything. Let's go," Dr. Meier replied. The three piled into Troy's aging Toyota van and sped away from the airport.

Twenty-five minutes later, the van pulled into the sheltered entryway of the Southern Palms. After an efficient check-in at the welcome desk in the open-air lobby, Jim and Dr. Meier settled into their separate rooms on the far side of the resort, away from the noise of the bar and the swimming pool. Though the night was dark and quiet, and Jim could hear the call of the Atlantic surf just a few dozen feet from his room. There was a knock at the door. Jim answered, and Dr. Meier walked in.

"It's late, and I'm going to say hi to a couple of guys in the bar that I know, and then I'm heading to bed. Let's meet for breakfast, OK?"

"Sounds good to me." Jim responded.

The two men said good night to each other, and Dr. Meier went back to his room. When he had locked and chained the door to his room, Dr. Meier punched in a direct dial number to the United States. Novokatnaia's curt voicemail answered. "I am not available. Leave your number. Thank you." At the sound of the beep, Dr. Meier said, "This is Meier. We are now in Barbados, and I'll just wait to hear from you. Some of your associates are here, and I am going to meet up with them now." He gave the telephone number for his room and hung up. At least he had Jim out of Ohio, and Barbados was remote enough that they were really out of harm's way. At least, that was Meier's hope. He did not know Novokatnaia's Russian associates waiting for him in the bar but could not really avoid them since she had pretty much demanded that he meet with them. Meier couldn't get the "what ifs" out of his mind. *What if Peter Randolph finds out the true story about who he is? What if he finds out about Jim? What if he goes to the press? What happens to me if he goes to the press? What if Jim finds out about himself? What if the FBI gets wind of what we've been doing?* Meier continued to worry. He could see his whole world caving in. He had never felt so stressed. He had all the backup plans in place the best he could, and tomorrow he would be able to get a better handle on things. He headed to the bar to meet with Marina's Russian friends. But Dr. Meier was beginning to have uneasy feelings about the whole enterprise, Marina Novokatnaia included.

————

On the other side of the continent, Durango's thoughts about Novokatnaia's latest order led him to other thoughts. *She's an absolute idiot if she thinks we can polygraph everybody! If there's a leak, it's going to look bad for me. If the polygraphs don't turn up a leak, it still looks bad for me. This is a no win situation. How the hell can I polygraph all 114 people who work here? Well, it's 111 now because we don't have to worry about Dave or Marta or that other guard anymore. Dave could be the leak, but someone had to leak it to him because there's no way he would have enough brains to access the data.*

Durango was familiar with Dave's credentials and job history. Dave had finished high school, flirted with a number of jobs before becoming a night watchman at the Pacific Beach

Boardwalk. How demanding could that job be? All he had to do was make sure the skaters didn't molest the tourists and make sure some of those bikers didn't mess with Slomo, Pacific Beach's aged but agile skating icon. Dave had actually stayed on that job for over a year before coming to work for Durango as one of security guards. Durango knew or thought he knew that Dave had a relatively low IQ and even less initiative. *So what had gotten him involved with Peter Randolph? It had to be money, but who would've been offering him money, and unless they already knew what was going on at GeneVision, why would they even offer Dave money? Who could be so interested in what GeneVision was doing that they would offer a security guard money for information?* Durango decided that he really needed to find out the identity of who was using Dave. *Maybe polygraphs could focus on that angle - - - who had talked to Dave about what? But I don't have anybody to do the polygraphing now that Marta is gone.* Durango knew nothing about Dave's former intelligence work.

Chapter 18

As the two disguise artists worked on Abby and Pete, transforming them into a second generation Chinese-Americans, Jason watched and waited. Jason realized that he did not have the complete picture of what was going on in GeneVision's facilities in California and Ohio but he easily had enough to make the play for hush money. He would simply email the head of GeneVision, the lady with the Russian name, tell her what he knew, and demand payment into the numbered bank account he and Dave maintained in Panama. It was a violation of federal law to clone humans, and GeneVision had definitely cloned three humans, one in California, one in Ohio, and one in St. John in the Caribbean. He and Dave had found the *piéce de resistance* during the early morning hours of GeneVision's New Year's party just a few months ago. Durango and the others had become much too drunk to realize that Dave, the designated sober guard for that night, had entered Durango's office for a not-so-routine look-see. While there, he found in the top, locked drawer of Durango's desk a document entitled, "Biologic Accelerator - - Documentation." The documentation that Dave had emailed to Jason from Durango's office, described in detail a genetic implant for a newly cloned infant that would drastically accelerate the physical and chemical development of a clone. The accelerator was set to work until the clone was biologically 20 years old. Thus, though Pete was biologically and developmentally twenty-five years old, he had actually been "born" only ten years ago. The first twenty years of physical development had taken only five years. This experimental procedure seems to have worked flawlessly. Pete's memories, unlike his physical body, were psychologically and behaviorally generated and he "adopted" them during that first five years of life. By the end of the fifth year of his life, he was physically and mentally twenty years old and had all the memories of a full childhood. Then for the next five years, intense schooling and training had brought him up to par with an ordinary twenty-five-year-old. Novokatnaia would pay anything to keep the acceleration technology secret. Dave had befriended Pete as much as a security guard could without drawing notice or creating suspicion and had learned from just talking to him and being around him that Pete was at least on the surface no different from any other twenty-five-year-old. Thus, Dave and Jason had two money winners - - the fact of the cloning and the fact of the Biologic Accelerator. Dave and Jason had worked several swindles in the past, and they immediately recognized a goldmine when they saw it. They also fully realized that this goldmine was fraught with danger. Though both Jason and Dave truly loved America and wanted to arrest its decline, they also truly loved money and saw their chance to get rich.

———

"How do we look?" Abby asked, bringing Jason back to the present. Before him stood two Chinese in their mid-twenties and both looking somewhat Americanized.

"Not bad, not bad at all," Jason said. "You two could pass for two Orientals escaped from the Dear Leader's Paradise." Jason's political incorrectness was overshadowed by his reference to North Korea's despot, but his assessment was accurate. Both Abby and Pete looked Chinese. Their skin complexion, faces, hands ——everything was beautifully Chinese.

"The job is complete," Abby said. "We are completely Chinese down to our privates." Jason now recalled that one at a time, each had gone into the Air Stream's bathroom for fifteen or twenty minutes for the application of special skin pigment and other adjustments to private areas of their bodies. Pete had exited the room smiling.

Pete's make-up magician said, "I've added some body padding to Pete so that he looks about twenty pounds heavier than he did before. I call that the Doubtfire technique." Pete did look a little heavier.

Jason then took several photographs of each of the newly minted Chinese, and after about ten minutes of working with the scanner, printer, and plastic document maker, Jason said, "Here are some documents." He gave each a packet of documents, driver's licenses, charge cards, and other things routinely carried by Asian-American yuppies. "Be sure you know your names," Jason said.

"My name Lin Dan," Pete said, faking a Chinese accent.

"Don't put on an accent. You are second generation. That means you were born here and you are as American as anyone else." Abby was dead serious and seemed to be admonishing Pete.

"No problem," said Pete. "What's your name?"

"My name was Zhou Mi, but when I married you, I took your last name. My name is now Lin Mi. Last names go first. And it's time for us to get going. We want to get to Ohio as soon as we can."

Pete hesitated. "What about our parents? Suppose someone asks us where we are from, where we were born, and things like that?"

Abby answered, "You have a bio to read in the car, and once you've read it, we'll burn it. I already know my history. But just so you know, your parents lived in New York, and you were named after a great Chinese singles badminton champion. After you were born, your parents went to Wuhan to visit relatives and were killed by the Wuhan coronavirus. You obviously survived."

"I did?" Pete asked.

Abby ignored him. "My parents live in Indonesia. They too lived in New York for a while but moved back to Indonesia to be closer to their families and to escape New York's crime."

Jason took Pete by the shoulders. "Pete, we might not see each other again. You have a lot to catch up on. A lot has happened in the last twenty-four hours. I hope you know now beyond the shadow of a doubt that obviously we're all on your side. You'll be safe in Ohio. You have a head start, and once you're in Ohio, you'll make the right contacts and then you'll need to fade away into the American landscape as you and the others figure out what to do."

"The others," Pete whispered to himself. "Thanks, Jason, and thank Dave when you see him. Will I get to talk to you from Ohio?"

"Yeah, we'll talk," Jason said without conviction and with a sudden far-away look in his eyes. "If we don't, it'll be because they caught up with me, otherwise, yeah, we'll talk. One more thing. Don't trust anyone except Abby until you meet Jim Fawcett in Ohio. You'll need to bring him up to speed. I doubt he knows anything at all."

The two men embraced, then everyone walked out into the dry desert air.

"Good luck, boy," Jason said softly.

"Thanks, Jason."

Abby and Jason bid each other goodbyes. Jason mounted the Harley. Abby got into the driver's side of the SUV. "Coming?" she said to Pete who was watching Jason head down the dirt road.

"Yeah, I'm coming." Pete got into the passenger side. He then saw that the SUV was outfitted with a very sophisticated navigation system and a radar detector but otherwise looked ordinary. "I'll program the GPS," Pete said.

Abby watched, amused, as Pete examined the unit. After a full minute, he still had not gotten started with the system. Abby then informed him, "It's not a GPS. It's a special kind of navigation system. It'll route us away from traffic jams and recommend the best routes. This particular unit will route us around tollbooths, roadblocks, and any places where the police might be checking cars. It'll alert us to any police presence within a mile or so. But its main feature is that it blocks photos of our faces and our license tags by emitting a certain kind of microwave whenever it detects cameras and then somehow makes any image captured by that camera show up as a light glare. It also blocks location services on our cell phones and laptops so that we cannot be tracked. To get it programmed, just push the AutoRoute button. I've already entered the destination name and programmed all the other stuff in."

"I've used a GPS in Dr. Jacob's car. I know enough to know that these GPS's always lose the signal and when they have the signal, the routes are often irrational. I hope you are not depending on this thing to get us around police checkpoints." Pete was demonstrating, he thought, that he had had enough experience with GPS units to know their shortcomings.

Abby laughed. "Pete, we won't lose any signals. This unit is not a market unit. The signal it uses is from DOD's Block IIIF Satellite. The Block IIF is the newest satellite that the government publicly acknowledges, but the Block IIIF is so secret that its existence is not even on the books. No lost signals, no weather problems, no nothing. It's pretty flawless. I'm actually proud of it," Abby said, sounding like maybe she had helped design it.

"Be careful. God opposes the proud," Pete said. "Did you help design it?"

"No, but I know the people who did. That's why I'm proud of it, and we -—I -—use it."

"We?

Abby didn't respond. They road in silence until Pete repeated, "We?"

"Pete, I'm part of an off-the-books organization that has learned who you are, and we are committed to protecting you from anyone who wants to harm you, and we're pretty sure that includes the U. S. government. So for now, Pete, let's leave it at that, OK?"

Pete quickly responded, "Not OK. Who is this organization, and why do you think the U. S. government even knows about me since I didn't even know about me until now?"

"Pete, I'm only a foot soldier in this organization, and I can't answer those questions, but I'm taking you to people who can."

"I thought you were taking me to Ohio and this Jim Fawcett."

"I'm taking you to people who will protect you and answer all your questions, but first we have to detour to Ohio."

"So being part of this Organization as you call it is how you got this unit and access to the satellite signal, right?" Pete asked.

"Yes to both," Abby replied. "Plus, we have some backups, too." Abby pressed a button and the sound panel in the dash lowered to reveal another device that Pete had never seen before. "This is sort of a universal communicator. " Abby said. "It'll connect us directly to various highway patrol broadcasts between here and Ohio and will provide telephonic connections to anyone anywhere. It will also let us listen in to any police or FBI communications within a hundred miles."

Pete gazed at the futuristic system. He wanted to read his computer file. "Will all this stuff allow me to use my disc? I'd like to read my computer file."

"No problem," Abby said.

He reached into his backpack and pulled out the HVD. "Dave said everything I needed to know was on this disk. Where do I put this into the system?" Pete saw the DVD drive, the flash drive, another drive that he could not identify, but he did not see an HDV drive.

"It should fit into one of those slots," Abby replied without looking.

Searching and still not seeing where to put in the HVD, Pete said, "I still don't see where it goes. You're the computer whiz. How about giving me a hint?"

Abby smiled. "OK, give it to me."

Pete handed her the HVD.

Abby looked at the disk she was holding in her hand. "My God!" she exclaimed. "How long have you had this out of the bag? Get it back in the bag now!" She was quite familiar with HVD technology and recognized this version of the HVD as the most advanced computer portable storage system available and that it could also allow GeneVision to detect their location.

Pete jammed the HVD back into the resin bag.

"Damn! That device is equipped with a secure tracking capacity. GeneVision can know where we are at any time if they have it programmed to track continuously. I can't disable the chip without triggering a self-destruct cycle." Abby was clearly worried. "I wish you had told me you had an HVD!"

"It was only out of the bag about ten seconds. I'm sorry. I've never even heard of an HDV before."

Abby said pensively, "HVD, Pete. There's no way to block its signal if it's out of that bag, and there's no way to disable it without destroying the data on the disk." Abby continued. "We're pretty much stuck with it. Just don't take it out of the bag until we figure something out. And I don't know if they could get a location on us or not from ten seconds."

Chapter 19

Abby looked worried.

Pete started, "How about — " He was interrupted by Abby.

"Let me think!" she said with irritation. After a few moments, she said, "We might be lucky if he is in town. A professor I worked with last year, Dr. Johan Schweers, is part of the Deep Ecliptic Survey for the Lowell Observatory. That's pretty close to here. His facility will be shielded from any outside penetration, so the HVD can't be detected as long as it is inside his place. He will have HVD capability and we can download all the data from the HVD onto something else and then get rid of it. We'll still have the data, but they won't be able to track us."

She drove and at the same time dictated some numbers to the navigation system. "This says we have 96 miles to go. We'll hit Interstate 17 in 2 miles, then it's a straight shot to Lowell. We just have to hope that they don't get us before we get to Lowell. I just hope that bag actually works."

Pete glanced at Abby with raised eyebrows, now wondering whether in fact the bag would protect them.

Abby dictated a number for a phone call. They both heard a voicemail answer over the car's speakers. After the voice mail went through its answering routine, Abby said, "Johan, this is Abby Adams. I'm in a little bit of a jam and wonder if you can help me. I know it's late at night but I'll explain. I'm driving north and will pass near to Lowell and wonder if I can use your computer to read a disk. And, yes, I know it's late." Abby was being deliberately vague. "Here's what I would like —- Johan, thank God you picked up!"

Abby switched to private mode and held the cell phone to her ear. After listening to Dr. Schweers, Abby said, "Yes I'm fine, but I'm on the road and need this big favor." She listened to Dr.

Schweers, nodded several times, then said, "Thank you for not asking. I'm on Interstate 17 about 90 miles south of Flagstaff, so I should be there in about an hour and a half."

She listened for about a minute, and then said. "You are very prescient. See you in a while." She clicked off the cell phone.

"You're kidding. Your name is Abigail Adams?"

"No, not really. That's just a name I use. You do not know my real name. Not yet, anyway, but there's still time to remedy that." Abby gave him her smirky smile. "Anyway, Schweers realizes that there is something unusual going on that I do not want to talk about on the phone. He knows not to ask. He and I have done each other some favors over the past couple of years. The only little problem is that he can't see you. I don't want anyone to see you. That way, even if they find out about him, he will never have seen you."

"What about your Chinese do?" Pete asked.

"My do?" Abby laughed. "I guess I'll tell him I'm going to Vegas. I really think once he sees my *en chinois*, he'll keep his distance and won't ask much of anything."

"You sound pretty confident."

"I am."

"I mean, confident that you can trust him."

"I am."

"How so?"

"A couple of years ago, I caught him using cocaine. I have a photo." She held up her cell phone. "Once someone catches you using cocaine, they can own you if they want to. For tonight, I own him." Abby spoke with a coldness that Pete had not heard in her voice before.

The two rode in silence for close to an hour. It was after midnight, and traffic on Interstate 17 was very light. Abby drove close to ninety miles per hour, protected by the system-generated alerts along the way, and took the Milton Road exit. After several minutes, Abby took the right fork in the road and then stopped the car before heading up the switchback road. "You need to get out here and wait for me. Stay out of sight. Behind those trees would be good."

"I don't like the idea of just waiting out here in the woods in the middle of the night."

"You're a big boy, but do you want a flashlight?"

They both laughed. "No," he said. "Clones are not afraid of the dark."

Abby gave him a curious look.

"I'm joking, Abby."

Abby reached into the side pocket of the car and pulled out another cell phone. "Keep this. My cell number is programmed as speed dial 2. My cell is also in the address book under Adams Restaurant. My phone will be on vibrate, so call me if there is an emergency. Otherwise, don't call. I've already set your phone to vibrate, otherwise to make no noise at all. When I come back down the hill, if I keep going, that means they are on to us, and you are on your own. If that happens, all the information you need is in the cell phone. That cell phone is fixed so that it cannot be tracked or traced, but don't use it unless you have to."

They looked at each other. Pete wondered what would it have been like with her if they had met in another life. He wanted to find out but concluded that knowing Abby that way was not his destiny. He pocketed the cell phone, exited the car, and disappeared quickly into the woods.

Abby gunned the SUV up the switchback road and wondered what would it have been like with this clone if they had met in another life. She sighed, resigned to what she felt must be a higher calling and one that called for sacrifice.

Chapter 20

Pete waited, hidden from view should any other vehicles come up this road at this time of night. He thought back over the past hours. Only this morning he had awakened to the violence of the largest earthquake California had had in recorded history. He had found out that his home was more of an elaborate Potemkin prison than a home, that Dr. Jacobs, whom he loved, was part of some cloning conspiracy, and that he, Pete, was the clone! He was a clone!! And not just any clone! Thomas Jefferson! A security guard and someone disguised as a state trooper had hustled him out of GeneVision's clutches. And, now hiding in the woods, Pete was in the grip of a group of people who used to work *with* the CIA, not for them, but with them, whatever that distinction meant, and were now doing their own thing. Apparently there were other clones, and one or more of them must be in Ohio. He was disguised to look Chinese and was in some futuristically equipped car on the way to Ohio with a pretty brunette who said that their computer disk enabled them to be tracked across the country, and that disk had volumes of information about the cloning operation, but he could not access that disk without giving away their location to people who wanted to kill them.

All of these thoughts were running through Pete's mind again and again when someone shook him by the shoulder. "Wake up, fellow."

In a nanosecond blur, Pete had Abby in a head hold before he was even fully awake. Then he realized that it was Abby. "Abby, shit—-!" Before he could finish the sentence, he found himself flying through the air. Abby had broken the head hold and flipped him!

"Abby, shit, you could have killed me." He held his neck. Abby held hers. They just stared at each other, each grimacing with neck pain.

"You were asleep. I was standing here for about a minute saying your name, trying to wake you up. I'm sorry. I didn't mean to hurt you." Abby was secretly heartened to see that Pete's reaction was really not fear and flight, but fight. Jason had told her as much, and now she had seen for herself that Pete was going to be a formidable opponent for anyone who wanted to tangle with him.

Pete now realized that Abby had martial arts training. Not only was she a looker, but now he knew she was lethal too.

Both still held their necks. "Abby, you could have broken my neck and paralyzed me. Clones have special necks," Pete said with mock seriousness. As they looked at each other, both gripping their necks, they both broke into laughter. And they continued eye contact.

Pete took Abby in his arms, and they deeply kissed. His hand found her breast, and he gently fondled it as Abby undid Pete's belt and reached into his pants. "I see that clones are well hung - - - and hard," Abby whispered.

After ten minutes of very physical love-making, Abby and Pete just lay there in the woods until Abby said softly, "OK, we'd better get dressed and hit the road."

"How 'bout one more time?" Pete said with a smile, reaching for Abby.

"Not now," Abby said as she stood and began to get dressed.

As they dressed, Abby said, "I didn't print anything out. I've got it on another HVD. I've also got the tracking HVD, and we have to get rid of it, but not here. Johan hacked into their satellite transmission and set it to transmit a location signal at variable intervals from twenty minutes to three hours apart.

Quite a piece of genius to do that! We'll have to assume that they already are after us, so we have to get rid of this thing as soon as possible."

"With all my personal info on it?" Pete asked.

"I zeroed it out. Nothing is on it at all, but the tracking is still functioning. I didn't want to disable it yet."

"Why the hell not? They are tracking us!"

"Don't sweat it. It's back in the bag. And they will be tracking the HVD, not us," Abby said, with the first full smile she had had since she learned a couple of hours earlier that there was an HVD in the car.

Pete smiled. He understood the possibilities.

He does catch on fast, Abby thought as she pulled onto Interstate 17, but this time she headed south, not north as before.

———

A tense hour and a half later, Abby had driven back into Phoenix and approached the Phoenix Sky Harbor International Airport. She did not stop at any of the passenger terminals, all of which were practically deserted at this time of night. Instead she headed straight to the twenty-four-hour UPS dispatch office.

"Wait here, Pete. I'll get rid of this thing and then we'll get started to Ohio for real."

"Where are you going to send it?" Once out of the box, the HVD could be tracked.

Abby smiled. "I know a Virginia address outside of Washington, D. C., that'll get these people off our tail." Abby quickly exited the car before Pete could think it through. She well knew that he would not like her selection of recipients.

The UPS counter attendant, once Abby succeeded in waking him up, was very helpful in providing an Express Small Package container. Abby took the HVD out of its insulating bag, packed it into the UPS container, sealed the container, and handed it to the UPS attendant. She dictated an address to the attendant who then affixed the computer-generated address label and bar codes to the package. Abby paid cash, and returned to the car. The whole transaction took no more than ten minutes.

During that time, Pete quickly accessed the contents of the HVD that Dr. Schweers had prepared. It was a detailed, technical description of File Forty. He, Peter Randolph, was File Forty. And then Pete saw it again.

> The human generation experiment has been completely successful. In all discernable aspects, clone Peter Randolph is Thomas Jefferson.

Pete exclaimed to himself, "I am Thomas Jefferson! Thomas Jefferson! I am a clone of Thomas Jefferson!" He was still trying to understand what it all meant when Abby opened the driver-side door and got behind the wheel.

"What's wrong?" Abby asked when she saw the look of shock on Pete's face. Then she saw the HVD link on the car's computer screen.

"Yeah," Abby said softly.

Pete finally broke the silence. "When will it go out?" he asked.

"They have a plane at 7 AM. That's about four hours from now, and that's the first UPS plane out. If no one from GeneVision gets here before it leaves, they will think you are on a passenger plane, and they'll spend a lot of time trying to figure out where you are going."

"Abby, how much of this do you know?" Pete asked, motioning to the HVD.

"Pete, I know that you are Mr. Jefferson, and so we both know how important it is to get you to safety."

"So, the government is after us. Anyone else?" Pete asked.

Abby looked thoughtful and after a moment answered, "For starters, GeneVision. Then, there's the press. But the real worry is our own beloved government. If they don't know the details about this cloning project already, they soon will. And then you can bet on it, they'll do everything they can to bring you and the others in, and not just bring you in, but bring you in for good. It'll be a one-way trip. You *are* Thomas Jefferson, you know. My God. Thomas Jefferson." She looked at Pete with admiration and some degree of awe. "Thomas Jefferson," she repeated reverently. "I am in the car with Thomas Jefferson. I had sex with Thomas Jefferson." She shook her head, finding it all almost too difficult to believe even though she knew it was true.

"So you're saying they'll keep us out of sight, in a government facility, or somewhere?"

"I'm saying that they'll drain every bit of data they can from you and then who knows? But it won't be good."

"They'll kill us?"

"What'd you think? If you were the government, and you had basically shredded the Constitution, routinely lied to 'we the people,' and pursued your own personal agenda at the expense of the very values on which this country was founded, what would you do when suddenly out of the blue, Jefferson, Hamilton, and Franklin show up?"

Pete just turned and stared out of the car window. *So there really are two other clones*, Pete thought. *Alexander Hamilton and Benjamin Franklin!*

"Hamilton and Franklin?" Pete asked, surprisingly calmly.

"Yes, Hamilton and Franklin. But, Pete, that's all I know. I know GeneVision was trying to clone Hamilton and Franklin, but I don't know where they are. But one of them is Jim Fawcett, and that's why we are heading to Ohio."

Chapter 21

Durango exclaimed with elation, "Finally, a break!" A technician had just informed him that the satellite had established communications with the HVD.

"Here it is," the technician said as he handed the printout to Durango. "The HVD is at 33 26' North, 112 West. That's in Phoenix, and looks to be directly at the Phoenix Airport. I love these things. They are more dependable than air tags." The technician was examining a military map of Arizona.

"So he's planning on flying away. Well, big surprise for Mr. Peter Randolph. Within two minutes, every screen in that little podunk airport'll have his picture on it as a dangerous fugitive. Get the manager of the airport on the phone right now, and email him the pictures we have of Peter Randolph. Tell him Mr. Randolph is wanted under the federal terrorist laws and that he might have a bomb on him. Then let me talk to him."

While the technician, eager to please his boss, scurried into action, Durango used his own cell phone to call CHP's Deputy Commissioner Westmoreland.

Westmoreland's phone rang and continued to ring. "Answer the phone, you pinhead!" Durango felt his blood pressure rising. Finally, a sleepy voice answered, "Yeah, hello."

"Westy, how are you?" Durango tried not to sound irritated.

"I haven't slept at all since we have a murderer on the loose using one of our bikes."

"Westy, I need to get to Phoenix. We have a very reliable tip that Mr. Randolph is in the Phoenix airport as we speak. I'm arranging to get him arrested as a fugitive in interstate flight. I need to get to Phoenix, so what I need is a motorcycle escort to Brown Field and then one of your jets to fly me to Phoenix. I don't have to tell you how important this is and how many important people are going to want this situation resolved ASAP. And, of course, you will be very favorably remembered by my people."

"OK, you've got it. I have people in your area so I can have a car there in ten minutes, and the jet will be ready when you get to Brown. But, is Brown open? Was the runway damaged by the quake?"

"The runway is operational. I checked, but the tower is closed until 8 AM."

"I'll arrange it. You won't need the tower."

The two men broke the telephone connection. Westmoreland was now more worried than he had been before because of the tension he had detected in Durango's voice. And Durango was tense to the point of cracking. But Westy knew that being "favorably remembered" meant a hefty sum coming to good old Westy from Durango's company.

"Sir, Sky Harbor has alerted all the gates, and they are actively seeking Peter Randolph." Durango's eager young technician smiled, knowing that he had done well. "They've electronically distributed his pictures to the active gates and have put his picture on the TV monitors around the airport, except there are certain screens under contract to the local cable service which they cannot preempt without permission from the cable company."

"OK, sounds good" Durango now began to relax a little. He could begin to picture in his own mind putting the cuffs on Peter Randolph and hustling him back to California where he would probably never be heard from again.

"Sir," a uniformed trooper filled the doorway. "We are ready to get you to Brown Field." Brown Field was a government airport outside San Diego used primarily by law enforcement and some military agencies. Special clearances at Brown Field were business as usual. Also, it would not raise any suspicions for a state plane to take off with some urgency.

Forty-five minutes later, Durango and two assistants were in the air for the short flight to Sky Harbor. Durango was still uneasy about the HVD transmissions since they had been erratic over the past hours. For some reason the GPS signals were not transmitting properly. Durango agonized that if Randolph got out of Phoenix that it could be almost impossible to find him.

Chapter 22

Marina Novokatnaia's red eye flight landed at Ronald Reagan National Airport on time at 8:30 AM. She immediately took a taxi to her luxury suite at the Hay-Adams where she prepared for the board meeting that was scheduled for 11 AM. She had been updated by Durango, and felt that he was not at all in control of apprehending Peter Randolph. Randolph was simply on the loose, and no one had any idea at all where he was. At least Dr. Meier was apparently able to get his little clone prick out of the country. She would make arrangements for both Jim Fawcett and Hans Meier to be taken to Russia where she would have no difficulty in keeping them under wraps.

Even though it was three hours earlier in California, she punched in Durango's cell phone number. It went immediately to voice mail. She left a short message. Marina felt frustrated that at a time like this Durango would turn off his phone. *Unless,* she thought, *for some reason he is out of range or has deliberately made himself inaccessible because something has happened.* Marina was thinking the worst could have happened. After all, she had received that ominous message that the White House was asking questions. *How could they have found out anything, and just how much did they know?*

————

Durango chose not to deplane in Phoenix but simply waited for the next transmission from the HVD. At 8:30 AM Phoenix time, sitting in the cockpit, Durango opened a radio channel to GeneVision's Communications Center, or what was passing for a communications center after the serious quake damage. The open channel signal was promptly received at the California communications site, and the California technician spoke to Durango. "The disk is apparently in the desert northeast of Phoenix, sir. That does not make any sense to me because there are no roads or highways at the location from which the transmission came. I don't understand, Mr. Durango, unless they dumped it or something. Plus, it's only transmitting intermittingly, not continuously. That's unusual for this unit, and I can't seem to do anything about it."

Durango spoke, "Yeah, that is strange. Anyway, I'll take it from here. Fax me the report."

The fax followed within a couple of minutes. Durango studied the fax which included the military map with the location of the latest transmission highlighted. He dreaded the answer but asked his pilot anyway, "Jim, is this a flight path?" Durango drew a line from Sky Harbor through the location point.

"It is a normal flight path for east bound traffic, but sometimes west bound traffic is routed out of Sky Harbor that way too to avoid too many planes in one area."

"Is there any way to find out what planes were in that area at 8:45 this morning?"

"I can ask the tower. I think they'll talk to us even though they don't like to give out that kind of information."

After a short conversation with the supervisor in the tower, Durango's pilot gave Durango the news: "There were three planes in that area, all east bound. A private charter plane bound for BWI - - that's Baltimore - - - a Southwest Airlines plane bound for Nashville, and a UPS plane bound for Reagan."

Durango thought out loud, "If they are trying to be clever, they are going to Nashville. Nobody would go to Nashville unless they were trying to be clever. If they are trying to get to D.C., then they are on the Baltimore plane. The only way the

UPS plane is relevant is if they know that the HVD is a tracker and ditched it, but there's no way they'd know that."

"They've been pretty resourceful to this point. To get him out of California so efficiently tells me that they have some sophisticated help." The ex-military pilot had flown Durango to a number of places, usually junkets, over the past five years, and Durango respected his judgment.

"Yeah, but what's on that disk is priceless not just to us but to Peter Randolph, too. He wouldn't just give up the disk, at least not without copying it over to another device. Those disks can be copied at high class computer centers, but in the middle of the night?" Durango was unsure which plane out of Phoenix to concentrate on.

"We'll play the odds. We'll eventually get another GPS fix. Let's go to D.C. Even if they fly into Baltimore, the objective is going to be D.C."

"Mr. Durango, there are a lot of scientific facilities and universities in Baltimore where they could be headed. I wouldn't rule out Baltimore."

"You're right. Let's go to D.C. and sit tight and then try to pinpoint where they are going. We can get a chopper over to Baltimore if we have to. Let's get to D.C. How quickly can we leave?"

"I'll talk to the tower and try to get us out fast. We'll have to fuel up and do a preflight."

Durango nodded and then checked his cell phone for messages and heard the clipped voice of Marina Novokatnaia. "Someone in the government is asking questions about the San Diego operation. Get rid of everything having to do with Peter Randolph. He has never existed! Understand? That means documents, computer files, everything. Zero out every computer. And when you find him, keep him totally out of sight and call me immediately. And why the hell is your cell phone not answering? Call me. I'll be in a meeting during the middle of the day."

Durango was starting to get a headache. Ten o'clock in the morning was too early for a headache. *How can I get rid of all the Randolph stuff while I'm going to D.C.? Somebody back in San Diego will have to handle that. But why does she want all traces of Randolph to disappear. He's just a clone, and even though that creates a pile of federal legal bullshit, the scientific achievement itself will overshadow the illegality of it. And didn't she learn anything from either one of the Clintons? Cover-ups just don't work. Too bad about Marta Norman. She could have sterilized the site. I'll just have to trust whoever took over from Marta to do the job.*

Durango continued to wonder, *Why would Novokatnaia erase all evidence of one of the greatest scientific breakthroughs of the century? Why not just take the heat and then enjoy the rewards and the glory? She's the first to clone a human. That's got to land her in the science hall of fame.*

Chapter 23

As Jim Fawcett walked on the beach in front of the Southern Palms, his nagging concerns deepened. *Clearly something was amiss. Things just don't seem right. Why had they left Ohio so quickly? Why was there so much ambiguity about the trip? Why had Meier picked only me to make the trip? Had Doc gotten into some trouble or done something illegal? Last night he looked fearful, pale, and completely stressed out. Anyway it was almost 10 AM and he had not come out of his room yet so maybe all he needed was a good night's sleep.*

Jim returned to his room and dialed Dr. Meier's room. There was no answer. Fifteen minutes later, he dialed again, and still there was no answer. Jim walked over to the poolside restaurant and ordered tea, yogurt, and mangoes. Thirty minutes later, after eating, he walked over to Dr. Meier's room, and knocked repeatedly on the door. No answer. He quickly walked to the front desk and asked them to ring Dr. Meier's room. Still there was no answer. It was now close to noon.

"He was supposed to meet me a while ago and I haven't been able to get hold of him all morning. I'm scared something may have happened to him. Can you let me into his room?"

"I'll get Security." The desk clerk had a brief telephone conversation, and the resort manager appeared from an inner office. The desk clerk explained the situation, and the manager said, "Send Security to the room, and tell them not to enter until we get there. Mr. Fawcett, come with me."

As they briskly walked across the resort property to Dr. Meier's room, the manager asked, "What is your relationship to the gentleman?"

"I am . . . ." Jim hesitated and then said, " . . . his son. He is my father."

The manager stopped walking. "But you two do not have the same last name, Mr. Fawcett." The manager looked Jim squarely in the eye.

"When my parents got divorced, I lived with my mother and took her last name." The manager said nothing, simply nodded.

Two uniformed security guards were waiting when Jim and the Southern Palms manager reached Dr. Meier's room. The manager knocked on the door, and there was no response. He knocked again, this time more loudly. There was still no answer.

"Open the door," the manager ordered, and one of the security guards unlocked the door. The safety chain was not in place and the guard opened the door halfway. "Dr. Meier?" the manager called out.

"Doc, are you in here?" Jim yelled.

There was no answer.

The four men entered the room.

Dr. Meier was still in bed. Jim approached the bed. He gently touched Dr. Meier's shoulder. Jim withdrew his hand quickly and looked at the other men. "I think he's . . . ." Jim's voice trailed off.

The manager looked closely at Dr. Meier without touching him, then grabbed the room phone and punched in a number. Jim could hear the answer at the other end of the line, "Front desk."

"Get Sergeant Barnes of the police immediately. If Sergeant Barnes is not available, call me back. I want him, not just anyone." He hung up the phone. "I'll have to ask you to leave the room," the manager spoke authoritatively to Jim. "Please go wait in my office."

Jim was shaken but attempted to keep his composure. "He's my father. I'll wait here."

"Under Bajan law, no one can be alone with the deceased until the doctor has made a proper examination," the manager said. "I am asking you politely to leave the room." As he said that, the manager looked fleetingly at the two Security guards. Jim got the message. He would be escorted from the room unless he left voluntarily. "Mr. Fawcett, *trust me*," the manager said deliberately, emphasizing the words. "Please wait in my office."

"I'll wait outside. I don't want you people in here either, so under your law, you must leave also. And I didn't hear you call for a doctor."

"Very well, we'll all leave, but again I'm asking you to *trust me* and wait in my office. Mr. Fawcett, there are times in our lives when we make critical decisions which determine much about our future. This is one of those times for you. *Mr. Fawcett, you must trust me*." He looked intently at Jim.

Jim looked at the manager inquisitively but could discern nothing extra in the manager's face or demeanor. The manager then looked at Jim reassuringly and said, "Come, I'll go with you." He turned to the security guards. "Do not let anyone in this room unless I am with them," he barked.

"Yes, sir," they both said in unison.

The manager then took Jim gently by the arm and began to lead him back to the resort's main office. After a few moments of walking, he said, "I know this is very difficult for you," the manager began, but Jim cut him off. "Don't try to cheer my up. Let's just wait for the doctor which you never called."

"Mr. Fawcett, I know the gentleman well, and he's not at all your father. I know it and you know it. So just stay quiet and listen. Dr. Meier is an important man and has come here on several occasions. He and I have had a special arrangement regarding his business. Mr. Fawcett, I know what his business is, probably better than you. He pays top dollar, I give him some extra favors, keep his stays confidential, and protect his privacy. The police who come will protect that privacy. They're not the regular island police. Instead they're special police that we use on special occasions. Dr. Meier did leave an envelope for you in my care when you first checked in. He instructed me to give it to you should anything happen to him. I suggest we don't talk further until we're in my office."

What the hell is going on? I was right - - - something is very much wrong with all of this, the quick exit from Ohio and now this! Jim's thoughts began to flow a mile a minute.

Chapter 24

At exactly 11 AM, Marina Novokatnaia entered the small, beautifully furnished Windsor Room of the Hay-Adams Hotel. The four other members of GeneVision's Board of Directors were already seated, and each looked worried.

"Let's begin," Novokatnaia began, but she got no further.

"If you will permit, Ms. Novokatnaia," the distinguished looking former Senator, Sue Ellen Chalmers, said flatly, "Under the bylaws, the President conducts all meetings, and though we have not operated by that particular bylaw in the past, I think we need to do so today. So, as the Board's President, I will conduct this meeting. I assume that is acceptable to you?" Senator Chalmers had been soundly defeated in her recent bid for reelection because her constituency finally got fed up with her accepting huge sums of money from so many out-of-state pressure groups and then shamelessly either voting the way those interests dictated or executing parliamentary maneuvers which would be of subtle, but substantial, benefit to those interests. The voters turned a deaf ear to her slick TV ads claiming that that was business as usual in Washington and that they should keep her there because she had seniority and "was connected." She had been asked to be on the GeneVision Board because she had done numerous favors for GeneVision in the American Congress. Both she and GeneVision clearly understood that money was the swamp-fuel of Washington policy-making. Without her clever tactics on the contentious Senate Committee on Health, Education, Labor, and Pensions, federal law would have seriously hampered GeneVision. Her gift to GeneVision was a green light to do relatively unregulated, secret work, though according to federal law GeneVision, of course, could not clone humans.

"Of course, that is completely acceptable, Senator." Marina, concealing her irritation, looked at the other three members of GeneVision's Board of Directors. Dr. Charles Marion, CEO of the largest biochemical supply house in America, had provided most of the biological and chemical materials used by GeneVision's several laboratories. He was a forceful man but did not know the full extent of GeneVision's work. None of the four knew, each willfully blind as far as Marina Novokatnaia could tell. Her intent was that the Board members would know only that GeneVision was carrying out some academically innovative genetics research at each facility.

Seated next to Marion was Dr. Afanasii Pakoslav. He was a retired currency speculator whose connections to various segments of Russian society made him a useful Board member. Marina smiled to herself. *Immortal, repeated glory.* What a ridiculous name this genius had. He would follow her lead if there were a problem on the Board for the two of them shared a vision of Russian resurgence in the near future. She and Pako briefly smiled at each other.

The final member of the Board was a law professor from Tulane University, Dr. Charles Delna. He had taught Soviet law before "the change" (as he referred to the pathetic collapse of the Soviet Union) and during his many trips to the old Soviet Union had become a drinking buddy of Dr. Pakoslav. The two, in violation of Soviet law, had in those early years met in Pakoslav's apartment in Saburova outside of Moscow and shared their common interests in wine, women, and currency manipulations. Their times together in Saburova were risky, but the two were discrete. In those times, a Soviet citizen could not legally host a foreigner in the home without the permission (and the surveillance) of the KGB. Delna was on the Board only because Pakoslav, in order to pay off "an old debt," prevailed on

Novokatnaia for Delna to be added to the Board. Pakoslav got his wish, but he steadfastly refused to reveal to anyone the nature of the debt. In Marina's eyes, Delna was harmless. As far as she could remember, he had never said anything of substance at a single Board meeting.

"Ms. Novokatnaia," ex-Senator Chalmers began, "Would you be so kind as to give us a summary of what you know regarding the earthquake and the state of the California facility?"

In order to project control and authority, Marina stood. "I have not had time to put together a formal presentation, but here is the situation as I understand it." Novokatnaia then gave the group a succinct, executive summary of what had happened in California. She did not mention that Peter Randolph's whereabouts were unknown and that GeneVision had launched a nationwide search to find him, nor did she mention that Jim Fawcett had been evacuated from Ohio to Barbados, well removed from American clutches. Nor did she mention that compliments of some of her Russian friends, Dr. Meier would meet his untimely demise in Barbados.

When Novokatnaia had finished her brief presentation, there was a period of silence, which seemed to Novokatnaia to last at least a full minute. Finally, Senator Chalmers asked, "And what about Peter Randolph? Is he still alive?"

Novokatnaia was visibly stunned. None of the Board members had ever been informed about the existence of Randolph. They were supposed to have been kept in the dark about that project as well as everything else pertaining to human cloning. For a brief moment Novokatnaia was unable to formulate a reply. Finally, she said in a volume hardly above a whisper, "How did you find out about Randolph?"

"Never mind how we found out. Is he alive?" Chalmers's tone was cold.

"Yes, he is alive, and he is in a safe place." Novokatnaia was confused for one of the few times in her corporate life. For the first time ever, she was unsure about how much the members of the Board knew.

"I think you need to give us a full briefing about Randolph." The voice was Pakoslav's. His tone was also cold, but he wore a smile on his face, the wary smile of someone who knows he has a venomous snake cornered. But his smile also conveyed confidence in Novokatnaia. A knowing glance passed from one to the other.

Novokatnaia, having recovered her composure, was now ready to face this unexpected rebellion of the Board. Marina chose her words carefully. "I have never informed the Board about the Randolph project because you four people need to have complete deniability about this project. The Randolph project is probably the most important scientific breakthrough in the history of science, and if I had informed you before now, you as Board members would have legally been required to shut down the project or face criminal liability. Science requires that this project go forward. As long as you did not know the specifics of this project, you had no criminal liability."

"Since we now know, you need to give us a full briefing, and it must cover each of our facilities," Chalmers pressed.

"Very well." Novokatnaia feigned resignation. She was still unsure about how much the four knew, and she was not about to tell them the full scope of GeneVision's projects. "I think the best way to inform you fully is to take you to our Ohio facility and give you a complete briefing, Ohio because the California campus has been partly destroyed. The Randolph project is complex, and you cannot get a full understanding without being on-site. Plus, you need access to all the technical angles, and that requires that you be able to query the scientists and geneticists themselves. I can arrange for all of you to be transported to Ohio immediately, be briefed, and return here. The whole thing will take only a couple of days."

Pakoslav spoke next. "That sounds like the best approach. I think if we're going to do it, we need to get to Ohio immediately. Today."

Novokatnaia moved swiftly. "I can get a plane this afternoon. Will that work for everyone? We can either stay overnight or return here tonight."

Chalmers and Marion nodded in agreement, and both said 'OK' together. Only Delna looked worried.

"What is the problem, Dr. Delna?" Novokatnaia asked.

Delna paused then said softly, "There's no problem."

"OK, then it is set. I'll have my office make the arrangements to charter a Lear, and we'll go this afternoon. Please plan on staying completely available so my office can give you the final departure plans. If there is nothing else, I'd like this meeting to adjourn so I can call my office and make the arrangements."

With that, the meeting broke up. Novokatnaia returned to her suite, but she did not call her office. When her call was answered, she spoke in Russian. There was no conversation, only a short monologue from Novokatnaia. When she had finished, the voice on the other end of the line simply said, " Korosho. Onee budut oomrut sevodnya." *Very good. They will die today.* The line went dead. Though it was not yet noon, Novokatnaia poured herself a pepper vodka and sank into one of the plush armchairs.

Chapter 25

By agreement, Afanasii Pakoslav and Charles Delna meet a half hour later at the Sushi Ogawa on Connecticut Avenue. This trendy place was loud, had Michelin-level sushi, and had recently become a meeting place for the two men when both were in Washington at the same time.

After they had ordered sushi and beer, Pakoslav asked, "Well, what do you think is going on? What did you think of the meeting?"

"Pako, you tell me. What is the Randolph project?"

"Charlie, you've got to trust me on this. There's some serious criminal shit that GeneVision is doing, and I am part of it. You saved my life a few years ago in Russia, so I 'm repaying that debt. I'll fill you in, but you've got to assure me that you will give me several days to get out of the country."

"Pako, what are you saying?"

Pakoslav looked irritated. "Charlie, I can't go into any details unless you give me your word." Pakoslav faked a laugh. "Don't worry. I haven't killed anyone or anything like that."

The two men stared at each other. Finally, Delna broke the silence. "OK."

"OK what?" Pakoslav's terse response was clipped.

"OK, I'll give you three days before I say anything to the authorities. And that is *if* I say anything to the authorities. And if you haven't killed anyone, I probably won't."

"Thank you, Charlie. You are a true friend, and I will never forget you." After a pause, Pakoslav continued. "Charlie, they have cloned a human being, and he is now older than twenty years old. And hold onto your seat. They did not just clone any human. They have cloned Thomas Jefferson."

Pako saw that Delna seemed to be completely speechless. Delna did not move a muscle, but intently stared at Pakoslav. "Go on," Delna finally said in a hoarse whisper.

"I don't know how they turned out a twenty-year-old clone, but obviously the process had to be speeded up somehow. Or started a long time ago. But that's just the tip of the iceberg. They have also cloned another human at the Ohio office, and as I understand it, they have cloned a third human on the island of St. John."

"I didn't know we had a facility on St. John." Delna whispered.

"It's not called GeneVision, but Novokatnaia runs it, too. It's called Caribbean Biologics. They have apparently cloned a human. I was told that all three cloning projects have been one hundred percent successful. And, Charlie, it is my belief that those other two clones are also some of your country's founding fathers."

Pakoslav saw that Delna looked stunned. "What else do you know, Pako?"

"Charlie, steer clear of Marina. My friends in Moscow tell me that she is connected to some big-time, rough players in Russia. In Russia, they have proved that there is nothing they won't do. She will not want this secret to come out. Remember the Tariverdiev murder in Suzdal? She was part of that."

Delna remembered it well. The "Cucumber Millionaire," one of Russia's most powerful tycoons, had opposed the Kremlin's seizing control of the media. Vladimir Tariverdiev had been gunned down in front of the media which was assembled to witness Tariverdiev's donation of one million dollars to the Suzdal tourist industry. The Suzdal murderers effectively made the point that the Kremlin linked mafia had complete power and could and would do whatever they wanted to do. "You think Novokatnaia travels with the Russian mafia?" Delna asked.

"I *know* it. She'll stop at nothing. Charlie, watch your back. Don't take any chances at all. I'm telling you this so you can sever all ties with that woman," Pakoslav said with certainty.

Delna began, "I think the Ohio trip —"

"Don't go to that meeting, Charlie. Absolutely do not go. Do not get on that plane, Charlie." Pakoslav's tone was ominous.

"Why not go back to Marina and confront her?"

Pakoslav put his hand on Delna's arm, "We have visitors. The two men at the door. They were at the Hay-Adams talking to Novokatnaia before our meeting. They are not here by accident."

Delna looked very uneasy. "Fuck, I don't like the feel of this whole thing. Clones, Thomas Jefferson, Novokatnaia lying to us, and now two goons —"

"Charlie, take it easy. I've been in this situation before," the Russian said. Pakoslav caught the waiter's eye, and the waiter came to the booth and put his hand fondly on Pakoslav's shoulder and asked, "What can I do for you, my friend?"

"I need a taxi," Pakoslav said to the waiter. "Make it two taxis, and I want them to pick us up out back, outside of your kitchen, not on the street." Pakoslav slipped the waiter $50. "This is important. My wife is over there with another guy, and I do not want her to see me with a man. I'm gay and it wouldn't be so hot for her to know. Capiche?" Pakoslav smiled up at the well-groomed waiter.

"Si, capiche. I understand." The waiter winked at Pakoslav and then winked at Delna.

Pakoslav and Delna pretended to talk and laugh for several minutes until the waiter finally returned and said, "The two taxis are ready. They are friends of mine so they'll take care of you. You might consider coming out of the —"

Before the waiter could continue, Pakoslav cut him off, "Thank you. I'll remember how you helped us. Just don't tell *anyone*, OK? She may have some private eyes following us for all I know."

"No problemo," the waiter said and walked provocatively back to the main cash register.

"I'll go first, and in a couple of minutes, you follow. Take care, tavareesh" Pakoslav used the Soviet-era term of friendship. "You are a true friend, Professor Delna, I'm sorry it must end like this. Keep this." Pakoslav slipped an envelope into Delna's coat pocket, then stood and walked into the restroom alcove from which he could enter the kitchen. From there, he exited into the dimly lit alley. Delna frowned and watched Pakoslav as he left the restaurant.

Pako just validated everything, Delna thought. *Luckily we got Randolph out of California. But what did Pako mean, 'it must end like this'?* Delna waited a little over a minute, noted that the two men had glanced over at his table several times, then Delna stood and took the same route that Pakoslav had taken. When he exited the kitchen into the alley, there was one taxi waiting. He opened the back door and peered inside the dark taxi.

The driver said quickly, "Your friend said when you came out to make tracks, so you'd better get in." The turbaned driver looked worried.

Delna quickly slid into the rear seat, and with the tires spinning, the taxi picked up speed down the alley, finally exiting onto 18th Street.

"Where to?" the driver intoned.

"To the Willard on Pennsylvania."

The driver nodded.

Delna was already thinking over what Pakoslav had said. *Don't go to that meeting, Charlie,* he had said. Why not go to the meeting? That's where he could learn more details of the whole cloning project. *I've known about the cloning, but I need the details,* Delna thought.

My friends in Moscow tell me that she is connected to some big-time, rough players in Russia. She will not want this secret to come out. Even if she plays rough, there's safety in numbers. He and Pako could bring the other Board members up to speed during the flight. *That's what I'll do, expose the whole thing on the flight.*

Pako had said she was connected to *rough players. There is nothing they won't do. She will not want this secret to come out.*

She'll stop at nothing. Charlie, watch your back. Don't take any chances at all. Pakoslav had spoken plainly and ominously. But what would she do? *Do not get on that plane, Charlie.* If she would snuff out someone as prominent as Tariverdiev, she would not even hesitate to take out a member — or members — of the Board.

Don't go to that meeting, Charlie. Pakoslav's emphatic words had been plain and ominous. There was a dangerous plot underway, and Delna was caught in the middle of it.

If the clones are who Pako claims, then I've got to protect them from the government. At least, we've already rescued Randolph. Delna had lately been living the serene life of a professor after some years working deep cover but had maintained contact with associates from an earlier life. They had successfully gotten Randolph out of California. They had not yet "liberated" the clones from Ohio or St. John and had not been able to create access to those two campuses. *I've got to get those other two clones,* he thought.

The driver pulled up in front of the Willard. Delna glanced at his watch. There were still some Southwest flights available. "Take me to BWI," Delna told the driver.

The driver looked in his mirror at Delna, "That's a good forty-five minutes from here." His tone was *are you sure?*

"I know. Make it faster, if you can." Then Delna pulled out the envelope that his Russian friend had given him, opened it, and as he read the contents, he felt the energy drain from his body.

Chapter 26

Jim and the manager of the Barbados Southern Palms Resort entered the manager's office. The manager motioned Jim to a rattan seat and then removed a picture from the wall, revealing a safe. After a few deliberate twists of the dial, the safe door opened, and the manager retrieved a thick manila package and handed it to Jim. "I'll let you read this in private," the manager said and left the room.

Inside Jim found two envelopes, one thick and one thin. Jim opened the thick envelope first and found a wad of Barbados dollars and a second wad of American dollars. There was no note, just money.

Jim then opened the thin envelope, deducing already that there was a note of some kind in it. He knew as soon as he began reading that his life was changed forever, but in ways that he could not possibly foresee.

Jim,

If you are reading this letter, I am either dead or have been taken from you. What I have to tell you is very hard for me because I have grown to love you as a father loves a son. About thirty years ago, some people, scientists, in the USA, wanted to do what they could to return America to what the founding fathers envisioned. These scientists thought that America had essentially abandoned democracy and individual freedom, that the federal government had become irretrievably corrupt and owned by moneyed interests, and that the growing gap between the rich and the poor was becoming not only immoral but also beyond remedy. They, therefore, began a bold and dangerous scientific project. They decided that to return to the world of the framers was not possible without somehow jolting the current political structure and system into some kind of disequilibrium. To do this, they launched a project to bring back the framers.

*They obtained DNA fragments of three of the framers - - - Benjamin Franklin, Thomas Jefferson, and Alexander Hamilton. They cloned those fragments. Jim, they brought back those three demi-gods. Jim, you are the modern Alexander Hamilton. It's hard for me to write the words, but by the miracle of cloning you **are** Alexander Hamilton.*

Jim suddenly felt empty. He felt his body shaking. He felt the tears stream down his face. The thoughts rushed through his brain, and he realized that the pieces fit. The absence of family, the schooling, his innate talents with currency matters and economics, the relationship with Dr. Meier, the sometimes hard-to-explain goings-on in Findlay. The Islam scenario. The sudden trip to Barbados. The special police who were not police. Jim cleared the tears from his eyes and read further.

I know this is hard for you to comprehend, and I know it is a cruel twist of fate to have you read these words rather than have me talk to you face to face. If only I could have told you myself and earlier! But that was not possible. Jim, I do love you as a son. I want what is best for you. I want you to live a life that can be happy and productive. I want you to marry and have a family. But because of who you are and because of the situation in your country, I'm afraid that none of those things will be possible for you.

Since you are reading these words, you are probably in some danger. There are some people who oppose the cloning project itself, but they are not your main worries. There are others whose very power and existence will be threatened once they learn that you exist. They will want to eliminate you and the others. They are the United States government. Therefore, you must go into hiding and plan very carefully what you are going to do. You need to contact Peter Randolph. He is, it is strange just to write these words, Thomas Jefferson. I know this is hard to take in and it is coming too fast, but you must believe me. Randolph is in GeneVision of San Diego. GeneVision has a large campus there, and it is the home of the Thomas Jefferson project. I have also heard that there is a third clone, Benjamin Franklin, but I do not know his whereabouts or even if there actually is a third clone.

I am leaving a large amount of money with you, some in Barbadian currency and some in American currency. I am also leaving a credit card for you in a fake name. It is tied to a bank account I have set up at the Barclay's Bank in Bermuda. All you need is the account number, and it is the same as the combination lock on your locker at the riding barn in Findlay plus the number of your cell phone in reverse. I do not write the number here for obvious reasons. The money and the card are in another envelope that should be with this note. There is also a fake New York driver's license. All this uses the name Irwin Clark. Do not use your real name. They can find you too easily if you do.

Now, for how you must disappear from Barbados. You must go to the end of the beach from Southern Palms, down where the local vendors make flying fish sandwiches and sell local food. Look for Angelina. She will get you out of the country. You can trust her. Do not trust anyone else on this island, even the manager of the hotel. He has helped me in the past, but he is for sale.

Burn this note. Waste no time. Godspeed to you, my son.

Love,

Doc

There were no more tears. Jim's eyes, his whole being, were dry, tense. He felt as weak and powerless and depleted as a human being could possibly feel. He had lost his father and learned that he was the clone of Alexander Hamilton. And he had learned that he was a fugitive from his own government.

At that moment, the Southern Palms manager burst into the room and whispered loudly, "The real police are here. You've got to leave *now*. There is no time to waste. This way." The manager led the way through the open office door and immediately headed toward the street. "I've already called you a taxi. You can take it and head to the airport." The manager opened the taxi door, and turned, but Jim was nowhere to be seen. One of the two suited men in the taxi exclaimed, "I thought you said you had him!" He held a .38 caliber Beretta.

"He was right here," the manager said with confusion, but the two police inspectors were already out of the taxi and headed towards the beach.

Jim was running full tilt down the beach to the local vendors' area. His one-minute head start would hardly be enough! He had to find some place to hide. He headed into the vendors' zone.

"Are you lost," a bronze woman called to Jim as he moved hurriedly from one booth to the other, looking for someone who looked like an *Angelina*," whatever an Angelina looked like.

"No, I'm just in a hurry! By the way, do you know someone who works here named Angelina?"

The woman frowned and said, "I think you need a good flying fish sandwich. Why don't you just wait right there while I get the burner started."

"I really don't have time to wait, so I'll just——"

"Take it easy, Jim," the woman said quietly. "I'm the one you are looking for. Just stay right here and we'll have a bite, you know, looking casual and all, and then we'll leave."

She must be Angelina, Jim thought. *She knows my name.* Besides, he was the only white person in the area.

The two made small talk. Angelina placed a delicious looking sandwich on a plastic plate and handed it to Jim. Jim started to take a bite, but Angelina stopped him, "You need to pay for the sandwich. This has got to look right in case anyone is watching. You see those two men coming down the beach?" She smiled, and Jim noticed for the first time that Angelina was quite good-looking. "Jim," she said, "those men." She gestured subtly with her mouth in the Dominican style of pointing.

Jim looked and saw two men in light shirts and police issue Bermudas striding briskly down the beach directly towards Jim and Angelina.

"Well, my guess is that they are looking for you so why don't you just step back here until they finish looking." Angelina motioned Jim into the small storage room behind Angelina's cooking area.

Jim quickly hid in the dark closet. He was concealed but could hear what was said outside. He heard the men speaking in low tones, first in English and then Bajan, as they slowly walked past the vendors. None of the vendors paid them any notice, and the policemen looked conspicuously out of place. Most of the vendors were dressed in shorts or jeans, and there were no tourists around since the tourists seldom learned about this location, preferring instead to drink high-priced smoothies and dry hamburgers at the little stands directly across the street from the Southern Palms. Jim continued to wait.

Finally, Angelina poked her head into the storage area, "They've gone back to the hotel. Let's go."

Jim and Angelina quickly moved to her small van parked about 100 feet away. They got in, and keeping faith with the relaxed Bajan driving style, Angelina slowly pulled away from the beach area. "Keep your white face hidden, and we should be OK," she said as she pulled into the light traffic. Jim slumped low in the seat.

Chapter 27

Late that afternoon, FoxNews broke into their regular news program with one of their many News Alerts. "We have just gotten a report that a private Lear jet has exploded in the skies over Pennsylvania. The explosion occurred approximately 60 miles south of Cleveland over a sparsely populated area. The plane was en route from Dulles International Airport outside of Washington, D.C., for Toledo, Ohio. FoxNews does not yet know how many persons were on Board, but we have learned that a company called GeneVision chartered the plane. That's all we have at this time, but we will follow this story and should have more information very shortly."

Marina Novokatnaia did not hear the news. Besides, she seldom watched FoxNews anyway, preferring CNN instead. Nor did she hear her cell phone as it urgently beeped. She was sound asleep from too many vodkas enhanced with Xanax.

Chapter 28

The UPS plane carrying the HVD from Phoenix had landed at Ronald Reagan at 1:05 P.M., and UPS with its normal robot-like efficiency had the package well on its way to its Winchester, Virginia, address soon after the flight landed. The GPS took the UPS driver to a modern, nondescript building in an industrial park. The lettering on the building identified the company as Winchester Business Consultations. The driver, pushing back her hair, entered into a sterile lobby which had only a large security desk flanked by a number of television monitors. Behind the desk sat a smiling uniformed guard.

"My name is Alice. I have a delivery for you. Can you please sign here?" The driver waited for the signature. This guy looked like no ordinary security guard to Alice. He was fit, alert, muscular, and handsome.

"Sure, no problem," the security guard stated and signed the UPS form. "And you please sign here if you don't mind." He pushed a form to her and smiled as if sending some kind of romantic message.

Alice, blushing, quickly signed the form. "OK, that's it. Have a good day," she said and turned and exited the building. The guard, with appropriate appreciation, but no more than that since he knew that he was under continual video-cam surveillance himself, watched the attractive UPS driver leave the lobby then pressed a button under the large desk. An answering voice said, "Yes?"

"Sir, this is the front desk. I think that package you are expecting was just delivered. I have it at the front desk."

"Great! I'll send someone out to get it," the voice said.

A few minutes later, a stylishly dressed young woman came through the inner door to the left of the security desk. "Here it is," the guard said, handing the woman the package. "And I still want to marry you."

"You're too wild for me," the woman said, laughing and retreating back into the door from which she had come. The guard always told her he wanted to marry her, but he told that to most women. He was popular as well as buff and fit. He was also married.

Chapter 29

Durango's pilot landed the plane at Ronald Reagan just as the next transmission from the HVD locator was coming in. Durango looked at the coordinates and consulted a Washington-Virginia-Maryland map.

"If I'm doing this right, that disk is now near Winchester, Virginia."

The pilot double-checked Durango's work. "Yep, it looks like that's where it is, Mr. Durango, and it's giving us an exact address. Winchester is about an hour and a half from here. If you leave now, you'll be there by 4 o'clock."

Twenty minutes later, Durango was on Virginia 267 headed toward Winchester. That was when he heard the news bulletin. He listened to the bulletin without paying much attention until the announcer said that first reports were that the plane that had exploded in midair had been chartered by GeneVision.

Durango immediately telephoned Marina Novokatnaia. There was no answer. *My God. Was she on that plane?* At that moment, his cell phone signal indicated a call waiting. Durango answered curtly, "Durango."

"Mr. Durango, this is Karen from San Diego. I am Marta's right hand assistant. We've gotten rid of everything connected to Peter Randolph. We shredded the documents then burned the shreds. All the computer files that mention him or that project have been destroyed. We electronically scrambled them, re-encrypted them, and then used BleachBit II to destroy everything. Some claim that's an upgraded program of what Hillary's lawyers used to get rid of her emails. Anyway, no one can possibly retrieve these files or reconstruct them, much less decrypt them."

Don't ever say 'no one can possibly,' Durango thought. "What about the backups?" He asked.

"We did them too, the same way. Mr. Durango, we got rid of everything. There's nothing here even remotely connected to Randolph."

"OK, sounds good. Just double check everything. Have you heard anything from the boss?"

"No, not lately." Karen's replied nonchalantly.

"OK, Karen, thank you," Durango said as he broke the connection.

His thoughts returned to the plane disaster. *She must not have heard about the plane yet. She didn't even mention it. Was Novokatnaia on that plane, and why would she be flying to Toledo?*

Chapter 30

Abby was driving, and Pete was asleep. They were on I-40 East somewhere in Texas when Abby heard the newsbreak that a GeneVision plane had disintegrated in mid-flight above Pennsylvania.

"Pete, wake up, and listen to this."

Pete had been only barely asleep and quickly grasped what had happened. "What the hell? I mean, that can't just be a coincidence."

"It means someone's playing for keeps," Abby responded.

"Like who? The government?"

"Who knows? Whoever it is, they apparently know about you and the others."

"Lucky for us, they won't be looking for a Chinese couple. As I remember it, Jefferson never looked Chinese." Pete smiled at his little joke but still did not feel safe.

Abby did not smile. She had worked in intelligence long enough to know that their disguises would work only so long.

Chapter 31

Angelina veered off the Barbados airport road and drove into the main entry for Grantley Adams International Airport, but instead of stopping at the main terminal, she drove off on a side road towards an unmarked building near the end of the only runway. Jim asked, "I take it you're meeting someone at a special place because they'll be looking for us at the terminal?"

"Exactly," Angelina said as she pulled up beside a small twin propeller plane with the words "Four Star" written on the fuselage in large blue letters. "You wait here." Angelina got out of the van and entered the building. Jim watched her walk into the building. He had been so scared and agitated that he had barely noticed that not only did she have a beautiful face but also underneath her loose-fitting clothes she had a striking figure to go with it. And she was close to Jim's age. *Ah, what could have been*, Jim thought.

After a long several minutes, the door of the building opened, and Angelina and a large, black man in a pilot's uniform, exited the building and walked quickly to the car.

"Time to leave Barbados," the man intoned in flawless English.

"Fill me in first on what's going on, where we're going, and who's after us," Jim said darkly, not budging from the van.

"We don't have time now but I'll fill you in completely when we get airborne," the man said.

Jim stayed put in the car, just staring out at the unnamed man and Angelina.

"Jim, you've got to trust us, and you've got to get moving." Angelina's voice was now urgent.

"I guess so," Jim said as he got out of the car. "I don't have a lot of choices."

Angelina smiled and embraced Jim. She whispered into his ear during the embrace. "You can trust him. You're flying to America and you're going to meet a couple of people there who'll become close friends. I suspect that you already know who they are. The ones after you are GeneVision, the very ones you used to work for. Absolutely stay away from everything connected with GeneVision. They'll stop at nothing to get you back in their clutches. Good luck, Jim."

"How can I thank you?" Jim started, but Angelina put a finger to his lips to quiet him.

"God be with you," she said softly.

"Time's up. Let's go," the pilot said, and he and Jim boarded the plane. The pilot shut the door, fired up the engines, quickly got clearance as "Four Star Air Cargo flight 332, bound for Miami."

Jim looked out the window as the twin engine began its taxi. He was almost positive that he could see the glint of tears in Angelina's eyes. He wondered why she would be so affected since she really did not know him at all.

As the plane taxied to the end of the runway, Angelina did have tears in her eyes, not because she knew Jim especially well but because she fully understood, probably more than he did, just how much it mattered who he was.

"You're a lucky guy," the pilot said. "Your old man put this escape hatch in place a few years ago in case anything ever happened that you might need to get away."

"What's your name, and who do you really work for?" Jim asked.

"Whom, and you won't know my name, and I don't know yours. I'm working for your old man because he saved my life one time, and I owe him. I owe him big, and I'm going to make sure that you get out of harm's way just like I promised him I would. I know you've got some powerful people after you, but I guess you know that, too."

"Yeah." Jim laid his head back, and, exhausted, he stared out the small window as the twin engine reached its cruising altitude.

Chapter 32

The beep from Abby's cell phone woke Pete. He listened, waiting for Abby to say something, but she just listened. Finally she said, "OK, that's not good. We can be there in a couple of hours." She then switched off the cell phone.

"What was that about," Pete asked as he raised his seat from the reclining position.

"Things are moving too fast, so we are not going to Ohio. The guy you need to rendezvous with is no longer in Ohio. He is headed for Miami, so we are headed for Miami, too. I figure we can be in Oklahoma City soon, and there will be a plane waiting for us there to take us to Miami."

"Who do we meet in Miami?"

Abby waited a long moment before responding, "You still don't get it, do you Thomas? That's who you are, Thomas. You are meeting a couple of people who are in the same boat you are in. Meaning, some dangerous people are looking for all of y'all to shut all of y'all up."

Abby's cell phone beeped again. "Yes," she answered.

"It's a friend," she said as she put the phone on speakerphone. She and Pete listened as the man on the other end of the line was saying, "— are dead. The head honcho, Marina Novokatnaia, was not on board, and she never planned to be on board."

Pete did not recognize the voice. It was smooth, cultured, with a southern accent, and richly baritonal.

The man was still talking, " That's why I think she was behind it. She's getting rid of people who know too much. I called the San Diego facility a couple of hours ago, and found out that all traces of Pete have been eliminated. The place has been completely sanitized. The same thing has happened in Ohio. It's like Jim never existed there. So I think you two need to be careful. Avoid any place with surveillance cameras if you can, but given the recent placement of those cameras all over the place, that's going to be hard to do. After another day or so, throw away your cell phone and just use pre-paid phones. We can communicate in the Movie of the Day chat room at Yahoo at the regular times. OK? Got all that?"

"Yeah, I've got it, Abby said. "Who meets us in Oklahoma City?"

The voice said, "That's the last thing. Don't go to Oklahoma City. You are only about an hour from Shamrock, Texas. There's an airfield there that was closed down a few years ago, but the runway is still functional. There will be a Four Star Air Cargo plane there to take Pete to Miami." The voice then gave Abby the directions to the airfield.

Abby said, "OK, I've got it, and we'll be there in less than an hour if I move it."

"No speeding tickets, Abby," the voice cautioned.

They both clicked off.

Chapter 33

Durango's cell phone beeped. The caller ID read "Private," but he answered anyway. "Hello," he snapped. His tone was testy and was showing the strain of the events that were unfolding.

"Mr. Durango, this is Karen in San Diego. Our systems are now up and running. We've got good news and bad news, and — "

Durango angrily interrupted, "Cut the chatter and just tell me why you called!"

"Mr. Durango," the tone was now more business-like and respectful. "Do you know about the crash?"

"Yes. I've got the news reports. Do we know anything else? Was Marina on the plane?"

"No, she wasn't on the plane. She telephoned our office a few minutes ago. She is totally devastated and was actually crying on the phone. I've never heard her so upset. We don't know anything else yet except what we can get from TV."

"OK, OK, what about the HVD?"

"We have been able to get a continuous readout from the HVD. The technicians here worked a miracle and reprogrammed the transmission from the HVD itself. We now have the same thing as a GPS signal from the HVD and can tell where it is at any minute. It is now at 4577 Van Dyke Drive outside Winchester."

"Yes, I've got the address already. I'm only a mile or two away and am going over there now."

"Be careful, sir."

Durango broke the connection.

In a few minutes, Durango had arrived at 4577 Van Dyke Drive. He read the sign on the building. Winchester Business Consultation. *That could be anything,* Durango thought.

He walked into the lobby, noticed its sparse furnishings, and walked up to the reception desk. The male receptionist looked relatively unfriendly as he greeted Durango, "What can I do for you, sir?"

Durango decided on the direct approach. "I just talked to UPS, and they informed me that a computer disk that was supposed to be shipped to me was delivered by mistake to this address. They said some packages had become damaged, and they had to reconstruct the addresses. My company in California had sent me a priority package, and I have their number if you need to verify this with them." On this last point, Durango, prayed that the receptionist would not accept the offer.

"Just a minute sir, and I'll check with my supervisor." The receptionist dialed a number and spoke into the phone. "This is Mark at the front desk. Did we receive a UPS package today with a computer disk or something like that in it that was delivered here by mistake? A gentleman's out here inquiring. I was out until just a short while ago so I don't know if we've received anything. I'll put you on speaker phone so he can hear you, OK."

The speakerphone broadcast the supervisor's voice, "Sir, why do you need to know if we've received a computer disk?"

Durango replied, "UPS told me it was delivered here by mistake. I'm just trying to trace it down. It's their mistake, not yours. I'm just trying to locate my disk."

"Just a minute. I'll come out."

In less than a minute, a stern looking woman walked out carrying an opened UPS package. "Is this yours?" she asked politely, as she held out the HVD.

"Yes, it is. That's our logo on it." Durango pointed to the intertwined letters G and V on the surface of the disk.

"Well, I'm glad it's yours. We didn't know what it was and have actually never seen anything quite like this before, and we had no way of knowing whose it was. If you can show me some ID, you can have it."

Durango showed the woman his driver's license and his business card with the same logo as the one on the HVD.

She examined Durango's license and business card. "Looks good. It's all yours, and frankly you've saved us from a lot of trouble trying to find out whom to give it to. Thank you." She handed the HVD to Durango and threw the UPS packing material into a trashcan behind the reception counter. "Here, put the disk in this," and she handed Durango a padded mailing envelope.

"Thank you very much, and I apologize for the mistake." Durango was all smiles as he

casually pocketed the disk and walked out of the lobby. He quickly got into his car and sped from the parking lot.

Durango realized that he did not have any of the packing information. He now also realized that the lady had kept the packing materials, including the shipping papers, and had smoothly given him an unmarked envelope. *I don't know who the shipper was. I don't have any of the shipping papers.*

Durango then noticed that the message light of his cell phone was blinking. He called his voice mail and retrieved the short cryptic message from Marina Novokatnaia. "Jim, this is Marina. You need to drop whatever you're doing and as fast as you can get up to Brighton Beach. Go to Dacha Outfitters and prepare things for some guests. Absolutely no delay at all on this, Jim. None. I'll fill you in once you're up there." That was the entirety of the message.

Brighton? Why go there? And what guests? Jim had been to Dacha Outfitters twice previously and was well aware that it was a safe house managed by GeneVision. Marina had made it clear that he should get to Brighton Beach, New York, as soon as possible. He then punched Dulles Airport into the GPS and picked up speed. He could take care of the HVD in Brighton Beach. *Brighton's an OK place except for all those Russian thugs,* he thought.

Chapter 34

Dorothea Smythe, who had earlier played her role as the receptionist's supervisor, was actually the head of Information Retrieval and Protection for Winchester Business Consultations, and Winchester Business Consultations was a front for the CIA. Its business was to encrypt and decrypt specialized data containers such as HVD's.

Smythe spoke to the three men and one other woman who were standing with her in their standard government issue conference room. "When they try to read the disk, everything will work fine, and there'll be no trace that we were ever there. It looks like someone had tried to erase the disk but they only deleted one layer. We know the disk contains business documents for GeneVision, that California company whose plane just crashed. Otherwise we haven't gone into the details of the disk. We have a good copy, so gentlemen let's see what's on it. But before we do that, you should know that it had tracking software embedded on it. That's why we couldn't pretend that we didn't have it. They knew we had it. What they do not know is that we now have the transmission algorithm for the tracking signals and can track the HVD ourselves. It'll be interesting to see where it goes."

A young technician entered the room and handed Dorothea Smythe a printout. She perused it, walked to a seat at the head of the table and continued looking at the printout, but now she was not just perusing it. She was reading it intently and carefully. After she sat, everyone else sat. Finally, she spoke. "The disk belongs to GeneVision. They are a genetics research company in San Diego. They are also the ones whose plane crashed a few hours ago. There are documents and something called "profiles" on the disk. We have not decrypted these profiles yet. They are apparently pretty well protected, so they must be important. But it's just a matter of time before we'll have it all done."

The door opened without a knock. Everyone stood as an elderly, bald man entered the room. With no pleasantries, Dr. Paul Leader, head of the Winchester front, said brusquely, "We have orders to send the disk to Langley. We have orders not to read the disk and to make no copies. Has anyone read the disk?"

"We've read the directory of the disk but have not decrypted the contents yet. They are apparently encrypted with sophisticated software so it would take us some time to do it. So, the answer it no, no one has read the disk," Dorothea said. "But why are we not allowed to proceed as we normally do in such circumstances? Why does Langley want it there?"

"I don't know, but you know how it works. When Langley barks, we dogs do tricks. They want the disk kept in our cyber-safe until their people get here to take it off our hands. They are sending a special team by helicopter, and they should be here in about thirty minutes. OK, that's all. This meeting is over. Needless to say, no one outside this room can know about this disk."

Chapter 35

Abby pulled the car over to the side of the road and killed the engine. The green highway sign read Shamrock Field One Mile. Abby said, "Pete, this'll be goodbye. When we get to the plane, waste no time. Get out of the car and immediately on the plane. No delay at all, Pete. The field is supposed to be abandoned, but if there are any cars or anything there, don't look their way. They must not see your face. We don't want them to know anything at all, even that a Chinese guy is getting on the plane. I'd love to be your pilot, but that's not in the cards today." After a pronounced pause, Abby said softly, "I've enjoyed knowing you." Abby's eyes welled up. She tried to smile, but there was no conviction in her smile.

Pete also felt that this was the premature end of something that could have been more, much more. His feelings for Abby had been instantaneous and had intensified during their hours on the road. But there was no option. He had no choice but to leave her and head into a very dangerous and uncertain future. He pulled Abby towards him and kissed her gently, then more strongly. She responded in kind, and then pulled away and quickly started the car.

As she pulled out onto the road and headed for the nearby airfield, her lament was barely audible, "Pete, it would have been great if we'd met in another time, but now you're part of something so much bigger that I'm afraid that you're going to have a lot of what-could-have-been times."

"Yeah."

Neither smiled. Abby pulled up next to a Four Star DC-3. Pete moved closer to Abby, embraced her tightly, "Abby, I hate this. Will I see you again?"

"I think this is it, Pete, but who knows. Good luck. I'll pray for you."

"And I for you."

Pete exited the car and had reached the first step of the DC-3 ramp when a voice called out, "Hold it, please!"

Pete double stepped up the ramp, but a man in a TSA uniform was immediately behind him. "This is a spot security check. We'll need to see your papers, and we'll need to check the plane."

The pilot unstrapped himself from his seat. "What's the problem? We're on a schedule." The pilot looked inquiringly at the TSA agent.

Pete knew this was not right. *What is a TSA agent doing at an abandoned airfield?*

"There's no problem. For the last year, we started doing spot checks at these western airfields because since Biden decided to open up the border, these little airfields are easy transport points for terrorists, drug smugglers, sex traffickers, all kinds of sorry people. You know, he did plunge the country into a fentanyl epidemic. We're just trying to do our jobs." The agent looked at Pete, "Sir, can you show me some ID?"

Pete showed the agent the fake ID.

"This looks fine to me. If you'll just sign here, Mr. Dan, you can be on your way." He handed Pete a slick, plastic clipboard with a form entitled, "TSA Instant Check." The form simply indicated that the signer had been the object of a TSA spot check, that the check had been handled professionally, and that the signer had no complaints about the check. Pete signed "Lin Dan" and handed the clipboard back to the agent.

"Thank you, gentlemen. Have a nice day." The agent exited the plane and joined a second agent who had remained at the foot of the plane ramp. Both men walked rapidly back to the tower.

"We're taking off. Strap in," the pilot said hurriedly. He had a worried look on his face. He fired up the two engines of the DC-3 and immediately taxied down towards the end of the runway, turned, and gunned the engines. The plane picked up speed down the runway, jerked a few times from side to side, and bellowed into the clear Texas sky.

After they had gained a cruising altitude of 15,000 feet and been directed by Air Traffic Control onto a certain route to Miami, the pilot said, "Those were not TSA agents. There's no such form as a TSA Instant Check form. I have no idea what that was all about. A signature won't do them any good. I guess they just didn't know that you are who you are and fell for the Chinese thing."

"Plus they didn't check the plane like they said they were going to, " Pete added.

"Anyway, we're not going to Miami. There's too much surveillance there. We're going to Melbourne, Florida, instead, and will meet your friends there."

"*Friends*? As in more than one?"

"'Friends' is what I was told. But first we have to make a little diversion to Natchitoches, Louisiana, where you'll change planes. Whoever is running this show decided that you needed to change planes to cover your tracks. So I'll fake engine trouble and land in an abandoned airfield outside Natchitoches, Louisiana. You'll be met and driven to some other airport and take another plane to Miami. Before anyone from FAA or Transportation arrives, I'll fix my engine and take off, fly to New Orleans, and have the whole plane checked out. By that time, you'll be who knows where. That's the plan."

"How far is Nacho—, Nagi—, ever what the hell that place is?"

"It's about 450 miles from where we are right now. Our cruising speed is about 170. We should be there in about two and a half hours, maybe less, because we have a tailwind."

Chapter 36

Meanwhile, at Shamrock Field, the agent who had conversed with Pete had secured the plastic clipboard that Pete had conveniently held and sped off in a Ford SUV. The second agent was on the phone. "We got a good print, and you should have it within minutes. We didn't get any DNA."

"Good work," the voice on the other end responded.

"Their flight plan shows Miami so our people will be ready for them when they land. We'll need the final word from you. But Miami is beyond their range so somewhere along the line they'll refuel and rest or even change planes."

"Don't interfere with them until they get to Miami. I want to know whom they're meeting. Just keep me informed about where that plane is and let me know twenty minutes before they land in Miami. Wherever they touch down in route, keep them under close surveillance." CIA Director Lucado then broke the connection, leaned back in her leather executive's chair. As a pilot, she realized that the DC-3 could land just about anywhere, and they could easily lose their quarry.

Chapter 37

Joelle Lucado was planning the next steps when her secretary buzzed her, "Judge Lucado, Mr. Miles is here with some reading matter which you are expecting."

"Send him in."

Joelle Lucado's top personal assistant, Fabian Miles, walked in. "Judge, we have a problem. This is the full contents of the computer disk that we got from the Winchester office. Several things before you read it, and you are not going to believe this shit. First, yes, there are human clones. Second, there are four clones. Third, each clone is a clone of one of the founding fathers. This whole thing's like a far-out piece of science fiction, Judge."

Fabian Miles, a brilliant, 29-year-old student from Wake Forest University's Law School, was snatched up by Lucado immediately after she read his penetrating analysis of the Biden foreign policy regarding Iran and restoring the Nuclear Agreement that Trump had trashed. Young, good looking, and innocent, Miles was Lucado's most trusted advisor and ordinarily did not need to go through the Lucado's secretary to gain entrance to Lucado's inner sanctum.

The Director of Central Intelligence was stunned by the magnitude of what was unfolding. "Who are the clones, I mean, who are they clones of?"

Miles responded, "You're not going to believe this shit, Judge. Hamilton, Jefferson, Franklin, and Washington."

Both remained silent.

Finally, Lucado muttered, "Shit, shit, shit. Unreal! This is not good. What do we do?"

Miles did not respond. He knew the Director was simply thinking out loud.

"OK, no one is to know except for you and me. OK, Fabe?"

Fabian Miles quickly answered, "Absolutely, Judge."

"OK, that's all. I think I'd better get back to the White House and tell Screamer One what we have." Screamer One was the Secret Service's code name for the President, reputedly a reference to his frequent temper outbursts when he actually sounded on occasion like the Sri Lankan southern screamer, the large, noisy bird known for waking up entire neighborhoods in parts of Asia early in the morning with a type a screaming that defies verbal description. The First Lady, an ornithologist by training, who was too often the target of the President's outbursts, had actually suggested the code name for the President. Before becoming First Lady, she had worked on a rescue team in Sri Lanka in 2005 after a devastating tsunami and eventually suggested to the Secret Service that Screamer would be the perfect handle for her husband.

As Fabian Miles was closing the office door, Lucado called out, "Fabian, one more thing."

"Yes, Judge?"

"Close the door, and come back in."

Fabian Miles closed the door and stood in front of Lucado's large, French provincial desk.

"There's a plane taking one of those - - -." Lucado paused. "- - - clones from Texas to Miami. They are in a DC-3 so they'll never make Miami without refueling at least once. They might try to put the clone on another plane. We can't lose that clone. It's critical that we get him. So I want that plane tracked. Don't use the military. Use *our* equipment understand? No FAA involvement. None. Find that plane. If anyone gets off that plane, grab them. Fabian, I want you to run that operation. Do whatever it takes to make it happen."

"On what grounds?"

"Shit, drug smuggling, anything. Just get them, all of them. The pilot, too. We don't know who the clone is. If there are several of them, we won't know which one is the clone. And, Miles, no one can know why we are tracking that plane. No one can know one damn thing about any clones, OK?"

"Got it. I'll take care of it." Fabian Miles left the room.

Once again the Director leaned back in her leather chair, took a deep breath and considered the magnitude of what she had just learned and the operation she had instituted to get the clones. Then, she took another deep breath, heavily got out of her chair, exited the building through her private underground tunnel, and headed to the White House.

I guess I'm going to be seeing a lot of Screamer One, she thought. Judge Lucado did not realize how little she would actually be seeing Screamer One.

PART TWO
Chapter 38

Pete had listened with fascination as the pilot, violating numerous FAA regulations, faked engine trouble, radioed distress calls, and within a minute had the plane safely on the ground at an abandoned airfield outside of Natchitoches, Louisiana. There was one hangar, in surprisingly good condition, with the image of a red badminton racket sporting a large H L monograph painted on the front wall. Just below the racket a sign read "Thomas Air Park."

The pilot said, "This field is still used by ultralights and powered parachutes. It's named for an old badminton player who used to fly his own plane to tournaments around the South. He actually did win a lot of seniors' events, but he was mainly noted for the length of his matches. His matches would last for hours. He was obviously in any match for the long haul." After a pause, the pilot added, "And that's the point, my friend. You've got to be in for the long haul." He paused to let those words sink in. Then he continued, "OK, this is where you get out. Double-time it to that car over there, and they'll take you to your next stop. Good luck."

Pete started, "I just want to thank —"

"Yeah, I know, but there's no time for that. Get going. Move it, friend!"

Pete quickly deplaned and sprinted to the open, rear door of the waiting car, jumped into the back seat, and before the door was closed, the car bolted out of the airfield and was quickly moving south along Interstate 49.

"What's the plan?" Pete asked.

"We take you to another plane. That's all we know," replied the skinny, tanned man sitting in the front passenger seat. Pete wanted answers, but these people obviously did not have them or did not want to give them.

After a few minutes, they exited onto Louisiana 6. Eventually the car soon slowed and entered the Natchitoches Regional Airport. Pete could see several sleek corporate jets on parking stands. The driver pulled up to one of the smaller jets, a Sino Swearingen SJ30-2, and said without elaboration, "Here's your plane. Good luck."

"Thanks," Pete said, with a little attitude in his voice, as he got out of the car and trotted the ten feet to the waiting jet. As he ascended the ramp, he noted that the plane looked small even for a corporate jet, had its engines already running, and sported a tail adorned with a bright orange and yellow sunburst insignia with some design or letters in the middle of it.

He was barely inside when a graying man wearing a blue polo shirt said, "Pick a seat and belt in. It's just you and me. We'll take off immediately. We're going to Florida, and that'll take this baby no more than a couple of hours." The man looked tired and worried as he secured the plane door, took a seat, and fastened his seatbelt.

Pete took in the surroundings. The interior of the plane was plush, had four seats centered on a combination coffee table and desk. Everything was beige. There was a small beige galley behind two of the seats, and at the end of the plane was a small door, probably the toilet. On one wall was a large screen television and on the other wall were five surprisingly large airliner windows. In spite of the luxurious cabin, Pete was feeling increasingly frustrated and out of the loop, as if he never knew who anyone was and was continually being handed off from one person to another. "And who're you?" he asked with irritation.

"I'm the guy who is trying to keep you alive, Pete. Once we're airborne, go back to the lounge and get rid of the Chinese stuff. You'll be meeting some people soon, and you might as well look like who you are." The man seemed friendly enough but his tone was all business.

"I'm not moving until you tell me who you are and what's going on." Pete was emphatic and remained standing beside the row of seats. The jet began taxiing then quickly turned and immediately began picking up speed.

"Suit yourself, but takeoff in this plane's a little steep so you might want to hold on to something if you insist on standing up the whole time." The man then turned away from Pete who watched the several buildings of the Natchitoches Regional Airport zip by as the plane quickly sought its takeoff speed.

The SJ30 roared down the runway of the small airport and launched itself into the Louisiana sky. Pete fell into a seat, fastened his seatbelt and prayed that these people were actually on his side and were not part of GeneVision. It was then that Pete saw on the man's shirt the small logo with which he was intimately familiar. It was the interlocking letters G and V of GeneVision against the orange and yellow sunburst background. Also visible beneath the man's sport coat was a holstered pistol.

Pete surprised himself by not panicking. *Had GeneVision captured him after all of his attempts at evasion? Who was this armed heavy? Where were they actually going, and why all the subterfuge? And why was he not already handcuffed?* Pete realized that if this armed man wanted to restrain him, there was little he could do to prevent it. At least for the time being.

Chapter 39

Jim awoke with a start as the Four Star Air Cargo DC-3 landed with a jolt and the loud reverse thrust of its engines. It taxied for a few minutes and then rapidly entered a cargo hangar, and the pilot quickly applied the brakes and cut the engines as the hangar doors closed behind them.

"You're here, my boy."

"Where is *here*? Jim asked.

"Not Barbados, son. This is Melbourne, Florida. This is where you get off, and I refuel and get back to the lovely beaches of Barbados." The pilot then continued, "I have some idea of what's going on, but I don't need to know everything. Like I said, your dad saved my life one time in northern Russia when we were both doing our part to bring down Soviet Communism. That was the old days. We kept in touch through the years. He was a great guy. He loved his country. I've lost a true friend, so bringing you here was the least I could do for him. If you ever need me, you know where you can find me." Then unexpectedly, he gave Jim a strong hug. "God speed, my boy."

Jim said, "There's no way I can thank you. I wish I could. You saved my life. What can I do?"

The nameless pilot laughed. "You are going to have enough to do without worrying about paying me back. Get going." With a genuine smile, he gently guided Jim to the airplane's small door. He accompanied Jim down the short ramp of the old DC-3. "These guys'll take care of you and keep you safe. Your dad set it all up."

Two men waited at the bottom of the ramp. The pilot and the two men greeted each other silently but warmly. "We all worked with your dad, Jim. But it's all no names from here on out. Your dad made it very clear -—no names. This was to protect us and maybe you, too. Anyway, you can trust these guys. OK, I'm out of here." The pilot abruptly turned and disappeared into the Four Star DC-3, reappeared in the doorway of the plane and saluted Jim, then immediately shut and secured the door.

"Jim," the shorter man said, "We loved your dad, and he put in place a plan to get you to a safe place and put you in touch with people that you need to know. We don't know who those people are, but we know that our part of the plan's to get you to a hotel at Melbourne Beach and there you'll meet the others."

"What do you mean, 'the others'?"

This time the taller of the two men spoke. Though he was white, he had an island accent. "We don't know. What we do know is that you'll meet three other people your dad said you needed to meet. That's all we know. We don't know who or why. Someone else'll bring them to the hotel. You're supposed just to wait there until they show up. I don't know whether that's an hour, a day or a week. Or even longer. Or maybe they're there now. It's a need-to-know operation."

"OK, then, let's go." Jim's tone showed that he was assuming control. The three got into a small Hyundai Sonata, left the airport, skirted the Indian River for several minutes, crossed a causeway onto the outer barrier island, and in another ten minutes pulled into the sheltered auto-way of a large high-rise structure on the Atlantic Ocean beach. The sign at the entrance read "The SeaShell." The driver popped the trunk and said, "Take the suitcase in the trunk. It has some stuff you'll need. The room's prepaid. When you check in, use the name Irwin Clark. Do you have that driver's license?"

"Yes, I have it," Jim said weakly as he checked the documents Dr. Meier had left him. It seemed like the distant past that he had just been talking to Dr. Meier, that he had found his mentor's lifeless body, met Angelina, hidden from the Barbados police, if that is who they really were, surreptitiously escaped to the Barbados airport, and flown to Florida. It was all a blur, all happening so fast, yet it all seemed so remote. Though he was generally authoritative, he was now tired and was showing the strain of what was going on. "If I run into problems, how can I contact you?"

"You can't, Jim. We don't work for Four Star or MLB Cargo. You won't see us again. If anything happens, I understand that you have cash. You've just got to be resourceful."

They all looked at each other briefly, then Jim said, "OK." He got out of the car, pulled the travel suitcase from the trunk, shut the trunk, hit the lid with his open hand, and the Sonata pulled away from the SeaShell onto A1A and disappeared into the night.

Jim walked into the hotel lobby and up to the front desk. "Irwin Fawcett, and I have a reservation," he said.

The clerk punched away on the keyboard and soon said, "I don't seem to have it."

Jim realized immediately his mistake, but the desk clerk rescued him, "I do have an Irwin Clark."

Jim felt incredible relief, "That's me. I'm Irwin Clark. I was using my middle name. Sorry. It's been a long day."

The front desk clerk, after a momentary confused look, said very politely, "I must've misheard. I'm sorry. Yes, Mr. Clark, your room's been prepaid, but I need an I.D. and a credit card to cover incidentals."

Jim gave her his newly acquired driver's license and a credit card. The credit card processed with no problem.

"Yours is an ocean front suite in the North Tower. Here's the keycard. I see that you'll have another gentleman joining you. Shall I ring you when he arrives? Would you like a cookie?"

Jim said, "Yes, please do. I know someone else is supposed to meet me here but I'm not sure whom my company is sending. What name did they give you?"

"Brad Miller, and it says here that he'll arrive either late tonight or tomorrow." She handed Jim a paper envelope that held one of the hotel's famous cookies.

"OK, thank you very much," Jim said and turned from the front desk, strode across the lobby to the elevators and took the quick ride up to his eighth floor suite. *Who the hell is Brad Miller?*

The suite was quite comfortable with two separate rooms and a bath. Jim was feeling more confident now and decided to treat himself to dinner at the hotel restaurant just off of the lobby. After all it had been a few hours since that quick flying fish sandwich in Barbados. He turned on a light in the living room of the suite, walked out onto the exterior walkway overlooking the parking lot, securely locked the door, and headed for the restaurant.

Chapter 40

It was 8:45 P.M. President Ray was reclining on the couch in the Oval Office. His headache was not yet severe but with the stress of the GeneVision situation, he was anticipating the onset of a major migraine. He was the first President in modern times to employ both a daytime secretary and a nighttime secretary. His nighttime secretary was a forty-year-old male African-American Marine sergeant who doubled as a "walking companion" for the President should the President want to walk in the Rose Garden at night. Since the widespread deployment of paid demonstrators and the use of face masks in demonstrations following Trump's 2016 electoral victory and the 2021 invasion of the Capitol, the Secret Service had insisted that the President not walk outside at night, but President Ray routinely ignored that advice. Thus, the Secret Service had conspired with the Chief of Staff in getting the nighttime secretary to be Sergeant Michael Habig. Just how Habig would actually protect the President from a long-range sniper or a small personnel missile was anyone's guess.

Joelle Lucado was escorted into the outer office where she greeted Sergeant Habig. "Mike, how are you?"

"Fine, thank you, Judge. The President said for you to go right on in when you got here."

"Thanks, Mike. What kind of mood is he in?"

"The usual - - - jovial and relaxed."

That was their standard joke. Neither had ever seen the President jovial *or* relaxed, much less both at the same time. Joelle knocked, and after the President had yelled something loud and indistinguishable, Lucado entered the Oval Office.

Never one for pleasantries, the President began immediately, "Joelle, you've got to know that I'm really pissed that the CIA hasn't been on top of all this shit. This Novokata woman has got to be brought in, and somehow we've got to get her off my bioethics panel."

"Mr. President, things are even worse than that. A lot worse, sir. Can we sit down and let me brief you on what we've learned?" The President grimaced as the two sat. Joelle Lucado briefed President Ray on the contents of the HVD which the CIA had retrieved in Winchester, Virginia. Uncharacteristically the President listened without interrupting to Lucado's five minute briefing. Lucado finally concluded, "Mr. President, this situation's more serious and has more explosive potential than anything to hit this country since the Civil War. It'll make 9/11 pale by comparison." She paused briefly, and then continued. "Mr. President, there is no way we could've foreseen that GeneVision was actually cloning humans, much less . . . ." Lucado hesitated, " . . .well, much less, Jefferson, Hamilton, Benjamin Franklin, and George Washington."

Again uncharacteristically, the President was silent. His face was drained of color. He felt weak. Finally he said, "Shit!" He glared at Lucado. "And what do you mean there was no way to foresee what they were doing? Lucado, it is the job of the CIA to foresee this kind of shit. You dropped the ball. For a while I've been pretty sure what was going on, and this completely nails it down. You fucked up, Lucado."

"Yes, Mr. President." Lucado ignored the President criticisms as she handed the President a thin notebook with the CIA seal emblazoned on the cover and the TS stamp across the top. "This packet's the preliminary report. I'll have something more comprehensive for you tomorrow. But that's going to take time because I don't want to even tell people on my staff about this except for one or two people who work directly with me."

"Good thinking, Joelle. So let me get this straight. First, GeneVision has cloned four of our founding fathers. Second, as a result of the earthquake GeneVision has lost track of the clone they had in California, and we don't know for sure where the other three clones are. Third, a Russian woman who is also on my Bioethics Panel runs the company. Novokatshitia or something like that. Fourth, her entire Board of fucking Directors has been killed in a plane crash. Fifth, you are tracking someone whom you believe to be a clone and whom you believe is bound for Miami, but you really don't know. Sixth, in the government the only people who know about the clones are two of your people, you, and me. Is there anyone else?"

"Not that I know of."

"Did anyone in Winchester look at the disk?"

"No. On my orders, Mr. President."

"And seventh," the President's voice was flat. "I'm in a battle to get reelected."

The two remained silent for a while, and finally Lucado gave voice to what each was thinking. "And eighth, a lot of people think you - - - we - - - are trashing the Constitution."

The President slowly rose from his chair, walked to the window and stood, staring out from the world's most powerful office. He gazed at the street in the distance. A small number of protestors walked slowly back and forth on the distant sidewalk. Finally the President spoke. His back was still to Lucado, and his tone was now cold and hard. "I've seen the footage of those fucking hippies ranting and raving against Nixon and the Vietnam War. There were thousands of them. It was right out there on that street. I remember those religious nuts demonstrating against Clinton. Hell, you'd think they never had a blow job themselves. I remember those naive, liberal idiots parading around out there against Bush. I remember the liberals after Trump's election. Idiots! Liberals still don't understand even today what this nation is up against. They never will. And they proved it during the first two years of Biden, and he had no balls to confront them. And they don't give a fuck. That's the sad part. They just don't give a royal fuck for this country. Well, I do give a royal fuck for this country!" Then the President turned to face Lucado. "Joelle, I don't want those fucking clones to see the light of day. I won't have people out there demonstrating about their fucking civil liberties, freedom of speech, privacy, email, and all that shit. Joelle, you bring those clones in, and I don't care how you do it. Just get those fucking clones!"

"Mr. President, we're already on it. We'll get them."

The President turned away, and Lucado, recognizing that she had been dismissed, quickly left the Oval Office. President Ray walked to his desk, stood, and suddenly grabbed a small crystal vase from the desk. He hurled the vase against the wall. It shattered loudly. "Damn them!" the President hissed through clenched teeth. "Damn those fucking clones!"

Chapter 41

Marina Novokatnaia paced nervously, unable to decide whether to flee or attempt to regroup. She knew that her clone from California was on the loose. She also knew that the clone from Ohio was in Barbados, but since she had heard nothing, she feared that he too might have escaped. The third clone was in St. John, and he was secure. The fourth clone was at GeneVision's facility in Atlanta. Marina Novokatnaia decided that the stakes were too high to flee and made three quick phone calls.

First, she telephoned GeneVision of Atlanta and directed that Augustine Ball, the George Washington clone, be taken to Brighton Beach, New York, and secluded at Dacha Outfitters, GeneVision's New York safe house. Then she called St. John and directed Josiah Folger, the Franklin clone, also be secluded at the Brighton Beach safe house. Next she again tried to reach Dr. Meier in Barbados and was again unsuccessful. His satellite phone just went to voice mail. Finally she called the Brighton Beach safe house and, once connected efficiently to the night security desk, she indicated that two guests would be arriving, Misters Ball and Folger and that they were held under lock and key. They, of course, could have absolutely no contact with the outside world and should be turned over to Jim Durango from the San Diego office as soon as he arrived at Dacha Outfitters.

It was then that her own phone beeped. "Madame Novokatnaia, this is the front desk. There're two gentlemen headed up to your suite. They looked like government types. I thought you should know."

Without missing a beat, Marina Novokatnaia scribbled a quick note, placed it on the bed, grabbed her purse, cracked open the door, and saw that no one was in the hall. She quickly went to the stairs, and just as she was closing the stairwell door, she heard the elevator chime signaling that the elevator had arrived at her floor.

She silently closed the stairwell door behind her and hurried down the stairs but did not stop at the first floor. She continued on down to the private parking floor below the hotel. She left the elevator and walked out onto the street. And on this night, luck smiled on Marina Novokatnaia. A taxi was idling directly across the street. She walked briskly to the taxi, opened the door, and asked politely, "Are you free?" When the driver, apparently Syrian, nodded positively and said something that sounded like "yas," Marina got into the rear seat and said, "National Airport, please." She had made it a life commitment never to say Reagan's name.

Within twenty minutes, Marina was in Reagan terminal where she dropped her cell phone in a trash receptacle and then took the Metro to Union Station where she was in time for the Acela Express bound for New York. Once she arrived in New York, she would take a cab to JFK. There she would take one of the morning flights to London and connect to Moscow where she would finally be free of a U.S. President whom she despised. She settled into her seat for the train ride from Washington to New York that would give her plenty of time to make several urgent telephone calls. After waiting about forty-five minutes to make sure that she had not been followed, she pulled out one of her prepaid burner phones and made four quick calls, each to wire considerable sums of money from GeneVision accounts and from her local personal accounts to secret accounts in the Channel Islands. The transfers would be untraceable. By protocols arranged long ago, the transfers would be routed through a number of financial shells, each of which would automatically trigger the next portion of the money's journey and then cease to exist after it had served its one purpose as a monetary conduit.

Finally, Marina telephoned GeneVision Atlanta. Once she was connected to the Director of Security, an older American who had worked for the KGB during the late years of the Cold War, Novokatnaia immediately asked, "Are things underway yet?"

"Yes, we'll have Augustine Ball—-"

"No names! And don't say where," Novokatnaia interrupted, "and don't say anything else specific."

The former KGB man understood perfectly. "Things are well in hand. I'll handle things from down here and the package should be delivered to the beach house very soon."

The conversation had taken only 25 seconds, but anyone listening to it would have gained valuable information if they had known what to listen for. These calls completed, Marina Novokatnaia settled in for the ride and watched the urban American landscape zip by. She realized that she might never see this landscape again.

She would have to be careful. She had a head start. No doubt, the note she had hastily left on her hotel bed, "Bob, I'm going down the street to buy some snacks and will be back in about 15 or 20 minutes. Love, M" had bought her some time, but if the two "gentlemen" were indeed government agents, they would figure out pretty fast that the note was a ruse. She had to assume that the FBI or some of President Ray's personal thugs were looking for her. But she knew she could be out of the country in less than twelve hours.

Chapter 42

After a long and leisurely beachfront dinner, including a bottle of wine and some flirting with two single ladies at the next table, Jim Fawcett returned to his suite. He used the electronic key to enter his room and clicked the light switch. But the room did not light up. He flipped the switch several times. The room remained dark, and before Jim's eyes could adjust, voice in the darkness said, "Jim, shut the door, and come in."

Chapter 43

At ten minutes before midnight, CIA Director Joelle Lucado returned to the Oval Office and was ushered in without a word by Sergeant Habig who could readily discern from the hour and from Lucado's demeanor that something very, very serious was afoot. The President's mood was as depressed as Habig had ever seen it, and Lucado was similarly dark and somber. Lucado anticipated that this meeting would be private and off the books. Habig had informed her that President Ray had ordered that the meeting not be recorded in any office documents. Lucado had telephoned the President in the President's residence and said that they should meet in the Oval Office immediately. She had alerted the President that the news was grim but that they should discuss it only in person.

Without preliminaries, both quickly sat at the glass-topped coffee table. "OK, Joelle," the President began. "Give me the news. I'm assuming that the Novokata woman is threatening to go public or something like that."

"Novokatnaia, Mr. President," Lucado corrected, "and it's so much worse than that. First of all, we can't even find her."

The President was clearly astonished and for once was speechless.

The St. Thomas mantle clock that dated back to the Coolidge Administration symbolically struck midnight. Both the President and the CIA Director remained silent for the duration of the slow chimes. Then Lucado continued, "I had a retrieval team go to pick her up from her hotel and bring her in. She was gone. She'd left a note in her hotel room telling someone named Bob that she would be back in fifteen or twenty minutes. They smelled a rat, but she did too, and she somehow got out of the hotel even though we had all the exits covered. We're canvassing all the taxi drivers who frequent the Hay Adams, but so far we don't have anything. But that's not our biggest problem." Lucado sighed and avoided eye contact with the President.

"You remember that disk that we recovered from GeneVision? Well, we've downloaded everything on that disk, and things are bad. As you know, there are four clones."

"Yes, how could I forget that? Get on with it, please." The President was clearly exasperated.

"The clone from California's the one we were tracking from — "

"Were? *Were*?" The President's tone was a mixture of panic and incredulity.

"Yes, *were*. They were on schedule to Miami and with no warning and with only several minutes notice to the tower, they landed in Melbourne, Florida. Their flight path took them a good ways north and west of the normal flight path because of storms coming off the Gulf, so they were already close to Melbourne. We had no one on the ground at Melbourne. We had the FBI go after the clone's plane, but by the time they found it, the clone was gone and so was the pilot. We're questioning the people who own the hangar, but apparently it was closed and locked up tight. It must have suddenly opened up and that plane rolled right in. Someone was there and got the clone away mighty fast. We're not sure which founding father this clone is."

"Founding father! Shit!!" The President clinched his fists. "Have you searched the area? No doubt you have."

"Well, yes and no. You've got to project these things down the road, Mr. President. It's basically Neustadt. Our choices are the only thing we have to work with. When this thing becomes public — "

"It won't, dammit! The fucking public will never know about these clones! Are we clear on that, Director Lucado? In case you missed it, Director Lucado, beginning with Biden, Presidents don't give a fucking damn about the public. We care about other things."

"Mr. President, we've got to face reality. The public's reaction will matter. This whole thing may well become public. Remember, we don't have Novokatnaia. We don't have the clones. The fact that this clone got out of the facility in California without a trace, the fact that he apparently had help on the ground in Florida, the fact that somehow he even got from California to Florida, all this indicates that there are some people who know what's going on a hell of a lot better than we do and that the clones have some real clever people helping them. My guess is that GeneVision has the clones and will use them for its own purposes."

"OK, OK, maybe you're right. What about the other clones, not the one from California, the others?"

"We think, *think*, Mr. President — we don't know for sure — that one clone was in Barbados. We were tipped off that a scientist from Ohio was connected with some super-secret experiment and had a son who was not really a son. He was supposedly a clone."

"Which one is the clone? The President interrupted. "The scientist or the son?"

"The son is the clone, President Ray. Well, the scientist suddenly flew from Ohio to Barbados with this twenty something year old boy clone, and the scientist died right after he got to Barbados." Novokatnaia paused, and after a fleeting twitch, her expression remained even. "Our contact in the Barbados police has told us that the boy clone then disappeared and may well have left the island."

"Shit, shit, shit! Now we have two clones on the loose! Which one is this? Do we know?"

"His name at the hotel where they were registered was James Fawcett. That's not one of the founding fathers, Mr. President. No one named Fawcett was a framer of the Constitution."

The President looked at Lucado with a menacing expression. "Joelle, don't patronize me. I'm the one with a degree in history. I know that there's no Fawcett framer. You, if I remember correctly, have a lightweight degree in communications from a college that has since ceased to exist because it lost its accreditation and folded. And a law degree from the law school with the lowest bar passage rate in the nation." The President smiled menacingly. "And, if I remember right, you finally passed the bar on the fourth try."

Lucado feigned surprise at the President's anger and responded, "Mr. President, I'm not being patronizing. I'm simply pointing out that now we have a name. That name, if it's attached to a clone, tells us that they know that they need to remain under the radar."

"We already know that! Illegal clones would have to remain under the radar anyway, especially given who they are." The President did not want even to utter the names of America's constitutional framers.

"Yes, Mr. President," Lucado continued. "At my insistence, NSA has been running Echelon searching for some digital fragments that will tell us where Novokatnaia is. We intercepted a cell phone call that originated near Elkton, Maryland. The call went to the GeneVision facility in Atlanta, Georgia."

"Christ, how many facilities does that company have?"

"We don't really know, Mr. President. Anyway, the conversation was garbled because the woman was apparently on a burner phone and was apparently on the move. We think she was either on Interstate 95 heading north or maybe on a train heading north. We've already asked for a tower dump from the phone companies so we can inspect all telephone, text, and email transmissions along that corridor for tonight. Because the quality of the conversation we intercepted was poor, the voiceprint cannot conclusively say that it was Novokatnaia. But whoever it was asked about 'the plans.' The voice in Atlanta then referred to a beach house and," Lucado consulted her notes and read, "Augustine Ball."

The President looked up abruptly. "Say that name again."

Lucado consulted her notes again. "Augustine Ball."

"Joelle, do you know who I did my M.A. thesis on?"

"No, Mr. President, I don't." Lucado looked irritated at what she thought was a digression and with effort managed to keep from rolling her eyes.

"George Washington. George *Augustine* Washington. His childhood, because we know so little about it, was my topic. We do know that his father, Augustine Washington, after his first wife died, married Mary Ball. George's mother's name was Mary Ball until she married George's father and took his last name. Augustine Ball has to be a clever name for George Washington's clone. The father's first name and the mother's maiden name. It can't be anything else!"

"My God," Lucado said softly. "Mr. President, that fits. And I bet they used that naming pattern with all the clones."

The President and Lucado remained silent for a full minute.

Lucado broke the silence. "We've tapped into GeneVision phones and emails in Atlanta, and there's no telephone or Internet traffic in or out of that facility now. None at all. That's very unusual even for it being nighttime. It's like they know they're being watched. Which goes to show that this Augustine Ball is damned important."

"OK, so where's little Augustine now?"

"Mr. President, he is not little. He's at least twenty years old, maybe thirty."

"If he's that old — if all these clones are so old — then they must have started this cloning thing twenty-five or thirty years ago. Outrageous! It's totally outrageous that they could have been doing it this long and we didn't know anything about it! Obama should have been paying attention to this instead of attacking the police! Trump should have been on this instead of just obsessing on himself. And Biden, well, it's sad, he was just incompetent, and his family should have kept him even from running for President. And for all these years, where the hell was the CIA? All they wanted to do was bug journalists, follow American citizens, read their email, and all the while this Russian bitch is cloning our founding fathers! I just can't believe it. Anyway, it goes right along with government being so weak that it hasn't been able to do one damn thing to protect our country."

"Until you got in, Mr. President." Lucado was simply incapable of not kissing ass when the opportunity was so inviting.

Stroked, President Ray continued. "And now that we're in office, well, things are different. We've taken care of the borders in spite of the Democrats pushing for open borders. How stupid can you be? And we've taken care of noncitizens taking advantage of our rights. I never did understand how noncitizens could get all the same rights that we get."

"Even more rights, Mr. President. In some states they get Medicaid where our own citizens can't," Lucado added.

The President continued, "Anyway, once we got in and made some changes, people can't hide behind 'privacy anymore." The President held both hands up to put 'privacy' in quotes. "That word is not even in the Constitution, and the whole notion that the Supreme Court could just read the right of privacy into the Constitution is a complete abuse of their power. It's total bullshit. And that one right is what the terrorists use most. The Democrats are right on this one. We should disarm the Supreme Court."

"And the cloners, Mr. President."

"Yes, them too. Our hands were always tied when we tried to find out what companies like GeneVision were doing."

"Mr. President, we actually never tried to see what GeneVision was doing. Remember, they contributed a good amount to your campaigns."

"Well I mean companies like them. We never suspected that GeneVision was doing anything like this. Anyway, where's that Augustine Washington clone right now?"

"Augustine Ball, Mr. President. In the air if they're still on the flight plan they filed. They're bound for New York. But, Mr. President, with all the airports up there, they can divert at the last minute, and we could lose them unless we cover every landing strip in New Jersey and New York."

"Then do it."

"We can't," Lucado monotoned. "We don't have the manpower, not even close."

"We can force them down at some military base in North Carolina or Virginia, can't we?"

"Yes, Mr. President, but then we will have a live clone on the ground. We need to think this through."

There was a knock at the door, and Sergeant Habig poked his head in, "Mr. President, Attorney General Trentini is here."

Lucado looked surprised that their secret midnight meeting was not so secret after all.

"Bring him in." President Ray turned to Lucado. "Joelle, I took the liberty of asking TT to be here. I figured that we're getting to some kind of decision point."

"We are, Mr. President," Lucado agreed.

Trentini entered the room. He looked fresh for it being the middle of the night. He wore a yellow golf shirt, bright green golf pants, and psychedelic shoes.

"My God, TT. Are you dressed for a Halloween party?" The President, always a conservative dresser, often commented on the way others dressed.

"Mr. President, I don't dare wear this stuff in the daytime, so I thought I'd wear it tonight." Trentini's tone was light.

"I can see why." The President frowned. " TT, we have a problem. There're four clones. Four, TT, and they're clones of four of our founding fathers. Benjamin Franklin, Thomas Jefferson, Alexander Hamilton, and George Washington."

Trentini tensed, "Oh, shit!

The President continued. "Franklin we'll capture shortly. Washington's in the air between Atlanta and New York. The other two are loose. We don't know where they are, except that one's on the north Florida coast somewhere. GeneVision, who Joelle reminds me, was one of the big contributors to my campaign, created these clones, and Marina Novokata runs GeneVision, and we've lost her, too. And somehow she's on my ethics council. And on top of it all, she's a damn Rooskie! The damn Russians are always, always, always, always involved in anything that turns out to be a pile of shit. Reagan at least was right about them. The evil empire."

TT was still recovering from the shock of learning that there were four clones of America's founding fathers. He looked thoughtful and said nothing. The President continued, "The way I see it, we have an unraveling ball of horse dung. Nothing good can come out of this. Clones running around claiming to be the founding fathers have too much potential for wrecking everything we're trying to do to save this country. God, that smart, slick, liberal, do-good, big government, socialist Democratic party fucked up things so bad during Obama's time that ever since then it's been a full time job just trying to get the country back on the right track. Trump and Biden royally screwed things up, so now it's up to me, and I've got a bunch of clones on the loose and a Russian on my ethics panel."

After a silence, the President continued, " Novokata disappearing means that we can't really deny what's going on because she can come along and show that we're lying."

"Novokatnaia, Mr. President." Trentini corrected. "She's not a problem. Once she tries to leave the country, we'll grab her. Joelle, you can handle that, can't you?"

Both were fully cognizant that neither Justice nor the CIA could legally detain Marina Novokatnaia even if she were to try to leave the country, that is, without an emergency order issued by the President.

"Mr. President," Lucado spoke. "These are both perfect cases for you to issue Medical Pickup Orders. They're on the books. We've never used them, but they're the perfect means to pick up both Novokatnaia and any of the clones we can find. No courts have ruled on medical detentions so once we get them, we can keep them, really as long as we want to, especially if we move them outside the country. I've got places in other countries we can put them. We can thank Bush for that. To protect us from the tremendous panic and all the additional cloning that'll result if the public finds out that the founders are back with us, I think you're justified in making a medical finding and issuing the orders and then keeping it all classified."

"OK, I'll issue a medical pickup order. One for each of them, and one for that Rooskie bitch. We'll make a finding that she has a communicable disease and that she must be detained, committed, what's the term?"

"Quarantined," TT said.

"Yeah, quarantined. We'll quarantine her at a government facility. Do it incommunicado, and Joelle, your people interrogate her and find out everything. Everything. Do whatever you have to do."

"Mr. President, a medical pickup order requires several signatures."

"I don't give a damn what it requires. Draft it. I'll sign it. You get the damn signatures! Now, this clone that flew out of Atlanta. Force that plane down, and if it won't comply, shoot it down. Same thing, extreme medical necessity. Draft the orders, I'll sign them, and let's get that clone."

"Mr. President, should we bring Defense in on this? Carsten's the proper channel for a shoot-down order," Trentini was referring to Secretary of Defense Carsten Shulla.

"We don't need him yet. The law lets me do this without him. Don't forget. I'm the Commander in Chief, and I can shoot down any plane I want to," the President said with arrogance.

Two years earlier, the President had claimed several new presidential powers that he asserted were inherent in his power as Commander in Chief. One of these new powers was the power to destroy an aircraft if it posed an extreme health threat to the American public. A second power he claimed as an inherent power as Chief Executive was the power to quarantine or detain without a warrant for an indeterminate period of time any person who posed an extreme medical risk to other persons. In the past, such detentions were gray areas of law and required certain formal medical findings before mandatory quarantining beyond twenty-one days could occur. The President had issued a directive in a signing statement to an unrelated bill that "the President has the power pursuant to the Commander in Chief clause and pursuant to powers of the unitary executive under Article Two of the Constitution to order the medical quarantining for a reasonable length of time of any person for whom there is a reasonable suspicion that such person poses an extreme medical danger to the public." The President, Lucado, and Trentini knew that no diagnosis was required for the issuance of such orders and that under the newly passed America First Defense Act, Medical Pickup Orders could be kept secret. Modeled on national security letters so favored by the Bush Administration in the days following 9/11, Medical Pickup Orders even prohibit the quarantined person *or anyone else* from telling any other person, including attorneys, about the quarantining. Though such a gag order was undoubtedly unconstitutional, the Ray Administration was not concerned over "prissy constitutional niceties" when it thought the nation's security was threatened. President Ray's take-away from the pandemic years was that by simply invoking the labels of "science" and "medicine," government can take extreme, autocratic measures and the American public will obediently comply as per the old Milgram experiments. President Ray did care about the public because he thought of the public as a herd of sheep, craving to follow and devoid of independent thought.

"The public doesn't have to know about this. Under the Act, it can all stay quiet." Lucado said.

"But it won't," TT said emphatically. "There's no way you can force a plane down, or, God forbid, shoot it down, and have it stay quiet. Maybe if you get the Russian lady, that'll work and stay quiet, but there's no way in hell you can force a plane down even at a military base and have it stay quiet. There'll be radio traffic, eyewitnesses, everything. Mr. President, you need to think this one through very carefully."

"You're right, TT," Joelle Lucado surprised TT by reversing herself so fast. "Novokatnaia's not a problem. We can nab her — if we can find her — and no one needs to know about it. But the plane with the clone, well, that's another problem. If it's a private plane, we can force it down under the guise that they are illegally moving a very contagious person."

"Is it definitely a private plane?" the President asked.

"Yes, we verified with the Atlanta FAA that the plane's a GeneVision Falcon 7X. That's a fast plane so we don't have much time. We have fighters in the air tracking it already."

"OK, then I hereby issue the Force Down Order, or whatever you call it, and if that does not work, shoot the damned plane out of the sky."

"Mr. President, that's going too far!" Trentini exclaimed.

The President leaped to his feet. "No, the hell it's not going too far! If we say force it down because someone on it has a disease —"

"Make it anthrax, monkeypox, Ebola or smallpox. Something lethal."

"— anthrax, it makes no sense not to shoot it down if it plans to land in a populated area. We need to destroy that clone because if we have someone claiming to be George Washington and then we have a company like GeneVision verifying that he is Washington, then gentlemen, we are in a deep, deep shit hole."

Lucado spoke with apprehension. "Mr. President, how are we in trouble? We need to get it out on the table."

President Ray spoke with passion. 'We're in trouble because the times today are so different. Those clones will undermine what we're doing to save the country. Rights which were practical back then are no longer possible. It's a new world, and people who represent the past are simply obsolete today. Like medical pickup orders, email wiretaps, cell phone tracking, drone assassinations, drone surveillance, EMP weapons, cyber weapons, et cetera, et cetera, et cetera. We're under attack right now for using technology to preserve our country and our freedoms from these Islamic idiots, Russians, Chinese, and who the hell knows who else. My enemies will jump on these clones and parade them around attacking us. Who loses? Not me, gentlemen, no, no, no, not me. The country. The country loses if we can't preserve our freedoms and the Constitution. An updated, relevant Constitution. That's what I want to do, and by God, I won't let one fucking clone stop me. Shoot down the damn plane if it won't land. End of discussion! Fuck it!"

Joelle Lucado and Theodore Trentini sat quietly. They along with the President realized that they were in uncharted waters and that once the Shoot Down Order was given, there was no turning back and things could spin wildly out of control.

"Plus," the President continued, "there's a Russian behind it. How the hell did we ever let that happen? Anyway, with a Russian behind it, you can bet that it's part of an anti-American plan hatched in the fucking Kremlin. Goldwater was right. We should have lobbed one into the men's room at the Kremlin. We missed our chance back then. And we missed our chance when Putin attacked Ukraine. Biden once again showed true weakness and no grasp of history."

"Mr. President, I think you've hit on it. In all likelihood it's part of a Russian scheme against America, and that alone justifies terminating that clone." Lucado was reverting to her CIA lingo. "I'll issue an Extreme Retrieval for Novokatnaia, and you issue a Force Down-Shoot Down order for that airplane."

"Done," the President said.

"Done," TT echoed.

Chapter 44

Hearing the man's voice in the dark room, Jim Fawcett considered briefly whether he should run, but he was not the type to run, and, further, he knew of no place to which he could escape. He said, "I'll shut the door when you show me who you are." Jim could now make out the silhouette of a man sitting in one of the two armchairs. The clock on the table beside the chair read 12:15 A.M. In the dim glow cast by the clock face, Jim could see that the silhouetted man held a small handgun.

"Jim, I'm on your side. Come in and shut the door."

"If you're on my side, why the gun?"

The man holstered the gun in a side holster and said, "I didn't know whether you would come through that door alone or whether they would've already gotten to you."

"Who is *they* and —"

Before Jim could finish the sentence, the man clicked on the table lamp, and Jim could now see that the man sitting in the chair was white, around 50 years old, athletically fit looking, had short graying hair, high cheekbones, lines of a frown etched on this forehead, hints of a beard, and a facial expression which spoke curiosity. He was fashionably dressed in a blue sport coat over a Hawaiian shirt and gray pants. Jim saw the man's coat had the interlocking G and V of GeneVision. Jim gazed at the man, shut the door, and continued, "Now the door is shut. Who is *they*, and who are you?" Jim quickly concluded that he needed to plan his escape since the man was apparently with GeneVision.

Without answering, the man walked to the door, opened it, and glanced quickly both ways down the corridor. Then he shut and locked the door, turned to Jim and said, "Jim, I'm aware that you're from GeneVision of Ohio and that you're on the run. I'm the one who arranged for you to be brought here, and I'm the one who'll do everything possible to keep GeneVision from getting to you. I'll also do what I can to keep the United States government from getting to you."

"Who are you? How do you know so much about me?"

"I'm Charles Delna. I teach linguistics at Tulane University in New Orleans, and I've been on the Board of Directors of GeneVision for several years. A few days ago, I stumbled onto some documents that were never supposed to see the light of day and found out that GeneVision had secretly cloned four people. Four very special people. You're one of those people. I know that you know you're a clone. Do you know who you are a clone of?"

"Yeah, James Madison," Jim said as his own credibility test of this man who had somehow gained entrance into his hotel room.

"False. Alexander Hamilton. I think you know that, right?"

"Yes." Jim paused before continuing. "You say there're four of us? Who're the others, and where are they?"

"Let's sit down. It's a long story." Charles Delna took one seat and motioned Jim to the couch across from Delna's chair. "Yes, there're four. Brace yourself. Y'all are founding fathers of the American political system. I don't know where numbers two and three are, but I do know where number four is. Would you like to meet one of your —" Delna paused, looking for the right word. "— colleagues?"

"Obviously yes. Can we set that up?" Jim now decided that he had no option but to trust this man who seemed to know so much and seemed to be so forthcoming.

"We can do it right now." Delna turned towards to bedroom and said a little more loudly, "Pete, come on out and meet Jim!"

Jim looked up towards the open door of the dark bedroom. There, filling the doorframe was a tall young man, middle twenties in age, broad-shouldered, and slim. His face, like Delna's earlier, showed curiosity but also fatigue. His hair was thick and black, his face long and pleasant looking. He walked into the room, approached Jim, and held out his hand. "You're Alexander Hamilton, otherwise known as Jim Fawcett. I'm honored to meet you. I'm —" Pete paused and with a catch in his voice said, "—Thomas Jefferson, previously known as Peter Randolph. I think, Alex, that you and I have a lot to talk about. You should know, and you, too, Dr. Delna, that I've never introduced myself as Thomas Jefferson before and don't think of myself in that special regard, but I think destiny requires that I should begin forthwith to do so. And you, too, Mr. Hamilton."

Jim Fawcett gaped, speechless, at the complete image of a young Thomas Jefferson.

"Golly," Delna softly exclaimed, staring at Peter Randolph. "You even talk like Jefferson."

Chapter 45

Marina Novokatnaia could not help but be nervous as she waited far back in the check-in line for the British Airways morning flight to Heathrow where she would connect to Aeroflot's flight to Moscow. She tried to appear nonchalant, reading *USA Today* and not glancing around too noticeably, but she had quickly become aware of the heightened security and the close inspection of passengers' passports. Nevertheless, her forged passport was of such thorough craftsmanship that she had complete confidence that she could easily navigate any passport control in the capitalist West. In addition, while on the train, Marina had applied what she had practiced so many times in Russia -—the use of the latest of Russian technology to defeat facial recognition cameras. This technology involved scleral contacts, facial altering makeup that appeared normal to the human eye but introduced slight distortions to cameras, lip modifications, facial dimension modifications via dermal stretchers, facial resymmetrification, and even hair restyling. The passport photograph had, of course, been preprogrammed to match her modified facial features. Marina resisted the urge to contact the Brighton Beach safe house to see if the clone had arrived or if Durango had arrived. She realized that even though she was using prepaid burner phones, those phones were not completely immune to NSA intercepts. Marina Novokatnaia was essentially isolated until she got to Moscow. And Marina was under no illusion about Russia. It was hardly paradise, but it was sanctuary.

Chapter 46

On the east coast of the United States, it was almost 9 A. M. The President had not slept at all and at his orders had been informed several times during the night about the GeneVision plane out of Atlanta. It had apparently not taken off until around 7 A.M. in the morning. No one knew the cause of the delay, but the Defense Department was now tracking the GeneVision jet as it followed its flight plan to New York's LaGuardia Airport. President Ray, Joelle Lucado, and TT sat without speaking in the Oval Office, waiting for an update on the plane.

"Mr. President, just to recap," Lucado said, "The plan's to force the plane down at Dover Air Force Base in Delaware - - -"

"I know where the fuck Dover is, and I know the plan," President Ray barked. "Don't give me a recap, Joelle. Just phone downstairs and get an update."

As Lucado reached for the phone on the President's desk, her own cell phone chirped. "Lucado," she snapped. She listened for about ten seconds, then said, "OK, OK, we'll be right down."

Lucado turned to President Ray. "Mr. President, they're in voice communication with the GeneVision plane and things aren't going well. The plane's refusing to comply. We need to get downstairs."

Without a word, the trio headed to the fifty-five hundred square foot Situation Room in the basement of the White House where they joined several technicians in front of an array of the world's most sophisticated communications equipment.

"Mr. President, you can hear the voice-com between our people and the plane." The uniformed technician at the central console explained what President Ray and his advisors were hearing. "This is real time. Our F-16 pilot is in contact with the target aircraft. We've established our own communications with the plane over a closed frequency so unless they know the frequency no one can intercept or listen in on the conversation. If you press this button right here, you can enter the conversation. For them to hear you, just keep the button pressed. If you let go, your transmission will be broken they won't hear you. They can't hear what we are saying now. OK, sir?"

The President turned to TT. "TT, you know how to work this stuff?"

"I do."

The President turned to the three technicians. "How about waiting outside and when we need you, I'll let you know."

"Mr. President, the protocol is—-"

The President's interruption was terse and cold. "Son, I *am* the protocol. Get out of here now!"

Without another word, the technicians quickly left the room.

There was no conversation coming out of the device. After what seemed like thirty seconds of silence, President Ray finally said, "Is that thing working?"

"The light's on," Lucado said. "It must be working. Maybe I should get one of them to come back in here."

"No. I don't want anyone else in here because if I have to, I'll have that plane shot out of the sky, and I want you two to be the only people here if I give that order." The President's jaw was clinched and his eyes were stone cold.

A clear command then crackled through the radio. "GeneVision 41, this is the Air Force F-16 on your wing. This is an interception. Do you understand? We are now ordering you to land at Dover Air Force Base at the same coordinates and runway we just gave you. You have been cleared, and you are ordered to land. Please acknowledge. This order is pursuant to -—"

The GeneVision pilot interrupted, "Negative, Air Force." The GeneVision pilot had a slight Georgia drawl. "We've violated no laws and your trying to force us down is an illegal action. We're sending this transmission out on open frequencies and to the Internet so that the world knows that you're attacking a civilian plane that has done nothing wrong."

"Damn!" TT exclaimed. "So much for a secret conversation! Now the whole world's going to hear it!"

The President yanked the mike from its stand and slammed the transmit button with his fist. "GeneVision, this is the President."

TT interjected, "Mr. President, you have to keep the button pressed down to talk to them."

Without missing a beat, President Ray continued, his fist on the transmit button. "This is the President of the United States of America. I've issued a Force Down Order. I assume you know what that is." The President's tone was caustic. "It means that my boys can force you to land, and if you refuse they can - - - and they will - - -shoot you down. As President I've authorized you to be shot the hell down. Do you understand what I'm saying?"

"Mr. President, if this really is you, you don't want to do that. Do you know who I have on this plane?"

"Yes, I do, and if you land I can assure you that no harm will come to you or your passenger. On that I give you my word. I'm sure you understand the need to handle this matter discreetly."

"Mr. President, if you shoot this plane down, you'll be committing a crime against America and a crime against the Constitution. I will not land this plane. We have no engine problem. We have no contraband on board. There's no health hazard on board this aircraft. We've broken no laws, and we won't break any laws. We'll land at LaGuardia, and you're welcome to meet us there along with our own people and the press."

After a short pause, the GeneVision pilot exclaimed, "Fuck! Mr. President, your F-16 just head butted us. Please call him off before he causes a midair collision."

"TT, what the fuck is a head butt?" President Ray look confused.

"The F-16 must have flown directly at him and at the last minute flew up and over him," TT whispered.

TT and Joelle Lucado could see that the President was losing control. For the first time in recent days, there was fear in President Ray's eyes. The veins in his neck were taut. His face was red. All three realized that the pilot of the GeneVision plane was speaking on a public mike and was building a record that would lead to condemnation of the President if the plane were shot down. The President suddenly, almost magically, became self-collected and thoughtful. "I had hoped to avoid any public panic, and I now assure the public that there's no danger if we destroy this aircraft. The only danger is if this aircraft is allowed to continue to a more populated area." The President continued calmly, "We're aware of what you had hoped to keep secret, that you have on board a lethal, micronuclear device that presents a substantial danger to the American public. If you don't follow the directions of your Air Force escort, I'll issue the order myself right now that your plane be destroyed. We've been able to discern that your device is not yet armed and poses no danger to the public if we destroy your plane—-" The President then yelled into the mike, "right now! Is that your wish? This is your last chance, GeneVision."

"No, Mr. President. That won't happen. You know perfectly well that I have no lethal device of any type on board. You also you know I've got Augustine, or rather, George Washington, on board."

The President took his finger off of the transmit button. "What an arrogant ass," the President hissed.

The President pressed the transmit button and spun his own public record. "My people have determined that the pilot is psychologically unstable. He has apparently decompensated, and that plane is carrying a lethal, radiological device. I cannot allow that plane to continue with that device on board. I've been assured that shooting you down will not cause the device to be detonated. I regretfully have no choice." The President stood, and as he did, so did Lucado and Trentini. "Air Force escort, this is the President. Shoot them down. I'm going to the zero-one frequency to give that order again."

The Air Force pilot responded, "Mr. President, GeneVision 41 has descended to an abnormally low altitude and has reduced air speed drastically, but there's no airstrip in the area. This maneuver could be to—-"

The President interrupted the F-16 pilot. "Fuck it! Shoot down that plane now!"

"Mr. President, I'm required to obtain the authorizing codes, sir."

TT placed a small computer monitor in front of the President. "Here are the codes, sir."

President Ray then press a red button on the console, identical to what he had been trained to do on the first day he took office. That button activated a special printer beside the President's desk and switched all the communications to an encrypted, emergency frequency. Everything said between the President and the pilot of the Air Force F-16 would be recorded and also printed out in real time on a Situation Room printer and a printer aboard the Air Force fighter. The President then invoked the procedure that had been put into place in the years following 9/11 to authorize the destruction of a civilian airplane over the United States. The President repeated the required codes of the day, and then pursuant to the law that required confirmation codes from an authorized Executive Branch official, TT read from another computer screen a parallel set of codes. Both the President's and TT's voices were validated by a voice recognition system that had been automatically triggered when the special transmission frequency had been activated. The Air Force pilot then registered the proper codes and acknowledged the validity of the President's order. Then the President added harshly, "Shoot down that GeneVision plane." The voice of an Air Force F-16 pilot came back, "Order confirmed." As required, he repeated the President's order. The two printers, one on the plane and one in the Situation Room, printed out every word of the fatal exchange.

There was some static, some electronic noises, then the pilot's mechanical voice said, "Mr. President, the targeted aircraft has been destroyed and what's left of it will hit the ground in sparsely populated land in Eastern Maryland at approximately West 75° 57' and North 39° 03'. Coordinates have been recorded to DOD Operations. Mr. President, prior to the shoot-down, radar detected what could have been a LALO jump, that is, a low altitude, low opening jump, sir."

"Could anyone survive such a jump?" The President's query was to no one in particular.

"Mr. President, are you asking me, sir?" The Air Force pilot responded.

The President realized that he still held the microphone in its open setting. "Yes, Air Force, I'm asking you," President Ray said weakly.

"Sir, it's possible an experienced jumper could survive but highly unlikely since the GeneVision plane was a jet and could not reduce its speed to the minimum knots required for a successful LALO jump. Sir."

"Could an inexperienced jumper survive?"

The pilot hesitated, then responded, "It's possible, sir, but highly, highly unlikely."

"Thank you, Air Force," the President said and killed the communications channel.

The President turned to TT and Lucado. "If someone jumped from that plane, we've got to find him. That's our top priority." President Ray stood and with his back to TT and Lucado, continued. "Secretary Shulla is still in the hospital, but he knows about this. I talked to him a couple of hours ago. He knows to seal off the area so no one gets near the wreckage of that plane except our people. Our people will recover all the bodies and everything else. He knows that I want that area completely sanitized immediately. Carsten knows not to let anyone — anyone — see anything, including the bodies. But, Joelle, I want you to be the one to coordinate the search for any possible survivors and anyone who parachuted out of that plane. Call in every resource you need from any agency of government. I'll give you complete authorization for whatever you need to do to find any survivors."

TT, surprised that the President had informed the Secretary of Defense about the GeneVision affair, spoke, "Mr. President, is Carsten completely in the loop on this? I thought he didn't know what was going on."

"He knows. I filled him in a while ago about what was going on, but he's still in the hospital so I handled the Shoot Down Order myself. The law allows that. Carsten believes that this whole thing's a terrorist situation. He doesn't yet know about the clones. I didn't want to put that on him while he's in the hospital."

The Secretary of Defense had suffered a heart attack a week earlier and was still recovering in the hospital. President Ray was actually elated that the SecDef was absent since the President wanted as few people to know about the clones as possible, and he was adamantly opposed to bringing in an Assistant Secretary of Defense while the SecDef was in the hospital.

"That plane had a device on board. The pilot had snapped. That's what this was all about, people. The Air Force and the FBI will secure that area to make sure no one gets their hands on that device." The President was sounding more confident.

"Mr. President, with all due respect, sir, this is looking like a monumental cover-up. Didn't we learn from Nixon and Bill Clinton and from Hillary's emails, the IRS under Obama, Obama's loads of cash to the Iranians, Trump's inciting a riot at Congress, the FBI covering up he Bidens' corruption, golly, the list goes on and on. Anyway, haven't we learned that cover-ups just don't work? Mr. President, sir, let's don't go down the road that those people went down." Lucado's voice was calm.

"Joelle," the President said with equal calmness. "You have no grasp of how many things in the past we do not know about because they were successfully covered up. Look at the Lynch-Clinton tarmac meeting. Look at Hillary's disappearing emails. Look at the Trump-Russia connection. Look at that Biden laptop. Now, our situation is different from those cover-ups. They were all illegal. Our situation is purely national security. There are times when the national security and the stability of the nation require us to withhold some things from the public. This isn't a cover-up. This is a necessary action to preserve the integrity and stability of the nation. GeneVision was embarking on dangerous and illegal experiments with human beings. We have to make it clear that that kind of thing just will not be allowed. If you want to call it a cover-up, that's OK with me, but the fact of the matter is that sometimes a President has to make difficult decisions to protect the security and domestic tranquility of the nation."

Lucado just stared at the President. She felt that it would be futile to discuss the President's rationalization.

"I hope that story sticks, Mr. President. You'd better issue a statement ASAP. But something else bothers me," TT said, moving away from the issue of the cover-up. "And that is that this whole thing was handled in-house rather than by the book, by the Defense chain of command. It looks like a plumbers deal, like what Nixon did."

"Come on, TT. I had to handle it myself because there wasn't enough time to go through all the steps, and there was a device on board, and the pilot had snapped. It's really pretty simple. We don't need to bring the Pentagon in on the clones stuff, at least, not yet, and Carsten would agree to that. Besides, he's in no condition to fight me on this." The President paused, looking to both Lucado and TT for assent. After an awkward moment of hesitation, both the Director of the CIA and the Attorney General reluctantly nodded their acquiescence.

"OK. Good," the President continued. "TT, put GeneVision of Atlanta -—no make it every GeneVision office in the country -—off limits, on lock down. Seize everything they've got, and detain everyone, absolutely everyone, who works for GeneVision."

TT gasped, "Mr. President, that means detaining hundreds of people! We don't have warrants or anything."

There was another awkward silence. Finally, TT caved, "OK, but what's my legal basis?"

The President responded. "Use the Medical Pickup Law. The foundation is that GeneVision was doing genetics experiments and somehow the pilot was affected." The President paused briefly. "Even to the point that he knowingly had a radiological device on board. Therefore, anyone at one of GeneVision's facilities could be affected so we have to bring them all in and make sure they are not dangerous to the national security. You've got my order, TT. I'm ordering that it be done. Get your people to draft whatever you need, and I'll sign. OK?"

TT responded, "Mr. President, exactly what is our basis for all of this? Is it that there was a dirty bomb on board that plane or is it there is a medical emergency?"

"It's both," President Ray responded quickly.

TT and Lucado looked doubtful. Lucado spoke, "Mr. President, there was no device on that plane. You just pulled that out of thin air."

"Lucado," President Ray said calmly. "Wd have to go with that as our rationale, at least temporarily. So it was both a medical emergency and our intelligence, which, of course, might later on prove to be faulty, that there was a radiological device on board that plane."

Lucado and TT did not respond.

"Well?" the President finally said.

"OK," TT uttered meekly.

"Joelle?" The President waited for agreement from Lucado.

"Yes, Mr. President." Joelle Lucado said faintly.

"Good. Good, that's all. Stay close. Thank you." The President's dismissal of his two close aides was peremptory and final.

The Attorney General and the Director of the CIA left the President alone in the Oval Office. The President turned on the flat screen to watch the news coverage. It was just what he expected. The President's few sentences over the open channel when speaking to the GeneVision pilot had led the news organizations to right where he wanted them.

"Such fucking sheep," President Ray said softly as he half sneered at the TV screen.

The blonde, female announcer was droning on, with a tone of wisdom and insight, " . . . plane was under the command of a pilot who apparently had suffered a severe mental breakdown. The aircraft was apparently also carrying some type of explosive device, but we don't know how powerful it was or even what kind of device it was. We really have only a few hard facts at this point, so here's what we know. The pilot was unstable. The plane was carrying some type of radiological device. The President personally asked the pilot to land the plane at Dover Air Force Base. The pilot refused. Apparently, the President personally gave the order to shoot down the plane. That's all we have right now in the way of hard facts. Anything else is speculation. We expect a statement from the White House at any moment."

The President actually laughed out loud as he thought, *Wow! The press is so, so, so superficial. What sheep!* He stood, snapped off the television, and stalked from the office.

Chapter 47

In the pastoral countryside of Maryland's Eastern Shore, FBI, Homeland Security, and CIA agents swiftly spread out in search for a possible John Doe survivor. The redundancy and inherent inefficiency of three agencies executing the search was lost on President Ray, who ordered all three into action against the advice of both TT and Lucado. The President was fast becoming obsessed with what he saw as a personal threat to his reelection campaign from the clones of the founding fathers. To support the Administration's fiction of medical necessity, agents from the Communicable Disease Center in Atlanta were also dispatched to the area. Homeland Security agents were employing radiation detection devices. All of the agents thought the search was genuine and were unaware that they were but bit players in the closely held, secret plot hatched in the Oval Office to capture and silence the clones. The highly classified ARGUS-IV system developed by the Defense Advanced Research Projects Agency (DARPA) was deployed to make the search practically certain to find anyone surviving the shoot-down. The ARGUS-IV system allowed an area that was too large for an effective search on foot to be searched in astoundingly high resolution from drones, not only detecting visual elements, thermal signatures, and life-imagery tags. In addition, the CIA dispatched five MDDD's (Micro Drone Detection Devices) to the area. An MDDD, no larger than a dragonfly, can transmit video pictures. Given its size, an MDDD can penetrate many buildings and other structures without detection. The new generation MDDD being deployed by the CIA in the search area was much more versatile and much more life-like than the experimental versions timidly used during the Obama years. Lucado figured this would be a good opportunity to further field-test this secret device, reminiscent of similar devices in the old movie, *Minority Report.*

The search for a possible survivor of the LALO jump systematically started at the shoot-down coordinates and expanded in ever-widening circles. No building or vehicle was left unsearched. The government agents asked owners' permission to walk through houses and barns and were usually permitted to do so by the concerned residents, most of whom were aware of the government's characterization of the search as an "emergency."

At a well-kept farmhouse close to the center of the target area, an elderly woman who looked as if she had been thrown off the train had answered the door with a Mossberg pistol grip, twelve-gauge shotgun. "What do you want?" Her tone was menacing. She pointed the gun directly at the two men in Military Police uniforms at her door. "I don't need no government people sneaking around my place. You got ten seconds to get the hell off my property." She cracked open the screen door and spat tobacco juice close to one of the agent's shoes. Her eyes were blood-shot, her dyed-red hair was in a dark hairnet, and her clothes were disheveled.

The agent in charge responded, "Lady, please put down that gun. We're here only to make sure everything's OK. Will you please put down that gun?"

"I take it you guys don't count time too well. You got about two seconds left," she said without lowering the gun.

"OK, OK, just stay calm, you win, we'll leave," said the second agent. He then said to his colleague, "Let's go. We don't need an incident. She's OK." He then turned to the woman, "Ma'am, we're sorry to disturb you. They might order us to come back here tomorrow, but we'll try not to disturb you." The two CIA agents backed away from the door.

The woman nodded without a word and watched the two men back away from the door and retreat to their motorcycles. She smiled as she overheard one say to the other, "She's obviously crazy. Did you see the look in her eyes?"

"No shit," responded the second. "We'll come back tomorrow."

The woman watched the two speed down her driveway back onto the main road and continued to watch them until they were out of site. "Government shitheads!" she exclaimed as she shut and locked the door.

Her husband, also armed, was standing in the doorway leading to their bedroom. "Good job, Shirley. If they come back, the dogs'll let us know. And they weren't MP's. I was an MP for seven years. They weren't no MP's. Plus MP's ride Harleys, not crotch rockets."

They both walked briskly back into the bedroom, shutting the door behind them. The blackout shades of the bedroom windows were lowered, giving them complete privacy.

"We should use the room in the barn," the man said, and his wife readily agreed.

Chapter 48

At the Melbourne Beach SeaShell, Jim Fawcett, Peter Randolph, and Dr. Delna had talked through the night. Dr. Delna had filled them in on everything he had been able to discover about GeneVision's operations. He had also explained to them that not only was GeneVision after them but the government was also almost definitely searching for them.

"You've got a lot more to fear from our government than from GeneVision. GeneVision's fast melting down, and the U. S. Government's just getting geared up. If the government finds you, you'll live the rest of your lives in some secret lab somewhere and no one'll ever know of your existence," Delna had explained to them, mincing no words.

Jim had responded, "I think Thomas'll agree with me that the same goes for you except it won't be a lab for you. It'll be a prison in some less gentle country."

Jim Fawcett and Peter Randolph had done most of the talking, leaving Charles Delna to listen in fascination. The two young men had sounded just as Delna had imagined Hamilton and Jefferson must have sounded. Erudite, articulate, learned, creative, arrogant, insightful, and humorous. Both Jim and Peter fully grasped their special places in current American history, and both men decided to use their "real" names, Alex and Thomas. Delna had objected on grounds that that was presumptuous and could be dangerous, but the two younger men ignored his objections.

As 10 A.M. approached, they admitted that there was no obvious way to find the George Washington and Benjamin Franklin clones. Because of the documents that Delna had stolen from GeneVision, they knew the names of the two clones and knew that one was in Atlanta and the other was on the island of

St. John, but they also realized that those GeneVision facilities had inevitably descended into chaos and that the whereabouts of the two missing clones were impossible to guess. They had not turned on the television or consulted any Internet sites so they knew nothing about the government's shooting down a GeneVision plane over Maryland.

"Let's get some sleep," Thomas suggested. "We'll deal with the lost clones later, but right now, I can't stay awake any longer. My temple needs some maintenance."

"'My temple needs maintenance.' What the hell does that mean?" Delna asked.

Alex answered, "He means that his body is his temple and that he needs to take care of it. Sleep, man, sleep. It's tonic, and we all need a dose." Alexander Hamilton turned to Thomas Jefferson, "You always did mix God and science."

Both men just stared at each other.

"Now, how did I know that?" Alex asked softly, and all three men looked at each other with wonder, aware that there was some kind of mutually shared linkage between the two clones.

"I'll take the couch," Charles Delna said. "You two clones can have the bed."

"Forget it," Alex said a little haughtily. "I'll take the bed, Thomas, you take the recliner."

"Let's flip for it," Thomas quickly proposed. "Fair is fair."

"It's my room. Good night." And with that Alexander Hamilton stalked to the bedroom, noisily shutting the door behind him.

"He always was an arrogant Brit," Thomas Jefferson said of his fellow fugitive. Dr. Delna did not hear the remark. For the first time in many hours, he was asleep.

Chapter 49

Van Eaton Turner was the Director of Caribbean Biologics (CB), GeneVision's facility on the island of St. John in the United States Virgin Islands. As soon as Turner had learned that things had fallen apart in San Diego and following a phone message from a frantic Marina Novokatnaia, Turner had put into motion his own escape plan, a plan that he had long had on the shelf for just such an eventuality. The plan involved gently informing Josiah Folger that he was a clone of Benjamin Franklin and that both of them needed to leave St. John to stay out of the clutches of those who would do them harm. Turner was savvy enough to realize that he was going to be in a mountain of legal trouble if, or when, the cloning project was discovered. Turner's plan was to get to the mainland and then to trade Folger to the FBI for immunity from prosecution. Turner would give Folger up in a heartbeat to keep his own freedom. If he and Folger by chance got separated, he could always contact Folger by cell phone and lead the FBI to him. Plus, he had installed a secret locator on Folger's cell phone. Though Folger might switch off the location service of his cell phone, the permanent locator that Turner had installed could not be detected or deactivated without a code, and Turner had told the code to no one else.

It was early in the morning. Things at St. John usually started early so that the middle of the day could give way to siestas. Turner telephoned Folger and suggested that they meet for breakfast. "Sure, chief," Folger had replied.

The two men took an outside table overlooking the tranquil waters of Cruz Bay at the Beachside Café of Caribbean Biologics. After they had ordered a heavy breakfast of bacon, eggs, grits, muffins, and passion fruit, they sat side by side, neither talking, taking in the spectacular view. Finally Turner decided to get started. "Joe, we need to talk. There are some things you need to know. Some of it you will not like. Some of it you'll like. Basically I need you to know some basic facts of life." Turner paused.

Josiah Folger turned to Turner and with raised eyebrows said calmly, "Dr. Turner, what took you so long?"

Turner was stunned. Finally, he said weakly, "What do you mean?"

"I know who I am. I've known for about a year."

"Tell me."

"I am Josiah Folger, a clone of Benjamin Franklin. I was brought to this age by some type of genetic acceleration process. There are also three other clones - - - Thomas Jefferson, George Washington, and Alexander Hamilton. And you know the amazing thing is not just that I'm a clone. It's that I actually think like Franklin. I've done nothing but research Benjamin Franklin since I figured out who I was. I react like him, I see things the way he saw them, and I seem to have his same mixture of crudeness, creativity, and craftiness."

Turner was astonished and speechless.

Folger continued, "How did I find out? Well, let's say that I hacked into the computer system, not completely, but I got into enough of it to learn a lot about me, or Project Twenty as I am referred to in the files."

Turner had recovered enough to try to regain control. "Then you know how important it is for you and me to get to a safe place."

"I know how important it is for *me* to get to a safe place. I'm the one they would like to get their hands on, not you."

"Bullshit. They'll want to interrogate me, probably in one of their CIA prisons and then they'll prosecute me, so I'll be on the run just as much as you will."

"So what're you proposing?"

"We'll take separate ferries over to St. Thomas, fly separately to Miami, then rendezvous at the Catch of the Day restaurant in Miami. It's only a half-mile or so from the airport. From there we'll decide how to contact the others. The other clones. We need to make sure they're safe. We don't use our cell phones. Turn off the location feature on your cell phone so the FBI can't track you. That's important, Joe. Keep your cell phone on, but don't use it. You've got to keep it on in case I need a backup way to contact you."

Turner pulled a cell phone out of his briefcase and handed it to Folger. "This is a no contract, preloaded phone."

"A burner phone," Joe interjected.

"Yes. The location service on it has been deactivated. Use this phone, not your own. When you call, keep the call under fifteen seconds. If you need to say more than that, use a pay phone if you can find one. When we're in the St. Thomas airport, even if we get near each other, no eye contact at all. None, OK?"

"Sure, no problem, Chief."

"OK, remember. Don't even make eye contact with each other if we run into each other before the restaurant in Miami. If anything happens to either one of us, the other goes on. Don't try anything heroic. No one will recognize you, but they might recognize me. If the FBI by some outside chance gets me and I can get free of them, I'll call you. Remember, even though they might detain me, they have to let me go within forty-eight hours since they don't have anything on me. Then I'll call you, and we'll figure out how all of you can stay free of the government. Here's a ticket for you." Turner handed Joe Folger a computer-generated boarding pass and airline ticket coupon. "You're flying American, and I'm on Delta. You have your passport, right?"

"Yeah." Folger pocketed the cell phone.

"We need to leave in about an hour to make the ferry and the planes. Be ready," Turner said. "We'll use separate ferries. I can be on the 8 o'clock ferry."

"OK, I'll take the 9 o'clock."

Both men got up to leave, having hardly touched their breakfasts. Turner then looked at Folger. "Joe, I'm sorry that I didn't tell you what was going on a long time ago. I want only what's best for you."

"Sure, chief, no problem. I'll see you in Miami."

Turner watched as Folger walked out of the small café and headed towards his small oceanfront villa. Turner felt like things were back under control. *Folger's a smart kid, but even smart kids know fear when the FBI's gunning for them. As soon as we're in Miami, I'll get us to a motel somewhere and start negotiating with the FBI. I'll have only a day or so since Folger'll start getting itchy after a while.* Turner put some money on the table, left the café, and went to pack his remaining clothes. He had already packed all the documents he would need to negotiate with the FBI from a position of strength.

———

Just before 10 A.M., Joe Folger walked off of the ferry into Charlotte Amalie, St. Thomas, where he immediately got a taxi for the fifteen-minute ride to the airport. As he chatted amiably with the taxi driver, Joe pulled out his new cell phone and pretended to place a call. "Golly, this phone is so undependable. The battery's dead, and I just charged it. Do you think we can stop at a phone booth so I can make a quick call? I really shouldn't wait to make this particular call, if you know what I mean. My fiancée."

"No problem, mon. Here. Deff don't kip yo gyal waitin," the driver said as he offered his own cell phone to Joe, "He ma cell fone."

"Thanks, dude," Joe said as he took the phone and dialed a number that he had memorized when he hacked into the Caribbean Biologics computer system. The reggae blaring from the radio was loud enough that the driver could not overhear Joe. "Hi, this is Josiah Folger. I'll plan to see you in a few hours. I'm out and about. I can't wait." He broke the connection and said loudly to the driver. "She wasn't home so I just left her a message. Thanks for the phone." Joe handed the driver back his cell phone.

"No problem, mon." The driver pulled up in front of the terminal. "Here we be."

Joe paid the driver. "Cool. Have a good day, dude."

"You, too, mon. Likkle more."

Joe paid the driver and walked into the terminal. He quickly ascertained that Turner was apparently not in the terminal, then hurried to the Cape Air counter and paid cash for a ticket to San Juan, Puerto Rico. *If anyone's looking for me, they'll think I'm coming from St. John, so I'll just come in from Puerto Rico. A big surprise for Dr. Turner. I hope he enjoys his fish at the Catch of the Day. If my instincts are right, he'll be the catch of the day.*

The Cape Air flight was not until 4 P.M. so Joe Folger had several hours to kill before he would start his trip to the mainland. Not being seen by Turner was critical. Folger quickly exited the terminal, hailed a taxi, and said, "Hey, man, can you take me over to Megan's Bay?"

"Sure thing." The taciturn driver pulled away from the terminal. When they finally arrived at the touristy beach, the driver said, "You want me to pick you up?"

"Yeah, how about 2:30?"

"Sure thing. I meet you right here in the car lot."

"Great. Thanks," Joe said, shutting the cab door and heading out onto the beach to mix with the tourists. As he walked onto the beach, he reflected, *this might be the last time I see this beach.*

Chapter 50

Thomas, Alex, and Dr. Charles Delna spent the day filling each other in on the events of the past week. Most of the time was spent in the hotel room, though Dr. Delna had ventured out of the room to the beach for an hour to give Thomas and Alex some private "clone time."

While Dr. Delna was out of the room and down on the beach, Jim's cell phone chirped, indicating an incoming voicemail. Jim's eyes widened as he listened to the voicemail. He turned to Pete. "You need to hear this," and he played the message.

"Hi, this is Josiah Folger. I'll plan to see you in a few hours. I'm out and about. I can't wait."

The two just gaped wide-eyed at each other. "OK, let's check something," Pete said quickly and started tapping rapidly on his laptop. After several minutes, he said, "Look at this," and he handed the laptop to Jim.

After reading the entry from an online encyclopedia, Jim said, "So Benjamin Franklin's father's second wife was Abiah Folger. Folger. And she was Benjamin Franklin's mother. That fits with our own names. Benjamin Franklin's father's first name was Josiah. The father's first name and the mother's last name. Josiah Folger."

"It's him!" Pete exclaimed. "He's found us. How he did it, who the hell knows, but he's found us!"

"How do you think he got my cell number, and do you think that was really him? Delna's saying the government's looking for us, so maybe the call was a fake."

"One thing's for sure. We have no way to contact him if it really is Folger. Whoever it is, at some point we'll have to meet him. We'll get a neutral place, not here. How 'bout we send the good doctor to meet Folger?"

"That sounds good to me."

At that moment, Charles Delna opened the door, shut it quickly, and turned on the television. "We've been talking so much that we haven't watched the news. I'm afraid things are not too good."

"Doc—-" Alex started.

"Hold it. This is important," Delna responded. The three listened to the news announcer.

"The White House is not commenting, but as you just heard from the tape we played, the American Air Force has shot down a civilian plane over Maryland. The plane was carrying some type of explosive device. We don't know anything about the device, what type of device it was or how powerful it was. Skip, has anyone verified that the device was definitely a nuclear device? I hesitate to use that word since we don't yet have corroboration. We just want to report the facts."

"No, Anne, there's been no mention of whether the device was nuclear or not, but the government did claim that it was radiological. That doesn't necessarily mean that it was nuclear. It could have been radioactive material or something like that. I would say that it probably was not a nuclear device since there's no indication that the Atomic Energy Commission or the Energy Department has been called in. And we haven't seen any HAZMAT presence at all. But, Anne, I have to add that the government has sealed off a huge area so our reporters can't get close to anything. In short, the government as usual is keeping the American people in the dark. So I think it's safe to conclude for right now at least that the device was not nuclear. It seems somewhat unusual to me, bizarre in fact, that the President was so directly involved in the shoot down. Perhaps more bizarre, Anne, we know that the pilot apparently suffered some type of mental breakdown. We have gotten hold of some transcripts of conversations with the pilot just before the order was given to shoot the plane down and stuff he was saying indicated clearly - - - well, the stuff that he was saying just did not make sense."

"Do we know who the pilot was or what kind of mental breakdown he suffered, Skip?"

"No, Anne, but the transcripts do show that he was clearly out of it. I won't try to make a medical diagnosis, but the pilot was clearly not in control of his faculties. For example, he claimed to have George Washington on the plane with him."

Thomas exclaimed, "Shit! They've killed George!"

Dr. Delna interjected, "We don't know that *our* George was actually on that plane. And if he was, we don't know for sure that he was killed when the plane was shot down."

"Shhhhh." Alex quieted the two men and pointed to the television where the news announcer's tone was excited.

" - - - was involved directly in giving the Shoot Down Order. It was actually the President himself on the line with the pilot. So, something was so important about what this plane was carrying that the White House itself gave the Shoot Down Order. That itself is totally unprecedented. The Secretary of Defense is still in the hospital, but the written procedure is that the Assistant Secretary acts as the Secretary in this kind of situation, and we have heard nothing from him. From the fact that the President himself gave the order to destroy the aircraft we can conclude that the device was something other than a routine explosive, but the White House has not released a statement yet. I'm going to our Pentagon correspondent, Jimmy Pielmeyer. Jimmy, what have you been able to learn? What was so critical that the White House rather than the Pentagon handled this matter?"

"Skip, we don't have anything on that at all. Let's remember that the Secretary of Defense, Carsten Shulla, is still in the hospital. He suffered a heart attack some days ago. The Pentagon is saying nothing at all about the type of explosive on board. What we've learned, however, is that the plane which was shot down was a very modern, fast jet, a Falcon 7X, owned by an Atlanta corporation with the name of GeneVision. Now, what's noteworthy here is that the plane that crashed two days ago in Pennsylvania also belonged to GeneVision, or if it did not belong to GeneVision, it was at least chartered by them. We don't know whether there's any connection between these two crashes. But it's mighty coincidental that two planes belonging to the same company go down in one week."

"What do we know about GeneVision, Jimmy?"

"Only what we've gotten off of the Internet, Skip, that it's a privately owned company doing genetics research. They have facilities in Atlanta, in Ohio, and on the West Coast. We've also learned that the CEO of GeneVision is Marina Novokatnaia. She's also on the President's Bioethics Board and is a respected member of some of the country's higher business circles. She also contributed heavily to the President's presidential campaign. We've tried to get to her for a statement but so far have not been able to contact her."

Delna turned the volume down. "This so-called analysis is obviously going to go on all day. We need to figure out what it means for us."

Thomas Jefferson spoke next. "The chances are good that if the plane was actually shot down that George is dead. There's no way that they shot down that plane because it has some bomb on board. Obviously the people in power are playing for keeps and wanted George Washington dead. But why?"

"You must not be too up on the news, Thomas," Delna said. "This Administration has torpedoed the Constitution, the very document that you four helped create. If you four are allowed to talk in public, you'll likely discredit everything that this President stands for and several Presidents before him. The Congress, too, is going to be running scared since, beginning mainly with the Democrats during the Trump years, both parties have basically abdicated from any pretense of national responsibility. They've abandoned their oversight role and become a gilded, entrenched elite. Just one look at campaign finances shows you that most of Congress is on the take. So what it adds up to is that both the Congress and the President will want to keep you four from talking in public."

"You are assuming, my good doctor, that we clones have the same views as our parents?"

Alexander raised his eyebrows in question.

Delna did not look surprised. "Well, what about it? Do you believe the same things that Alexander Hamilton the first believed, Alex? And what about you, Thomas, do you agree with Jefferson about liberty, freedom, the danger of government, and the corrupting alchemy of power? Do you two believe that the separation of powers system is worth salvaging? Do you two believe that we should go the way of a huge, controlling government? Do you two believe that we should embrace the cancel culture and junk the first amendment and the marketplace of ideas?" Delna looked intently from one to the other.

"Those questions are all a little premature. We need to know exactly what this Administration stands for," Alex said.

"I do know what they stand for, and I know what I stand for. I can't explain it, but to a tee, I have the same views as the first Thomas Jefferson." Thomas said.

"Me, too," Alex said. "I have the same views that Alexander Hamilton the first had. I can't tell you why, and it is not just me adopting some role. It just *is*."

Thomas continued, "And I might have been under wraps to some extent out there in San Diego, but I haven't been living in a cave. The American government is by no means monolithic. There are good people in it, and some of them are in positions of great power —"

"I guess you're talking about the Supreme Court," Alex interrupted.

"Well, not necessarily. Even a corrupt or misguided executive branch of government can have good people in it. Take the old Obama Administration. Though in general it was clearly off the rail and corrupt, it still had some good people in it. Anyway, we're getting sidetracked." Thomas continued.

"This is hardly getting sidetracked," Charles Delna, ever the professor interjected. "Since 9/11 every President has engaged in so many actions in violation of the fourth amendment that not even the Soviets could have matched what our Presidents have authorized. And forget Congress. Those bastards have been sold out to the high rollers for several decades."

"That's a grand overstatement, Professor Delna. The Presidents have violated the fourth amendment? Like what specifically?" Alex asked.

"For starters, like issuing a half million or so NSL's, national security letters, requiring various companies to turn over millions of files on individual citizens who weren't suspected of doing anything at all. That was the beginning of the federal government's all-inclusive databank. And don't forget that, in spite of what past NSA directors claim, the NSA listens in on any phone calls it wants to without any court orders. And don't forget that the government is reading emails, texts, tweets, monitoring the contents of the cloud, tracking Internet usage, holding people without trials, setting up secret interrogation prisons in foreign countries. Gentlemen, the deep state is real. Should I go on?"

"A lot of that deep state stuff is bull shit, but OK, you've made your point, Dr. Delna, and I know all about the NSL's and secret interrogations and all that stuff, but there are reasons for all this. The United States was attacked on 9/11. Don't forget that. And don't forget that today's enemy is a small core of political Islam and that the enemy is not located in any one country. Some of its people are here in our country and we cannot keep them from inflicting harm on our country with the traditional methods. And yes, I'm well aware that the Biden Administration let a lot of terrorists and criminals in during its open border orgy. So we have to use more aggressive methods. And protecting the nation is primarily the President's responsibility. End of story." Thomas was adamant, and Delna remembered that the original Thomas Jefferson when he became President, like America's recent Presidents, also believed in broad executive power.

"You've spotted the key thing. The government's trying to keep the terrorists from doing something. In other words, the government's mission is preemptive, and this mission can be used to justify just about anything. For example —"

"Hold on," Alex interrupted. "We ought to listen to this."

Alex turned the television volume up, and the news announcer was saying, "—and so the White House is about to release a statement about the incident over Maryland, and we'll go back to our White House correspondent, Skip Sergeant. Skip?"

"Anne, we'll have the statement in just a minute. About the Maryland scene itself - - - our people cannot get near it, and air space over the area has been closed so we don't have any images and really know very little about what's going on in Maryland. Everything's very hush hush, and - - - OK, here is Mark Johns, the President's Press Secretary."

"Good morning, everyone," Johns began. "I have a short statement, and that's it. No questions at this time. Here's the statement: 'A Falcon 7X aircraft, privately owned by a company named GeneVision, filed a flight plan from Atlanta, Georgia, to LaGuardia Airport in New York City. En route, the pilot showed signs of instability and was suffering from delusions.

The federal government obtained information that an explosive device of unknown power was on board this plane. We know for certain that the device was not a nuclear device. On the President's order, four Air Force F-16's attempted to escort the plane to a safe landing at Dover Air Force Base in Delaware. The pilot of the private plane refused to cooperate with the Air Force escorts. The Air Force then attempted to force the plan to land, and the pilot of the private plane refused to change course and caused several near collisions with the Air Force F-16's. This may have been deliberate on his part. When it was determined that all other options had failed and that the private plane was heading to heavily populated areas, the President personally gave the order that the plane be destroyed. This was either a terrorist event with a pilot who was pretending to be unstable or an event with a pilot who had actually become mentally unstable. We have not ascertained exactly which type of event it was.' Ladies and gentlemen, that's the statement, and that's all we have at this time." The Press Secretary hurried to the exit.

"Mark," one reporter shouted. "Had the pilot been subjected to one of GeneVision's genetics experiments?"

Mark Johns whirled around, showing undisguised irritation. "No questions at this time, but I'll say this. GeneVision was carrying on some unauthorized genetics experiments on human subjects, and it's completely possible that in some way the pilot's mental and emotional integrity had been compromised. We clearly couldn't permit him in his unstable condition to enter a heavily populated area with an explosive device on board any more than he already had." With that Mark Johns quickly left the pressroom.

Pandemonium reigned in the pressroom. No one realized that the shouted question had been planted in return for a promised scoop in the future should the government learn anything definitive about GeneVision's "unauthorized genetics experiments."

Chapter 51

Dr. Delna, Thomas Jefferson, and Alexander Hamilton sat motionless, each trying to comprehend what they had just watched on the television. No one spoke a word for some long moments. Finally Thomas spoke. "George Washington, if he was on that plane, is now dead. And clearly the government's playing for keeps."

"Let's take it one step at a time," Delna said. "Was GeneVision engaged in any genetics experiments that you know of that could cause a mental breakdown?"

"Not that I know of," Alex responded.

"Me neither," Thomas added.

"Other than human cloning, were there any genetics experiments at all that you knew of going on at GeneVision?"

"No," both men said together.

"Was GeneVision doing any psychological experiments or pharmaceutical experiments that you know about?"

"No," Thomas said.

Alex added, "In Ohio, they were doing nothing scientific at all that I could see except carrying on some environmental projects concerning the use of experimental alternative fuels, including vegetable oil, but they were doing nothing medical or genetic that I know of."

"Except you," snickered Thomas.

"Yeah, and you, too," Alex said.

"But we don't know what they were doing in Atlanta. They could've been doing different kinds of genetics experiments there, and we would have no way of knowing." Delna was clearly attempting to keep the three from jumping to erroneous conclusions.

"And we're not scientists or physicians so we wouldn't be aware if they did have some clandestine experiments going on." Alex said. "So we can't even guess intelligently that the pilot was not having some kind of breakdown and that it was just a coincidence that he said he had George Washington on the plane."

Pete then said, "After the earthquake, I was able to access some of the computer files, and one of the files referred to a George Washington clone being in Atlanta."

Delna had turned his attention to the television where the news announcers seemed animated about something. "Let's listen to this," he said to Thomas and Alex.

" — was recorded by a private citizen outside Dover, and they turned it over to us. As we've said, this tape is the first one we've had access to, and it seems to be a complete transcript of the historic conversation between the unidentified pilot and the President of the United States. Let's listen." The television channel ran captions with the audio transcript.

> GeneVision 41, this is the Air Force F-16 on your wing. This is an interception. Do you understand? Rock your wings if you understand. We are now ordering you to land at Dover Air Force Base at the same coordinates and runway we just gave you. You have been cleared, and you are ordered to land. Rock your wings if you understand this order. This order is pursuant to -—

> Negative, Air Force. We've violated no laws and your trying to force us down is an illegal action. We're sending this transmission out on open frequencies and to the Internet so that the world knows that you

are attacking a civilian plane that has done nothing wrong.

This is the President of the United States of America. I have issued a Force Down Order. I assume you know what that is. It means that my boys can force you to land, and if you refuse they can - - - and they will - - -shoot you down. As President I've authorized you to be shot the hell down. Do you understand what I'm saying?

Mr. President, if this really is you, you don't want to do that. Do you know who I have on this plane?

Yes, I do, and if you land I can assure you that no harm will come to you or your passenger. On that I give you my word. I'm sure you understand the need to handle this matter discreetly.

Mr. President, if you shoot this plane down, you'll be committing a crime against America and a crime against the Constitution. I will not land this plane. We have no engine problem. We have no contraband on board. There's no health hazard on board this aircraft. We've broken no laws, and we will not break any laws. We'll land at LaGuardia, and you're welcome to meet us there along with our own people and the press. Fuck! Mr. President, your F-16 just head butted us. Please call him off before he causes a midair collision.

I had hoped to avoid any public panic, and I now assure the public that there's no danger if we destroy this aircraft. The only danger is if this aircraft is allowed to continue to a more populated area. We are aware of what you had hoped to keep secret, that you have on board a lethal, micronuclear device that presents a substantial danger to the American public. If you don't follow the directions of your Air Force escort, I'll issue the order myself right now that your plane be destroyed. We've been able to discern that your device is not yet armed and poses no danger to the public if we destroy your plane right now! Is that your wish? This is your last chance, GeneVision.

No, Mr. President. That won't happen. You know perfectly well that I have no lethal device of any type on board. You also you know I've got Augustine, or rather, George Washington, on board.

My people have determined that the pilot is psychologically unstable. He has apparently decompensated, and that plane is carrying a lethal, radiological device. I cannot allow that plane to continue with that device on board. I've been assured that shooting you down will not cause the device to be detonated. I regretfully have no choice. Air Force escort, this is the President. Shoot them down. I'm going to the zero-one frequency to give that order again.

Mr. President, GeneVision 41 has descended to an abnormally low altitude and has reduced air speed drastically, but there is no airstrip in the area. This maneuver could be to allow someone to do a LALO jump.

Fuck it! Shoot down that plane now!

The news anchor just sat there, shaking her head. She now had a panel of supposed experts with her, and they all wore pained, shocked expressions. Delna muted the television.

"Well, what do you think?" he asked.

"One thing's clear," Alex said. " The President knew who was on board from the get-go. But they referred to him as Augustine. That I don't understand."

"I can answer that one. When I read the files, I saw that George's name was Augustine Ball." Thomas frowned. "It still blows my mind that they would actually shoot the plane down rather than take him alive."

Delna spoke. His tone was dark. "They're better served with him dead. Alive, he's too dangerous. If George Washington were to blow the whistle on this government, on this administration, on Congress - - - well, they didn't want to even risk that. So they killed him."

Thomas paced across the room to the window. "And that means they'll kill us too if they get the chance. I think, gentlemen, we're in a much worse situation than we thought. We need to figure out where we can go into hiding and how."

Alex's cell phone beeped. They all looked at each other. Alex looked at the caller I.D.

"It just says "Private." Alex responded.

"Then don't answer it," Delna said.

"I think we should answer it," and with that, Alex answered. "Yeah? Who is this?"

"Listen closely. I will say this only once. At 9 o'clock tonight go to the chat room named after my friend's house. I will look for you there."

Then the connection was broken.

Alex was simultaneously stunned and excited. "That was Josiah Folger! He said for us to meet him in a certain chat room tonight."

Delna was himself stunned. "How do you know that was him?"

Alex responded, "Listen to this." He played the earlier voicemail message from Folger.

> "Hi, this is Josiah Folger. I'll plan to see you in a few hours. I'm out and about. I can't wait."

Delna sat softly in the recliner. "Gentlemen, this can change everything. We'll now have all of you together for the first time."

"Yeah," Thomas said. "For the first time in over two hundred years."

Chapter 52

"Mr. President?"

"Yes, Phyllis." The President responded to the speaker on his desk. Phyllis, his administrative assistant, also operated as a strict gatekeeper, and no one got to the President without first going through Phyllis.

"Joelle Lucado's on her way up here to see you. She says it's urgent."

"OK. When she gets here send her on in. And see if you can get an update on Carsten from the doctors. Talk to him yourself, not just the doctors."

"Yes, Mr. President."

The President swiveled back in his tall, executive chair, tapping his finger nervously on the plush chair arm. *I think we can control this if I can just get hold of those other clones. There is no way in hell that I'm going to let them stay loose. I've got to be careful to create the right record for the public. Thank God the media are so simple that we can just lead them around by the nose. Deaver was right - - - they are just so shallow.*

There was a soft knock on the door, and Phyllis stuck her head in. "Mr. President. Dr. Lucado is here."

Lucado waited for Phyllis to close the door then spoke. Her tone was tense and thin. "Mr. President. We're trailing one of GeneVision's directors. He's from the island of St. John where GeneVision has a facility. He landed in Miami about an hour ago."

"My God. They're everywhere. OK, tell me more."

"His name is Van Eaton Turner. He runs the St. John operation. We've followed him to a restaurant outside of Miami where he's apparently killing time. My people tell me that he is obviously waiting for someone."

"How would they possibly know that?" The President asked skeptically.

"He keeps looking at his watch. He keeps looking at the door. He hasn't ordered any food yet though he's been there over 30 minutes. He's only had iced tea, sweetened. But the main reason we know he's meeting someone is that he's called American Airlines twice to ask about inbound flights from St. Thomas. He flew Delta. Now, why would he be interested in American flights?" Lucado occasionally took on a Socratic tone when talking to the President.

The President gave Lucado a menacing glance that told her to cease her didacticism. "Because someone else from GeneVision is coming to Miami, and they didn't want to travel together."

"Exactly, Mr. President. I feel that we should keep Turner under surveillance until they make contact, and then we'll have them both."

"Just get them, Joelle. We can't let him and whoever he's meeting get to the press. Any idea who he's waiting for?"

"Mr. President, logic says it's another clone. We think the other three GeneVision facilities were each dedicated to a specific clone, and it makes sense that the other person, the one Turner is waiting for, is their clone."

"St. Johns's?"

"Right."

"But why would they bring him here to the mainland? That doesn't seem to make sense." The President looked puzzled.

"We'll know that when we arrest both of them. Our current thought is that GeneVision's probably trying to hide their clones," Lucado said.

"But GeneVision hardly exists anymore. The FBI now occupies the California facility. Their Board of Directors is all dead."

"There's still Novokatnaia, and we still don't have her."

"Just get those clones." The President said, emphasizing each word. "All of them. The clones and that Russian bitch."

"Right, Mr. President," and with that, Joelle Lucado turned to leave the Oval Office.

"One more thing, Madame Director."

Lucado turned back toward the President.

"Have they identified the bodies, the remains, or whatever's left from that plane carrying the clone?"

"Sir, we've identified the remains of the pilot, but that's all I've got now. They're still working the scene. The debris is spread out. And we don't know for a fact that there was a clone on board."

"OK," was all that the President said. Lucado turned, smiled to herself, and left the room.

"Damn, this is unreal!" The President stood, walked to the windows overlooking the White House lawn. For several long minutes he just stared out at the perfectly manicured lawn.

As soon as Lucado was in her car headed back to the CIA headquarters, she punched in the speed dial for Fabian Miles. "Fabian," she said when he answered after one ring. "Where is our package? Has it arrived safely?"

"Yes, Madame Director. On the base," he said laconically. They both broke the connection without another word.

Chapter 53

Alex fired up his laptop. "It's time to find that chat room."

"Hold on." Delna said. He opened his small suitcase, reached under the clothes and pulled out a flash drive. "Install this program first. It'll encrypt everything you type in but decrypt it automatically when it reaches its destination. It'll also make your computer completely invisible to everyone else."

Alex took the flash drive from Delna and held it gingerly, examining it closely. "There's no label." He glanced at Thomas and looked directly at Delna with an implied question.

"A VPN?" Thomas asked.

"No, it's a lot more powerful than that. A friend whom I trust implicitly gave it to me. It works. You can trust it completely," Delna replied.

"Well, while we are being forthcoming, maybe you can explain this." Thomas reached into his pocket and pulled out a small slip of paper and unfolded it. On the top were written the words "A at M" and the numbers "766-969586868589."

"And this, Mr. Delna." Alex held an ATM card in his hand from The National Bank of Vanuatu. "What the hell are you doing with a bank card from Vanuatu? It's time for you to do some explaining."

Both of the young men looked at Charles Delna. Delna responded without hesitation. "I guess you need to know, but I didn't want to get into it until the time was right."

"That time is now. Talk!" Alex demanded. "Having this type of bank card isn't normal for a college professor, and what kind of number is that? It sure doesn't look like any normal telephone number. And who the fuck is A and what the fuck is M?" Alex's voice had a threatening edge to it.

"This ought to be good," Thomas muttered and sat down on the long sofa.

Alex remained standing. Delna remained in the recliner facing them. "First of all, I am a college professor. And I am on the board of GeneVision. And I am definitely on your side, not theirs."

"Tell us about the card." Alex said. "And this, too." He held up a disposable cell phone.

"It's a card I use to keep extra money that I want access to if things get difficult here in America and —"

"What the fuck does that mean?" Alex was clearly irritated. "We're on the run from everyone, the government, GeneVision, the FBI, everyone, and you're holding out on us!"

Thomas interjected, "Let's have the short version, Delna. Give it to us short and simple."

"I also worked for a secret agency of the government."

"Oh, shit!" Alex glared down at Delna. For the first time, Alex's face showed the violence he was capable of.

Thomas stood and grasped Alex by the elbow. "Let's hear the whole story before we kill him. And Delna, make no mistake. We *will* kill you if we have to." Thomas' dark tone was matter of fact but left no doubt that he could and would kill. "We're the first human clones, and not just any clones. We're from the past, this country's getting more and more screwed up, and if we have to kill to stay free, we will." Thomas leaned close in, just inches from Delna's face, and slipped each word. "Trust me, Delna, I will kill you without a second thought. So for your sake I hope this is good!"

Delna stayed seated and did not seem shaken by Thomas's threat. In fact, he smiled as he thought, *well, thank God. They are tough enough that maybe they can actually stay alive.* "OK, the short version. I have been with an organization that works from the State Department known as the Procurement Project. It's well hidden, really invisible, way down in a State division known as Administrative Operations. 'The Project,' for short. We take on special projects in this country and in other countries."

"And we're now your fucking government project?" Thomas interrupted in a threatening tone.

"Let him finish, Thomas," Alex said flatly.

"At the Project we try to make contacts with people in other countries who can help us, and we try to get high value people from other countries who're in the United States to switch their loyalties to the United States. And we eliminate persons whom it's unadvisable for the CIA or other agencies of the government to eliminate. None of this has anything to do with GeneVision or you two, or you three if you include Josiah Folger. I have the credit card in case DOJ or the Congress starts some investigation and wants to target me, and I have to disappear. A lot of stuff I've done might not be completely legal. Everyone I know in The Project has a card or two for emergencies. And the number is a new contact in Moscow. A friend that I can trust completely. M is for Moscow. A is for Andrei. The number is obviously changed so that no one can call it. It could just as easily be a defunct inventory number or auto rental in Minneapolis and a confirmation number, you name it in case it fell into the wrong hands."

"Which it did. My hands." Alex said, still not convinced.

"Don't think you are so clever, Alex." Delna now had an edge to his own voice. "I knew you had that information as soon as you took it. Do you think I'd be so stupid to leave it where you could find it unless I wanted you to? I figured a few minutes in the bathroom was long enough for you to rifle through my stuff and find it. My question was to find out how honest you two are and how clever you are. On honesty, it didn't take you long to come clean with the number and the card. Clever? Not too clever, Alex. You could have made it work for you a lot better than you did. The way you handled it, I could tell you anything and you wouldn't know whether it was true or not. You don't even know that it's true what I just told you. It's lucky for you two that I'm on your side."

Alex and Thomas looked at each other just long enough for Delna to know that they were still undecided about him.

"Look. You really don't have any choice. There's no way you two can kill me. Take my word for it. You can watch everything I do and listen to every call I make. If I wanted to turn you two over to the feds, I could have done it a thousand times already. I'm totally on your side. I think you need to install this program and find that chat room."

"For all we know, this program is a tracking program. There's no way we can know what this software is doing. So we don't install it. We take our chances and go without it," Alex said with finality as he tossed the drive into the nearby trashcan. "We'll depend on the VPN."

He began to search the Internet for the chat room named after Monticello and after about ten minutes he had found it. Delna had watched him with the laptop and realized that Alex was quite good at finding things on the Internet and even used some shortcuts that Charles Delna himself did not know. Delna also noticed that Alex was using a powerful search engine that Delna had never heard of.

"What's the search engine?" Delna asked.

"It's a new generation engine that GeneVision developed," Alex answered tersely without looking up.

"Here it is," Alex said. "Now all we have to do it makes our presence known and wait for Joe Folger to show up."

Alex typed in Have two new relics from the past. Looking for third. "Now we wait."

In less than 30 seconds, their wait was over. I have a third. It's in Orlando, Florida. I can ship it to you. I'll call you.

As Alex was getting ready to type in a response, Delna said, "Don't respond. The less said the better. He said he would call. We know he has the number. Let's wait for the call. When he calls, give him the number for the throw-away phone and hang up."

Thomas and Alex glanced at each other. Then Thomas said, "OK."

"Incidentally, that's why I have it. You asked." Delna said with sarcasm. "You did ask, you know."

Alex's phone rang. Alex put the phone on speaker and answered, "Yeah?"

"Get me a better number. I'll call back in an hour."

Alex said quickly, "No need. I have a better number now," and he gave the voice on the other end of the line the last four numbers for the disposable cell phone.

"Good job, Alex," the voice said condescendingly. "How about the rest of it?"

"It'll be at the same place where you and I chatted."

"OK." The connection was broken.

"He obviously knows what's going on. He called me Alex."

Back at the laptop, Alex was still logged into the chat room. He typed in the rest of the number for the disposable cell phone. "Now he has the complete number."

Within a minute, the disposable cell phone beeped. Alex answered, "Yeah?"

"Tell me a city and a public location where I can ship the item to," Joe Folger said.

"Melbourne Beach, Florida, and — hold on."

"He wants a public location where we can meet." Alex covered the phone and said to Thomas.

"Tell him on the beach in front of the Hilton," Delna said quickly. "It's safe, and we have good visibility there. And there're no cameras on the beach."

"But there are lots of cell phone cameras."

"No government cameras, and that's what matters," Delna responded. "But there's one webcam."

"I'll give it to you in the room," Alex said into the cell phone. They wanted the telephone link to be as brief as possible with as little hard information as possible, given the vast monitoring abilities that the National Security Agency has unleashed on Americans.

"Tomorrow before noon," Folger said and broke the connection.

The three men stayed quiet for a short while. Finally Charles Delna broke the silence. "Guys, we are on the verge of something historic. You three being here, alive, and now all three of you are going to be together. That's dangerous, but it's inevitable that it's going to happen. Now back to The Project. I've experienced some of this kind of stuff before. Trying to keep out of sight, trying to avoid government detection, things like that. So tomorrow, I'll be the one to go to the beach to meet him. I'll be able to pick him out."

"Yeah, but the FBI will be able to pick you out. After all, you were on the board at GeneVision. If they're onto us, they'll find you pretty quick out there on the beach." Thomas looked worried.

"Just wait. You'll see. They won't recognize me at all." With that, Delna stood, "Gentlemen, I'm going to bed, and I'll take the double bed. You two can fight over the couch and the recliner." Delna walked from the room and partly closed the bedroom door then turned back to face the two young framers, "Guys, I think things are going to get rough. If you have to choose between honesty and cleverness, choose cleverness. Nobody follows a dead clone no matter how honest he is. Good night, clones." With that, Delna shut the door.

Thomas and Alex just stared at the door. Thomas looked at Alex. "Is he legit? What do you think?"

Alex thought for a moment, then said, "Once we find Joe, if this guy doesn't turn us in, he's legit. Until then, let's watch out."

"Yeah, we really don't have a choice. If he's dirty, he's already got backup, and they already know where we are. If he's legit, then we're in luck because he'll know some shit about what to do," Thomas sighed.

"OK, dude. I'll take the couch," Alex said as he sprang for the couch just ahead of Thomas.

Chapter 54

In the lobby of the SeaShell, a man at the check-in counter sounded desperate. "Ma'am I don't have that much cash on me. My big rig's in your side lot, and all I want to do is keep it there for today while I get some rest. ICC regs won't let me drive any more today."

"I'm sorry, but your credit card was rejected and the charge for parking the truck on the lot's $12 a day and the room's $150 a night, and that's a special price. Unless you can figure something out, I'll have to ask you to leave." The clerk indeed did look sympathetic. "I don't have anything else I can do. They've told us not to let anyone park without paying up front. I'm sorry, sir."

"Is there any way you can just let me stay here for a while?"

The clerk responded, "Well, stay in the lobby for a while, then move down on the beach, and I'll try to keep security away from you."

A muscular African-American man had witnessed the exchange as he waited for his turn at the check-in counter. He said, "Excuse me, but I couldn't help overhearing. If it's a matter of the room money and the parking money, I'll pay for him." Both the clerk and the man looked at the African-American man with surprise. "I'll pay for him. Give him a room. Here's the cash." He handed over two hundred-dollar bills to the clerk.

"I know my card's good, dude. I think the bank screwed it up."

"No problem. I've been there, man. Rufus Forest," the black man said as he held out his hand.

"Dan Brass," the truck driver said as he shook hands with Rufus Forest.

"Just fill this out, " the desk clerk said with relief as she handed the truck driver a pen.

After the truck driver had registered and his benefactor had talked briefly to the desk clerk, the two men started from the counter.

"Wait," the desk clerk called out emphatically.

The two men turned around. "Your cookies," the clerk said as she held out four cookies on a napkin. "Compliments of the SeaShell."

"Thank you, ma'am," the truck driver said as he took the four cookies, and the two men walked out of the lobby into the hot and humid Florida air.

"Man, there's no way I can ever thank you. My name's Danny Brass. If there's ever some way I can help you, here's my card. I drive that rig over there." He motioned to a shiny eighteen-wheeler on the far side of the parking lot. On the side of the truck, Rufus read 'Danny Brass Trucking, Savannah, Georgia' is bright red letters. "Keep my card. If you ever need something I can do to repay you, call me. It's got my cell number on it."

"No problem." The card read "Danny Brass – Over the Road – Hire – Lease."

"My name's Rufus. Anytime I can help somebody out who's in a jam, I try to do it. I've been my own jams, too many of them. Anyway, take care, OK?" Rufus pocketed the card.

"Sure thing. Thanks again, brother."

"How about my two cookies?" Rufus held out his hand.

Brass laughed, "Here, take all four," and the trucker handed Rufus the four cookies.

The two men parted. Danny Brass headed towards his truck. Rufus went back into the SeaShell and headed for the bank of elevators.

Chapter 55

Alex, Thomas, and Delna finished their room service breakfasts. Alex and Thomas watched the FoxNews coverage of the ever-evolving Middle East situation. The coverage was punctuated with cursory coverage of the government's shooting down GeneVision's plane. Delna read the complementary *USA Today*. A knock at the door startled all three men.

"I'll get it. You two get into the bedroom." Delna checked the .99 mm Hellcat tucked in his rear belt. When the two young clones were out of sight in the bedroom, Delna went to the window and ascertained that there was only one person in sight. He stepped over to the door, looked through the peephole and called out, "Who is it?"

"It's time to party," a voice responded softly.

Delna opened the door. There was a large, burly looking African-American man standing there, smiling. "Are you going to ask me in, CD?" the black man asked.

Delna's big smile showed the relief that he felt at seeing his longtime friend, Rufus Forest. "Roof, you mother. Come in!"

Rufus Forest walked in, and Delna quickly looked outside, then closed the door, locked it, and pushed the no-entry button. The two men hugged. "I'm so glad to see you. Did you make double sure no one followed you?"

"No problem, brother. You sounded pretty down on the phone. What's going on?" Rufus settled into the recliner. "You said this would make that Znamensk job look like child's play, so what's up?"

Delna looked at Rufus, allowed his shoulders to slump, and grimaced. Their friendship had spanned several decades. Over thirty years ago when Delna was teaching at a small community college in rural Maryland, a young, black kid with an oversized chip on his shoulder had been in one of Delna's classes. In that class, Delna had seen tremendous promise but an equal lack of motivation in the young kid. One day a semester later in the college gym, Delna and another young faculty member joined a group of students in a four-on-four pick-up basketball game. The chip-laden, young black student was on the other team. He had a couple of inches on Delna and had a hip-hop swagger to go with his perpetual trash-talk. When Rufus saw that his former professor was playing against him, he said quietly so that only Delna could hear it, "White boy, you gonna eat some shit." On the first play of the game, from over four feet away Rufus blocked Delna's attempt at a three pointer, following which Rufus smiled, just as he did after each of a number of blocks during the game. In addition, Rufus scored at will against Delna and the other three on Delna's team.

Following that game, Delna had approached Rufus, and the two attempted to communicate for the first time. Delna eventually found out that Rufus's parents had both been killed in a highway crash when Rufus was eight years old. After his grandmother had tried to raise him for a couple of years, she died, and Rufus then cycled through a number of foster homes, got hooked on drugs and lived on the streets, until on a dare he signed up for a state program which would pay community college tuition for one year. Rufus had seen it as an opportunity to sell drugs to a whole new population of white kids who wanted to buy but were afraid to travel into the inner areas of Baltimore City to make the purchases. Delna had seen great promise in Rufus. Rufus was clever, daring, a risk-taker, and seemed to be a natural out-of-the-box thinker.

During that semester, Delna himself had become involved with The Procurement Project and quickly realized how helpless he would be if the government were to turn its back on him.

When driving back to his apartment one Sunday night after being on Maryland's Eastern Shore at The Project's training facility, Delna came upon a street brawl. As he got closer, it became clear to him that there were five blacks attacking one person. The victim was down and was a bloody mess, and the five were showing no signs of letting up. Delna stopped his car, walked toward the group, and fired one shot into the air from his .38. The five whirled around. The obvious ringleader said, "Honky, you'd better fuck off. This ain't none of your fucking business."

When the five spread out like a pack of wolves and slowly advanced on Delna. Delna without hesitation shot the ringleader in his left knee. The thug screamed in pain as he grabbed his knee and collapsed to the ground.

"Who's next?" Delna calmly asked.

"Fuckhead, you gonna die," snarled the tallest thug as he pulled out his own .38.

Delna shot the .38 out of the thug's hand, then in the same calm voice said, 'You don't hear too well, do you, Shitface?"

"You broke my hand, cocksucker." The injured thug was practically whining.

The man on the ground was holding his shattered knee. "Let's blow. Get me to the ER."

The four quickly picked up their wounded colleague, piled into their shiny, new Maxima and sped away. Delna then discovered that the badly beaten victim of the gang attack was his former student, Rufus.

Delna took Rufus home where Delna and his wife, Olive, rehabbed Rufus for two days, and then Delna made a deal with Rufus. Delna would set Rufus up as a private detective. Though Rufus could have other clients, they were only secondary. Delna would always be his priority client, and Rufus was to learn how to beat the government at the privacy game - - - fake identities, fake passports complete with chips, disguises, evasion techniques, money laundering (which Delna's lawyers called asset protection), and similar skills. Delna's direction to Rufus had been, "Do everything to protect me and help me be invisible if I ever need to be." Rufus assumed that Delna was engaged in illegal monetary schemes. Rufus only had to graduate, stay off drugs, stay out of jail, and tell no one anything about Delna or their business relationship. The deal seemed just enough outside the law to appeal to Rufus. Rufus readily agreed to the bargain, and Delna had two of his associates give Rufus a crash course in every skill he would need,, and Delna set him up in business . Delna impressed on Rufus that in the world he was entering he should be friendly with everyone but prepared to kill anyone. Rufus's response had been "No problem."

Several years later, after Rufus had shown himself to be reliable and resourceful, Delna had filled him in on Delna's Procurement Project connection. Rufus's only response had been a big toothy smile as he said, "Man, I learned about that a long time ago. You told me to protect you. The first thing you do to protect someone is to find out who they are and who they gotta be protected from."

Thomas and Alex emerged from the bedroom. "So who is this?" Thomas asked.

"Who are they?" Rufus asked.

Everyone just stared at each other. Rufus broke the silence, "CD, you're not changing your sexual orientation, taking up with boys now are you?"

Delna and Rufus laughed. Thomas and Alex frowned. "OK, Roof, it's a long story, and you have never heard anything like it, I can guarantee you," Delna said with a smile.

"OK, so what's happening, dude? Hit me."

"Wait just a minute. Who is this guy?" Thomas asked.

"He's the one who's going to make sure none of us get caught," Delna answered.

Charles Delna then told Rufus the complete story, at least as far as he knew it. Rufus did not interrupt or ask questions. He had learned to be an attentive listener and to save his questions.

Rufus turned to Thomas and Alex. "Did he miss anything, boys?"

Thomas and Alex then took turns filling in some details, some of which Delna had not known concerning how the two had escaped GeneVision and some facts concerning their lives at GeneVision.

"Is that all?" Rufus asked, then laughed. "Like that ain't enough."

Alex then said, "I hate to sound ignorant, but it's my life at stake here, so Professor, tell me more why I should trust this guy."

Before, Delna could answer, Rufus gruffly said, "Boy, if you're a fucking clone, you'd better trust Charlie Delna. CD is your one hope. CD, can I tell them about you?"

Delna nodded, "Tell them everything you want to."

Rufus then told Thomas and Alex how Charles Delna had saved his life, set him up in business, and then told them about Delna's being part of the Procurement Project. After he finished, he added, "I would give my life for this man in a minute. I would do it without a second thought. He's the trustworthiest sonofabitch you'll ever meet. He'll never sell you out. If you two want to stay free, you're in luck because there's nobody better than him and me at beating the fucking government. He's got the field experience." Rufus smiled, glancing at Delna. "And I got the brains. I just don't know if the government can be beat. If the government wants you, they'll find you, sooner or later. We just have to make sure it's later. Much later."

Thomas stared at Delna. "If the Procurement Project's part of the State Department, then what's to keep them from knowing what you're up to? Sooner or later, you're in their net."

Delna and Rufus glanced at each other, and then Delna explained. "OK, we were not exactly complete about the Project being part of the State Department. It's sort of part of the State Department in that the Project's classified budget for the Project is funneled through State, but State really doesn't know anything about the Project. The Project's totally off the books. It's beyond black. President George Bush set it up as a secret, independent entity that would answer to him and only to him. After Obama was elected in 2008, Bush decided that Obama couldn't be trusted to know about the Project so during the transition period before he left office President Bush severed any connection it ever had with the White House and buried the Project deep inside the State Department. The result? The Project is completely free-floating, off the books, completely off the grid. And, by the way, that's not the only thing Bush kept away from Obama, but, anyway, that's the Procurement Project. Since then no President has known about the Project."

"Your Procurement Project will be secret only until someone scrutinizes State's budget closely," Alex observed.

"Who runs it?" Thomas asked.

"No one. Several of us were able to save our ways of operating, our contacts, and all that kind of stuff, and every now and then we talk to each other, but no President since Bush has been solid enough to know about the Project. He kept it from Obama, and there's no way we would ever have told Trump or Biden. One was unstable, and the other just incompetent. The result is that it is sort of in limbo now. It still exists but is not doing anything to speak of."

Alex then said what both he and Thomas were thinking, "*To speak of.* What does that mean?"

Neither Delna nor Rufus responded.

Thomas added, "It's a rogue agency above the law. Outside the law. I can't believe it!"

"Maybe, but let's focus. Given what's going on in our government today, it's also your only hope of staying free of the government's clutches," Rufus said emphatically. "You're incredibly lucky that it *is* rogue."

Delna took up the explanation. "Those of us in the Project who are still alive confer with each other and when we agree that we have a President who can be trusted with knowledge of the Project, we'll fill him in completely. Or her. Unfortunately we haven't had such a President since 2008. But enough about that. We've got an immediate thing to take care of. Meeting Joe Folger on the beach." Delna then filled Rufus in on the upcoming meeting with Folger on the beach.

Alex looked at Rufus. "Maybe you should be the one to find him. They'll be looking for the three of us."

"Well, I'm the obvious one not to do it," Rufus answered. "There ain't too many brothers on the beach. And we've got to assume that they know that Delna and me are buddies." Rufus picked up the book bag he had brought with him. "No, we'll use this stuff and send one of you surfers down there."

"Surfers?" Alex and Thomas asked together.

"Yeah, surfers." Rufus then opened the small book bag. "How 'bout this stuff, CD?" Delna took from the package all sorts of items that Thomas and Alex did not immediately recognize.

"The major surveillance method the FBI and CIA will use to find us is facial recognition. But facial recognition is getting antiquated and can't handle good disguises. Therefore, we'll disguise our faces when we go outside." Delna gripped a small bottle and held it under the light of the table lamp. After a close examination, he announced, "This'll work fine." He looked satisfied. "The latest thing in facial recognition technology is triple-band fusion, but even triple-band won't be able to identify any of us if we apply this stuff right."

"OK, have either one of you two ever surfed?"

"I have," Thomas said, then added. "A lot. When I was Peter Randolph, we went out to Pacific Beach and surfed whenever we could."

"How good are you?" Alex asked.

"Dude, I rock," Thomas swaggered as he replied.

"We'll see who can surf," Alex muttered.

"Dude, forget it," Thomas said to Alex.

"OK, here's the way we do it." Charles Delna intended that his serious tone would bring everyone back into a serious demeanor. "And this isn't California, dude, so keep your mind on one thing, and that's to keep from being found out. So, if they're looking down on the beach, they'll be looking for loners. Therefore, two of us go down, me and Rufus."

"But you two dudes can't surf and don't even look like surfers." Thomas objected. "And y'all are sort of old," he added with a smirk.

"That's where you're wrong, Thomas boy, well, at least, partly wrong," Rufus answered. "In about thirty minutes, we'll look like old surfers from the sixties." He paused, then added, "Well, not quite that old, but seasoned." Turning to Delna, Rufus said, "Let's do it, CD."

"What's CD mean? Thomas asked.

Alex quickly answered. "You're so dense, Thomas. It means Charles Delna. That's his name, dumbass."

Delna and Rufus went into the bathroom, spread out the various materials from Rufus's book bag and began to work on their faces.

When they emerged from the bathroom, thirty minutes later, Thomas and Alex looked at them in shock. Rufus and Delna had turned into leftover hippies from years earlier, clad in board shorts and wife beaters, with the long hair around a large receding hair line for Delna and a small Afro for Rufus, some arm tattoos for Delna, and, most remarkably, completely different faces.

"The faces, how did you do that?" Thomas asked incredulously. The men's faces had been fundamentally altered.

"We've used the latest in FTT. That's facial transformation technology. It's special makeup that filters the light reflected by the face so that the internal dimensions of the face are slightly modified, like the distance between the eyes, the distance from the nose to the mouth, symmetry, things like that." Rufus continued to explain. "You see, facial recog is based on intricate facial dimensions. Change the dimensions, and facial recog won't work. We also used light reflective masking to change the apparent size and configuration of the cheekbones, eyes, lips, everything. This is a lot easier on you white boys than on me because my skin absorbs the light, so unless I do a Michael Jackson, it's harder for me to disguise myself, but I think it works OK for this little venture on the beach. Besides, facial recog doesn't work too well on my kind anyway." Rufus smirked at his own politically incorrectness.

Alex's expression was one of pure amazement. "Is it waterproof?"

"Yes," Rufus answered, "but not for long, so we won't go in the water. We'll carry surfboards, but we won't go in. They have boards for rent at the front desk. We'll get a couple of boards there."

"The surf's pretty small today so get funboards, not shortboards," Alex said.

Thomas looked surprised. "I didn't know you surfed. You didn't say anything. And where can you surf in Ohio?"

Alex smiled, "We have some pretty big waves in Ohio. I've been surfing all my life, *dude*," Alex smirked. "California's not the only place with waves."

Thomas looked doubtful. "Ohio? Waves?"

"OK, here's the plan," Delna said. "We go out and make contact. When I see someone that I think's our boy, I'll talk to him. You two need to watch it all on the webcam on the computer."

Thomas and Alex glanced at the laptop screen. It was logged into a webcam that gave live coverage to the beach in front of the Hilton.

CD continued, "That's why I picked that particular beach. You can watch it all. You can already see that one guy down there reading." CD pointed to a figure reclining in a beach chair. "Well, the whole time he's been supposedly reading, he hasn't turned a page. My bet is that that's Folger. You two, take note, and don't make those kinds of elementary mistakes. Anyway, the whole time I'm on the beach, you've got to be watching, and if either one of us changes our boards from the right side to the left, that means, there's trouble and you two should get out of here fast. We'll make contact in that same chat room if we can. But if anything happens, you two'll be on your own."

"Here's some money and some ID's," Rufus said as he handed Thomas a wad of cash and a small packet of fake ID's. "There's a fake passport for each of you. They are perfect passports and will get you out of the country if you need to take off. Good luck."

"Wait!" Thomas exclaimed. "How come you have these passports? I thought you just found out who we are, but now you produce fake passports for us, already prepared."

"When CD first called me, he said bring two passports, and he sent me your photos. I never question CD. When he says do something, I do it, but I didn't know what all was going down. Kid, that's going to have to do. It's time for us to get down to the beach."

Alex and Thomas just looked at each other.

Rufus and Delna headed for the door.

"Wait a minute," Thomas cried out. "Remember we're just clones. You need to give us some ideas. Where would we go, and all that?"

"Y'all are the smartest clones around. You'll figure it out if you have to." Delna said, and he and Rufus walked from the room.

When they had left, Alex remarked, "They look pretty genuine. No shoes and all."

"That's cool. No self-respecting, burned out hippy would wear shoes." Thomas said as they both pulled up chairs and glued themselves to the screen.

"Dude," said Alex.

Chapter 56

The British Airways plane landed on schedule at Sheremetyevo International Airport in Moscow. Marina Novokatnaia walked with the other passengers along the long marble walkway leading to Moscow's inhospitable passport control, but once there and unlike the other passengers who were mostly tourists and business people, she immediately went to an unmarked door at the far right end of the passport control lobby and knocked twice. The door opened, and the Head of Russia's FSB, the reincarnated KGB, embraced her.

" Dobro pojalovats v Moskvu, Madam Novokatnyeyu."

"Thank you, Mr. Chairman."

Sergei Andreeyovich Verionsky was a Putin colleague from the old days and not only headed up the FSB but was also was Chairman of the little known Komeetet po Bezopasnostee Geneteekee (KBG), the Committee for Genetics Security. This secret Russian directorate was established with the express purpose of penetrating Western genetics research programs, and Marina Novokatnaia was one of its most valuable agents.

"The information you've been providing us has been most useful for our own programs. The President is eager to hear your briefing."

"I'm looking forward to that meeting, too," Marina said without conviction. She realized that with the escape of the clones, some in the Kremlin would consider her to be quite dispensable since she had lost control of the clones of America's founding fathers. However, a proven skillful survivor of Kremlin treachery, Marina Novokatnaia had withheld just enough data to cover unanticipated developments.

"Marina, I know, and you know that I know, that your reports have never fully explained the acceleration aspect. You claimed that acceleration was achieved by use of a process which you subcontracted from the Mayo Clinic's Human Cell Research Unit in Florida. As you know, that operation's so closely guarded that we cannot independently verify that they even have developed such a process. We'll need you to be more forthcoming on this particular item."

"As, yes, dobyereeye, no proveryaet. Trust, but verify. Gorbachev's pet proverb," Novokatnaia interjected testily.

Ignoring her hostile tone, Sergei Verionsky added with a smile, "Maybe, just maybe, there's some room for you and me to get on the same page. After all we're pursuing the same objective, are we not?"

"And what might that be, Seryozha Andreeyovich?" Novokatnaia asked with a decidedly friendlier tone.

"Longevity, Marina, longevity," Verionsky said with a broad smile.

Marina Novokatnaia suddenly knew that she now had to make a quick decision which could well determine whether she would be relegated to a third-rate academic position somewhere in Siberia. If she lost control of the genetic acceleration process, the Kremlin would no longer need her. If she shared the process with Verionsky, he would then own her, and he could even expose her as having had the secrets of genetics acceleration from the beginning. In that case, she would be tried for treason and undoubtedly be found guilty. But Marina was no novice to the ways of the Kremlin. From the czarist days through the Communist rape of the country and continuing into the Putin era of rule by thugs and oligarchs, a central operating tenet inside of the Kremlin is *vsegda emyeetye dver spasyeneia* - - - always have an escape door. Marina had long ago determined that she would never enter into an agreement with a Kremlin official without covering all of her bases. She had developed a full scientific description of the genetics acceleration process, complete with diagrams and references. The catch was that the analytical description and diagrams were seeded with subtle inaccuracies. Of course, Marina's own scientists at GeneVision had thought they were drafting the document to mislead the United States government, but Marina's hidden purpose was to use it to mislead her own government should the Kremlin ever attempt to get control of the genetic acceleration process. This was to be a high stakes game. If Russia's own geneticists spotted any flaws or omissions in the document, Marina Novokatnaia would immediately be branded as an American spy and simply disappear into some labor camp. But when genetic acceleration failed to work properly in Russia, only Marina Novokatnaia among Russia's geneticists would be familiar with the process itself. That was her high stakes gamble.

So Marina took the step, which would determine her personal future and quite possibly the future of Russia's own genetics research program. "Chairman Verionsky, how will we, how will I, be assured of this longevity that you speak of?"

Verionsky replied, "I'll do nothing to endanger my own longevity. I'll co-sign everything with you. That way we're both equally at risk."

Novokatnaia quickly replied, "That's ridiculous. That's just a ruse for you to have complete deniability under an investigative tactic. No, Sergei Andreeyavich, I have something else in mind. Let's go to my apartment and discuss it properly. I've already alerted my staff to have yazyk and basturma prepared. Come, Seryozha Andreeyavich, be my guest."

Beef tongue with beet horseradish and Georgian kebabs were a delicacy, and Verionsky was not about to decline. Plus, he was intrigued that Novokatnaia had implicitly admitted that she had possession of the genetics acceleration process. With that process, he could vault Russia's genetics research program into the global forefront and become a billionaire along the way. He did not mind having Novokatnaia share in the spoils, at least for a while. "Marina, you truly know the way to a man's heart. I would love to join you."

"I have no interest in your heart, Chairman Verionsky. My interest is in longevity and, of course, Mother Russia."

"I think we have the same interests, Madame Novokatnaia. So here's what I think we should do. First, you —"

A knock at the door interrupted Verionsky. "Stand out of sight, Madame Novokatnaia." When she was standing where she could not be seen, Verionsky partly opened the door. An agent of the FSB stood before him. "Here's the baggage you requested, sir."

"Thank you. I'll take it." Verionsky took the one suitcase from the FSB agent and shut the door. "You're traveling light, Marina," Verionsky said as he lifted the suitcase to chin height to indicate its light weight.

"I left rather hurriedly, Sergei," Novokatnaia replied. "Now, what were you saying?"

"Let's continue that at your villa, Marina."

Escorted by Chairman Verionsky, Marina Novokatnaia bypassed passport control and the crowds of sullen travelers in the baggage claim area, and the two strode purposefully to Verionsky's late model Land Rover SUV. However, as Verionsky opened the door for her and handed her suitcase to his driver, they did not escape the keen surveillance of a Sheremetyevo security guard. Oleg Morozov watched Verionsky's car speed out of the VIP Parking Arena onto the M-10 Leningrad High Speed Motorway, the heavily traveled route from Sheremetyevo into Moscow proper. When the car was out of site, Morozov pulled out his cell phone, punched in a local number long ago provided to him by his American handler, and at the mechanical answering tone, he said, "Marina Novokatnaia and Sergei Verionsky have just departed Sheremetyevo for the city." He broke the connection. For years, Morozov's position as security guard of Sheremetyevo's VIP Parking Arena had proven a source of useful intelligence for the Americans. Morozov smiled to himself as he pocketed the cell phone. This would mean an additional bundle of cash to supplement the paltry salary the Russian government paid him.

Chapter 57

In Washington, D.C., no more than fifteen minutes later, Fabian Miles telephoned Joelle Lucado who was taking a break for tea in her office and at the same time pouring over the data the agency had compiled on GeneVision. She had taken personal control of the GeneVision situation and was not yet willing to trust anyone else in the agency other than Fabian Miles with the details of the clones and the scope of the GeneVision problem. "Judge Lucado, can I see you for a few minutes? I have a report from Moscow."

"Yes, come on over," Lucado responded.

Moments later, Lucado said, "Come in" in response to the soft knock on the private door leading from the large conference room that connected her suite to Fabian's office.

Miles entered Lucado's office and walked over to Lucado who was standing at her Louis XIV tea table beside the window overlooking the formal gardens she had insisted be planted outside the CIA's otherwise unadorned building. "Here it is," Miles said, as he handed her the single sheet of printout.

The four-sentence message from Moscow Station read as follows:

Marina Novokatnaia arrived at Sheremetyevo International Airport and was met by FSB Chairman Sergei Verionsky. She had only one suitcase. She bypassed passport control. The two departed Sheremetyevo twenty minutes after her arrival and are apparently headed into Moscow.

"Well, so she finally surfaces. I guess it'll be pretty easy to get her off the Ethics Council now," Lucado laughed. "So the race begins."

"What do you mean, Judge, the race?" Miles asked.

Director Joelle Lucado sighed deeply, walked to her desk, sat heavily, and picked up two photographs. "These are the clones, Fabian. We got these photos from our searches of the GeneVision facilities in California and Ohio. At least, we think they must be the clones." She handed the photos to Miles.

Lucado continued, "The race is to see who can get them first, us or the Russians."

"My God!" Miles exclaimed. "It would be a national calamity if our framers were in Russian hands!"

"It would be a lot worse than that, Miles."

After several minutes during which the two simply pondered the various scenarios, Lucado finally said, "Well, Screamer's the President. I've got to tell him what's going on. But first, I want to talk to Cordero."

Secretary of State Douglas Cordero was an intelligent Chicagoan who had lost in his bid to become a U. S. Senator. Though crooked enough by Chicago standards to pass muster, Cordero came off as an egghead and was perceived as arrogant by too many voters to win a Senate seat. As Secretary of State he was a one-man brain trust and was well thought of internationally. He was also a dependable ally of President Ray. Though he disapproved of Ray's emotional outbursts, Cordero approved completely of Ray's zeal to protect national security even if it meant "finessing" the Constitution. It was Cordero who had tripled the manpower and quadrupled the budget for the State Department and along the way had unknowingly increased the budget for the Procurement Project. In addition, State had Administrative Operations, its own small intelligence operation. Though Lucado's own budget had gained only modest increases during President Ray's years, the CIA's poor record during and following the Iraq War as well as its difficulties in dealing with global terrorism had rendered Lucado powerless to resist State's encroachment. The President agreed that State should have its own intelligence unit, independent of the CIA and independent of Homeland Security. Administrative Operations was that program, but Lucado had deep suspicions that within that umbrella agency there were even blacker programs which were so far off the books that even the CIA had not yet been able to identify them.

Miles registered surprise. "Why bring State into it now, Judge?"

"Because once Novokatnaia officially surfaces in Moscow, it becomes an issue for State to handle. You know, they actually have some assets there. We aren't the only ones on the ground in Moscow. We've got to bring Cordero up to speed. I want to meet with him first and bring him up to speed before we all get in front of Screamer. I'll call Cordero myself. That way, he can hardly refuse. I have to figure out if I should bring anyone else in on what's going on. OK, Miles, thank you."

Fabian Miles headed for the door, then paused and turned back to face Lucado. "I thought the President said that no one else should be brought in at all, Judge. Has that changed?"

"No, Fabe, it hasn't changed, but my oath is not to Screamer."

Fabian Miles left the room, and within fifteen minutes Joelle Lucado was in an unmarked car headed for the Executive Office (EO) Building across the street from the White House. In response to her request that the two talk, Secretary of State Cordero had suggested they meet in the basement conference room that State maintained in the EO Building for off the record meetings. Other than the two Marine guards on duty, no one was allowed in that part of the EO basement. There was no record of who used this basement conference room. The Basement, as the room itself was commonly called, housed meetings, which "never occurred." Cordero's instincts told him that this was to be such a meeting.

PART THREE
Chapter 58

CD and Rufus left the SeaShell's wooden, beach walkway and stepped onto the sand of the beach. The Atlantic was cooperating with the surfer ruse. The powerful, glassy waves were challenging even the best of the surfers, and most of the people on the beach were watching the show.

"The Hilton's a short walk down the beach," CD said.

"Let's make it look right," Rufus replied. "I think we should go on out and catch a few waves and gradually end up down in front of the Hilton. The flow's in that direction."

"No can do. We can't take a chance with this make-up. It's supposed to be sort of waterproof, but we can't take the chance. We can't screw around with that."

Rufus laughed. "Maybe you've gotten too old to catch a wave?"

CD just grunted in response.

Rufus and CD walked along the water's edge until they reached the Hilton's beach. Since they had scanned the beach earlier on the Hilton's web cam, the numbers on the beach had picked up substantially with lots of young twenties and thirties taking advantage of the perfect temperature and surf.

"It looks like a group of college kids is here," Rufus said, "and that's going to make it pretty hard to pick out our boy."

"Look at those T shirts, and look at those tattoos. These aren't college kids." Most everyone on the beach except Rufus and CD sported numerous tattoos. The few men near CD and Rufus who had on shirts wore T-shirts emblazoned with the words "Rugged Cross."

"Just our luck. This is some kind of religious biker group," Rufus said. "We'll never find our boy in this mob."

"Think again. I already see him. Look over there," CD motioned slightly with the tip of his board towards the water's edge where a young man sat with two biker girls who were sporting "Prayer Warrior" T shirts. The young man wore a Rugged Cross T shirt, but he had no tattoos. Except for CD and Rufus, he seemed to be the only other person on the beach with no tattoos or body piercings.

"Another thing," Rufus observed. "He's at the farthest possible point from the video cam. That makes it harder for us if we have to use it, but it makes sense if he's trying to stay out of sight. He sounded on the phone like he had some tradecraft. But for someone who's been living in the islands, he's surely not very tan."

"But notice that he's facing away from the video cam, and has the two girls facing it. If the feds are monitoring the cams, they won't even notice him."

"Let's hope this make-up job works since to talk to him we'll have to face the camera," Rufus said.

"OK, what's the plan, genius?" CD asked.

"You're the field agent. You tell me," Rufus responded as the two faux hippies from the past looked out at the breaking surf. "And remember, CD, we stand out as tatt-less."

"OK, yeah, that's a problem we can't do anything about. Anyway, I say we just go up to the three of them, and I'll take it," CD said. "You just play along. I'll ask him if his name's Jim or Peter or Thomas or Alex." CD looked at Rufus inquiringly.

Rufus laughed loudly. "You've got to be kidding me. You'll be leaving a trail a mile wide if the feds come down here asking questions. If that's not him, he'll surely be able to get them started looking for us. They'll know we're here in Melbourne Beach —"

"Indiatlantic," CD corrected with feigned seriousness.

"Whatever. And they'll saturate the area and find all of us. And remember, if that's not Joe, it's probably a religious guy, and he'll be a credible source for the fucking feds."

Several bikers walking by heard Rufus's language, and a large, burly guy with at least twenty tattoos and arms as large as tree trunks said, "Watch the language, fellow." He smiled but was physically imposing enough to be taken seriously.

"No problem," Rufus said softly. "I'm sorry."

"No problem," the biker said as he walked on. Then the biker turned and walked back to Rufus. "You're not one of us, so who are you? The press or something?"

"No, I'm just staying at the hotel."

"No you're not. You just walked here from way down there. I saw you. That's two strikes, cussing and lying. Three strikes and you have to become one of us, fellow." The biker was still smiling but did not walk away.

Rufus said, "OK, yeah we're staying in town but we wanted to use the beach down here, and sometimes the hotels get sort of weird when people not staying there use their beach."

"That's three lies, Jim." CD used a false name for Rufus. "You're out. You have to become one of them now. They look like Christians. Are you ready for that, Jim?"

"I'm already there, Tony. I've been a Christian ever since I could think," Rufus said.

The biker laughed, "My name's Dreamer. Y'all just have fun, OK, and don't run away with any of our women, especially that one." Dreamer motioned to a shapely brunette lying on the beach. "That's BeeBee. She's my wife."

"Dreamer. Why that handle?" CD asked.

"Because I have a lot of experience with dreams," Dreamer said cryptically.

"Who are y'all? A motorcycle gang?" CD asked.

"We're a club, not a gang," Dreamer said seriously.

CD then said, "Dreamer, we're looking for someone we were hoping to meet down here. It's a young guy about 25 or 30, and he's not a biker. So he's not one of yours. Can you help us out, Dreamer?"

"Yeah, that guy over there talking to Debbie and Sandy. He's no biker. Just look at him, and he was down here when we got here. OK, I gotta go. I'm getting hot, so it's time to get in the water." Dreamer and his two friends walked to the water's edge, felt the temperature, then without hesitation ran a few steps and plunged into the surf.

"OK, let's go talk to Joe." CD said.

Rufus just shook his head, and the two started towards their quarry. "And, Roof," CD said, "First of all, no cussing. You won't blend in. Second, just follow my lead."

Rufus muttered something under his breath, probably unrepeatable in present company, and trying to look loose and natural, he and CD ambled through the bikers and eventually made their way closer to the water's edge where the young man was talking to the two biker girls. The girls were both sitting in the sand with their backs to the surf, facing the young man whose back was to the video cam which was perched high above the beach on the Hilton's barrier wall. Rufus and CD came up behind the young man, passed by him, and kept walking a few steps and stopped. Still looking out at the surf, pointing casually at a large breaker, Rufus and CD talked together casually for a few moments. Then they turned and were facing the young man whom they realized for the first time was smoking marijuana. CD took a few steps toward him, and said, "Hey, dude, maybe you can help me. I'm supposed to meet someone down here. Do you know anyone around here named Thomas or Alex or Joe or Pete?"

Rufus rolled his eyes and fought the urge to slug CD.

The young man replied, "Dude, I don't know anyone down here except these two lovely ladies."

Rufus said, "We're supposed to hit some waves with them, but we just talked on the phone and don't know what they look like. Hey, but that's cool, you don't know 'em?"

The young man in a less friendly tone, "Man, I don't know 'em. And I'm sort of busy now."

"I thought weed made you mellow," CD said under his breath to Rufus.

The young man took a deep drag off the joint and said, "Dude, this guy who paid me to come down here said maybe some old guys might come around asking questions. But he didn't tell me his name or nothing like that." He then handed the joint to one of the girls.

"Hey, buddy, I stopped smoking weed three years ago. I'm high on Jesus now, and you can be too." The girl handed the marijuana joint back to the young man.

"Cool," he replied as he took the joint and took another deep drag.

"What do you mean, someone paid you?" Rufus asked.

"This white dude gave me fifty dollars to come down here, mix it up, and wait around for a couple of hours, and see if anyone came around asking questions."

"Who asked you to come down here?" CD asked.

"I don't know his name. It was just some dude on the boardwalk up there."

"When did you talk to him? And can you tell me what he looked like?" CD asked.

"Man, I don't remember what he looked like. He looked like anybody else, you know, two arms, two legs —"

"OK, no problem, we just —" CD started to press the young man again when someone tapped him on the shoulder.

"Who might you be looking for?" The speaker was a young man with a thick biker headband, an earring, and multiple arm tattoos and carrying a surfboard. He was dripping wet and had obviously just come out of the water.

"Nobody, never mind," CD replied. He spoke softly to Rufus, "Let's get out of here before we draw a crowd."

"Good idea," Rufus replied. The two started off.

"Hold on, dude," the newcomer said. "Pray tell, might I ask, who might you be looking for?"

CD caught the strange phrasing. "Well, dude, I am supposed to meet some friends here. I'm particularly looking for someone named Joe. I talked to him on the phone but I don't know what he looks like."

The newcomer replied, "I think I know where we can find this guy named Joe. Come on with me." The fellow produced a cap from his board shorts, pulled it low over his face, turned, and without waiting for a reply, walked directly towards the Hilton. CD and Rufus quickly caught up with their new acquaintance, and ten feet before they reached the entrance to the Hilton grounds, CD said, "OK, before we go further, how about you telling me who you are and whether you know our friend."

"Get your hat down over your eyes, man. There are people around. I'm your friend. I'm Joe Folger. I know you're not Thomas or Alex, and I'm pretty sure that you," turning toward Rufus, "are also neither. Last I heard, they were both white. Sorry, good sir. I guess I was doing a little racial profiling there." He smiled slightly and, looking back at CD, continued. "Now, if you happen to be FBI or in league with Van Eaton, then I'm history anyway, but better now than later. Later on, I'll know my friends. Right now, I don't know them and have no idea where they are. So look, you two, I know you can take me in if you want to. If you're on my side, prove it. But I warn you, I've made a bunch of friends down here, and I don't think they'll let you take me in without a hell of a fight." Joe Folger motioned to a group of unsmiling bikers who were standing nearby watching the encounter. One of them nodded knowingly to Joe.

CD and Rufus followed Joe's gaze. " No problem. We're the only friends you have in this country, Joe. And the other two," CD paused, then continued, "clones are not far from here, and they're safe. Now tell me, who is Van Eaton?" CD vaguely remembered the name from some GeneVision briefing papers that had crossed his desk.

"How about Turner? Does that name ring a bell?" the young man asked.

"Yeah, Van Eaton Turner. I think he's with GeneVision, and they are -—were -—the ones holding you?" CD ventured.

"Good. But that proves nothing. You need to prove to me that you're who you claim you are. Tell me something I don't know."

CD looked thoughtfully at the young man. "That's easy. Just come with us, and you'll know for sure. In the meantime, chew on this. That pot smoker down there can I.D. you and us. That wasn't too smart for someone who is supposed to have flown a kite."

"That guy's so buzzed that he won't remember what we look like, and besides he's not all that credible is he?"

"And what about the girls. They weren't buzzed. They'll know what we look like. If the feds talk to them, we're had."

"Man, I might have been out of the loop for twenty years or so, but I know that there's no way that a bunch of Christian bikers who used to be outlaws will tell the feds shit."

CD was getting exasperated. He was just getting ready to argue further when Rufus cut in, "OK, you two. We've got company. Don't look now but there're two new guys on the beach walking around, and they ain't bikers. And there're two others coming out of the Hilton."

"How the hell did they know we were here?" CD exclaimed softly.

"They probably don't know we're here, but they must know Joe's here. Assuming this is Joe."

CD said without turning around, "Where are they now? How far away are they?"

Rufus said, "They're about a hundred yards away and coming this way, but I'm more worried about the two coming down the boardwalk from the Hilton. They're headed right for us."

"What're y'all so serious about?" It was Dreamer. CD and Rufus were so involved that they had not noticed that Dreamer and a fellow Harley rider had joined them.

"Dreamboat, I need a favor."

"Before we get into favors, you've got to call me my right name. Dreamer." Dreamer looked at CD, waiting for an answer.

"Dreamer? Yeah, whatever. Dreamer."

"Not whatever. Dreamer."

"Dreamer, there're two guys coming down the boardwalk, and they're looking for my friend here." CD motioned to Joe. "He's done nothing at all illegal but they're from the government and they want to take him in for questioning. He's a Christian. Can you get him out of here, like just some of y'all leave and have him in the middle or something?"

"That's not a problem. I knew they were feds as soon as they came out of the hotel. And there're three others, too."

"Where?"

"Those two guys, and that girl over there." Dreamer nodded toward a girl standing on the edge of a group of bikers some distance away.

"How do you know she's a fed?"

"Because she was talking to her breast." Dreamer smirked. "I usually pick up on it when a female talks to her breast."

Rufus interjected, "Time to go, boys, How about it, Dreamer? Can you get our boy out of here?"

"No problem." Dreamer turned to Joe. "Do you have a name?"

Joe nodded, "Yeah, Ben."

"OK, go." CD said quickly. "Ben, get in touch like you did before. The same room. And, by the way, Ben, that's the proof that we're on your side. We'll wait to hear from you."

Dreamer took Ben by the elbow, nodded to his fellow biker, and said to CD, "This is Cuffs. We'll take care of Ben. Later." Dreamer, Cuffs, and Ben began to make their way away from the boardwalk and the two approaching agents. With Ben between them, Dreamer and Cuffs headed down the beach and quickly melted into the crowd of bikers.

CD looked at Rufus, "I guess Cuffs has had a lot of experience with cuffs. Let's see if this makeup does the job. There's no way to go but straight ahead." The two men headed up toward the boardwalk where the two federal agents, clad in long pants and Hawaiian shirts, were coming directly towards CD and Rufus. As they approached CD and Rufus, one of the agents said, "Excuse me, but can you tell me who these people are?" He gave a sweeping motion to the throngs on the beach.

Rufus replied, "It's a fucking biker club, dude."

He and CD continued walking, but were not more than several steps past the two federal agents when one called out, "Do you mind if we ask you two a couple of questions?"

Rufus and CD stopped, paused, then turned around, and Rufus said, "Yeah, no problem, dude." They were now well out of the webcam's scan area.

The taller agent took the lead, "I noticed you were talking to a couple of girls and a gentleman on the beach. We're looking for a gentleman who is about that age and height. Do you mind telling us who he is and whether he's staying at the Hilton?"

"Man, I don't know who the dude is," Rufus replied. "We were just asking him about all these bikers since I ain't a biker, and he don't look too much like a biker. He said he was staying at the Crown Plaza."

"No, I think he said he wanted to stay there but he got a deal at the Radisson and so he went there, but he wanted to use the beach here," CD said.

"No, Adam, I think he said it the other way around," Rufus said, knowing that they were just giving the agents more places to check out. "And then he said he was staying across the river at the Holiday Inn."

CD played along, "Yeah, Devon, he did say he was staying at the Holiday Inn, but he also said one time that he was staying at the Radisson. And he said he's staying with some other guy who actually got the room."

"You already smoked too much weed. You can't even remember what he said," Rufus said.

"The fuck I can't. He said he was staying downtown."

Rufus responded, "No the fuck he didn't. He said — "

"Fellows," the taller agent said irritably, "Just tell us what you know about him."

"Sorry, but we don't know anything other than he was doing a lot of weed. What's he done?"

Without answering CD's question, the agent asked, "Where was he going?"

"What do you mean, where was he going? He was just sitting there."

"Well, he's not there anymore. Did he say where he was going?"

They all looked at where the young man had been.

CD responded, "He didn't say shit. He was stoned, man, and just talked about girls. They were standing right there. It was sort of embarrassing."

Rufus, "I think that's him in the water." Rufus pointed to three figures in the water.

The shorter agent pulled out a pair of high-powered field glasses and spotted the three in the water. "Yeah, I think that's him. No tattoos and he's got two girls with him. You won't believe this, but it looks like they are baptizing him."

Rufus burst out laughing. CD frowned.

The taller agent then said, "OK, gentlemen, thank you for your help, but before you go, take a look at this picture. Is this the guy in the water?" The agent held out a picture of Joe Folger. The picture was grainy and was apparently taken with a passport control camera at some airport.

CD replied, "Yeah, I think that's him. I can't be too sure because the guy down there," and CD motioned to the pot smoker in the water being baptized by the two girls, "that guy's face was like you get when you been doing too much weed, you know what I mean?"

Rufus joined in, "Yeah, and all white dudes look the same to me, but I remember he said that he needed to stay out of sight, but he never did say why."

CD added, "Yeah, and he seemed sort of nervous to be so high on weed."

"Thank you, gentlemen."

"No problemo, dude," Rufus said with a toothy smile.

With that, the two agents retreated back up the boardwalk. One of the agents began talking into the small microphone beneath his shirt collar. Rufus and CD had to trail behind them since that was the direction in which they were already going when they had first encountered the agents.

"They have his picture," Rufus said quietly.

"Yeah, they had to have it sooner or later, but they apparently don't have the files from St. John yet."

"Or they were destroyed by GeneVision when the meltdown started," Rufus said.

"You know we're being followed, don't you?" CD said.

"Yep," Rufus said.

"It's those two bikers who just stopped. They're leaning on the boardwalk railing waiting for us to move on."

"OK, so what do we do?"

"Nothing. I'm not worried about them. I'm more concerned about those two agents. I guess they're just going to watch our pot smoker until he leads them back to where he's staying, wherever that is. They're surely not going after him now." CD motioned to the two agents who had now taken a table on the Hilton's oceanside bar from which they could watch their target. CD and Rufus walked through the bar area without acknowledging the two agents, walked through the Hilton lobby and out onto the automobile drop-off area. There were about a dozen bikers in the area.

CD said quietly to Rufus, "You know, Ben was pretty smart. That pot smoker does look a little like him and will at least delay them for a while." Looking at the bikers, he said to Rufus, "Get us a ride if you can."

Rufus said, "No problem." He walked up to one of the bikers. "Do you think a couple of y'all could take us down the beach?"

The unsmiling biker that Rufus had approached said, "Man, I ain't no taxi. You got legs. Can't y'all walk?" He scowled at Rufus, almost challenging him.

Rufus then noticed that this biker did not have on a Rugged Cross shirt but rather wore Satan's Gang colors. At that point, a tall, bearded biker who had been tailing them came out of the Hilton, walked up to Rufus and the Satan's Gang member and said in a deep, bass voice, "Timeout, come on, if you're going to ride with us, you can't be an asshole." Turning to Rufus, he said, "He's a one-percenter. Look at his colors. He's with Satan's Gang, and I used to ride with him. See my colors? I'm Rugged Cross, and Timeout, bless his outlaw soul, is with us for a couple of days to see if he wants to come over. Anyway, I'm Killer. Where do y'all want to go?"

Rufus said, "Thanks, Killer. We met Dreamer and Cuffs down on the beach."

Killer responded, "Yeah, I know. I was standing right there with Dreamer when you talked to him. He told me to watch out for you, that you were obviously in some kind of trouble."

"Yeah, well, we need to go down the beach about a mile or so."

"No problem. Hey, Low Side, you take the black dude, and I'll take the old white guy. Timeout, stay cool, man, and we'll be back in a minute."

"How bout I take the black dude?" Timeout said.

Killer smiled broadly, "Man, you'll be on board before it's all over. I know it."

Timeout said, "Fuck that, Killer. Don't push it."

Killer just laughed and grabbed Timeout around the shoulders and squeezed him, "Please don't cuss, Timeout. You're going to mess up our reputation. We bikers have an image to maintain."

CD and Rufus both did double takes. They were both thinking that with all the leather, tattoos, body piercings, and cigarettes, the image was beyond damage from a cuss word or two. For the first time, Timeout gave the hint of a smile. He turned to Rufus. "OK, get on, my black brother." He motioned to a shiny Harley V-Rod Muscle.

Killer said to CD, "You're the lucky one. You get to ride B with me," and he motioned to a white bike. It was the only white motorcycle in sight. It bore the trade name *Indiabike*.

"He always did show off," Timeout said as the four put on their helmets. "You don't have to wear these in Florida, but they say if you don't, there ain't nothing up there to protect. It's got a mic so we can talk to each other. Just stay with the sissy bar," Timeout said to an uncomprehending Rufus. Sensing Rufus's confusion, Timeout explained, "That's the high bar back of you to keep you from falling off." Timeout shook his head in disbelief.

With the usual loud pipes, the Harley and the Indiabike sped out of the Hilton's lot and were quickly doing 60 mph down A1A. After a couple of minutes, they neared the SeaShell hotel. CD said through the helmet mic, "Slow down in front of that hotel, but don't turn in."

"You got it," Killer responded with a nod of his head. Killer slowed the bike. CD was alarmed to see that the door to their sixth-floor suite was wide open.

"Pull in at that restaurant, OK?" CD said into Killer's ear.

Killer pulled into a small sandwich shop across the street and down about a half block from the SeaShell. From there, they could clearly see the SeaShell and the balcony outside CD's room. CD awkwardly dismounted and turned to Rufus and Timeout who had pulled up beside them, "Roof, did you see that?"

"Yeah, we got problems."

"OK, let's just watch from inside for a few minutes." Turning to Killer, he said, "We need to stay here and watch the hotel. Thanks for bringing us down here, but you two better go ahead and leave. There might be some trouble, and I don't want to get you involved."

"Man, you just don't get it, do you?" Killer said. "Dreamer said to take care of you, and we're going to take care of you. That's all there is to it. How 'bout it, Timeout?"

"Who are they in trouble from?" Timeout directed his question to Killer.

"Dreamer said the feds." Turning to CD, he asked, "Is that right?"

CD said, "Yeah, that's right. But it's even worse than that. You don't want to know. Take my word for it."

"Well, if it's the feds — before I found Jesus, I would say the fucking feds but I don't talk that way now — then I'm going to do what Dreamer said. I'm sticking with you all the way," Killer said.

"I'm in. The fucking feds ain't too high up on my list of people. The only good fed's a dead fed," Timeout said.

Rufus and CD looked at each other. "OK, guys, thanks," CD said. "We do need some help, I admit. How bout I fill you in later on what's going down?"

Killer said, "OK, but no drugs, no crimes, none of that stuff. We'll keep you out of their hands, but we won't help you commit any crimes."

CD replied, "Right. No crimes. We haven't even committed any crimes. It's complicated."

"No problem," Killer said.

"Shit!" Rufus said. "Look at the room!"

The other three looked up at the balcony on the SeaShell's sixth floor. Three men were standing outside.

"Clearly FBI," Timeout spat on the pavement of the sandwich shop parking lot. "I hate those fuckers!"

"Did you leave anything in the room?" Killer asked.

"Yeah, two people that we want to make sure the feds don't find. They're with us. The feds are really looking for them more than us. They might be looking for me, but they don't even know about Rufus, I mean Tony," CD explained.

"OK" was all that Killer said with an inquisitive glance at Timeout as he continued to watch the three agents. All three wore sunglasses, Hawaiian shirts, and long light-colored pants. Two of them approached the outside elevator to leave the sixth floor, and one stayed behind, standing on the balcony outside the room.

"Let's go inside so we're not so obvious," CD said, and the four entered the sandwich shop and took a table near the window. After ordering coffee, CD said, "Roof, we need a plan. We need to know if they have Thomas and Alex, and if they don't, then where are they?"

Rufus responded, "And how will we get back in touch with them?"

CD replied, "The same way we did it before's the only way I can think of offhand." CD did not want the two bikers to know about the chat room.

At that moment, a black Buick with dark-tinted windows drove into the passenger drop-off of the SeaShell and two men got out. "That's the tall dude from the beach," Rufus said. "And the other one looks like the guy that asked us those questions."

Another identical, black Buick pulled in behind the first car, and another man got out from the passenger side of the car. He spoke briefly to the first two agents. One pointed up to the sixth floor room then walked to the rear door of the second car, opened it, leaned in and roughly pulled someone out of the back seat. It was a kid in a T-shirt and bathing suit. He was handcuffed with his hands behind his back. The agent walked him to the first car, and for an instant, his face was turned in the direction of the sandwich shop as he was roughly thrown into the back seat.

"That's the pot smoker! They got him." Rufus exclaimed. "Can you see in the car? Do they have the girls? They're the only ones who might be able to I.D. us."

"If they touch one of our girls, they'll pay. Remember, Jesus turned over the tables in the temple when those government idiots messed with His stuff." Though the biblical facts were muddled, Killer's intent was clear.

CD thought fleetingly about that interpretation of Jesus's turning over the tables at the temple and doubted that there were any government agents in the temple, but at that moment, the Buick with the pot smoker sped out of the lot and raced down A1A.

"We need to know where he's going. Killer, can you follow him?" CD asked.

"Timeout, find out where he's going. Call me when you know something, but don't do nothing stupid," Killer said to Timeout.

Without a word, Timeout left the shop, fired up the Harley, and sped out onto A1A, did a quick U turn and headed off after the Buick.

"This could be dangerous for him," CD said.

"He's a big boy." Killer replied. "Besides, a bunch of his friends are just up the road a piece. He'll call them if he needs help."

"What do you mean, his friends?" CD asked.

"Satan's Gang. Outlaws." Killer responded.

At that moment, Killer's cell phone buzzed. After a brief conversation, he broke the connection. "We've got another problem, well, not really a problem. Dreamer and some of his boys have taken your beach friend — Ben? — out to where we are having a service tonight. He's safe, but Dreamer says we need to get you three together."

"A service?" CD responded. "What kind of service?"

"A church service for the homeless. It's called Once A Month Church, and it's something the local Rugged Cross guys do on the last Sunday of the month wherever we are. At five in the afternoon, we have a service for them and then feed them. It's a cool deal."

"I didn't even realize it was Sunday." Rufus said.

Killer looked at him, "Man, you need to do some serious business with God, or you're going to regret it later on. The stakes are high. You at least need to know that it's Sunday."

Rufus turned to CD. "CD, we do have a problem. All our stuff's in the room. They have it now."

"We didn't have any identification stuff. All they got was clothes. Oh, and the makeup stuff."

"Yeah," Rufus said, "The makeup stuff. And that's not all. They got DNA so they know about you now, and they know about me, or they will as soon as they run the DNA."

"You guys use makeup?" Killer asked with a wide smile.

"Not that kind of makeup, Killer. It's stuff to keep the feds from recognizing us. Like those guys we talked to today on the boardwalk. They wouldn't know who they were talking to. It's sort of hard to explain, but we really don't look exactly like what you see right now when you look at us."

Killer just smiled. "OK, if you say so." He did not seem as disturbed by the references to DNA as he was to the references to two men wearing makeup.

CD's cell phone beeped. The display read "Private." "Yeah," CD answered tersely.

After a moment's listening, CD said, "OK, don't say anything else. Hold on."

CD turned to Rufus, "Our boys are safe, at least, for now. He has a disposable cell phone. We need to get with them."

Killer interjected, "Some of us can pick them up. Where are they?"

"And then we can all meet at the Once a Month Church," Rufus said and turned to Killer. "Where's that going to be?"

"It's only about three miles up the road, at Ocean View Park."

CD said into the cell phone, "OK, Ocean View Park. There's a church service there tonight at five, in the park. A biker club's doing it. We'll be there."

"OK," Thomas said at the other end of the line and broke the connection.

"We can't go back to the hotel to check things." Rufus said.

"I can go. They don't know me." Killer said.

"It's too dangerous. They'll grab anybody who walks into that room. The feds are playing for keeps, Killer. You need to know that." CD looked at Killer for a long while, then said,

"I need your help, Killer, but trust me. You're better off not knowing what's going down."

"You hear me asking?"

"Then let's go to church," Rufus said.

"I'll need to get another bike. I can only get one of you on the bike."

"No problem," Rufus said. I'll stay here a while and watch the hotel. Send someone for me in a half hour or so."

"Done," Killer replied, and he and CD stood.

"One more thing, Roof. If we get in trouble, use the chat room."

Killer and CD left the sandwich shop.

Chapter 59

CIA Director Lucado's private briefing of Secretary of State Douglas Cordero in the Basement Conference Room of the Executive Office Building proceeded uneventfully until there was a knock on the door. Lucado answered the door, and to her surprise Fabian Miles was there. "Madame Director, " he said with some urgency in his voice. "Can I see you for a moment?"

"Yes, of course." Lucado, with a feeling of dread, nodded to Cordero. "Douglas, can you excuse me just for a minute?" She stepped into the hall.

"Judge, I'm sorry to come over here, but I didn't want to risk using the phone. We have Joe Folger. They got him! That's the name of the Franklin clone. At least they think they have him. He denies that that's who he is. They captured him in Melbourne Beach, Florida. They're doing a DNA match or will be doing it as soon as they can. They'll use drugs on him to get what they can out of him as soon as they can, but he's totally spaced out on marijuana so they have to wait a while. You know how it is." Miles looked dead serious.

"I assure you that I do *not* know how it is," Lucado said icily. After a pause, she continued. "Do we have a DNA sample from the clone to compare this new sample to?"

"I don't know, Judge."

"Find out, Miles. I'm going across to see the President now, so wait until after I get back to Langley before you update me unless it's critical. I don't want to be with Screamer when I get the news."

"Yes, Judge."

Lucado reentered the Conference Room. "Douglas. I think we just might have caught a break. My agents in Florida have apprehended someone whom they think is one of the clones.

They're in the process of identifying with certainty whether it's the Franklin clone or not. Douglas, we need to get next door and bring the President up to speed on this."

Lucado stood, but Cordero stayed seated. "You're mighty cavalier about having the CIA pick up someone on American soil, Joelle. Don't you think there's going to be an outcry by the public?"

"The public will never know about this, Douglas, and if they do find out, the law allows us to operate on American soil since 9/11."

Cordero replied, "Yeah, but that law is secret, and that in itself is a serious breach of American legal precedent — enforcing a secret law on an American citizen. Sort of Russian, wouldn't you say?"

Lucado squared up and pointed her index finger at Cordero. "Douglas, don't lecture me! We're in a war for this country's very soul. We have to do some things to protect the country that we couldn't do if the country weren't under threat. That's elementary logic. You're on board with that, aren't you?"

"I'm on board *if*— " Cordero repeated the word, "*if*— we're under some threat. I'm not sure that clones, even if they exist, are a threat to this country. They might conceivably be a political threat to this Administration, but, Joelle, this Administration is not the country."

"This is getting absurd, Douglas. Of course, this Administration isn't the country, but its charge is to ensure the security of the country."

"I thought the President's oath was to uphold and defend the Constitution," Cordero responded.

Ignoring that, Lucado answered, "And let's not forget, Douglas, that State's conducting its own intelligence operations which as you well know are completely illegal."

Cordero this time did show some slight surprise. "Like what?" He asked.

"Like your little Administrative Operations program." There was a silence as Cordero considered the implications that Lucado knew about the joint State-Defense spy unit. "Yes, Douglas, I've known about that little club for years."

"And it's completely legal. President Obama re-authorized it during his first week in his second term in a secret Executive Order. You know that. So what's the problem, Joelle?"

"The problem, Douglas, is that State isn't equipped to do intelligence gathering. On occasion, your little operations have forced us to withdraw from very productive stuff that we were doing. This fragmentation of intelligence gathering is the very thing that the creation of the Department of Homeland Security was supposed to prevent. And, yes, I realize that Homeland Security became so politicized during the Trump and Biden Administrations that it's now nothing but a bureaucratic swamp. But, Douglas, you're muddying the waters by getting into stuff that State isn't qualified to get into. Spying and infiltrating is CIA business, not State business. And on top of it all, State has shown that it is reckless, careless, and negligent in how it handles national security materials. Remember Hillary? Remember the many ways that her gross mishandling of emails hurt our nation's security? Remember her basement server? How much the nation actually got hurt as a result of her recklessness is so serious that we cannot even let the public know about it."

"OK, Joelle, but remember, your CIA had Brennan and Clapper. Loose lips, blatant dishonesty, loose logic, and appalling misjudgment."

"That's ancient history," Lucado quickly responded.

"Whatever," Cordero answered dismissively. "We're on opposite sides on this one, but let's see what we can agree on.

How about this? First, the clones are plausibly a threat because if they are indeed clones of some of our framers and if at the same time, they are wacky in their views, then they could present a complication to our prosecuting the war against Islamic extremism, Russia, and China. They could constitute a divisive and destructive force in our political system. Second, given this potential divisiveness, they must be apprehended, if for no other reason, than to confirm that they're genuine and that they aren't loons. Third, it's not a national security issue, at least not at this time. Can we agree on these three points?"

"Yes, I think so, Douglas. But the President is looking at this less dispassionately. He wants those clones dead or alive. Preferably dead, I think. Remember, he knew that the clone on that plane was George Washington, and he pretty quickly gave the shoot down order. I was there. He was almost panicked until he got hold of himself."

"I know. You covered that when you briefed me, but we don't know for a fact that there was a clone on board, and if there was, we don't for a fact who it was a clone of. We can't just assume George Washington."

"It's pretty much beyond a reasonable doubt, Douglas," Lucado said conclusively. "Why else would he have shot down that plane? There was a clone on it. That clone is now dead. Period. Anyway, let's stick to the three points. We need to hustle over to the President's. By now, he's probably mad because I'm late. Let me handle it, Douglas. He might be ticked off that I brought you in on this whole thing without clearing it with him first. I took a big chance briefing you without his knowing about it, Douglas."

Douglas Cordero just nodded.

The two left the conference room and walked through the tunnel under the street leading from the Old Executive Office

Building into the West Wing of the White House, passed through White House security, and entered Phyllis's office. "He's waiting," Phyllis said without a smile. "And he doesn't like to wait. He is the President, you know." She smiled knowingly. "Go on in."

Lucado rolled her eyes. Cordero's expression remained frozen.

Lucado and Cordero entered the Oval Office. The President was standing with his back to the door staring at the bronze bust of Benjamin Franklin. "Come in," the President said without turning around. "I hope you've made some progress, Joelle." The President's tone was somber. He turned around and was clearly taken aback to see his Secretary of State. After a slight pause, he recovered, "I guess it was just a matter of time before we brought you in on things, Douglas. I'm glad you're here." The President's tone had unexpectedly turned friendly. He respected Douglas Cordero and seldom resorted to theatrics with him the way he did with Lucado. Cordero as a man was not easily bullied by President Ray's macho rages.

Cordero replied, "Thank you, Mr. President. And, yes, I do wonder why I wasn't brought in on this from the very beginning. Joelle has briefed me, and this is clearly a matter that I would expect to be part of from the get-go."

"I'm sorry, Douglas. It all developed so fast that I admit I haven't organized our sessions or my advisory system on this matter as well as I should have. But," the President smiled and held out his outstretched arms in welcome, "you're here now, so let's go forward." Turning to Lucado and without waiting for Cordero's response, the President motioned them to wingchairs and took a seat himself. He then asked, "So how about it, Joelle? Any progress?"

"As a matter of fact, yes, Mr. President." The Director of Central Intelligence then filled the President in on the capture in Florida of the man who was possibly the clone of Benjamin Franklin.

"Excellent!" the President exclaimed with his clinched fists in the air. "Let's make sure that no one gets wind of this, and I want to be briefed on every development as it happens, Joelle," the President said. "As it happens," the President repeated. "Understood?"

"Yes, of course, Mr. President."

"And Joelle, I want this Benjamin Franklin or whoever it is to be kept under the tightest wraps we have, just as if he were a terrorist, because he may well be."

"Mr. President, I also have a lead on Ms. Novokatnaia. She has surfaced in Moscow, and she's with Sergei Verionsky. He's the head of their intelligence. She was allowed to bypass passport control, so that tells us that she's been one of their people all along."

There was a silence in the room. Finally, Douglas Cordero broke it. "This looks like possibly a major security breech, Mr. President." He stared hard at Joelle. "And the conservative media outlets could start with that Russian collusion bull shit again, but this time it could be directed at us." The reference was to the media's and the Democrats' fabricated allegations of Trump's collusion with the Russians during the 2016 presidential election.

"It might be a security lapse," Lucado quickly said and in an effort to assign blame, she continued. "Everybody on that Bioethics Board was supposed to be vetted by Justice, and Novokatnaia herself was supposed to be checked out by State since it was widely known that she had Russian connections in her background." Lucado stared coldly at Cordero.

"The vetting was done by the Secret Service as always," Cordero said with disdain. "This wasn't at all a State operation, Joelle."

"You two can have your little turf fights somewhere else, but not here in my office," the President said huffily. "Right now, you two better share absolutely everything you have on these clones, Novokatnaia, GeneVision, and the whole ball of wax. You share it with each other. You share it with me. And you share it with TT. You hear what I'm saying? And not one leak. Not one. If there's a leak, someone will be hung up by the balls. Understood?" As most male bullies, the President often used anatomical references in the presence of women.

"I guess that lets me off the hook," Lucado said in monotone.

"No leaks! Not one! Understood?" The President's face was beginning to turn red.

"Right, Mr. President. There won't be any leaks from my end," Cordero said with a smile.

Lucado added, "No leaks at all, Mr. President."

"OK, good. If you don't have anything else, I've got to get ready to meet the new Governor of Florida. They've had some real losers as governors. Remember the one who was indicted for propositioning a child at South Beach? How stupid can you get! He was himself indicted for money laundering, so then Florida has a third governor in the space of two months. Then they had one who was a Republican, then he became an Independent, then he became a Democrat. What a lust for power! The new one's Italian, so he's probably crooked, too. You remember that guy who was being groomed for the presidency who said that all Italians are genetically criminal?" The President snickered then quickly cleared his throat and adopted a more serious tone. "No offense, Douglas."

"None taken, Mr. President. That was the Mercedes man, as they called him, and that remark ended his political career. And rightfully so, I might add. His was an arms merchant, and that put him into all kinds of nefarious circles."

"You've got to wonder why so many Florida politicians are child molesters. It must be something about the weather." President Ray looked truly perplexed for a moment, then stood, "OK, keep me totally informed."

With that, the President turned his back on Lucado and Cordero and walked to his large, orderly desk. Turning his back was a way President Ray showed superiority and also the way he terminated conversations and meetings.

Cordero and Lucado left the Oval office and began to retrace their steps to the Old Executive Office Building. When they had reached the tunnel, Cordero began, "Joelle, I think—"

"Not here, Douglas," Lucado cautioned him and slightly raised her eyes toward the ceiling light fixtures. She knew that they were more than just light fixtures because she had personally ordered the installation of listening devices and cameras in those very fixtures. "Wait."

Chapter 60

The Once A Month Church meeting was at Melbourne Beach's tranquil Ocean View Park. The Once A Month Church was an institution begun by several nondenominational churches in the Melbourne area. Modeled on a similar undertaking on the North Shore of Oahu, its primary purpose was to show the homeless that Jesus cares for them. As fate would have it, or as some looking back might say, as God rigged it, the members of Rugged Cross and also Ben, CD, and Rufus had all been on the Hilton's beach at the same time. CD briefly wondered, *do things, or at least some things, happen by orchestration?* CD was already apprehensive that his getting the bikers involved was putting them in great danger. That he had not disclosed to them what was actually going on, he had decided, was simply a necessary evil. He had no qualms about it. The fleeting question which hit CD as he held on for dear life as Killer sped down A1A was whether saving the clones justified the evil which might have to be done in the future.

When CD and Rufus arrived at the Once A Month Church service, the service was in full sway in front of a large banner of a cross with the letters O M C. There was a rocking, energetic local band sporting the name Emu, and it was playing some sort of loud country-religious music, and the bikers were singing along, or at least they were making noise, with a surprising number swaying back and forth with hands uplifted in praise. Many of the Rugged Cross bikers had come through their own private hells to arrive at the realization that God was indeed real and willing to work in their lives once they embraced Jesus. Some of the homeless people were not doing much singing, but they did look interested in what was going on, and most were clearly into the service, with hands raised and bodies swaying.

Killer had called Low Side, a Rugged Cross friend, to pick up Rufus at the sandwich shop. The biker wore that name because a year ago he had leaned his bike too far down on its side. The result was a near-fatal accident and two months in the hospital in traction. Low Side and Rufus approached CD and Killer. "Where's Dreamer, and where's Ben?" Rufus asked.

Killer searched the crowd for some sign of Dreamer. "I don't see Dreamer nowhere," Killer said. "If he was here, we'd know it. He's not here."

CD frowned. He was feeling the most discouraged he had since the clones saga began. "Roof, this is no good. We've lost all three clones, and all we've tried to do was keep them safe. And now we've lost them. Shit."

Rufus was about to answer when Killer placed a hand on Rufus's arm and spoke sotto voce. "Don't look now, boys, but our friends from the beach are here too. There's two of them over there near that palm tree."

"And there's the girl agent over there," CD said softly to Rufus as he subtly motioned to a female standing near a clump of palms. "We've walked into a trap."

"How did they know?" Rufus wondered aloud.

A biker-preacher was now telling the crowd how every issue was a trust issue. "Y'all might not have a big house you can call home, but y'all are like us bikers," he said in a booming voice as he preached directly to the group of homeless persons. "You don't have a whole lot, and things right now might not be all that great for you. But if you just put all your trust in Jesus, things will get better! Never, never forget," he boomed, "You're a child of God! You're God's child, and He loves you! He loves you! He loves you! OK? Amen?" A chorus of Amens responded. The biker-preacher continued, "Friends, let's celebrate God! Let's read Psalm 42 together. Psalm 42 is a treatment plan for worry.

If you feel that life has put pressure on you, then let go, and let God, and watch the pressure evaporate! Do you feel like you're in a pressure cooker? Well, ask Jesus take the top off that pressure cooker!" There was a large projection screen, and the words of the Message version of Psalm 42 were projected for the crowd to read. "And if you don't want to read, then just listen to these words." The assemblage of bikers and homeless persons started reading Psalm 42.

"Here comes Dreamer and your boy," Killer said. Dreamer, Cuffs, and Ben were about a hundred yards away and walking toward CD and Rufus. CD tried to warn them off, but there were too many people in the way and the distance was too great for a clear line of sight. Just as Ben saw CD clearly, the two agents near the palm tree also saw Dreamer and Ben and started toward them. Dreamer and Ben, unaware that a government noose was closing around them, continued casually walking towards CD and Rufus.

"Call him, Killer. Tell him to get out of here!" CD hissed to Killer.

Killer punched in Dreamer's speed dial number. CD and Rufus could see Dreamer pull his cell phone out of his front pocket. "Yeah, Killer. I can see you. What's up?"

"The feds are here, over to your left. They've seen you. Get out of here!" Killer said quickly.

Without replying, CD and Rufus could see Dreamer say something to Ben, and both of them turned quickly and headed for the parking lot. The two agents suddenly broke into a run after Dreamer and Ben. Two other agents that CD and Rufus had been unaware of emerged from the crowd of singing people and started running towards Dreamer and Ben. Dreamer shouted something, and a wall of bikers materialized between him and the agents. The four agents drew their guns. "What are you gonna do, shoot all of us?" The husky voice came from a large, tough looking prayer warrior who was now standing with her huge arms crossed on top of her even larger breasts. She stood directly in front of the agents on the path leading to the parking lot.

"Stand aside, lady. This is none of your concern," one of the agents said sternly.

"That's Laura," Killer said. "There's no way they'll get past her. It'll take more than a few shots to bring her down."

Another tough looking biker stepped forward.

"That's Carol Ann. She can easily take down any five if it comes to a fight," Killer said.

"If you want a brawl, being it on," Carol Ann bellowed.

Several other prayer warriors quickly joined Laura and Carol Ann, and then more and more stepped forward until the path was totally blocked by dozens of female bikers and their men such that the agents could no longer even see their fleeing quarry. The male bikers stood behind the women as the bikers instinctively realized that the federal agents would probably not shoot the prayer warriors but would not hesitate to use lethal force on the scruffy males.

The band started playing "White Flag," but more and more of the church crowd had turned and was now watching the face-off between prayer warriors and the four federal agents.

"Ma'am, step aside. This is a federal investigation, and you'll be arrested if you interfere. Everybody listen up. That guy with your biker is a criminal. He's the only one we want. We won't touch you guys at all. None of y'all bikers will be arrested. Only the guy they are protecting. He's a dangerous criminal, and we have a warrant for his arrest. Now step aside."

A homeless man in the crowd yelled encouragement to Laura, Carol Ann, and their sister prayer warriors, "Get it on, sister!" Others chorused "Amen."

The prayer warriors did not budge. "Asshole, one thing we know. You feds eat shit!" The shout came from a biker who had just trotted up from the parking lot. It was Timeout. He was now the only male on the front line with the prayer warriors.

Rufus exclaimed softly to CD, "That's Timeout!"

One of the bikers called out, "Timeout, get the fuck out of the way! Let the ladies handle this."

"Fuck that!" Timeout spat out in the directions of the agents.

Killer said to Rufus and CD, "I think you two better come with us. Me and Low Side will get you out of here. Come on."

The four started to move in the direction of the small parking lot behind the band. All eyes were now on the increasingly loud confrontation between the bikers and the agents. No one was noticing that Killer was leading CD, Rufus, and Low Side out of Ocean View Park to the parking lot.

"Last warning," the agent yelled. "Move aside, or you will be arrested, and I promise you will do some hard time," the taller agent barked at the bikers. "I know there's a ton of warrants out for all of y'all so I can make sure it's a hot day in hell before you ever ride a bike again. Now step aside."

No one moved. Then all four agents produced stun guns, and headed in a deliberate, coordinated wedge towards the prayer warriors who did not budge. Timeout yelled to the agent who was the closest to the bikers, "You fucking use that taser, and you die, shit-face." He pulled from his jacket a large, black revolver and pointed it at the agent who was nearest him.

"Drop the gun! Drop it now!" The voice was from a woman standing no more than twenty feet from Timeout. She was dressed as a biker but was clearly an agent who had infiltrated the Rugged Cross Motorcycle Club. She leveled her Glock 17 9 mm at Timeout.

"Women can't shoot," Timeout said. He was momentarily confused by the biker turned agent but continued to point his revolver at the taller, male agent who was approaching several bikers who were blocking the way to the parking lot.

At that moment, the sound of two motorcycles boomed from the parking lot. The tall agent, now wielding a taser, shot 50,000 volts into Laura's ribs. She immediately stiffened and collapsed to the ground, convulsed, and breathed in irregular, jerky spasms. Another agent immediately tased Carol Ann.

"You asshole!" Timeout shouted and fired at the first agent who yelled, staggered backwards, and fell. Only a millisecond after Timeout had fired, the female agent shot Timeout multiple times. Timeout fell, writhing on the ground, without making a sound. He attempted to rise, still gripping his revolver, and the agent then shot Timeout five more times. Everyone, bikers and agents alike, just stood motionless, stunned at what they had just witnessed. Timeout remained in a contorted position and did not move. An agent then ran up to Timeout, knelt and felt for a pulse, then felt at another place on Timeout's neck. The agent then grimaced and just shook his head.

The bikers then erupted in a stampede for their bikes as the other agents rushed to assist their own agent who had been shot by Timeout. The homeless beneficiaries of the Once A Month Church service ran in the opposite direction, directly for the beach.

The woman agent yelled, "324, are you OK? Talk to me." She continued to point the stun gun menacingly at any bikers who were nearby, but they were more interested in fleeing the scene than in seeking revenge for Timeout. Some of the bikers had already reached the nearby parking lot and were headed out of the park at high speed. The agent bent over to her wounded colleague.

"I'm OK. The vest took the bullet, but shit, it hurts." The tall agent still sat on the ground, patting his chest. Like all the other agents on the scene, he wore a high tech alumina-polymer vest under his aloha shirt. It was more bullet-resistant than Kevlar, but like Kevlar, it was hot and generally uncomfortable.

"Then, stop complaining, 324," the woman said with a slight smile.

"Sure thing, Mary, I mean, 390."

The other agents had now joined Mary and 324. Mary counted the agents and said, "OK, all 22 of us are here."

One agent said softly, "This should be an FBI operation. We aren't trained for this kind of shit."

Another agent said not so softly, "Me too. I didn't become a case officer to do crowd control"

The group of CIA agents all looked toward the parking lot where the bikers were quickly exiting. Among them, Dreamer and Cuffs were already out of sight. At that moment, in with dozens of motorcycles, Low Side and Killer, carrying CD and Rufus, sped from the area.

"Look there," an agent yelled, pointing to Low Side and Killer out in front of the other bikes. "Those two bikes have men riders. All the other riders are women."

"They're the same two men that we met at the beach," 324 said as he grimaced under the bruise of the bullet's impact with his protected chest. "I was watching them before all hell broke loose. They're obviously hiding our fugitive. OK, here's what we do. I'll take a car and report to the Director. 390, you come with me. Everyone else, we have the highways monitored. They're already on alert for the bikers coming their way. Don't pursue the bikers, but report to the highway checkpoints that you were assigned as backup locations. Any questions?"

There were none until one agent asked, "Deadly force?"

"Yes, deadly force as needed, but the objective is to apprehend the subjects alive." Then 324 added, "But I don't care what happens to the bikers." 324 motioned to a tanned, good-looking agent with tattoos and no shirt standing nearby, "Bob, brief everyone on the outer perimeter plan. 390 and I'll catch up with you." 324 and Mary walked to their Buick without a word and headed to the safe house where the pot smoker from the beach was being interrogated with the assistance of sodium thiopental. It took only minutes for them to leave Ocean View Park several miles behind them.

Back at Ocean View Park, as Bob began his briefing, he and the other agents heard in the distance the faint sounds of motorcycles. The engine sounds were gradually getting louder.

"They're coming back," one agent said. Several of the agents stared at Timeout's body on the pavement.

Another joined in, "Thank God, they're Christians. Maybe we can reason with them. But I think we'd better cover up that body."

Bob pointed to two agents, "Put the body in the trunk, and do it quickly. They'll be here in a minute."

As two agents stuffed Timeout's lifeless body in the trunk of a nearby company car, about thirty motorcycles roared into view. They did not slow down at all until they were directly upon the agents. The bikers were led by a menacing looking, bearded man with a flowing ponytail. Few wore helmets. The bikers then without a word and losing little speed completely encircled the agents. The bikers kept riding in an ever-closing circle around the agents who were now being herded like sheep. The roar of the engines and the angry faces of the bikers were propelling the ordinarily disciplined agents into confusion, then fear. These bikers had done this before to rival biker gangs, but government agents had never before seen the Circle of Death, a trademark tactic of Satan's Gang, the nation's deadliest motorcycle gang.

"Fellows," Bob tried to shout over the den to the bikers. "We can hardly ask for forgiveness." He laid down his gun and walked out from the herded agents towards the circling bikes. They were going so fast, that it was now a blur of metal, man, and leather. Bob held out his hands, palms up, in a universal appeasement gesture and yelled. "I'm a Presbyterian so I know where you are coming from," he shouted. "What happened was terrible and wrong, and I'm truly sorry. Let's—"

Bob never knew that these bikers were not Rugged Cross. The first shot fired from the circling bikers hit him in the chest, the second in the face, and a third in the throat. He was then riddled with bullets before his body even hit the ground. For the better part of a minute, the normally tranquil beachfront park was filled with guns firing and men and women screaming and cursing. And dying. Several of the agents got off some shots at the bikers, but in less than thirty bloody seconds, the Circle of Death had done its work. The bodies of eighteen slaughtered CIA agents lay strewn in the middle of the park where just minutes earlier, Timeout's own body had lain and before that, songs of praise had been lifted up to the heavens.

"Timeout, we did this for you. We're done here. Let's go," the bearded leader of the Satan's Gang said calmly, and the gang from hell virtually flew down the otherwise peaceful street, leaving behind the first casualties of the United States government's search for the clones.

Chapter 61

The massacre at Ocean View Park galvanized the various government agencies searching for Ben and the bikers. State and federal agencies in Florida were now on high alert as they were determined to apprehend every member of Satan's Gang as well as every member of Rugged Cross. The state and federal agents were now operating under the implied rubric that deadly force should be used if there was any justification for it, whether it was actually required or not. At the I-95 highway checkpoint outside of Melbourne Beach, four CIA agents had pulled two semis across the road to block traffic. Bending to threats from a convincing CIA agent and also to the promise of new equipment as a reward for their cooperation, the Brevard County Sheriff and the Florida State Police had in an unprecedented concession agreed to allow CIA agents instead of state law enforcement personnel to man the checkpoint. Moreover, the CIA agents were authorized to dress as Florida state troopers. Surprisingly quickly, the various exits off of and entrance ramps for I-95 were also manned by various law enforcement personnel. Tourists were allowed to pass after a thorough inspection of the interiors and the trunks of their vehicles. But bikers on the busy highways had to endure lengthy detentions and questioning. Many, later shown to have had no part in the events at Ocean View Park, were detained for days and some for weeks. The government was especially looking for anyone who resembled the individual in the fuzzy photograph of Ben that had been emailed from Langley. The only thing these agents had been told was that the photographed individual was armed and dangerous and that if he presented a threat or attempted flight, they were to use all necessary force to apprehend him and to use deadly force if apprehension was not possible. The CIA's line, ordered by

Director Lucado, was that the individual was part of a right wing terrorist network. The agents on the scene had no idea that he was in a sense one of the nation's framers.

Chapter 62

Joelle Lucado leaned back in the plush leather chair behind her large mahogany desk. She was bone tired and increasingly anxious that things were not coming together on the clones the way she wanted them to. It was late in the afternoon and still no word from her Florida agents. Her anxiety was slowly morphing into fear. Her people had someone in custody, but who was he? That someone had to be one of the clones, or if not a clone he was somehow connected to the clones. She had ordered her agents to make the subject talk, and now all she could do was await the results. Her scrambler desk phone beeped. She grabbed the phone.

"Yes?" she answered. Her secretary informed her that "Florida Center" was holding. "OK, put it through," Lucado said and to her surprise heard the relief in her own voice. Just getting a report, any kind of report, would be better than not knowing the status of what was occurring in Florida.

"Yes, Florida Center, go ahead."

"Madame Director. We administered drugs to get the subject to talk. Even though he's clearly a pot smoker and still has a lot of THC in his system, we went ahead and shot him up because our experience shows that the drugs sometimes work better when combined with a certain amount of THC. He's apparently just a college kid from Daytona State College who someone — we don't know who — paid to make contact with someone else on the beach. We don't know who this detainee is for sure. He gave us his name, and we're currently checking it out. What's important is that someone in their mid-twenties paid him to just stay on the beach for a couple of hours. He doesn't know the person who paid him. He never saw him before. He did give us a description of the person - - - mid-twenties, lots of brown hair, somewhat on the heavier side, but not too much, green eyes, a good tan, soft-spoken, in other words nothing very useful other than age. That's all we got from him. This guy's just a stoner college kid. He wasn't our target, Madame Director. But the other individuals we cannot identify could well be."

"OK. Anything else?" Lucado's flat tone betrayed her disappointment.

"Yes. My partner and I observed two older men — they appeared to be in their forties or early fifties — speaking to our pot smoker for about five minutes or so. Our pot smoker didn't know who they were. They asked him if he knew a certain person but he couldn't remember what names the two men had asked about. But while he was talking to these two men, the younger fellow who earlier had paid him to just stay on the beach came up and briefly talked to the two men before we lost him." The agent paused.

"Is that it?" Lucado asked incredulously. "And what did you mean, 'he *was* not our target'? You didn't let him go, I hope."

"No, we didn't let him go, but, but, well, we pumped him with some more drugs to get everything out of him, and he —." The voice on the phone paused. "Well, Madame Director, he expired."

"You killed him?" Lucado exploded into the phone. "You actually killed him?"

"Yes ma'am," The flat answer was without elaboration.

While he was waiting, with dread, for Lucado's response, she heard another agent in the background at Florida Center say, "I can't get anyone on the radio. No one responds at all."

Lucado could hear in the background, "Just keep trying."

Joelle Lucado meanwhile, no longer sitting, paced for a few moments, then stopped and said, "OK, get rid of the body. How many people know about this, Florida Center?"

"Me and three others, Madame Director. We're all seasoned. You don't have anything to worry about."

"I want all four of you in my office tomorrow morning. Understood?"

"Yes, ma'am, but two of us are running this operation down here, so if possible, maybe we can put off our trip to Washington until we get some resolution here. Would that be possible?"

"What do you mean, *resolution*? Do you have more to tell me?"

"Yes, there's more," the voice continued.

"Oh, shit." Lucado sat heavily.

"Me and my partner ran into two guys on the boardwalk who were leaving the beach, and they were trying to avoid talking to us, at least it seemed that way. These two were both probably in their forties, white, but one of them might have been black, and they were sporting fake tattoos, like they were trying to blend in or something. We talked to them briefly, and got some facial grabs for ViScan, but so far we don't have an identification. My hunch is that somehow they are involved. Next, we got a tip that two guys who seemed to fit the descriptions of our two clones were staying at the SeaShell Hotel and had been seen by the maid in the suite rented by an older white male who fit the description of one of the guys we encountered on the beach. We went to the room, but it was empty. We did get items of clothing and other personal items and are putting that through a DNA screen now."

Lucado broke in, "Did it look like they'd left the room in a hurry, or was everything in order?"

"There was no indication that it was an escape or that they knew we were coming, but they weren't there and haven't returned to their room. And there's more, Madame Director. As you know, we have a good number of agents assigned to the operation down here. You put 32 of us on the scene here. That turns out to have been a good idea because we could put tails on a number of people on the beach who didn't fit in with the biker crowd. Well, several of those tails led us to a bikers' church service a few miles from the beach—-"

Lucado rolled her eyes, interrupting. "A church service?"

"Yes, Madame Director. At that church service, we spotted two persons who obviously weren't bikers. We think they might well be our targets. Then, four other persons arrived, and wouldn't you know it, two of them were the same two middle aged men we had encountered at the beach. Plus another young man arrived, riding on the back of one of the bikes. He could well be the young man who hired the pot smoker, I should say, the *late* pot smoker." Lucado could hear someone in the background laugh. "We have photos of everyone, and once we've finished enhancing them, we'll run them through ViScan. Hopefully, we'll then know who everyone is. Plus, one biker pulled out a revolver, and we terminated him."

One of Joelle Lucado's priorities on taking over the CIA was a crash program to develop the next generation of facial recognition software. She had fought hard for the expensive project and for the CIA's power to develop the supporting database. The ViScan project put the CIA firmly in the business of operating on American soil, and the FBI still resented the encroachment on what they regarded as their own turf. ViScan, developed by a skilled multidisciplinary team inside of the CIA, was the result of Lucado's skills at bureaucratic infighting and her conviction that the nation could do nothing other than benefit from being able to identify wrongdoers more efficiently. ViScan could scan faces at the rate of over 70,000 per minute, comparing them to the expanding CIA database of faces. But the true breakthrough with ViScan was that it could also identify persons from body posture, gait, and other kinetic, physical characteristics (dubbed PhyChar by the acronym-prone CIA) generally outside of a person's conscious control. The only problem with that particular segment of identification was the tiny size of the current baseline database, but the CIA was quickly expanding its PhyChar Database, which would link a person's biometrics to other CIA databases. Lucado hoped that with the search for the clones and persons who were aiding them ViScan was now going to show its value.

"Of course, I want the results as soon as you've got them. But you were at this biker gathering and saw the people you hypothesize to be our targets and the other two men. I'm assuming, since you haven't said, that they all got away. Is that right?" Lucado asked with a tone of accusation in her voice.

"Yes, but we have the main roads blocked. I've already deployed agents as a backup to block the main roads leading from the area. Madame Director, we'll intercept the subjects. Now that the bikers have fled the scene, I'll have the other twenty agents or so being redeployed to assist with the roadblocks. The State Police, thanks to your negotiating with them, have been totally cooperative."

Joelle Lucado clipped her words as she said, "I don't like this. I don't like it at all. You have twenty agents at an outdoor church service, you have the subjects in your sights, you kill some biker, and the subjects get away. And while this is going on, you kill a college kid by giving him too much truth serum. Is that the bottom line? Have you killed anyone else?"

The voice from Florida replied icily, "No we haven't terminated anyone else. Madame Director, all hell broke loose. That biker shot me. The only reason I'm alive is that like all the rest of us, I was suited up. One of our people took him out, and that's when things fell apart. The bikers all went running for their bikes, and there was no way in hell to contain the situation."

"So our only hope now is that by some stroke of stupidity, it won't dawn on those bikers that the roads will be blocked."

"Yes ma'am."

"OK, that's it for now. You don't have anything else, do you?" Joelle asked quietly. The energy and strength had been drained from her.

"No ma'am. That's it."

"OK," Joelle said and hung up the scrambler phone. One of the perks of being Director of the Central Intelligence Agency was that she had a well-outfitted apartment on the premises for occasions and nights just such as this. The strain of dealing with the Florida operation, with Screamer, and with that pompous Douglas Cordero had left Lucado exhausted. She buzzed Fabian, "I'm gone. You should take off, too. Tomorrow no doubt will be another rough day."

"Good night, Madame Director."

Chapter 63

Though the Rugged Cross was a Christian organization, its members in their former lives had had substantial experience skirting the law, and they now called on those practiced skills to avoid the roadway checkpoints that the CIA had erected to trap the bikers and apprehend the clones. After Timeout was shot, instead of immediately fleeing Melbourne Beach, the Rugged Cross bikers had returned to the large high school football stadium where the school's principal, a former biker and a member of a local church, had allowed Rugged Cross to set up camp. After a long contentious meeting -—contentious as only ex-outlaws can make it -—Cuffs and Dreamer finally persuaded most members of the motorcycle club to split up and ride alone, in pairs, and in threes, and to take different routes out of the Melbourne area and to meet in Atlanta in two days. Others of the bikers would hole up in Daytona Beach, New Smyrna Beach, Ormond Beach, and other beach towns where bikers were a familiar and welcome sight. Dreamer explained the strategy to his followers as "spreading out and melting into the scenery."

Dreamer had safely delivered Ben to CD and Rufus. Ben was standing with the two older men, and for an island boy in the midst of a group of bikers and former outlaws, he was astute enough to say nothing and draw as little attention to himself as possible.

"OK, most of us are here, but some are still missing. We can't wait any longer. They can catch up to us." Cuffs looked around the group as if mentally counting. "This is a mass exodus, guys. For those of us who're going to get out of Dodge, we need to do it now!" Cuffs was adamant that no time be wasted. "For y'all who are staying around here, just scatter and God ride with you!"

Dreamer then said, "Everybody, we stay in touch by cell phone. Nobody has done anything wrong so don't be timid if you get stopped. Stay off the interstates as much as you can. Don't speed too much, but don't go too slow either or you will attract attention." Dreamer said, then added, "And take off those colors."

"Well, hold on a minute," CD shouted. "Guys, y'all got to remember that it's not the local cops that's after you. It's the CI of A, and they mean business. They're dangerous. If they want to, they can listen to your cell phones, and no doubt they'll be watching from the air, so be smart. That's all I can advise. If they stop you, tell the truth. You can say you were here at the beach service, when things got ugly you took off, but you don't know nothing about us, and you don't. That's the truth. You don't. It's that simple. So whatever you say can't hurt us, and we're leaving you now. We'll be on our own, and we'll take care of ourselves."

Rufus looked at CD with a questioning look. He fully realized that without the motorcyclists, they would be hard pressed for transportation out of the Melbourne Beach area. CD noticed Rufus's uncertainty and subtly nodded at him to hold off questioning.

"OK, that's it, let's blow this joint," Cuffs said to the group. He then designated two's and three's and also some solitary bikers to take different routes. Some would exit the area going north, some south, and some directly west, crossing over to the mainland from the barrier island where Melbourne Beach was. Cuffs also staggered their departures over the next several hours so that drone surveillance would hopefully not detect the exodus.

"So now what?" Ben asked CD.

"We look for a boat. We stay off of the roads. There's so much boat traffic around here that there's no way that they have enough manpower to check them all. We leave tonight." CD sounded more confident than he was.

"Yeah, just like that, we just go find a boat," Rufus said.

"We buy it. It'll be legal. When we finish with it, we sink it. No one ever knows."

Ben said, "Then, let's do it. We can't stay here. Let's go!"

CD said, "We still have the problem of contacting the others. Alex and Thomas."

"I like that you're getting our names right, Professor," Ben said. "And contacting them is no problem. While y'all were organizing our exit, I've been talking to Alex and Thomas in the chat room. It's all set, where and when, so let's go."

CD smiled in surprise. "Ok, but where to?"

"And when do we meet up with them?" Rufus asked.

"Soon enough, fellows. Let's go." Ben was obviously not going to be forthcoming.

"Everybody, just hold tight!" It was Killer's voice, and he had a note of urgency uncharacteristic of this reformed outlaw. He was holding his cell phone. "You'd better listen up."

They listened to a live news alert in progress:

> "It looks like an organized, deliberate massacre. The scene is bloody, and there are a number of dead bodies here, and that's why we are not showing full pictures. If you have younger children in the room, you might want them not to hear or see this broadcast. We don't know who is responsible for what has happened here. There're now multiple ambulances on the scene taking the wounded to nearby hospitals, and more ambulances are on the way. The persons who have been shot for the most part are apparently not bikers. They look like regular businesspersons and tourists.

Several look like bikers. We do know that there was a biker church service in this park late this afternoon, and presumably any bikers who were shot are members of a Christian biker club. But quite frankly we don't know who the other persons are. So, to recap, there has been a mass shooting in Ocean View Park. There appears to be numerous casualties. We don't know who they are, and police have now cordoned off the area so we can't get close. We'll bring you more as soon as we know more, but for now we have our networks' terrorism expert with us. It's a horrible and gruesome scene here. Waldo, is this yet another Islamic terrorist event?"

Waldo, the man described as the network's expert then pontificated,

"It looks that way. But we don't know for sure, and no group has yet claimed responsibility. A Christian church service in a local park. A soft target if ever there was one. Heavy weaponry. Lots of casualties. No rhyme or reason for the senseless slaughter. So even though we don't know the specifics, it appears to be another Islamic statement, but it could maybe be some other terrorist organization since the southern border has been completely open since 2020. Either that or bikers. It could have been two biker gangs shooting it out. We just don't know at this point."

The bikers, CD, Rufus, and Ben were completely stunned. For a moment, no one said a word, and then several started at once.

CD broke the silence, "We can thank God that journalists are so clueless."

"Don't be so hard on them, CD. They're just entertainers," Ben said. "They're concerned with money and ratings, not truth. Everybody in this country knows that by now. Don't worry about them."

Everyone started talking at once.

"They're already trying to pen it on us."

"It sounds like there were a bunch of agents there and they got attacked."

"It could have been terrorists."

CD then said, "Since Rugged Cross is implicated —"

Cuffs shouted, "We are not implicated. We got out of there once Timeout got shot."

CD continued, "Yeah, but nobody knows that. For all they know, you were the last ones on the scene. So what I'm getting at is that every biker leaving this area is going to be stopped. I think we either sit tight or we'll have to come up with a better plan to get out of town."

Dreamer then said, "Well if no bikers leave town, that'll mean that they'll know whoever did it is still in town, and they'll cover the area, and sooner or later, they'll find us."

"They'll search all of us, and no one has any guns in this crowd, or at least those of us who do, we can get rid of them," Cuffs said. "And there's that principal. He'll probably go to the police. My guess is that Satan's Gang did the killing."

"The principal won't talk. He's a biker and a Christian," Dreamer said.

"If none of us have any guns, they'll know for sure that we just got rid of the guns, so that doesn't help much," Killer said.

"There might be a way," Rufus said. "Who has a disposable cell phone I can use?" Rufus held a wrinkled business card.

"What's that?" CD asked pensively, eyeing the card.

"I met a truck driver. He drives 18-wheelers. That's his occupation. We struck up a conversation at the SeaShell. If he's still around, he just might help us."

CD immediately saw where Rufus was headed. "And you're thinking that he can haul us out of here in his truck." It was a statement, not a question.

"Exactly." Rufus smiled.

"Well, why wouldn't he also think we're just a bunch of murderers? We have to assume he's heard the news about the massacre. And if so, he would just turn us in," CD said.

"I hope not. It's better than just staying here waiting to be picked up." Rufus said.

"What are y'all talking about?" Dreamer asked.

"Dreamer, did I hear that you have your CDL? You can drive a big rig?" CD asked. As he spoke, he pulled a disposable cell phone out of his pocket and handed it to Rufus.

"I did it for 12 years," Dreamer replied.

Rufus punched in the number from the business card and held the cell phone to his ear.

Chapter 64

Lucado had just started to leave her office for her on-premises apartment when Fabian Miles burst into her office. Before Lucado could scold him for not knocking, he blurted out, "Ms. Lucado, you'd better see this!" He snapped on her office television, and the two watched Melbourne's local news description of the Ocean View Park massacre. Neither said a word as the reporter described the gruesome discovery of what had taken place in the oceanfront park.

As they watched in stunned silence, Lucado's office phone rang. Joelle sprang over to the desk. "Yes?" she answered through gritted teeth. After just a few seconds, she fairly screamed, "I'm watching it now! I want everyone involved in this pile of shit in my office first thing tomorrow morning!" She slammed the phone down. It bounced off her desk.

"I hate this job! I hate those clones! If it's the last thing I do, they will surely die!"

Fabian Miles, ever the diligent servant, said, "You'll have to brief Screamer, Judge Lucado."

"Fuck Screamer!" Lucado started from the room and shouted back to Miles, "I don't give a shit what happens, don't disturb me any more tonight. The world can go to hell for all I care!" She slammed the door behind her.

Chapter 65

Not only the CIA, but also the entire law enforcement community of northern Florida went into a Rapid Response Mode following what quickly became known as the Ocean View Park Massacre, yet another in America's long list of mass killings. The CIA chief in Florida decided to ignore Lucado's impetuous order that everyone should appear in her office the next day. All local, state, and federal law enforcement agencies sprang into action, and within an hour, major roadblocks were in place, and within two hours, numerous checkpoints and blockades had been erected on every major road in northern and central Florida. Every motorcycle and vehicle was being checked, and licenses and identification papers were being subjected to rigorous scrutiny. All motorcyclists were being thoroughly questioned, photographed, and fingerprinted in an unprecedented use of police power, and many were being detained incommunicado pending further investigations. Curfews were instituted in many localities. 18-wheelers were also being stopped, and their contents checked. For the first time in American history, the federal government with the cooperation of a state was claiming and exercising a massive stop and search police power that went light years outside of the Constitution.

Rufus's new friend from the SeaShell, Danny Brass, willingly leased his 18-wheeler to Rufus, no questions asked. Rufus and Dreamer picked up the truck from Brass who pocketed the $10000 and headed off to Savannah in a rental car. He and Rufus agreed that Rufus would soon telephone Brass with a location of the truck somewhere in the southern United States and that Brass would pick it up. Within an hour of taking possession of the 18-wheeler, Rufus and Dreamer had loaded many members of Rugged Cross with their bikes into the enclosed cargo space and had concealed the human-bike cargo behind boxes of large but lightweight hot tub covers, complements of Danny Brass. The manifest showed that the hot tub covers were bound for various places in the Midwest. The covers provided a shield from floor to roof eight layers deep so that if the police demanded that the trailer be opened, they would see only a load of spa covers. To see any bikers would require moving no fewer than fifty spa covers, something the bikers hoped the police would not bother doing. The bikers had minimum ventilation, but they agreed that that was a slight price to pay to escape from the numerous government agencies which were angrily searching for them and would without doubt unleash major unpleasantries on the bikers if found. Friends in Florida's Brevard and Volusia counties hid a number of bikers who were not loaded into Brass's 18-wheeler.

After encountering seven roadblocks where the Florida state police with the assistance of unidentified federal agents were polite and seemingly thorough, the big rig with Dreamer driving crossed into Georgia without incident. However, CD and Rufus had already learned from news broadcasts that the roadblocks had spread into neighboring states, though the Georgia troopers were less polite and noticeably less thorough than those in Florida. Every twenty miles or so, Dreamer stopped the truck and a couple more bikers set off on their own. The bikers had shed their Rugged Cross colors and for all practical purposes were just regular, scruffy-looking, all-American guys and gals. As it turned out, they had presumed correctly that the roadblocks were searching specifically for members of the Rugged Cross Club and for Ben. A number of the bikers were reluctant to take off their Rugged Cross colors until CD convinced them that the CIA would use truth serum on them and their women and would probably imprison them without trials just for being Rugged Cross. The bikers, CD explained, would surely be considered to be terrorists, and once that label was attached, all bets were off as to what might happen to any bikers in federal clutches. They could even be taken to "black sites' in other countries and kept there for who knows how long. Forget the presumption of innocence. And the massacre provided all the justification that the government needed to do whatever it wanted to do.

Finally, CD had convinced them not only to shed their Rugged Cross colors but also to ditch them entirely, which they had done at piecemeal stops at rest areas and other locations with public dumpsters. To minimize the chances that the police might find the discarded colors, they searched for and had little trouble finding dumpsters with particularly noxious materials in them. The difficulty was not so much finding the dumpsters but in stuffing the clothing down into the dumpsters below the other refuse. Some of the bikers had alternate colors that they could dun, and the other bikers simply had to invest in new wardrobe at truck stops along the way. Once CD had explained and re-explained several times to the doubting bikers what actually transpired in the CIA's black sites, none of the bikers resisted, and all got rid of the Rugged Cross colors. Though it might have been lost on some of the bikers that CD was familiar with what happened in the black sites, it was not lost on Ben.

With one of the bikers switching off with Dreamer to drive the truck, the trip from Melbourne Beach to Atlanta, which would normally take about eight or nine hours, took thirteen hours. Contending with the roadblocks, numerous stops to let off pairs of bikers, stops for disposal of incriminating clothing into various smelly dumpsters, and avoiding the much faster Interstate 75 all added hours to the trip, but no one complained, either about the time or the cramped and hot conditions inside the cargo unit.

At a truck stop on the outskirts of Atlanta, CD, Rufus, and Ben stood facing Dreamer and Killer. There was a strong but heavy feeling of camaraderie and dread in the air. They all knew that the entire federal government was searching for them. And so far they had beaten the government. Their common adversary and shared plight had steeled their friendship. And now it was time for good-byes. And they also knew that they might never see each other again.

"Dreamer, keep dreaming," CD said. "And never let those dreams die."

"I'm good with dreams, CD. I just don't want nightmares." Dreamer had picked up the "CD" from hearing Rufus. "I'm not worried about me. I've been on the run before. I'm more worried about y'all and the kid," Dreamer said as he motioned towards Ben.

"All I can say is, thank you, Dreamer. Thank you, Killer." Ben's eyes were misting. "I'll never forget you." He paused, then continued. "Whatever you hear about me and my two friends that you've never met, please always know that we want what'll work out best for you." He paused again, then added softly, "And our country."

"The country can take care of itself. I just hope y'all can take care of yourselves," Dreamer said.

Ben looked directly at Dreamer. "I'm not so sure the country can take care of itself. The damage done to our country recently by our politicians is still with us."

Rufus then interjected, "OK, that's enough good-bye stuff. CD, we need to hit the road."

"Right," CD said.

The five men hugged, then Killer looked at Dreamer and said, "Hammer down, bro," and without delay, the two reformed one percenters jumped on their bikes and roared out onto

Atlanta's perimeter road. CD, Rufus, and Ben watched them until they were out of sight.

"OK, you two," CD said. "We have an asset in Atlanta that you two don't know about."

Ben did not look surprised. Rufus said, "You've got to be kidding. I know your wife is here. She's always been your main weapon, CD."

Ben said, "Your wife? You never mentioned her."

"There's a lot you haven't mentioned too, Ben." CD said. "Anyway, yes, my wife of thirty years. She taught art history for fifteen or twenty years, then retired from that and has been running a nonprofit that has been aiding Honduran childcare agencies. She's well connected in her own right, apart from my connections. She has a lot of other expertise and experience that's going to help us a lot. I think she'll be able to help us do what we need to do." After a pause, CD added, "And, believe me, we'll need all the help we can get."

"So, does Mrs. CD know about us?" Ben asked.

"Well, first of all, she kept her own name. She's Olive Jones. And second, no, she doesn't know anything about you clones."

Ben looked somewhat surprised. "Is she *the* Olive Jones - - - as in *The Olive Jones History of Art*? The one who did the art history book that revised and updated the Jensen book?"

CD answered, "One and the same. She's one smart gal," he said with a smile. "OK, enough of that, let's get rid of this truck."

"Wow," Ben exclaimed. "Amazing."

Rufus looked squarely at CD. "Are you going to tell Ben about her other expertise and experiences, like how she's so well equipped to help them stay clear of the government?"

CD turned to Ben. "Let's just say she knows a lot about how to foil the government's attempts to find us and she's got her own special skill set."

Ben did not look doubtful but did look interested. "That's sort of cryptic sounding, CD. What are these other experiences and expertise that she has?"

"She's done her share of undercover work for the government, Ben. Let's leave it at that for the time being." CD realized that he should not have used the words 'for the government.'

"No, let's don't just leave it at that! Explain, CD!"

"Ben, she knows how to keep us off the grid."

Rufus then intervened to reduce the heat. "Ben, I know Olive, and I know how she operates. You can trust her completely. She might have done some undercover work for the government, but, like CD here, she's not a government pawn. You've got to trust us and you've got to trust her, Ben."

Ben paced, frowned, and turned back to Rufus and CD. "I guess I trust your honesty. I just don't see a plan. This all seems so ad hoc, and ad hoc won't work. But whatever. Let's go."

The men took the truck to a less frequented truck stop, parked and registered it with the short-term parking attendant, and telephoned and left a voicemail message for Danny Brass where he could pick up his 18-wheeler. It had served the bikers well. Not one of the Rugged Cross band had been apprehended in the widespread search by state and federal authorities. And Ben, Rufus, and CD were also still free. CD just hoped that the other clones were also still free, but he felt that the clones along with Rufus and himself, and by extension his wife, were now living on borrowed time.

"Our ride will be here any minute now. Olive is sending someone for us. It's possible she's being watched, so even though we have a small house in Atlanta, we're actually not going to my house," CD said.

"Right," Rufus continued for CD. 'We're going to my aunt's house in Buckhead. She's out of the country for a while, and she gives me the run of the house and let's me use her car when she's gone. No one can see the house from the street. I don't think that will automatically make us exactly safe, but at least they can't watch us without our knowing it."

"Unless they use drone cameras or smart technology," Ben added.

They had not noticed the Atlanta Airport shuttle that had pulled into the truck stop parking area until a shapely young woman in a chauffeur's uniform got out. She walked directly up to them and said, "Does one of you answer to 'Ram'?"

"Yeah, that's me," CD said then glanced sheepishly at Rufus and Ben who were shamelessly admiring the newcomer.

"OK, I have directions to take y'all to Buckhead," she said with a pleasant Southern drawl. "So, let's get going. I want to drop y'all off and then make a quick run out to Hartsfield before I call it a day." She started for the van without waiting for a response.

"Ram? Where did that come from?" Ben snickered.

CD's tone was serious as he replied, "That's a private message from Olive. Look, this driver doesn't know anything, not even our names, so no talking in the car except about the weather."

"No problem," Ben said.

Rufus nodded in agreement.

After a thirty-minute ride through the dense Atlanta traffic, the van pulled up in front of a deceptively large brick and wood, Tudor style house in a well-to-do Buckhead neighborhood. CD paid the van driver, thanked her, and after she had departed, Rufus reached into a drainpipe, pulled out a key, and let them into his aunt's house.

Looking around at the beautifully furnished house, CD remarked, "Well, gentlemen, I don't know if this is going to be our new home for a week or two or just for a day or two, but at least for now we can half-way relax for the first time in quite a while."

"Dude, I haven't been relaxed since I left my place in St. John," Ben said. For the first time, CD and Rufus could hear the fatigue in his voice. "I need a shower."

"OK, this way, everybody." Rufus ushered Ben and CD down a hallway. "That'll be your room, Ben, and CD, you and I'll take this room. When the other two get here, Ben, one'll be in there with you, and one can have his own room down the hall."

"Ben, before you shower, see if you have a message from the other two, OK?" CD suggested.

"I already did. They know where we are and they'll get here sometime tonight if they can." Ben smiled at CD and Rufus.

"Why didn't you tell us?" CD asked with some irritation in his voice.

"I've been with them in the chatroom for the last couple of hours, and —" Ben didn't have a chance to finish before CD interrupted.

"For two hours!" CD exploded. "Listen, Ben, you've got to keep me informed about everything. That means everything, Ben!" For the first time, CD sounded genuinely irritated. "If I'm going to keep you clones from getting caught, you can't be holding out on me."

Ben looked squarely at CD. "Fuck that, CD. This is not about you. It's about me. It's about Thomas, and it's about Alex. We're the future, not you. Now, I appreciate your help. I need it. I need you, and I need Rufus. But don't take us on as your personal pet project. You don't run this show. We do. Understood?"

"Well, fuck that." CD virtually screamed, his face now red with anger. "You're crazy, not just fucked up. You're full out crazy, off the rail. You don't know the first thing about who's looking for you or just how dangerous they are."

"The hell I don't," Ben shot back. "I've been planning my freedom years before you even knew I existed. So have Thomas and Alex." Ben was exaggerating, but CD had no way of knowing that.

"You two cut it out!" Rufus stepped between them. "We've got to be one team, not a collection of prima donnas. Ben, you clones are going to need CD more than you can imagine. You got absolutely no idea what you're up against, and, CD, just cool it."

CD started to say something, but Rufus grabbed his elbow. "Step back, CD. Let's clear the air a little later, OK?"

Ben left the room without saying a word. CD glared at Rufus. "We can't let them screw everything up and get caught. The stakes are too high, Rufus."

"I know that, CD, but I think these boys know what they're doing. And he's right. It's about them, not you. Not me. They're our charges in a sense, but they're not our troops. It's not a command situation, CD. It's a team situation, and we've got to give them some leeway at the same time that we educate them about how to stay off the grid." Rufus spoke calmly. "You've got to expect that they're going to have their own unique link with each other, and we can't really share in that."

"Yeah, OK, I guess," CD said, but his face was still red, and his voice was still clipped. "I'll see if I can contact Olive." CD busied himself on his laptop. CD and Olive had long ago established a way to communicate privately. They fully realized that, given both of their histories, their emails would be read and their telephone conversations listened to. They simply communicated through laptop encryption by posting to a certain, heavily used Norwegian travel forum that they had discovered some years earlier. The posts appeared instantaneously. Both, of course, rotated through special usernames and had their own coded way of communicating with each other. After reading on the forum for several minutes and typing in a short message, CD said to Rufus, "Olive will get here tonight or maybe tomorrow."

Before Rufus could respond, the sound of the doorbell startled both men. "That's the back door," Rufus said softly. They looked at each other. Rufus tucked his thirty-eight revolver into the back of his pants and activated the video-cam which watched the rear door of the house. CD stood just out of sight with his own revolver drawn.

"It's Thomas and Alex," Rufus said after he had zoomed in with the video camera. He started for the rear door.

"Be careful, they might have been tailed," CD cautioned.

Rufus opened the door and quickly asked, "Are you alone?"

"Yeah, we weren't followed. At least I hope not," Thomas said, and he and Alex stepped into the house. "Where's Ben?" Thomas asked immediately.

"Taking a shower. He'll be out in a minute," CD said.

The four reflexively hugged, then CD and Rufus brought Thomas and Alex up to speed, and as they finished, Ben walked into the room, having showered and put on some fresh clothes.

For the first time in over two hundred years, Thomas Jefferson, Alexander Hamilton, and Benjamin Franklin were together again. They just stared at each other. No one spoke at first. Rufus and CD realized, as did the three younger men, that something of monumental importance and without historical parallel was unfolding at this very instant in this very room. To a man, they realized that the three young men standing there could well shape America's future. Rufus motioned to CD, and the two quietly left the room, leaving the three alone. Three of America's founding fathers had returned.

Chapter 66

Stories, speculations, and fears about Russian infiltration of the Ray Administration, a private plane being shot down by the White House, and clones roaming the streets exploded through the nation's print, electronic, and social media. Extrapolating from the bizarre reference to George Washington and its link to a genetics company in Atlanta, the electronic media filled its programming with the usual speculative what-ifs. Social media maxed out with invention and gossip. Inside the Washington beltway, or "this town," as insiders referred to it or "the swamp" as others referred to it, some thought it all was just another wild publicity stunt out of Hollywood to prep the public for some secret to-be-released movie, but others were paralyzed with the fear that clones, probably numbering in the thousands, might already be amongst us, ready to sap our biological strength and pervert our species.

The White House embarked on a desperate attempt at spin control and imposed a complete news blackout on the subject of the mysterious GeneVision plane that it had shot down over Maryland and instead issued cleverly worded statements concerning the "purely formal" link between Marina Novokatnaia and the Ray Administration. The Administration completely disowned Novokatnaia and assured the nation that she was not privy to any critical or classified information. The public, long trained to recognize presidential lying, was hardly mollified. The White House hinted but refused to explicitly admit that it had been duped and misled by "the Russian dominatrix" and attributed its colossal misjudgment to "Novokatnaia's own well concealed lack of qualifications and professionally hidden links to Russian gangsters." The Administration intended for the Novokatnaia disaster to distract the public from what it considered to be the more serious clones issue, but given the media's feeding frenzy on the clones story, the attention of the public was uncharacteristically not so easily diverted. The flaw in the White House strategy was that by releasing nothing but untruths about the clones or the plane it had shot down, it created an inviting void that the media rushed to fill with its own inventiveness. Many among the public recognized the media coverage as simply the latest river of "fake news."

A leading news network aired its own three-night special entitled "Clones in Our Midst?" The tone of these broadcasts was that genetic research in general held all kinds of possible benefits for mankind but that human cloning itself was not only immoral but was fraught with all sorts of dangers. Another news network entitled its one-night town hall special "Human Cloning: Should We?" Its pre-screened audience was overwhelmingly opposed to the very idea of human cloning which they described as "immoral," "dangerous," "sinful," and "ungodly," and one person from the audience even claimed that "human clones would not have souls and thus would inherently be evil." When the moderator asked the man how he knew that a clone would not have a soul, the man just mumbled a bunch of nonsense, and the audience actually laughed. Public television as usual had the most informed coverage albeit with its usual leftist tinge. Its moment of drama on its own town hall meeting was when a Catholic bishop during the discussion somehow got onto abortion and asserted that life only begins at conception and that that is why abortion is wrong. The physician on the panel pointed out that clones are obviously alive, but since there is no conception in the cloning process, the assertion that life only begins at conception was as obsolete as stagecoaches. The bishop simply asserted that cloning was a "biological abomination."

When asked for the biblical basis for that conclusion, the bishop threw up his hands in disgust and stalked from the room.

In Atlanta, the clones themselves got many a laugh over the various attempts on the news channels to deal with an issue of monumental importance but about which the commentators were still in the dark. Olive and CD had been communicating and quickly agreed that Olive was quite possibly under surveillance and that she should not yet come to Atlanta.

Chapter 67

President Ray sat at his large mahogany desk in the Oval Office and was in the final ten minutes of preparation for his address to the nation on "a topic of national significance," as the advance statement described the President's speech. It was set to air live at 8:00 P.M. on all of the major news channels and networks. The make-up magicians were powdering President's Ray's face as he tested the microphone with "One, two, three. How's this?" The President and his advisors had quickly agreed that the address should be from the Oval Office in order to signify the gravity of the situation, but they never reached real consensus on the content of the speech. Cordero thought the Administration should take a conciliatory tone and speak directly to the clones, wherever they were, and ask them to meet with the President to forge a new style of politics in the nation, one bridging the gap between the needs of a modern America and traditional constitutional principles. Lucado and Trentini had favored a hardline approach in which the President would hold out the olive branch to the clones but at the same time reject the notion that their genetic heritage somehow put them "one up" on any other American. President Ray in the end rejected all of his advisors' advice and was alone in favoring the speech that he was now set to deliver.

The image consultants were making sure that the several items on the President's desk — a picture of the President's wife, an American flag, and a scroll of the Constitution which the President would grip during a particular part of his address — were perfectly arranged and each visible and identifiable to the cameras.

"One minute, Mr. President. Everyone places, please." The White House's own Press Secretary stood in the wings behind the number one cameraman.

"Thirty seconds, Mr. President."

And then at ten seconds, the director gave a countdown, the "live" light came on, and the President began.

"My fellow Americans. I am speaking to you from the most important office in our beloved country, indeed the most important office in the world. This flag here on my desk (the President paused and in a practiced Reaganesque gesture gravely nodded in the direction of the small flag) reminds me every day that America is not a place. No. Rather, it is an idea. It combines freedom, individual initiative, and a genuine concern for our fellow men and women wherever on this planet they might live.

"Because we value human dignity and human freedom, America has since 9/11 taken major steps to make sure that our national freedom remains secure. But not only that, we want everyone everywhere to share in that great ideal of human freedom.

"The Declaration of Independence, penned by Thomas Jefferson, remains the world's outstanding statement of freedom. And Thomas Jefferson realized that a strong federal government would be needed to protect those freedoms. He, and then Abraham Lincoln after him, and then Franklin Delano Roosevelt after Lincoln, realized that the first duty of a President is to preserve and protect the security of the nation. If our nation ceases to be secure, those freedoms will evaporate."

The President paused and held up the scroll of the Constitution. "I will do everything I can to protect this nation and preserve its security because if I were to shrink from that duty one bit, this document, this Constitution that we all cherish, would be weakened and eventually become a relic, a testimony to our failure as a people.

"That will not happen as long as I am in this office. You have placed a trust in me to take those actions which must be taken to protect the nation."

The President reverently placed the copy of the Constitution on his desk, still in full view of the camera.

"Presidents beginning with George W. Bush have taken strong actions and recommended to the Congress strong measures to make sure that America survives the threat of Islamic terrorism. Recent Presidents, namely Presidents Obama and Biden, may have waffled on these matters, but even they advocated strong measures to preserve the nation's security.

"So why am I talking to you about such a heavy and important subject? There has occurred a development that now poses a new threat to our democracy. There are many rumors and much speculation concerning cloning and concerning whether GeneVision, a company with facilities in several of our cities, has indeed cloned humans. Not only would such cloning of humans violate federal law, but it would also pose a major threat to our code of morality and what we stand for as a God-honoring nation.

"Because there is now so much wild speculation concerning this matter, let me tell you what the facts are. Here is what we know. First, we have no evidence that humans have been cloned. But second, GeneVision was on a path that would have undeniably led to human cloning if our law enforcement officials had not discovered what they were doing. Third, GeneVision had embarked on a desperate mission to pretend, *to pretend* mind you, that it had produced human clones. This was as effort to manipulate public opinion so that when they finally did clone the first human, we would have grown accustomed to the idea and would, therefore, be more likely to accept it. It was also the beginning of a campaign to increase the value of GeneVision stock. My fellow Americans, what GeneVision was doing was a cynical and devious plot to break our laws, violate our code of values, and at the same time financially profit from this dangerous, and, yes, evil scheme.

"Part of this strategy of pretense was what led to the shooting down of the plane over Maryland last week. We faced the unprecedented situation of a GeneVision pilot who had become psychologically unstable and who had at his disposal some type of lethal, explosive device, quite possibly radiological. I personally gave the order to destroy that plane to make clear that this nation will not tolerate illegal actions. When a private plane is ordered to land by the federal government in this age of terrorist threats, it's very simple. That plane must land. There is no plan B. All responsible pilots know this and routinely comply. Under our law, there is no alternative barring, of course, an emergency such as an inability to land. That plane may have been on a terrorist mission. We do not know it's intentions, and its pilot refused to cooperate with us when we attempted to find out its mission. Among other things, we do know that plane may have intended to land in New York and parade out before the eager cameras a twenty-five or thirty year old person whom GeneVision corporate officers would claim was none other than George Washington." The President subtly shook his head in disbelief.

"We quite frankly do not know the purpose of the lethal device, and, given the delusional and erratic behavior of the pilot, we had no possible way to know what would happen and no way to forecast the loss of life should he just decide to detonate the device.

"Unfortunately we had to destroy that plane because indications were that it had an explosive device on board which they were prepared to detonate in a heavily populated area. So let me be clear. We quite frankly do not know exactly where they planned to use that lethal device. We do not know the intent, but we could not take a chance on the purposes and objectives of that flight. There is no way we could allow that flight to continue over densely populated areas of the northeast. As your President, one of the heavy burdens of my office is to protect the security of the nation even when that duty forces me to take drastic steps. I will never, never, be derelict in my duty to protect this nation. Other Presidents have been. I will not. Therefore, the young man whom that company was going to pretend was a clone was killed in the process and his body, along with that of the pilot, was burned beyond recognition. To date, we have not been able to identify who in fact this pretender was, but I assure it, there was no clone on that plane."

The President frowned, then forced a slight smile. "Now about the speculation that twenty- and thirty-year old clones are lurking in our midst, you and I know that this is simply not possible. Even if it were possible today, it was not possible twenty or twenty-five years ago when such a clone would have had to have been produced. Documents we have uncovered from GeneVision make clear that that company was unleashing its sinister strategy to pretend that it had cloned others of our framers. This would, of course, cause the stock of that company to skyrocket. This appears to have been the major objective of the conspirators. Those who designed this plan conspired to make a killing in the stock market. This could all occur within a matter of days. They knew that it would be impossible to expose the falseness of their claims before they raked in millions, perhaps billions, of undeserved dollars. Once the plot was exposed, the company would collapse, and its stock would quickly become worthless. All of you who are watching me or listening to me tonight, persons on fixed incomes, persons on pensions, regular stockholders, persons holding mutual funds — all of us would take the financial hit while the rip off artists from GeneVision with their millions of dollars would be long gone to countries with whom we have no extradition arrangements.

"But, my fellow Americans, there is more to this story. There are several other persons whom the perpetrators of this plot have used in their scam to make millions of dollars. Frankly, we do not know who these persons are or where they are. I ask now that they report to their nearest FBI office, and of course, we are able to give them immunity from prosecution. Then we can once and for all close the door on this cynical plot and on the wild speculation that this country has lost its way and permitted human cloning."

The President turned to the side and faced a camera on his left side in order to demonstrate that he was addressing these other perpetrators directly. "And to those of you who were part of this scheme, I say this. The plot is over. The plan failed. If you come in and help us put the remaining pieces of this puzzle together, we can offer you leniency and immunity. You owe it to this great nation to help us turn the last page of this sad book. If you do not come in, then there will be no leniency. If you do not come in, we will hunt you down, and make no mistake about it, we will find you and bring you to justice."

The President turns back to the front camera. "And so, my fellow Americans, this act of greed, as well as the threat of death from the skies to everyone living in the northeastern part of our great country, has been averted. Our republic has been spared the disaster of a radiological bomb. Our republic will be spared the nightmare of pretender clones. We will not allow human cloning as long as I am President, and I will send legislation to Congress increasing the criminal penalties for human cloning. We as a nation will continue to cling to those ideals our framers enshrined in the Constitution. This flag—" and with an open hand, the President motioned to the small flag on the President's desk. " — will continue to stand for human freedom. As President Ronald Reagan said several times, 'We are man's last best hope.' My fellow citizens, I ask you to join me as we proudly keep that flag flying as we keep that hope alive. Thank you, and God bless this great country, the United States of America."

The red light on the camera went off, and the President, accompanied by his aides, quickly left the Oval Office.

Chapter 68

"Can you believe that?" exclaimed CD as he muted the post-speech analysis from the talking heads.

"I guess he wants us to come in," said Thomas dryly. "Cool chance of that."

Alex quickly observed, "They clearly know that we are clones and that we're "out there" somewhere. Otherwise, there's no way the President would have said all those things about there being no clones."

"Yeah," Thomas said, "And if they actually do have any documents from GeneVision, they know about us."

"Unless GeneVision had already created false documents in anticipation of a governmental inquiry," CD said.

Ben, who had remained silent for the duration of the President's address to the nation, now spoke with a serious tone befitting his identity. "Gentlemen, we must look at the big picture. The President of this country has just told numerous lies to the nation about the shooting down of the plane, about the GeneVision operation, and about us, us clones. It's clear to me beyond any doubt whatsoever that the policy of this administration is to apprehend and silence us once and for all. And why? Because American government after some years of constitutional drift has now so thoroughly departed from the constitutional ideals on which this country is based, but that's only part of it. That's the political part, the freedoms, the separation of powers, and all those principles that we fought for so hard two centuries ago in Philadelphia and in the states. But there's also the economic part. This Administration with the complicity and timidity of Congress has continued the reckless spending and big government policies begun by the Bush-Obama presidencies and continued since then, especially with all the climate stuff, and this President realizes that, one, if it's shown that we clones are indeed genuine re-creations and manifestations of those founding fathers and, two, that we think the direction of the country is economically and politically dangerous and contrary to the Constitution, then this Administration will be driven from office. My prediction is that they won't even make it to the next election. The President's objective is to get rid of us. Period."

After a silence during which the other men digested Benjamin Franklin's pointed analysis, Thomas asked, "Are we all of one mind that the economic policies of this Administration are, as Ben says, dangerous and against the free enterprise system? I think that's what you are saying, right, Ben?"

"Yes, exactly. This Administration's spending and taxing policies substantially weaken the free enterprise system and shift far too much of the nation's economic activity from the private to the governmental sphere."

Thomas continued, "So are we of one mind on that? Are we all agreed with that conclusion? Alex, you historically wanted bigger government than either of us. Do you think the government has gone too far, going back to Bush and Obama? Or really, even all the way back to LBJ.

Alexander Hamilton was quick to reply, "With no doubt, the current policies and the current trend are, given the current tax code, fiscally irresponsible. Plus the reckless policies of the Biden Administration, substantially higher taxes, radical new types of taxes and fees, a beefed-up and audit-prone IRS, and all of this creates a drag, a brake, on the economy and dampens the willingness to take business risks and economic gambles. Only through risks and gambles does the nation's economy move forward."

CD interjected, "Well what about the banks, Alex? You always wanted powerful banks. They are at the core of the new big government drive. Are you reversing your position on the banks? If I remember my history correctly, you were in bed with the bankers."

Alexander Hamilton responded icily, " I was never in bed with anyone. Back then we weren't bought and sold like your politicians today. And apparently, CD, your history about banks is faulty. The banks back then were banks. Today, they're self-promoting investment houses that carry on some banking activities, even to the point that they can become too big to fail. The politicians allow the banks to also be investment houses because that produces more money for the banks, and the politicians in turn benefit by getting larger contributions from the banks. Or, to put it in auction terms, the politicians let the banks do all these non-bank activities so that the prices at the auction skyrocket. What, you may ask, is being auctioned? Politicians. It's a strange kind of auction. The politicians who are on the block actually get the money, but what about their souls? Well, clearly the banks get their souls, their allegiance, and their protection. It never worked like that before. So, no, CD, I want strong banks. The operative word is banks. What we have today parading under the label of banks might indeed do some banking business, but their major business is the buying and selling of influence. They are monstrous houses of legalized greed cloaked under the banner, *banks*. They are a cancerous growth on our political democracy."

Ben brought the group back to the major topic at hand. "All well and good, my dear Alex, but a more immediate problem is that we're apparently going to not only be hunted but we're to be the target of a public campaign to discredit us, to make us pariahs."

"Ah, yes, pariahs," CD said, "the only word in English taken directly from the Tamil language."

They all stared at CD curiously. "You people really should study linguistics," CD deadpanned.

Ben continued, "Anyway, we need to do two things, gentlemen. First, we need to tell the public that we indeed do exist. We need to tell them *who* we are. And we need to explain to them why we cannot tell them *where* we are." He looked from one to the other.

Thomas asked, "And second?"

Benjamin Franklin continued, "And second, we have no choice but to expose to the American public just how far afield from American constitutional values their government has gone. It has simply veered so far off course that I have the distinct fear that it may well be impossible to get it back on track."

After about an hour's discussion, they agreed that they needed to mount a public campaign. Thomas summarized their approach. "So what we'll do is use the Internet and social media from a virtual location that the government cannot trace or shut down. We'll lay out the facts, and this will hopefully discredit the current Administration since their story is total disinformation. We won't go after the policies until we've established our bona fides. Is that pretty accurate?"

"Yes," Alex and Ben said in unison.

"CD?" Thomas asked, after CD and Rufus said nothing.

After hesitating, CD said, "I think that generally makes sense, but I think we're deluding ourselves if we think it'll unfold just like that. The government has immensely powerful means of finding you — us — and their M. O. is to take no prisoners. You can see this by their downing the plane and killing the George Washington clone. Plus, there's one more factor we haven't even talked about."

Ben quickly took up the discussion. "Yes, the head of GeneVision, that Novokatnaia woman, has simply disappeared. We have no idea whether she's in government hands or whether she's gone underground. But that's a major variable that we haven't factored in."

"And we can't factor it in because we don't know where she is or whether she's even alive at this point," Alex said.

"I can guarantee you that she's alive," CD said. "And the smart money's on her being in Russia by now. I've seen that woman operate. She doesn't leave loose ends out there to trip her up. My guess is that she had a well-designed escape plan in place, and when she thinks the time is right, she'll resurface in Moscow."

Ben raised his eyebrows and smiled. "I think this can well help us, gentlemen." He continued smiling, then nodded and continued. "She has no reason to surface unless it's to use the cloning issue. In effect, she'll verify that there are clones, and at that point we're in business with the American public."

"Compliments of our Russian mid-wife," Alex snickered.

"I don't follow your logic, Ben," Rufus said.

"Gosh, I forgot you were here — you talk so much," Ben said, and they all laughed. Rufus didn't bark much, but his analytical bite was sharp.

"She has no reason to surface other than to validate her work." Ben explained. "She can't deny it publicly because she knows we're out here, and, if she denied the cloning, as soon as everyone learned that we exist, she herself would be discredited. But that might not matter if she is in Russia. She'll be better off if she takes the offensive and admits to human cloning and extols its virtues."

"And in the process, the Administration is exposed as a bunch of liars," Alex said.

CD broke in, "If — *if* — gentlemen, she is indeed in Russia, and *if* the Administration doesn't thoroughly discredit her. I think that could be pretty easy to do. And if the President's successful in turning this into a foreign policy crisis, the public will rally behind him, at least for a few months. They won't rally behind a Russian lawbreaker. And they won't rally around a bunch of clones. That is, they won't unless the story we give them is absolutely convincing. But they will rally around the President as soon as he plays the national security card."

"Which he just did," Rufus added.

"We need to test the waters," Thomas said.

"Meaning what?" Ben asked.

"Meaning that we need to post something and see what kind of reaction we get. Nothing detailed, nothing major. Something like a one-time blog saying 'There are three of us clones, and we're in hiding because of the great apprehension and misunderstanding surrounding us. It's true that we were cloned at GeneVision facilities. As you can readily understand, we cannot surface now, but we'll surface once the government assures us that no harm will come to us and that we'll be protected. We love this country and want only the very best for it.' Something like that."

CD frowned. "Yeah, we can post a statement like that, and then watch to see how swiftly the government traces it."

Rufus interjected, "They'll get a dead-end because we'll make it a one-time post, we'll alert the major media, and we won't physically be anywhere near the posting location. The government now has the capacity of knowing the physical address of every item posted on the Internet. They can get this through the digital trace that's now attached to everything that goes out on the Internet. We have no alternative to using a real, physical computer to make the initial upload from a specific location. However, that upload'll go to a virtual computer, and that virtual computer will then distribute our statement to the nation's electronic and social media. The virtual computer will send it out on a delayed basis so that when it's first seen by the nation's media, we'll be long gone from the physical location, like a coffee shop or a hotel lobby, that we used to upload it to the virtual computer. "

"The virtual computer idea works, but when did the government get the capacity to know the physical origin of every single thing put on the Internet? When did that start?" Ben asked. "I had no idea the government could do that."

"It started sometime after 2010. It's called Guardian Two. It was created as part of the government's effort to find bin Laden," Rufus said. "As I understand it, the system is practically unbeatable."

"Can they digitally back-trace stuff from a virtual computer?" Thomas said.

"Not as far as I know," Rufus said.

"OK," CD said. "We write the statement and then one of us goes to where there's free Wi-Fi, uploads it to a virtual computer, and then high tails it."

"We could use the darknet," Ben suggested.

"Darknet? What's that?" Thomas asked.

Rufus responded, "It's essentially an Internet underground where at one time nothing was traceable, but the NSA can now monitor and trace what happens on the darknet. It was mostly used for illegal drug transactions, porn, extremist political and lifestyle groups, and that sort of thing. Ben, I'm surprised that you even know about the darknet, and I hope you've never spent any time on it. Gentlemen," Rufus looked from one to the other, "we will definitely not use the darknet. That would discredit us with the public, and it would all be traceable anyway. No, what we'll do is keep it simple and assume that at least any physical location from which we upload anything can be identified."

"So at least we need some place without surveillance and cameras, like a coffee house or something," Alex said. "Some place where we can upload something to a virtual computer and then disappear."

"How do we get it to the right people in the media? How do we keep it from being intercepted?" Alex asked. "I agree that it's essential to get it in the hands of the right people before the government gets to them."

Rufus answered, "That's not a problem. We just broadcast it all over the place from the virtual computer. It's as easy to send it to a thousand recipients as to just one."

Alex then stood and looked at Ben and Thomas. "I think it's time for us to come out of the closet."

Chapter 69

The President of the United States had underestimated the independence of Secretary of Defense Carsten Shulla. The morning following the President's address to the nation, Shulla telephoned for a time slot to see the President.

"Tell him I can do it late this afternoon, Phyllis," President Ray said hastily. "Give him a fifteen-minute slot. I just don't have time to do more than that. I've got that Ladies Travel Club photo-op and then I want to spontaneously surprise the hedge fund managers by showing up at their seminar at Treasury. There's a lot of money to be had from them. So give Carsten fifteen minutes, no more."

Phyllis was back in the President's office in less than thirty seconds. "Mr. President, Secretary Shulla is, well, sir, he's angry. He's yelling on the phone. He said to tell you, sir, that if he has to wait until this afternoon, he'll just go ahead and resign."

"Oh, damn it. He's such a prima donna hothead. OK, I'll talk to him." Phyllis headed for the door as the President snatched up the phone.

"Carsten, how are you? I know —"

Carsten Shulla interrupted the President. "Mr. President. Either I'm Secretary of Defense or I'm not. If I am, then I've got to be in the loop on everything, including this clone stuff."

"Carsten, you were in the hospital. I had to move fast."

"Cut the bull shit, Mr. President." President Ray had never heard Carsten talk like this.

"Careful, Carsten," the President said slowly and darkly.

"Mr. President, I know you have voice-activated recordings made of every meeting. I want access to all the recordings on this clone issue. I know you've met several times with Joelle and TT.

I 'll use those recordings to bring myself up to speed. Frankly, I don't trust your people to brief me accurately."

The President exploded, "Carsten, that won't happen. You can fucking forget any fucking recordings! I'll have Joelle brief you, but any more threats and you're history." The President was practically yelling in the phone.

Carsten bellowed into the phone, "That won't work. I don't trust Lucado as far as I can spit. Mr. President, I'll have my letter on your desk in one hour." Carsten Shulla slammed down the phone.

"Well, fuck you! I can fire people just as fast as that Trump did!" The President of the United States shouted and slammed down his own phone. The small crystal Tula samovar given to President Ray by the President of Russia flew from the President's desk and shattered into hundreds of sharp pieces. The President never did see the inscription on the bottom of the samovar. It read in Russian, "Once the samovar cracks, you will blow on cold water." If the President had bothered to have this Russian proverb translated, he would have learned that when something bad happens, you should beware of more bad things happening — to you.

One hour later, the letter that Phyllis quietly slipped onto the President's desk read, "I hereby resign my office as Secretary of Defense because of matters of health. Signed, Carsten Shulla."

When President Ray returned from hobnobbing with the hedge fund millionaires, he snatched up the letter, read it, and uttered, "Son of a bitch! No problem. One less person to fuck up my plans!"

Chapter 70

During the next two days, the clones stayed in their Atlanta sanctuary, and after many revisions, they had finally crafted a statement for social media. They vetoed any idea of video. They clearly could not yet risk letting the government know what they looked like. Rufus and CD's major contribution was cooking delicious Southern meals for the group. Olive was still absent. After she quickly ascertained that she indeed was being watched, she had used her tradecraft to shake anyone who had hoped to tail her. Neither CD nor Olive were sure if this would accomplish anything more than revealing just how extensive the resources were that the government had thrown into its search for the clones.

———

At the White House, Phyllis entered the President's office without knocking. Though she occasionally knocked, she was the only person in the White House who dared to enter without knocking. "Mr. President, everyone's here. Should I show them in?"

"Yes, Phyllis, thank you." The President stood but remained behind the large desk. He often did this to distance himself from others and to symbolize his authority. He attached great importance to the physical positioning of the attendees at his meetings. The President was convinced that relative position not only said much about authority and influence but also influenced the flow of communications in meetings. The President's theory was that if one sits at the head of the table or at the foot, that person was a focal point, unlike someone who sat along the side of the table. And never use a round table as it was too egalitarian.

For the first time, the President was bringing FBI Director Jonathan Fogg into the small circle of advisors dealing with the clones issue. President Ray motioned Fogg, Lucado, and Trentini to the three chairs side by side facing his desk from which he intended to orchestrate this meeting. However, the President was well aware that Lucado, Fogg, and Trentini were powerful personalities and could be difficult to manipulate. The President was not looking forward to this meeting, but Joelle Lucado had insisted that the four needed to meet to make sure that they had one game plan, and the President suspected that Lucado's goal was to gain total control the search for the clones and ultimately control of the clones themselves.

"Well, lady and gentlemen, let's figure out how we can get these clones to come in from the cold," the President said with fake jovialness.

Lucado surprised everyone with her quick pounce. "Mr. President, we don't — at least I don't — want this to become a turf fight, but I think that the CIA's clearly better positioned and better resourced than any other agency of the government to apprehend these clones. The FBI should surely be part, maybe the most prominent *public* part," she emphasized the word *public,* "of our effort, but my people are now spread throughout America and unlike the FBI, my people aren't so easily recognizable and don't have the sorry history of bias and duplicity that some prominent FBI agents and directors had in the Obama, Trump, and Biden years. We need to monitor, listen, penetrate, and surveil, Mr. President, and we need to do it quietly and without public knowledge. And we should know that those clones will never voluntarily come in without conditions that we cannot and should not meet."

"Mr. President," Fogg began. "The FBI —"

The President quickly cut him off. "No turf fights, Fogg. We can get into that some other time."

"Mr. President," Lucado continued, confident that the President had already decided to allow the CIA to take the lead in the search for the clones, "They'll undoubtedly have conditions."

"Like what?" TT asked. As Attorney General, TT surprisingly had acquiesced to Lucado's power grab. Fogg's and the FBI's pursuit might arguably still be justice in spite of damage done to its mission during recent presidencies, but the Attorney General's pursuit was politics, specifically the President's politics. As far as TT was concerned, the FBI might conceivably have been de-weaponized, but the office of Attorney General itself continued to be one of the President's most powerful political weapons. TT continued the practice that that office served the President, not the rule of law.

"Like being given a public forum, being given the chance to address the nation on parity with the President," Lucado responded and then continued, "Like asking for an international DNA verification procedure."

"If they're the real thing, and that's a big if," TT said. "Even though they're from GeneVision, maybe they're not clones."

"Bullshit, they're clones, and we all know it," President Ray said impatiently. "Let's move on."

Fogg decided that the risk of incurring the President's wrath was worth a turf fight. Clearing his throat, he said, "Mr. President, the FBI has to take the lead in this or else we run the risk of a public backlash once it becomes public that the CIA's operating so aggressively on American soil. As long as the CIA was searching out Islamic terrorists and Muslims, no one minded, except maybe the ACLU, some liberals, and other naive groups. But if we're unleashing the CIA onto Americans, even if they're clones, well, that could be a lot dicier. We've got to take the long-range view. Once we've got the clones in custody, it becomes a legal situation, and if the CIA uses its usual devices and does things the way it usually does, prosecution will be next to impossible. Any evidence the CIA gets will in all likelihood have been illegally seized and, therefore, inadmissible. Mr. President, we've got to do everything from here on out strictly by the book so that once we get them we can convict these clones. This isn't a turf fight, Mr. President. It's about good policy and legality, not turf."

"Convict them of what? What can we charge them with?" President Ray asked. "And do we really want to prosecute them and give them a public forum? Why not just put them away somewhere?"

No one responded to the President's question, but the implications of illegality were not lost on anyone.

"How about some kind of conspiracy? How about other crimes under the terrorism laws?" Fogg responded weakly.

Lucado and Fogg bantered back and forth about how to charge the clones, what to charge them with, and whether the CIA's secret but invasive procedures would poison any future investigation or prosecution. TT and the President watched and listened as the President allowed the two to fight for turf.

After about five minutes, the President had heard enough. "OK, here's what we'll do. Our objective is to find those clones as soon as possible and once we have them to prevent them from talking publicly. We'll isolate them in a CIA holding tank somewhere. We won't prosecute them," the President announced.

"Mr. President —" Fogg began, but the President cut him off.

"I've heard enough, Jonathan. We can't give them a soapbox. If they get hold of due process, lawyers, and all that shit, we'll lose control, and they'll make it a public spectacle. It'll be just like 2018 and that circus orchestrated by that California Senator --—what was her name, Weinstein, Feinberg, whatever -—we can't risk it. Those clones could completely jeopardize our fight against the Islamic extremists, and on my watch that won't happen. Joelle, pull out all the stops. I don't care what it takes, find those damn clones. I don't need to know what you do or how you do it, just get it done."

"Mr. President —" Fogg's protest was abruptly silenced by the President's raised hand.

Everyone in the room knew that the President has just licensed the CIA to trample civil liberties so long as the President had plausible deniability. They also realized that he, not they, would be plausibly innocent of wrong-doing and that they, not he, could well end up being guilty of numerous violations of the law.

"This is the — I repeat, *the* — top priority. I want all possible manpower and technological power focused on getting these clones. And, needless to say, but I'll say it anyway," the President paused for effect. "This is a matter of national security so don't let anything or anyone stand in your way. Understood?"

"National security, Mr. President?" the voice came from the doorway. Douglas Cordero strode into the room.

"What are you doing here, Douglas, and why didn't you knock?" the President said sharply.

"I think, Mr. President, the question is why wasn't I here from the beginning?"

The President then demonstrated that he was a master at recovery. "Because, Douglas, I wanted to keep you out of what could get very, very dirty. Until you barged in, you weren't going to be tainted if things got out of control, but now that you're here, please do come in. Pull up a chair, Douglas."

"Thank you, Mr. President." Cordero muttered as he pulled up a chair and sat to the right of Attorney General Trentini. "Mr. President, I think things might already be getting out of control. I got a most interesting telephone call from Carsten."

"Oh?" the President scowled.

"Yes, and I know you like us to get to the bottom line, Mr. President, so here it is. He says that your national security argument is all lies. He says that you shot down that plane in order to silence the clone that was on board. He even says you have personally ordered numerous illegal acts in pursuit of these clones. He says that you've already committed so many illegal acts that it's only a matter of time before this Administration falls."

"He's lost his mind!" the President exclaimed. Lucado, Fogg, and Trentini sat in stunned silence. "Did he happen to tell you what these 'many illegal acts' are?" The President asked.

"Yes he did. Shooting down the plane is just the most public one."

"Well, it sounds like he himself has probably committed treason if he's spreading lies about things which incidentally he knows very little about. Clearly treason!" the President said. Tossing around the word *treason* had become passé following the unrestrained use of that word during the Russian collusion years.

"I think, Mr. President, Carsten probably knows a great deal about the whole thing." Then Cordero dropped the bombshell. "You see, he's listened to the tapes that record all your meetings."

The President wondered, *How the fucking hell did he get those tapes?* President Ray went visibly white and then in a noticeably thinner voice said, "Those tapes aren't complete. Some of our conversations were at other places, and a lot of the conversations we had in this office were on the order of brainstorming. I'm not worried about the tapes."

No one in the office believed the President, but they all realized that the tapes, if they indeed were in Carsten's hands, were incriminating.

"Mr. President, is this meeting right now being taped?" Lucado asked.

"No, I ordered the machinery dismantled," the President said.

So that's how he could order us to do anything and even put the clones into isolation. There's no record of his involvement. We hang, and he watches from the wings. Now it made a lot more sense to Lucado.

"Was it in fact dismantled?" Lucado asked.

"Yes, I verified it myself," the President responded.

"Great!" Cordero muttered.

The President, obviously not hearing Cordero, stood and said, "OK, here's where we stand. The tapes simply are not incriminating. Alone, they cannot be used as evidence because they were surreptitiously made."

"Mr. President, it's not about criminal prosecutions only. It could be about your impeachment and the political collapse of your Administration. In an impeachment, anything can be used as evidence. If those tapes show that we've violated various civil liberties, then we are finished," Trentini said. "And don't kid yourself. There will absolutely be ways to get those tapes into evidence once the trials begin." TT shook his head and grimaced. "I can't believe it! What have we ourselves gotten into?"

"Maybe you're right," the President said with unexpected equanimity. "But for now, let's stay focused on the clones. Lucado, you find those clones. Quickly. Fogg, you be ready to process the clones as terrorists once CIA finds them. Joelle, you hand them off to Fogg as soon as you've got them. TT, have your people prepare a terrorism prosecution just in case we go down that road. On the matter of the tapes, we'll meet tomorrow and decide how to handle it. In the meantime, no one but the five of us is to know anything about the tapes or what we have discussed today. Everyone understand?"

"Carsten knows about the tapes. He might even have made copies," Lucado said.

There was an extended silence, and then the President said, "I'll handle the tapes thing tomorrow."

The others deliberately did not glance at each other though they all feared the tapes becoming public.

"Mr. President, I thought you said there would be no prosecution," TT said.

"TT, prepare the case. I haven't decided whether to go forward with it, but we need to have it ready to go."

"OK, Mr. President."

"Then, that's all. Thank you for coming," the President said in dismissal. "Joelle, please hang on for a minute on another matter."

After Trentini, Cordero, and Fogg had left the room, the President came around the desk and swiveled a chair so as to face Director Lucado. "Joelle, are you completely with me on all this stuff? It could get very nasty, and we're taking some real risks."

"Mr. President, I'm in."

President Ray continued, "We need to do what we're doing because our nation has never been threatened like we are now. Deluded Islamic terrorists and Russians and the Chinese are bad enough, but the clones could completely undermine our efforts to beat our enemies. We have no option but to go outside the fourth amendment to find our enemies. And the clones, too, Joelle. It's a new day, and the old way, the fourth amendment as written two hundred years ago, just won't cut it in today's world. Hell, with email, cell phones, tweets, Instagrams, Snapchat, Tik-fucking-Tok, encrypted stuff, and all that, the fourth amendment, search warrants, probable cause, and all that stuff we learned about thirty years ago in law school, all that stuff is just outdated now."

"Yes, Mr. President."

"Plus, the threat is insidious and immense. Where will they strike next? Our subways, malls, airports, train tracks, ports, schools, and universities, everything is so vulnerable. We're a nation of soft targets. Not to mention our electric grid, our financial grid, our interconnected computer systems, and all that. Our public buildings here in Washington. Just since I became President, everyone one of these things has been targeted by the terrorists, Russia, and China in one way or another, and only because we've been able to carry on advanced surveillance and intercept their communications have we been able to prevent what would have been total catastrophes. I have to protect them all, and I can't do it if some clone claiming to be Thomas Jefferson is sabotaging everything I do."

"Mr. President, maybe they won't question your need to take actions to preserve the very nation that they helped start. You know the saying — the Constitution is not a suicide pact. We can't just assume that they'll oppose what you're doing," Lucado said.

"Maybe they won't, but we can't take that chance. We won't know until we bring them in. Joelle, you find them. And Joelle—-" President Ray paused and stared hard at Joelle for an awkward ten seconds before completing his order. "Take care of Carsten Shulla. We can't have him out there being a loose cannon." The President glared at Lucado, waiting for her agreement.

"I'll have him put into a government hospital for observation," Lucado said without hesitation.

"Whatever it takes. Whatever," President Ray said, then added, "But I want him silenced once and for all."

"What are you saying, Mr. President?"

"I'm saying that I want him silenced once and for all." President Ray looked intently at Lucado who held his stare.

"Yes sir, Mr. President," Lucado finally said. Then with neither saying another word, she stood and walked from the Oval Office. She walked with the knowledge that she was on the verge of violating Americans' civil liberties and privacy arguably more than had ever been done before. She also understood that the President had authorized her to dispose of Carsten Shulla, something she fully intended not to do. On the clones, she was definitely in agreement with the President that they had to be found, but beyond that her thoughts were unsettled. *Once I find the clones, then what? Maybe I can use the clones. If I can't, then I'll give them to Fogg, and wash my hands of the whole damn thing.*

When she arrived back at her Langley office, Joelle immediately put into effect a total nationwide search for the clones, focusing primarily on the area east of the Mississippi River. But more effective than a physical search for the clones would be the CIA's digital search for the clones.

Lucado emailed and then telephoned the Director of the Domestic Security Office (DSO), a little known subdivision within the National Clandestine Service of the CIA. DSO has a special relationship with its counterpart agency in the NSA, and those two agencies together created a harmonious relationship across bureaucratic lines. Their joint mission was to carry out clandestine operations within the United States, something that the CIA had by statute been prohibited from doing until that statute was tacitly ignored beginning soon after 9/11. DSO and the NSA jointly developed and operated Guardian Two, known within the trade as G2, the nation's most potent surveillance weapon in its counter terrorism activities. G2 could search through all types of electronic communications with incredible speed and identify communications "of interest." Developed after 9/11, G2 could simultaneously intercept, decipher, and execute a threat assessment on practically all communications and web activity taking place within the United States at any one time. The NSA's Echelon system was the precursor to Guardian Two, but Guardian Two was light years more powerful and faster and differed from Echelon in three important ways. Guardian Two could adjust the interception criteria on its own according to what it found. It had its own dynamic intelligence. Second, G2 could determine the relative threat posed by an Internet activity. And third, G2 was teaching itself to identify and decipher invisible text hidden inside of graphic images. G2 was learning to read steganographic communications.

"Fogarassy here. Hello, Madame Director," Louis Fogarassy answered in his deep basso profundo voice. A computer engineer and émigré from Hungary, Fogarassy had been Director of the DSO since its creation.

"Hello, Louis. How are you doing?"

"I'm fine, Joelle. What's going down?"

Joelle cut to the chase. "You've been briefed on the clones. Well, it's time to use G2. Louis, the President defines this issue as a top national security matter and has in effect invoked his inherent powers as Chief Executive and Commander in Chief. That means we can look at everything, emails, texts, tweets, Instagram, Snapchat, the servers and archives of Facebook, everything that Google has, and all the social media, cell phone calls, game platforms, everything, including pictures."

"I hear you loud and clear, Joelle. Do you have some documentation? Do we have a finding?"

"I'll email it to you as soon as we hang up. It's in the works. Louis, I don't know if they're using anything other than cell phones, but we need to pull out all the stops. This is a national security threat."

"Joelle, this is the first time we will have used G2 on this scale. And we've never used the steganographic decryption routine other than in controlled tests. That's a new capability, and it's still in beta. Just so we all realize that the results won't be definitive."

"Louis, I seriously doubt they use embedded texts anyway." Lucado paused, swiveled in her chair, then continued. "But, Louis, this isn't a shake-down cruise. Make it a top priority. The clones are a security threat. I doubt my people in the field can find them, but G2 can. At least, I hope it can. So give me a progress report ASAP, OK?"

More concern now crept into Louis Fogarassy's voice, and his accent thickened. "Joelle, it'll take more than a few hours to get the personnel in place to keep up with G2. She's just too fast. I'll need a pretty substantial team to monitor, check, and so on. It's not like just pressing a magic button. We have to introduce the parameters for the digital searches, create the search algorithms, validate them, open the various packet switches throughout the nation, and on and on. There are thousands of cell phone companies, ISP's, communications junctures, cell towers, server archives, and so on. Joelle, it'll take a couple of days for G2 to be running at a hundred percent.

Joelle Lucado said, "Louis, I know all that. You've got five hours to get it to one hundred percent. Pull people off whatever you need to. I'll give you more people if you need them. Just get it done."

Louis started to protest, "It can't be done that —"

The CIA Director cut him off, "Louis, fuck it! Five hours, Louis. Five hours!" With that, Lucado broke the connection.

Fogarassy muttered something in Hungarian under his breath. The couple of aides standing nearby couldn't translate the words, but they knew from his tone and his grim face that they had just heard some serious Hungarian swearing.

Chapter 71

President Ray realized that to divert the public from the clones issue, he needed to refocus attention on his domestic agenda. He had been heavily criticized for being in favor of big government, even of being socialist. Being socialist was still unacceptable to most Americans in spite of continuing noise from extremist elements in the Democratic Party, but President Ray made no secret about it — unlike Reagan, Ray was convinced big government was not the problem. The problem was too little government. Sheep need to be led. Government was the authoritative source of leadership, and under strong leadership the people would follow. Government had to shape society, not vice versa. The public surely had a right to opinions, but the government had no duty to follow those opinions.

To get his domestic agenda front and center, President Ray called his Chief of Staff, Lee Brown, into the Oval Office. Lee Brown was the first woman chief of staff in presidential history. She was stunningly beautiful, outwardly pleasant, an incisive analyst, and when necessary, utterly ruthless. She was also a dog lover and owner of two Bichon Frises, and it was this that first brought "The Dog Lady" to Ray's attention. After getting a degree in organizational theory from a now defunct Caribbean university, she had worked for several Senate committees and had eventually gone to work for the relatively unknown John Ray. They had in common that they had both at one time volunteered at dog rescue services. She had stayed on Senator Ray's staff during his time in the Senate and then came to the White House with him. No domestic policy initiatives got to the President without first being thoroughly vetted by Lee Brown. The Ray-Brown relationship was reminiscent of the Sherman Adams-Eisenhower style where Chief of Staff Adams controlled the flow of what got to the President, and everything for Eisenhower had to be reduced to one page. On rare occasions, unlike Sherman Adams, Lee Brown would reluctantly allow up to three pages. Also unlike Adams, Lee Brown played a major role in the development of domestic policy. In that sense, she was a throwback to the Haldeman-Ehrlichman team that controlled so much of the domestic policy-making during the Nixon Administration. However, President Ray had excluded Lee Brown from the discussions regarding the clones.

After Joelle Lucado had left the Oval Office, Lee entered from another door, and the President quickly switched gears from the threat of the clones to the need for strong governmental action on insurance and taxes. President Ray did not intend to get into a discussion about the clones with Brown. As a psychological matter, he recognized his own dark proclivities when it came to using his power and abusing civil liberties, and he frankly wanted to keep that side of his personality as far from Brown as possible. Lee Brown, ever perceptive, fully recognized President's Ray's excesses, and though she did not know the details of the search for the clones, she had like so many in the White House become aware of that consuming issue.

"Lee," the President began. "We need to go forward with that matter of nationalizing the insurance companies as well as instituting a national sales tax. We've got to have that tax to pay for all that climate stuff. I know I've sort of neglected those things, but we need to get back on top of them. We had legislation ready to send to Congress when we talked last time, right?"

"Mr. President, the national sales tax thing is ready to be introduced once you give the go ahead. Our people in Congress are completely ready on that. Everybody knows it's in the works. We can have one of our people introduce it on the hill at a moment's notice. Our people in both houses are ready to move on both bills. The insurance bill needs some tweaking, but it can be ready in a few days."

"OK, good, then let's go full speed on both of them. I need to refocus attention away from the clones. I'm sure you know something about that, but I want you to focus on policy, not clones. OK?" The President did not wait for Lee Brown's response.

President Ray continued, "The media's pretty easy to lead around by the nose, sort of like a big, dumb ox, so let's put it out there for them to munch on. They'll lead the public right into *our* nice, green pasture." The President emphasized whose pasture it was and after a short laugh, turned serious. "And on another matter, how did Cordero just walk in here a few minutes ago? Weren't you or Phyllis there to stop him or announce him or warn me or something?"

"Mr. President, he just walked by and when Phyllis tried to stop him, he just kept going and said the President said for him to come right on in. He *is* the Secretary of State. We can't just grab him. I'm sorry, Mr. President."

"Where was my marine guard? The one who's supposed to be outside the door."

"He was there, but Cordero just brushed past him. He *is* the Secretary of State, Mr. President, and he's in and out of here all the time. It's not like he was somebody off the street or something."

"OK, whatever. Let's just get the legislation up to the Hill. Get one of our lackeys, sorry, our friends, in the House to introduce these bills. Thanks, Lee."

"Mr. President, one more thing. Don't you think you need to bring me up to speed on this clones thing? It's dominating the news, and it's not going to disappear."

As he frequently did, President Ray stood, walked to the window and looked out over the White House lawn. Then he turned, and reversing everything up to this point, surprised Lee Brown as well as himself by saying, "Yes, you need to be in the loop on this one. I need your advice. Have a seat, Lee."

The President sat in the ornate, large wing chair in which he customarily sat, and Lee Brown sat in the smaller wing chair across from him. Darjeeling tea on a silver service and small pastries were on the coffee table between them. The President stayed silent for a period, then poured both of them tea. He made himself comfortable in his chair, and then gave Lee Brown a full briefing of the clones issue, ending with the contentious meeting he had just had with the leading members of his Cabinet. He omitted any reference to Carsten Shulla.

Lee listened to the President without interrupting or questioning. When the President finished, Lee remained silent for close to a minute. She and the President did not make eye contact. Finally she said, in a surprisingly strong voice, "Mr. President, of course, I have lots of questions, but for now just one. Do we have any idea where the clones are?"

"No, Lee. We have no idea at all. I wish we did. One might be in Florida. I think we'll know pretty soon though because Lucado will use all of her resources to find them. Everything. Even tools that we've not used on Americans before, like -—" the President paused, then changed direction, "Well, never mind the details. Just know that we're pulling out all the stops to find them."

"Mr. President, these clones aren't necessarily a threat. Why, they can be a godsend. For example, if— "

The President cut her off, "Lee, these clones are bent on bringing down this Administration, and on that there can be no doubt. How do I know this? Look at it. A Russian agent engineered the whole thing, and we now know that she's got to be in Moscow. If her company could make these clones, then they could well be programmed."

"Mr. President, that sounds like the *Boys of Brazil* or something like that." Lee smiled inwardly but kept her facial expression grim.

"That's not too far off, Lee. I realize that we don't know for certain that in fact they're programmed, but the national interest requires that we assume that they are. I won't let clones — robots — screw up what this government is trying to do, or worse than that, endanger our national security. That's why we have to find them and bring them in no matter what it takes. And we will. There's no possibility that we can't find them and bring them in. None at all."

The President stood and started pacing the room. "This country can be so great, so prosperous, so safe, so secure. Our Administration's on the very precipice of bringing services, programs, benefits, and opportunities to our people that are so much greater than anything they've ever had before. That's our number one priority. With this national sales tax, just think of what services and programs we can offer our people. Decades ago LBJ talked about a war on poverty. And just look at how much poverty has increased, especially under our own Democratic regimes, and mainly because of our enablement policies." The President was talking faster and waving his arms around animatedly. "Well, we can actually wage that war! And we can get rid of these insurance companies. Everybody knows that they're nothing but bleeders and leaches on the people. And now these damn clones are throwing a monkey wrench into the works." The President's face was turning red, and the veins in his neck were beginning to stand out. "Well, they don't understand that I won't let them do it. I can stand between them and the damage they want to do, and stand I will." The President paused, then pounded his large desk. "Damn them! Damn them to hell! That's where they came from, and that's where I'll send them back to."

The President then seemed to realize that he had been ranting. He smiled at Lee and with a suddenly relaxed, almost happy tone of voice, said, "Anyway, Lee, I care. I care deeply about this country, and sometimes I get carried away. We just have to keep our priorities straight, and the number one priority is protecting this nation from the destruction that robot-clones can cause. And right along with that is our other number one priority, that national sales tax and getting rid of the insurance companies."

Lee stood as she wondered whether the President realized that he had intoned several number one priorities, but she knew not to point this out. "Mr. President, thank you for getting me up to speed on this. We can get it all done, sir."

"Thank you, Lee. Yes, we'll get it all done, and first of all, we'll bring in those clones." He uncharacteristically walked Lee to the door.

Once Lee Brown had exited the oval office, the President walked briskly back to his desk, jerked the phone off its cradle and dialed Joelle Lucado.

Chapter 72

The clones, led primarily by Thomas Jefferson, finally arrived at a work product which would inform the public that they indeed existed and that they were "normal people." Rufus had identified a small Wi-Fi equipped coffee house adjacent to the Perimeter Mall complex of Atlanta. It would take him only seconds in that coffee house to upload the clones' statement onto a virtual computer in cyberspace, and that virtual computer would in turn distribute the statement to media outlets and social media. That would take the virtual computer less than a second, and then it would cease to exist. Tracing the statement back to the coffee house or even back to Atlanta should be impossible. They all agreed that Rufus was the best choice to go to the coffee house and upload the document to the virtual computer. Within minutes, the world would hear from the clones themselves that the first human clones in history were Thomas Jefferson, Alexander Hamilton, Benjamin Franklin, and George Washington, and that three of them were still alive and well.

"Wish me luck, boys," Rufus said as he walked to the front door.

"Are you armed, Roof?" CD asked. "You may not have a permit and you don't want to get in trouble with the police, but you don't want to get in a fire fight and not have any fire."

"I do have a concealed carry, and I'm as armed as I want to be," Rufus said.

"What does that mean?" CD asked.

"I'm taking this," Rufus said and pulled small, strange looking pistol from his waistband.

"What the fuck is that?" Alex asked with eyes wide.

"It's a no-noise tranquilizer gun," Rufus said. "I don't want to kill anyone, but I might want to put somebody to sleep. You never know when you might need this," he said as he fondly stroked the small pistol.

Thomas laughed, "If you're going to a fire fight, maybe you should have something with authority. Not some water pistol." Everyone laughed.

Rufus smiled and said, "To each his own." He placed the tranquilizer pistol back in his waistband holster. "See y'all later," he said and left the safe house.

Rufus drove his aunt's 2010 Hyundai Accent to the coffee house. Before he left their Buckhead hideaway, Rufus sprayed the Georgia license tag with a reflective coating widely available on the Internet so that traffic cameras, red light cameras, crime cameras, and any other types of surveillance cameras would be unable to read the plate. All that would show up would be a reflective glare. Not even the A U of the Auburn University specialty license tag would show up. Rufus drove about fifteen miles over the speed limit, and that was still slower than the majority of cars and trucks on Atlanta's speed-tolerant I-285. Arriving at the coffee house, he said a prayer for safety for him, CD, and the clones. He released his seat belt, got out of the car, and started towards the coffee house.

"Hold it, buddy," a voice called out from behind him.

Rufus froze, then caught himself, paused, turned nonchalantly, and was face to face with two uniformed Fulton County policemen.

"Yes sir, officer?" Rufus politely asked.

"I don't want to give you a ticket, buddy, but you just parked in a tow away zone."

"Golly, officer, I didn't realize it was a tow away zone. I'll move it right now if you'll let me."

One of the officers responded, "Good idea. This time, no ticket. You can usually find parking on that side street," the officer said as he pointed to a street one block up the road. "Sorry the sign's hard to see at night. Have a nice day." The officers continued their walk down the street.

After finding a legal parking place on the side street that the officer had indicated, Rufus entered the coffee house, took a table, ordered a black coffee with a scone, and flipped open his laptop. On the laptop Rufus had everything ready to upload. He wanted to keep his time in the coffee house to a minimum. There were enough bearded whites and blacks in the coffee house that Rufus felt that he could easily blend in. He was already concerned that two policemen now had reason to remember him.

The coffee and scone came, and the waitress said, "These scones are the best around here. You probably already know that, but anyway, they're on special today. You get two for the price of one. You can't beat that deal."

"Great! Let me have two. Thanks for letting me know." Rufus handed her a five-dollar bill. "You keep the rest of it. Thank you." The change would amount to a substantial tip for the waitress.

The waitress didn't move from the table, "Some people have complained that the Wi-Fi signal today's a little sporadic. We've just put in a signal enhancer. But it might not be working right. Let me know if you have a problem."

Rufus really did not have time for a talkative waitress. "OK, thank you very much." He then deliberately looked like he was engrossed in whatever was on the screen of his laptop, hoping that the waitress would take the hint and move on. She didn't.

"Nice laptop," the waitress began.

Rufus cut her off, "Yeah, thank you. Hey, let me get this work done. I'm bidding, and the item closes in a few minutes, and I don't want to lose it."

The waitress looked disappointed in losing someone to converse with but said, "Sure, I understand. The last few minutes are what count. Well, good luck. What're you bidding on, anyway?" She asked. "Just kidding," the waitress added after Rufus gave her an unbelieving look, and she walked back to the counter and left Rufus alone.

Rufus then activated the virtual computer and clicked on UPLOAD to upload the clones' statement. The statement quickly uploaded, and within minutes the clones' existence would be the lead news story throughout the world. Rufus reviewed in his mind the contents of the statement as he packed up his laptop.

Newspersons and Internet prowlers were already reading the statement as Rufus was leaving the coffee house:

> There has been much speculation lately about whether clones of some of our founding fathers actually exist. Some of the speculation has been way off base, and some of it has been accurate. We are releasing this statement to confirm that indeed there are three of us so-called clones. One was generated from the DNA of Thomas Jefferson, one from Alexander Hamilton, and one from Benjamin Franklin. There are only three of us. We were created by the cloning process at three GeneVision facilities in California, Ohio, and the American island of St. John. We are all three in our twenties, and all three of us unconditionally love this great and compassionate country. We are, however, not willing to reveal our whereabouts at this time because it seems that there is a determined search underway by the federal government to find us and to muzzle us. Somehow

it seems that some persons in powerful positions in the government think we are in some way a threat to them. Nothing could be farther from the truth. Therefore, all we are doing with this statement is letting everyone know that we exist, that we love America beyond all words, that like all Americans we cherish our freedoms and way of life, and that we will come forth when it is clear that we will not be in danger from the government.

We could not decide whether to announce this next thing but feel that the public has a right to know. There was a fourth clone, and he was the clone of our first President, George Washington. Unfortunately last week he was on the plane that the government shot down. His death is a national tragedy. It was completely preventable. We do not know the details, but this sad incident demonstrates that there is indeed a mortal threat to each of us. Whether that is because we are clones or whether it is because of whom we are clones of, we have no way of knowing.

Finally, fellow Americans, we are just like many of you. We pray. We listen for God's responses to our prayers, whether they are whispers or whether they be shouts such as we see in the Psalms. We love God. He is first in our lives and in our hearts, and He commands us to love everyone — everyone with no exceptions — and to serve the truth. Indeed, Jesus came to testify to the truth. That is what we desperately want to do. We try to live our lives according to His plan and His purposes for us. We have all the emotions that you do. We have all the imperfections that many of you do. Like you, we have our weaknesses, we make mistakes, we do things we shouldn't do, and we fail to do things that we should do. If we were there talking to you in person, you would not know that we were produced by a slightly different biological process from that which produced you. Like you, we have hopes, fears, aspirations, and dreams. Right now our major dream is that we can come out into the open and tell you about the exciting observations we have about our great country.

God has clearly blessed this great country, and our constant prayer to Him is that He will not give up on America but will continue to bless and protect America.

The waitress had her back to Rufus as he quietly exited the coffee house. He walked quickly to his car and within two minutes was back on I-285 headed back towards Buckhead.

Chapter 73

Four minutes later, Joelle Lucado answered her private telephone on the first ring.

"Madame Director, you wanted to be completely updated." Louis Fogarassy's voice had an urgency and excitement in it that was uncharacteristic of him.

"Yes, go ahead," Joelle Lucado replied.

"G2 already has a hit on a coffee house in Atlanta for an Internet upload claiming to be from the clones! Our people are on the way now and should be there as we speak."

"Get it on my screen, Louis," Lucado snapped as she clicked on a large flat screen monitor on her office wall. The flat screen would receive real time data generated by Guardian Two as well as relevant information from her field agents in Atlanta. Without missing a beat, Joelle buzzed Fabian Miles.

Her assistant was in her office in less than thirty seconds.

"Fabian, get me the leader of this Atlanta operation," Lucado said, motioning to the screen.

"He's on the line now, Judge Lucado," Fabian said. "I've been watching the G2 process and called him as soon as they had a hit."

Lucado snatched up the phone, "This is the Director. Where are you now?"

The voice on the phone replied, "We're about a hundred yards from the coffee house. We have it surrounded but we're trying not to cause a stampede. There's a lot of people in there now."

Joelle spoke coldly, "Listen and listen closely. No one — no one — gets away. Take them dead or alive. You got that? No one gets away."

"Yes ma'am. Dead or alive," said the leader of the CIA team preparing to assault the coffee house.

The CIA agents had no way of knowing nor did Rufus have any way of knowing that this particular coffee house was a monthly meeting place for the Georgia First Militia, an extremist conservative group that favored secession from the United States and hated all things federal. That night the Georgia First Militia was having one of its meetings. Two bearded men rushed in from the kitchen, and one of them said with a note of panic, "We've got company. There's a bunch of fucking FBI pigs outside all covert-like, and they're headed this way." The two men had been watching the streets around the coffee house on monitors installed in the kitchen to protect this justifiably paranoid group from federal agents or anyone else surprising them during a meeting.

"How many?" a heavily tattooed, bearded man called out.

"There's got to be about twenty or thirty. There's a whole piss load of those bastards."

"I'm out of here," one of the militiamen shouted and ran through the kitchen to the rear door. Immediately there was a disorganized, mass exodus as many of the militiamen and women broke for the kitchen.

Just an instant later, an armored CIA agent jerked open the front door of the coffee house and shouted, "Federal agent! Everybody freeze! Nobody moves!" He got no further. A shot rang out, and the agent grunted and dropped. Immediately the CIA team launched three tear gas canisters into the coffee house. The four militiamen who were still inside began to cough violently, but given their hatred and fear of the government, the men of the Georgia First Militia if nothing else were prepared. The men quickly donned gas masks. Two other agents appeared at the door, and again the militiamen fired on them. One went down.

The other agent yelled to the leader of the CIA detachment, "They've got gas masks in there. We need the D." The reference was to D541, a nerve gas developed at Plum Island, New York, that the government had never before used inside of America's borders.

The CIA man in charge of this attack knew that they already had in custody most of those who had tried to escape out the rear of the coffee house. He remembered the clear command from Director Lucado, *No one gets away. Take them dead or alive. You got that? No one gets away.*

The CIA agents efficiently cordoned off the area. The leader used a megaphone, "You're in violation of Georgia and federal law. You've got one chance to drop your weapons and come out with your hands up. If you refuse, you will be killed."

The answer from inside was a barrage of gunfire aimed at the agents.

"Get the door!" the team leader ordered.

"Yes sir!" responded an agent who was holding a specialty rifle. A quick burst from the SSK .950-caliber JDJ destroyed the front door of the coffee house.

The CIA team leader then gave the order, "Everybody, masks on!" The agents all put on special issue gas masks. These masks, unlike those worn by the militiamen, had special seals and gaskets, which would protect them from the D541.

The team leader saw that everyone was ready, then ordered, "Hit 'em with the D!"

D541 would put anyone to sleep within ten seconds of breathing it. Two unique properties made this gas particularly valuable to the CIA. Regular gas masks were not effective against it because the gas could quickly penetrate the gasketing material used in most masks. Also, the gas would just as quickly dissipate and within a few minutes of using it, there would be no evidence in the environment that it had been used. Five canisters of D541 were fired through the hole that used to be the door to the coffee house.

"Those fuckers are gassing us!" Shouted one of the militiamen.

"It's coming through the mask. I can't breathe!" screamed a second militiaman.

Then a violent explosion gutted the inside of the coffee house. A crimson smoke plume but no flames rose ominously into the dark Atlanta sky.

"What the hell!" the CIA leader exclaimed.

The destruction of the coffee house appeared to be substantial.

"Get in there, and see if there are any survivors!" the leader ordered.

It took only a few minutes to see that there were four dead militiamen, some missing body parts. All were either still wearing gas masks or had obviously just ripped them off. There were also four dead employees lying in contorted positions behind the main counter.

Joelle Lucado and Fabian listened in shock over the open channel to what was going on in Atlanta. Both were stunned and anticipating the worst. Finally Lucado said quietly into the earpiece of the team leader, "What's the report?"

The disembodied voice came back from Atlanta. "We have at least eight dead people in that coffee house, Madame Director. We used the D541, and then there was an explosion. I think they set it off themselves."

"Send me pictures of the dead. Are they all men? How old are they?" Lucado asked.

"Six men and two women. They look to be in the twenties or thirties," the team leader replied. "Four apparently were employees at the coffee house, and the others were patrons. "Hold on just a minute, Madame Director." After a short pause in which he was obviously getting a report from one of his team, the team leader said, "Madame Director, it looks like we have 7 to 10 casualties, almost all of them male and in their twenties and thirties."

"Sequester the bodies. Make sure we have them." Lucado could hear sirens over the open channel. She continued, "Don't let the local cops or the state get the bodies. And send me the pictures right away." Lucado's tone was flat. She felt bone tired and began to wonder why she ever took the job of being the nation's chief spy mistress.

Chapter 74

It was after midnight when CD awakened to urgent banging on his bedroom door. "Yeah? What's going on?" he called out.

"You need to get out here and see this!" Ben called out. "The coffee house Rufus went to has been bombed. I think it happened right after Rufus was there. We just turned the TV on, and all the local channels are covering it."

CD jumped from bed and ran to the living room where everyone was quickly gathering. Rufus was already glued to the television and ignored the others. Everyone took their cues from him and watched silently as the announcer described the scene near the Perimeter Mall complex.

"So here is what we know and what we don't know," the announcer was saying. The split screen showed the announcer in the field and the lead anchor who was sitting in the station's newsroom. Bringing out a lead anchor in the middle of the night was never done casually. The media was already considering this to be anything but a routine occurrence. "This coffee house that you see behind me here is located one block from Perimeter Mall. That's in the Roswell section of Atlanta. Apparently there was some type of police raid on the coffeehouse. At least two agents were wounded, and we believe there may have been one fatality. At some point there was a large explosion from inside the coffee house, and as you can see the place was pretty much demolished. There's been no statement from the police yet so we don't know if anyone was still inside when the explosion occurred. I don't see how anyone could have survived the explosion from the looks of the destruction. Now we do have one eyewitness to whom we have spoken but who does not want to appear on camera. This person says that there were about twenty or thirty government agents involved in the raid. He says they weren't in state police uniforms. This eyewitness claims that they were federal agents. If they were in fact federal agents we would assume they were FBI. Our witness says that the agents fired tear gas into the building before the explosion and that they were all wearing gas masks."

"Bob," the anchor broke in. "Was this in fact an FBI operation? Or was it DEA? Do we know who conducted the raid? And do we know why?"

"We don't know at this time, and right now there doesn't seem to be much of a federal government presence here at all. The agents we see are from local police jurisdictions. Our report is that there were about twenty or thirty agents in the neighborhood who were part of the raid. Right now we can actually see only a few agents, and no spokesperson has come forward. We have learned that the coffee house is owned by an LM Enterprises, but all we have at this time is the name of the company. You can see the crime scene strips behind me. The Fulton County police are here and have kept everyone at a considerable distance from the coffee house. In a very unusual move, they've closed the air space above this area of Atlanta so that we can't get our news choppers close enough to get a good visual of the devastation."

The station anchor asked, "A lot about this occurrence is looking very unusual. I can't remember air space above a crime scene ever being closed to the media, except for 9/11. Do we have any idea of why the air space has been closed or what might have precipitated the raid?"

"We have no idea, and until we get a statement, it's all just going to be speculation, but, of course, in this new era that is what we journalists do. I should add that the only other time I can recall air space being closed to the media was that recent downing of the plane over Maryland, you know, the one ordered by President Ray. That and 9/11."

Rufus leaned forward and turned the volume down. "I was right there just a few minutes before they did this raid. It's like they knew I was there within minutes of my posting that thing on the Internet."

"Probably just coincidence, Rufus," Alex said. "We can't jump to conclusions. Let's stay with the facts. For example, did you see other people at the coffee house or other people who would have been of interest to the government?"

"Yeah, there were around fifteen people there, and I guess they looked like the normal coffee house collection," Rufus said. "Nothing stood out as unusual."

"Hold it," Thomas said. "It looks like they're going to have a statement."

Rufus turned the television volume up, and they listened to someone who appeared to be a spokesperson:

". . . and I was in charge of this operation. This was an operation conducted by a special task force composed of members of the FBI, the DEA, and several other agencies of the federal government in cooperation with agencies of the state of Georgia and the City of Atlanta. The government had intelligence that this coffee house was the headquarters for a multi-state drug ring and that substantial interstate shipments and transportation of illegal drugs were routinely planned at this location. We had a reliable tip that the ringleaders of that operation would all be at one place tonight, and we decided that this was the time to conduct a raid and shut down this illegal drug cartel. During the operation before we were able to enter the establishment, someone from the inside shot and killed one of my agents, and then within a few minutes more shots were fired, and another of my men was wounded. The members of the drug ring were obviously heavily armed. We fired tear gas into the building. It was a nonflammable tear gas and had nothing to do with the explosion, which occurred shortly after the shots which wounded our agent. The explosion was apparently caused by a device in the possession of the members of the drug ring and definitely not by anything we were using. We had no explosive devices of any kind on the scene, and we had no flammable gases of any kind on the scene. We will release the names of the killed and wounded agents later, after we have had a chance to notify their families. There were casualties inside the coffee house, but we do not have a definite count yet. All were killed by the explosion which they themselves set off and not by our use of force. I want to emphasize that the explosion was set off by the people inside the coffee house, not by anything we did. We were hoping to be able to apprehend everyone peacefully and bring them to justice, but their resort to violence and lethal force prevented that. That's all I have now. I'm not going to take any questions at this time."

Rufus turned the volume down. "It's too much of a coincidence. They knew I was there within minutes of my upload." Rufus looked intently at CD. "Do you think they have the capability of monitoring Internet traffic real-time enough to connect it with the clones?"

CD replied, "I've heard rumors of a program that exceeds the capabilities of Echelon, but I don't know anything about it. I've only heard rumors. But what I heard was that they're developing a capacity to monitor the content of all Internet traffic in a large region of cyberspace all simultaneously and that the software can adjust itself like artificial intelligence to sift out what the government is looking for more efficiently than anything we've ever had before."

Rufus responded gloomily, "If that's true, then how are we going to communicate without letting them know where we are?"

Ben spoke up, "That's not going to be a problem, gentlemen. While I was planning my escape from St. John, I thought I might have to communicate with various people, like Alex or Thomas. I knew that Alex and Thomas existed, or at least I was fairly sure. So I developed a means of setting up a cyber-energy grid which can exist parallel to us but which cannot be detected unless one has a key to the grid itself. Now, in that grid there are potentially thousands of virtual computers. You communicate with only one of those computers, and it in turn activates another virtual computer or two or three — it's all randomly determined — and those secondary computers do the heavy lifting. All of the virtual computers used in any particular project exist only for nanoseconds and after their task is completed, they cease to exist at all. Since a virtual computer has no physical existence, once its virtual function terminates, it is untraceable and cannot be located. It's like it never existed in the first place."

"So it sounds like a super version of the virtual computer Rufus just used, right?" CD asked.

"Yes and no," Ben responded. "What I am talking about exists in an energy dimension that the Higgs Boson particle pretty much proves exists all around us. But the virtual computer Rufus used existed somewhere in cyberspace, and the NSA can monitor and penetrate cyberspace. I seriously doubt they have utilized the new non-baryonic principles of physics that I have used."

Everyone just stared at Ben. Finally Thomas, clearly awed, said, "He is truly Benjamin Franklin. Who else could have created whatever it is that he just described?"

"Amazing!" Alex whispered.

"How do you communicate with it?" CD asked. "Don't you have to use the Internet?"

"Yes, sure you use the Internet," Ben replied. "You just use coded language that the target virtual computer knows. To anyone reading it, it just looks like regular Facebook tripe. The government's snooping programs will just skip over it. It's actually encryption. It's called VisiCryption. It does not look like encryption. It looks like regular English. Since it does not look like encryption, the government won't give it a second glance. It's pretty much failsafe."

"Can you get us onto the main social media sites?" Thomas asked.

"Yes, I'll do that," Ben responded. "But it'll take a little coding. I'll get it done as soon as I can. Now, my system works for one-way communications, posting statements, stuff like that. I don't yet have it ready for real-time, conversational texting back and forth."

"What about the various types of instant messaging and routine social media stuff?" Alex asked.

"We shouldn't use any of that stuff. My system cannot handle those ways of communicating without a lot of coding that I don't have time to do. There's too much danger that the NSA can rather easily monitor and back-trace that stuff. Because of certain technical aspects of how messaging works, it would carry identifiers of our locations that my grid-embedded, virtual computer might not be able to eliminate."

Rufus frowned. "I like the sound of it, and if your system works, Ben, then we'll be able to communicate freely, but do you know beyond the shadow of a doubt that your system will actually work?"

Ben smiled confidently. "It works."

Rufus nodded. "OK, good, but I think our immediate problem is that they know we're in Atlanta. They'll be pulling out all the stops to find us. By now, they probably know what I look like because there were two policemen at the coffee house who stopped me, and we talked briefly. Obviously, the federal government will get their statements."

"I hear you, Roof," CD said. "I think it's time we leave Atlanta."

"And go where?" Alex asked.

There was a soft knock on the front door, and it was followed by six staccato knocks. Everyone looked alarmed. Everyone except CD.

CD smiled, "Relax everybody." As CD walked into the hallway and towards the front door, Rufus pulled out his cell phone and looked at the image on his security cam app. He just smiled and said softly, 'CD, you still have the touch. Always a step or two ahead."

The three clones just stared uncomprehendingly at Rufus.

CD walked into the room holding the hand of a slim, tall woman with black hair tied into a tight French twist, blue eyes, and with a smile on her face. "So these are the clones," she said matter of factly as she placed her laptop bag on a nearby end table.

"Everyone, I want you to meet my wife, Olive."

"Wow," Benjamin Franklin said with some enthusiasm, giving the very attractive woman a full-length appraisal. "I'm indeed honored and charmed, Madame."

Thomas quickly said, "Please excuse him, Mrs. CD. He has a lecherous streak."

Olive continued to look at Ben and said, "Then there can be no doubt. You're Benjamin Franklin. Right?"

"Indeed, Madame." Ben bowed slightly.

Olive had an amused look on her face, then looked at Thomas and said, "And you're Thomas Jefferson." It was a statement, not a question. She continued, "And you," she said as she shifted her gaze to Alex, "are Alexander Hamilton. Gentlemen, it is I who am honored and privileged."

"Are you positive that you weren't followed?" CD looked at Olive inquiringly.

"Yes I was followed at first, but I got rid of them. They were obviously not very experienced."

"How did you shake them?" Rufus asked.

"They're now following Dooky," Olive said with a smile as she shed the black French twist to reveal luxurious blonde hair. She then expertly took out the blue contacts to reveal her light green eyes. Now a totally different looking woman stood before them.

"Wow," Ben said in admiration. "You're even more stunning and devious than I thought."

Thomas and Alex just laughed. "Dude," Alex muttered.

"Dooky is Olive's sister. They're not twins but they look enough alike that it's a dependable way to shake a tail," CD explained. "Olive, did you bring anything?"

"I brought myself, darling. Isn't that enough?" She gave CD a knowing look.

CD simultaneously smiled and grimaced. "Did you bring anything else?"

"I did. My wisdom and my contacts, darling. You asked me to think through whether we're safe here in Atlanta. In a word, we aren't. Atlanta's no longer a feasible base. I've got a friend who can fly us to a small town in Louisiana where we can set up shop. It's a place that they would never think of, and it should be as safe as just about any place I know about. It's Natchitoches, Louisiana. When I realized that Atlanta is ground zero for the feds, I asked a friend of mine with a private plane to fly us to Natchitoches. She readily agreed, and we should pack up and head to their private airfield. It's about 10 miles outside the Perimeter Road."

"That sounds like a mighty big change in plans." Alex's tone showed doubts.

"It sounds plausible, Olive, but how do we get to this private airfield?" CD asked the question that everyone was thinking.

"Honey, I have taken the liberty of reserving a garbage truck that can transport us. We can all fit inside, and there's no way the feds are going to search the contents of a garbage truck."

"Perfect," Ben said. "Let's do it."

"OK, I agree," Alex quickly said. "Atlanta's no longer safe, and it's only a matter of time before they find us if we stay here."

"The sooner, the better," Thomas said.

"I like it, CD said. "Olive, how soon can we get that garbage truck to take us out of here?"

"I can give the word, and we can be out of here in less than an hour. I'll go ahead and alert our pilot. I think you will all like her," Olive said as she glanced at Thomas, then quickly moved her gaze to the others in the room.

————

The statement from the White House in response to the clones' announcement on the Internet that they indeed did exist and were on the run from the government was terse:

> "We now have definitive information from GeneVision, a company with several facilities in the United States dedicated to human cloning, that indeed several human clones have been created. That company is now under the control of federal

authorities following this flagrant violation of federal law and our long-standing national commitment that we would refrain from human cloning. However, in no way is the United States government in pursuit of these clones. Rather we welcome them, and we encourage them to come into the public arena at whatever time they think is most appropriate. We offer them full protection from those who might attempt to exploit or persecute them. If they are indeed clones of some of our founding fathers, we honor them for their heritage. At the same time, we note that they are full human beings in their own right and are not just copies of people who lived over two hundred years ago. They have violated no laws. Thus, we welcome them and will do everything possible to guarantee them life, liberty, and the ability to pursue happiness, the same inalienable rights that we all hold dear."

The White House spokesperson read the statement and did not take any questions. Simultaneously with the release of the statement, the Justice Department released a voluminous report on GeneVision's operations as far as the government had been able to piece them together. The DOJ report included a full discussion of the role of Marina Novokatnaia. A warrant was issued for her arrest, and the Justice Department applied to Interpol for assistance in locating and arresting her.

While this was happening, the President had yet another meeting with Joelle Lucado and Attorney General Trentini. "You know, Joelle, for a couple of decades, Presidents have been reluctant to use this power. Taking out someone, especially someone of Novokata's stature, and using our clandestine assets in such a way is not only dangerous to our people on the ground, but the Russians may well retaliate. As we all know, they don't hesitate to kill people in the West."

"Her name is Novokatnaia, Mr. President, and yes, it's a major step, but I don't see that we have a lot of alternatives." Joelle paused, looked at her hands, and then continued. "Novokatnaia has the knowledge herself, and she's linked to the people and the knowhow that could lead to the Russians initiating their own cloning program."

"If they're not already doing it," the President interjected. "And, Joelle, I know her fucking name."

"Well, we don't have any indication that they are already cloning."

"But now that she's shown who she really is, they absolutely will clone. You can be sure of it. That's just what we need — the Russians on a cloning binge. It's no telling where that could lead. Lenin, Stalin, Beria, another Putin, evil unleashed again."

"They are the real deplorables," TT said. "It was Hillary Clinton who first used that phrase."

Lucado said firmly, "Mr. President, we need to go ahead and take her out. There's no alternative."

"Take Hillary out? You can't be serious, Joelle."

"No, Mr. President. Novokatnaia. We should take out Novokatnaia. And we need to do it ASAP, before they get everything from her. They probably anticipate that we'll try for her so they're probably debriefing her as fast as they can. We can get to her. I have assets in place that can get to her, but after this kill, those people will have to be withdrawn. Then we'll be half blind for a while to what's going on inside the Kremlin. But getting rid of Novokatnaia is worth it."

"Half blind?" President Ray asked. "*Half?*"

"You don't need the details, Mr. President," Lucado said.

"I don't want the names of the people. Just tell me what you mean by 'half blind.'"

"We have a number of people close to the top Kremlin leaders. It'll take some time to set up the job on Novokatnaia. Once done, we'll have to get our people out of Russia within a couple of hours. That'll leave us with only several people left in low profile positions in the Kremlin. And realistically, there'll be a scramble in the Kremlin to vet everyone there so even those few assets might be in some danger."

"In short," the President summarized, "We'll cut down the number of spies we have in the Kremlin to just a few people whereas right now we have more than a few people there?"

"That's right," Lucado said.

"TT?" The President waited for the Attorney General to give his approval.

"It's a go, Mr. President. I guess we have to do it. It's a national security imperative to keep the Russians from cloning Stalin, Putin, and the others. There's no viable alternative," Trentini said flatly.

"You don't sound like you like the idea, TT," the President said with a question in his voice.

"I don't exactly like it, Mr. President. I fear it could result in developments that we can't foresee or control. But it's legal, and we need to do it," TT responded.

"Well, I'm signing the order. It's important enough to take that bitch out not only to stop the spread of the technology, and it might not even do that, but also to send the Rooskies a message that they'd better not start a human cloning program."

"They probably fear a cloning gap, Mr. President," Lucado said with a smirk.

"This is no time for attempted humor," The President snapped.

"That wasn't a joke, Mr. President. They'll want to make sure that their cloning technology is superior to ours, and with Novokatnaia in their clutches, they are already ahead of us," Lucado responded.

"We'll go ahead with it," The President said as he took his seat behind the large presidential desk and quickly scanned the single page in front of him. The title on the page was "Presidential Finding and Authorization for Special Procedures." The document stated in cold legalize that Marina Novokatnaia was a "compelling, substantial, and immediate danger to the United States" and authorized certain government agencies to eliminate her. The President signed the document in duplicate and handed both copies to Attorney General Trentini.

"There. It's done," President Ray said.

"These copies will never see the light of day, Mr. President," TT said solemnly.

With no further conversation, Trentini and Lucado left the Oval Office.

The President turned and walked to the window overlooking the lawn where decades before President Eisenhower had honed his putting skills. *Oh, for the bliss and serenity of those days,* thought President Ray.

As Trentini and Lucado left the confines of the White House, Lucado smiled as she turned to face TT. "We've started the search, TT. I'm hoping we'll have those clones in hand in a day or two and maybe we can get this whole thing under some control."

TT looked directly at Lucado, "Joelle, we're going down a dark, dark road, and I don't think for a minute that bringing those clones in will get this thing under control. We can't just kill them. We can't kill everyone. First this George Washington clone. Now Novokatnaia. Next, the other clones? This is becoming an America that I don't know."

"Very dramatic, Trentini. We do what we have to do, and it's not always pleasant," Lucado said caustically. She turned quickly, walked the final steps to her waiting car, leaving Trentini standing alone. TT just stared after Lucado, wondering whether she was just as devoid of scruples as the President seemed to be. He walked to his own car, got in, and said to his driver, "Take me to the Vice President's home, Robby, but don't go too fast. I need some thinking time."

"Yes sir," said TT's driver. He could always discern when not to engage the Attorney General in small talk. Those times were becoming more and more frequent. He put the 90-inch Lincoln limousine into gear and slowly pulled away from the White House.

Hours before the government's report on GeneVision was released, under CIA direction, the CIA and the FBI had secretly begun Operation Copycat, the largest joint search and arrest operation in American history and the first mass drone search. The original CIA-FBI plan had called for the epicenter of Operation Copycat to be Atlanta, Georgia, but Lucado had argued that the clones would not use air travel to get out of Atlanta but instead would try to change their base of operations to some other nearby city. Consequently, hundreds of government drones were targeting Charlotte, Birmingham, Orlando, Jacksonville, and New Orleans. Luckily for the clones, this strategic decision substantially reduced the CIA-FBI presence in Atlanta.

Chapter 75

As the clone entourage was hurriedly preparing to escape their Atlanta safe house, Alex's voice yelled from the living room, "Here we go again. The fucking — oh, sorry, Olive — White House has put out another statement."

They all gathered around the large flat screen and listened to the coverage from CNN International:

> With much fanfare, the White House today announced the broad outlines of its radical proposal to institute a national sales tax as a means ultimately to lower personal income taxes and eliminate chronic deficits. Though the detailed bill was given to the President's Democratic colleagues in the Congress, it has not yet been released to the general public or even to the opposition party. And the new proposal is coupled with a plan to nationalize the nation's insurance industry. In all, the combined proposal reportedly numbers over three thousand pages. The new tax will be combined with some ambitious spending cuts in foreign aid and cuts in the defense budget. It is expected that the fight over the new tax and insurance package will be long and bitter. The Republican opponents of the proposal are already labeling the tax as 'big government gone wild' and 'woke socialism'. The Democratic sponsors of the bill in the Congress have already justified the proposal as a means of advancing social justice and recognizing the virtues of diversity. They also assert that the money raised by the new tax will fund an aggressive climate rehabilitation program.

So went the coverage of the President's new proposal. The group stared at the television screen dumbfounded.

Alexander Hamilton's face reddened, "Holy Shit!" he exclaimed.

Thomas quickly said, "Gentlemen, there's a lady present so let's please guard against excesses of expression."

Alex immediately and energetically launched into a long analysis of the economic danger of the new tax and concluded with an animated condemnation. "Are these people deliberately trying to bring down America? This is echoes of Biden's stuff. Are these people deliberately sabotaging America or are they just so misguided that they actually don't understand the effects of what they are advocating? This country was at its most prosperous when our taxes were at a minimum. Then the great decrease in American prosperity began with the creation of real estate taxes, death taxes, state sales taxes, all kinds of excise taxes, school taxes, sin taxes, gasoline taxes, social security taxes, Maryland even had a rain tax — can you believe it! — and of course, the unconstitutional federal income tax, telephone usage taxes, worker's compensation taxes, Medicare taxes, Obamacare taxes, hidden, of course, under other taxes, and on and on and on. This national sales tax will divert huge amounts of money from the private sector into the governmental sector. It will take on the aura of an ever-giving fountain of cash, a license and invitation to Congress and the President to spend, spend, spend. There is not a chance in hell that deficits will be reduced. Deficits result not from a lack of money but from a lack of will, a lack of integrity, and a lack of accountability. Congress continually demonstrates that it lacks all three. That's why their approval rating is chronically in the toilet. Gentlemen, Congress is the problem. Our immediate problem as clones may be the President, but the nation's systemic problem is clearly Congress.

It has shamelessly abdicated its constitutional role in the checks and balances system. It confuses investigations with policy-making. The latter excites the media, and therein lies Congress's lusts. Our Congresspersons and Senators are shamelessly and selfishly dedicated to their own reelection and don't even deign to genuflect to the national interest."

Thomas said in a monotone, "It's been like that for decades. Congress greedily on the take from big money unions and big money business and American oligarchs. Their priority is their own reelection, not the national interest or their institutional obligations. They have abandoned any semblance of loyalty to the institution of Congress. And it's not just the Democrats. Don't forget how once it became clear that Biden's 2022 climate bill was going to pass in the Senate with what's her name's tie breaking vote how the Republicans, preaching about the vice of government spending, hid shiploads of their own expensive pork inside of Biden's climate bill."

Ben said with an empty smile, "Why, Alex, there's more. Don't forget all the surtaxes, surcharges, gross receipts taxes, marijuana taxes, alternative minimum income taxes, and capital gains taxes. I could go on and on and on, too. And fees coming out of the wazoo!"

Thomas moaned, in visible anguish. "I love this country more than I can tell you. Somehow it comes from within me. And I despair. I guess I don't have much hope when I watch Congress. They are basically grasping aggrandizers on the take, and —"

"And," Ben interrupted, "the Supreme Court has opened the floodgates of money by allowing corporate interests and unions to more easily buy Congresspersons and Senators."

"You mean the *Citizens United* decision? What a short-sighted, anti-America decision by out-of-touch elitists!" Alex's tone was bitter and sad.

"And they ruled term limits unconstitutional, and without term limits there is even less hope," Thomas said. "And that ruling was constitutionally flawed."

"Don't they realize that when such a high percentage of the GDP goes to government programs that prosperity is stifled, innovation is discouraged, and private initiative is depressed? Don't they understand this at all?" Alex exclaimed, his face reddened with anger.

Rufus and CD looked at each other. CD gave Rufus a slight nod.

"How much of the GDP has now been diverted?" Ben asked.

Alex quickly answered, "If you mean, what percentage of the GDP has been diverted into government spending, official reports say it is around 45%. That's federal spending and does not include the states. If you add the states, the figure has to be way over 50%, probably over 60%, which puts us ahead of the Scandinavian socialist countries. And today, the national debt is probably above 115% of the GDP."

Thomas interjected, "Then doesn't it make sense to have a national sales tax to make some inroad on the debt?"

Alex replied, "Not with the result being a decrease in private initiative, innovation, prosperity, and an increase in both jobs and business flowing out to the Pacific Rim. Not with the rise of China's economy. It would make sense only if it supplanted the federal income tax and was combined with completely reprioritized spending. For example, entitlements like Medicare, Social Security, federal health insurance programs, have got to be re-thought. Sadly, Medicaid too. There's no option if the country is to gain even a scintilla of economic credibility."

"What about the insurance part of the plan?" Olive asked. "You haven't mentioned that."

Alex quickly responded, "That one's a no-brainer. Nationalizing insurance will shift an enormous amount of business from the private sector to the governmental sector. The result? Even more taxes and the elimination of private business. That's clearly bad for the country."

Ben interjected, "And if insurance is nationalized, that inevitably means a national health system. And as far as health insurance itself is concerned, everyone knows that single payer systems result in drastically increased wait times for medical attention and also in much longer times to get new drugs to market."

"And right to life decisions and things like hospice will be in the hands of government bureaucrats, not parents, not families, and not doctors," Alex added. "Just look at the U.K."

Thomas joined in, "And the actual coverage will be worse and the service will be substandard. Even though private insurance companies are parasites on society — even worse than the lawyers — at least competition keeps them from being totally out of control. And the answer is careful criminal regulation of insurance practices and an ombudsman structure to at least put some restraints on insurance companies' malpractice."

Rufus and CD glanced quietly at each other. CD nodded imperceptibly, and Rufus said, "All true, but what can we do about it? Or more directly, what can Thomas Jefferson, Alexander Hamilton, and Benjamin Franklin do about it?"

"I know exactly what you are hinting at, Rufus," Alex quickly said.

"I didn't say a word," Rufus said in mock innocence.

They all laughed.

"Gentlemen," Ben said. "I suggest humbly that we relax our pace and take this one step at a time. Why are we clones here — living — at this particular time? I believe that it is no accident that we're here, right now, at this particular time and place. What earthly purpose or purposes are we to serve? Are we willing to become the targets of enormous acrimony with our lives clearly at issue?"

Alex took up the discussion again, "You are suggesting that the fight is now and that no one's better equipped to join the fight than us because of who we are." It was a statement, not a question. Alex continued, "And that the government will do everything in its power to find us and silence us."

"Not exactly." Benjamin Franklin responded, frowning and smiling at the same time. "I'm suggesting something fundamentally different. I'm suggesting that we aren't present at this moment in time simply by cosmic accident. Rather, the deliberate hand of Providence is all over this. We should attune our actions and thoughts not to the policies, the dangers, the threats, and all of that. Instead, gentlemen, we should attach ourselves immovably to the cause of Truth. Truth. God's purpose for putting us on the scene now, today, is to bring this nation back into line with Truth — political truth and God's truth. We have no choice but to act. Else we turn our backs on God Himself!" Ben's tone had become emphatic. "And that I refuse with all of my being to even consider."

Everyone in the room sat perfectly still. Some historians had painted Benjamin Franklin as the least spiritual, or at a minimum the least Christian of the prominent framers, yet here was his genetic replica resolutely aligning himself side by side with God Himself.

"Yes," Ben continued. "I know this might surprise some of you since the book on me — or should I say, the first me -—is that I had little use for God. Nothing could be farther from the truth. As my biological father said, 'I believe in one God, Creator of the Universe. That he governs it by his Providence. That he ought to be worshipped. That the most acceptable Service we render to him is doing good to his other Children.' The first Benjamin Franklin said that, and I stand by it. I just never wore my Christian credentials on my outer garments. Outer garments are but plumage cloaking the heart itself. Outer garments conceal; they don't reveal. My love for God, in my first time around was between my Creator and me. But today's a new era, and things are different. Maybe I'll have to be a little more overt this time around. Just as the hand of Providence was all over our Revolution two hundred plus years ago, His hand covers our actions today. As I said back then, God is omnipotent, omnipresent, and beneficent. Today, I'm thankful that we're willing to be led by His mighty, blessed hand!"

"Let's be objective," Thomas Jefferson said. "How do we know that, objectively speaking, ours is indeed the cause of Truth? We just have a different opinion of what kind of nation is better. Sweden, Norway, England, and some other quite civilized nations employ a lot of governmental controls, and those nations are still free and vibrant."

Alex answered, "One way we know that we proceed under the mantle of Truth is by looking at the people who oppose us. Specifically, look at Congress. That collection of scoundrels repeatedly promises and espouses one thing then delivers something else completely. They repeatedly betray Truth and shamelessly prove themselves as untrustworthy to their very core! They rail against deficits yet without fail create them, ever larger and larger. Our fortune is that those people have been brought together so that we can easily identify them. The misfortune is that the American people continue to allow them to exercise power over the country."

Ben then said, "That might be a little extreme, Alex. It's all a question of discernment. There's a more reliable way to discern that ours is the cause of truth and that the government is a collectivity of deception and un-truth. Look at their very deeds. They shot down an unarmed and innocent airplane. In doing that, they knowingly killed -—murdered -—the second George Washington. George Washington! Gentlemen, we all realize how much our cause would be strengthened were the great man himself here with us! Would that he were! They have spread blatant falsehoods and lies about us in public statements. They attempted to silence us at the Florida church service and were apparently prepared to kill us. They arrested a completely innocent and harmless tourist on the beach in Florida because they thought he was one of us, and the way I understand the law of arrest, the government cannot just arrest someone unless it has probable cause of criminality. That poor young man had done nothing criminal."

"Other than smoke weed." Alex interjected. "Correction. In Florida that's not criminal."

Ben continued, "They committed a massacre at the coffee house in Atlanta. They routinely detain people for long periods of time without charges and without trial, like the Guantanamo holding station and black sites in Eastern Europe. They seize people and sneak them out of the country and put them in foreign prisons where our judiciary cannot rescue them, where they're beyond salvage. They routinely listen to telephone conversations, intercept text messages, and monitor Internet traffic. But all of that, gentlemen, is not the worst of it. On top of it all, they believe all of it is right and good and, thus, they feel that they are justified to lie about it. They routinely lie about all of it. What they're doing and what they propose to do are all dressed in lies and falsehoods. If they would simply level with the people, ironically they might find greater approval and respect. There's a very plausible case to be made that privacy in the era of terrorism has become obsolete, but they haven't bothered to make that case with even a hint of intellectual honesty. Their actions offer up only one conclusion about our President and our Congress. With several exceptions, they are irretrievably dishonest! Whether they're running for office or already in office, lies are their hallmark. The lies range from a secret plan to end the Vietnam War to read my lips to you can keep your insurance to a YouTube video caused the deaths of the four Americans in Libya to not a dime of ObamaCare will go to abortions, and don't forget all the lies from Fauci, Trump, and Biden, and various state governors about the pandemic. I could go on and on, but here's the point. Dishonesty and truth do not cohabit! Dishonesty and truth do not coexist. That's how I know that theirs is not the side of truth and that ours is."

"Like the national sales tax, you name it," Thomas said.

Ben continued, "I could go on."

"And probably will," Alex quickly added.

Ben did. "The list of abuses is long and extends over decades. I submit that these actions bespeak evil. It isn't merely the policies that wreck our beloved nation. It's the stark dishonesty in which those policies are conceived and sold to the public. I submit that these actions establish a pattern of abuse and are an assault on truth itself. Deception and truth are incompatible. Congress and recent Presidents have aligned themselves squarely and decisively on the side of deception. The so-called "leaders" of both parties wallow in in-your-face duplicity and dishonesty. Just look at the 2016 campaigns of Hillary Clinton and Donald Trump. And look at the embarrassing choice of Biden and

Trump in the 2020 election. Truly a national disgrace! One clearly incompetent and the other unstable, and both steeped in deception and distortion. Yes, gentlemen, I submit that this is a war between Truth and Deception, and God has placed us here at this time and in this place to fight for Truth. 'On such a full sea are we now afloat, and we must take the tide as it serves —'"

"'Or lose our ventures,'" Thomas interrupted. "Brutus."

They all reflected for some moments, and then CD said, "I agree with your take on it, Ben, and that means we need to act with some dispatch."

Olive said, "'And now it springs forth; do you not perceive it?'"

"Isaiah," Thomas said.

"Yes, the time to come out swinging is now," Ben said. "Truth brooks no lethargy."

Alex then surprised them all. "I have drafted a statement that we can disseminate. It basically puts into writing what we have just been saying. I have already signed it. See what you think," Alex said as he dropped the draft into each of their cell phones.

They all read silently, the Thomas said enthusiastically, "I like it. It's perfect. Let's put it out there."

"Yes, but I have one addition," Ben said. "We should all sign it, not just Alex."

They all quickly agreed, and Ben and Thomas signed the statement.

"I hate to break this up, gentlemen, but our limousine's here. Time to go," Olive said with authority. "I suggest that we simply stop at a hotel on the way to our plane, use the hotel's business facility and launch the statement to the virtual computer from the hotel. They surely won't mount a mass assault on a hotel, and they'll never look a garbage truck."

Within minutes, they were all treated to the rear loader of a battered, green sanitation truck and were cozily ensconced inside the refuse containment unit. Within minutes, they had stopped at a large, five-star hotel and successfully publicized the clones' latest statement condemning the Administration's national sales tax and insurance proposals.

Within minutes, the clones' statement and the question of their very authenticity was fast creating a public firestorm. The lead-in for most of the cable coverage of the statement was a visual of Hamilton's signature at the bottom of the statement. Handwriting experts quickly compared the signature to the original Hamilton's signature and found striking similarities. Thomas's and Ben's signatures were also almost identical to the signatures from the original Thomas Jefferson and Benjamin Franklin. Not only the signatures themselves but also the clones' condemning of Congress set off a media frenzy unlike any other media excess in recent history. The White House, woke media institutions, and liberals in Congress all assailed the statement as "Right Wing Trash." More conservative members of the political parties and conservative news outlets engaged in self-serving and superficial analyses, validating yet again the clones' opinion that the news media are for the most part primarily entertainment in the pursuit of profit, not at all seeking analysis in the pursuit of truth.

In addition to its "Right Wing Trash" statement, the White House also issued a more temperate call for the clones to explain in "budgetary detail" specifically what they would change about the Administration's domestic agenda. The White House also renewed its call for the clones to "come into the open, to stop hiding, but to come to Washington and join in this important public debate in person."

The White House statement continued, "We will absolutely guarantee the safety of the clones and have asked two Justices of the Supreme Court and leaders of both parties to serve as protective escorts for the clones if they'll come into the open." Addressing the clones directly, the White House spokesperson had said, "You must understand that as long as you're hidden, our public debate cannot really move forward. No one knows whether you're real or whether you're just someone cleverly playing tricks on the American public. Are you real or is this all some grand media stunt? Therefore, the President asks you to please join him in trying to fix what's broken about our American system so in unity we can go forward. The President personally guarantees your safety and proper reception in Washington and asks for an open discussion so that we can together create a unity agenda."

———

The discussion in the confines of the garbage truck was as dynamic as it had been anywhere else. After reading the White House statement, Rufus's voice echoed in the metal containment vessel. "We need to respond. They're willing to talk, to have a dialogue. Isn't that progress?"

"If they're serious. And that's a big *if*." Alex sounded doubtful.

"A unity agenda! We've heard that before, and it was a lie then. Do they really expect anyone to believe it now? Are they that much out of touch?" Ben shook his head in disgust.

"That last part of the President's statement sounds like it could be an honest desire to have private conversation in person." Thomas continued. "But at the same time, that part of their statement sounded very strange to me."

"But how else can they invite us to private conversations?" Alex asked.

"Let's give it a day," CD suggested. "Then we'll have a better feel and some perspective. And let's remember that the public, not the government, is our audience."

They all nodded in agreement.

Chapter 76

The President's late afternoon briefing on the clones involved CIA Director Lucado, Attorney General Trentini, Chief of Staff Lee Brown, and surprisingly the Vice President. The President began the briefing. "We don't need to go over everything. And I surely don't want to talk about their semi-fascist statements. Just tell me if we're any closer to finding them."

Lucado answered, "No, Mr. President, but your strategy to flush them out should work. I think that in a couple of days we should be able to locate them."

"Do we even know if they're in this country? Have they conceivably left the country?" The President asked.

"Mr. President," Lucado responded, "We can't say right now, but I assure you that if they release a few more statements we'll have them."

"Then, let's push that dialogue approach. They'll have to respond," the President replied testily.

"Mr. President, on the policy front, we need to respond vigorously and connect them with the fringe right wing." Lee Brown was pushing for an all-out attack on the clones instead of a more moderate White House approach.

"Let's hold off on that, Lee," the President said with some finality. "My objective is to get them, not to debate them. To get them we need to make them use the Internet to release more statements. Let's just make them talk. If they talk, we'll know exactly where they are. Right, Joelle?"

"Yes, basically," Lucado hedged.

"Agreed, Mr. President," Lee responded. "But policy statements will make them respond. And the public might be tempted to buy what they're saying unless we shoot it all down."

The President responded with some impatience creeping into his voice. "I hear you, Lee, but now's not the time for that. Here it is, everybody. We drill it home that they've got to come in before we can talk policy. We don't even know who they are. This could be some huge hoax. Before we talk policy with somebody claiming to be Alexander Hamilton's twin, we need to know just exactly who it is. So no policy talk. Just 'come in' talk. Clear?" The President looked at each person for assent.

Each nodded in agreement.

"Vice President Armstrong? You haven't said a word. Most unusual. Are you in agreement? *Complete* agreement?" The President clearly wanted a verbal answer from the Vice President.

After some hesitation, the Vice President said, "Mr. President, you're the President. Not me. I follow your orders. If apprehending the clones is the policy, that's the policy."

The President, clearly irritated, spoke slowly, enunciating each word distinctly. "Are — you — in — complete — agreement — Mr. — Vice — President?"

Without hesitation, Royster Armstrong gave the response that he had prepared much earlier in anticipation of that very question. "No, Mr. President. I don't agree that that policy is the wisest or proper course of action. I favor an honest dialogue, not a trick or a ruse just to 'get them,' to use your words. These people are potentially an historic development in the history of America, and we need to recognize that this instant in history could be a critical juncture for us. But Mr. President, I recognize, of course, that you, not I, set the policy for the Administration. I think the policy is dishonest and unwise. Given my views, I'll resign if you want me to."

The President exploded. "And blow the whole thing to hell by freely talking to the press? No way are you going to resign, Armstrong. And no public statements. You're a member of this

Administration, and you will adhere to our policy line. Do you agree to that? If you can't agree and if you intend to undermine our policy, given the national security implications of having these people on the loose, not knowing who they are or what havoc they'll create, your actions will be considered a threat to the nation's security and will be considered in breach of office. Do I make myself clear, Mr. Vice President?"

After an awkward hesitation, the Vice President replied, "Yes, Mr. President, no public statements and no resignation." The others in the room looked on, shocked and speechless. The President had essentially threatened to initiate impeachment proceedings against his own Vice President. Or worse.

The Vice President locked eyes with the President. The President could read nothing into the Vice President's words or his facial expression. On the other hand, Royster Armstrong very accurately saw in President Ray's eyes a ruthlessness that conveyed that the President would do whatever it took to bring the clones in and then to silence them and also to silence anyone who stood in the President's way. But Armstrong was not worried about impeachment at all. That would be too public. Ray would never risk it. The Vice President was instead worried more about what nonpublic actions President Ray might take to silence his own Vice President. If truth were to be known, Royster Armstrong actually favored "getting" the clones too, even silencing them, but he would have hidden his iron fist in a velvet glove. He saw President Ray as uncouthly just shaking an iron fist. Armstrong had no doubts about Ray's deep fear and desperation.

"Good. Then let's get it done." The President rose, and with a wide sweep of his hand, he royally dismissed his team.

Chapter 77

"Which Way America Indeed?" screamed the massive headlines on the front page of the *Wall Street Journal*. The *New York Times* went with "Clones Blast President, Congress," and the *Washington Post* used a five-inch headline "Clones Issue Extremist Challenge to Nation." The White House press secretary refused to discuss the clones statement because "there's no way of knowing who actually wrote that extremist nonsense and whether the author has any credibility whatsoever." But at the same time, the White House renewed its offer of safety and protection for the clones were they to come "out of hiding." Two hours later, the White House spokesperson in commenting on the national sales tax program as an aside said, "There are legitimate views about the national sales tax proposal. Deficit spending's killing our nation, and a national sales tax is essential if we want to reduce our deficit spending pattern. Incidentally, these hidden people claiming to be clones oppose the national sales tax. I noticed that they didn't propose anything themselves. They proposed nothing at all in the way of reducing deficit spending. As such, the statement is more of the same extremism and nonsense. It gives us nothing constructive, and we don't even know who really wrote it. But it sounds like the same old rubbish from the other party."

Chapter 78

As the clones made their way out of the bowels of the sanitation truck, they were met by a teenage boy who said, "Y'all need to wait in here," as he motioned to a nearby concrete building. "Omi's not ready for y'all to board the plane yet."

"Who is Omi? Alex asked.

"She's your pilot," the teenager said as he led them to the small building.

Once they were all inside, Alex surprised them. "I have another short, follow-up statement ready to go out. I wrote it a couple of days ago. I think we need to issue it, that is, if y'all agree."

"You've surely been busy," Thomas observed.

Everyone quickly read the statement. It was another hard-hitting condemnation of both parties long-standing tax-and-spend mentality. Part of the statement read as follows:

> To be specific, President Ray should abandon the idea of a national sales tax, abandon the idea of a government takeover of the insurance industry, and instead initiate serious discussions aimed at reigning in government spending.

> We are not optimistic that President Ray has the sufficient vision to do any of these things, but he does not bear even most of the blame. We think the problems are more structural and systemic in nature. The basic problems are two. First, there is the lack of spine in the Congress to rise above party, restrain the Executive, and embrace the traditional economic values of America, private initiative, and limited

government. Instead of allegiance to the institution of Congress and the protection of its position in the separation of powers system and loyalty to what is in the interest of the nation, most in Congress have allegiance to whoever and whatever will get them reelected, and their loyalty is to those entities that will fork over the money and cushion their lifestyles.

Second, there is the shift away from Congresspersons focusing on and representing their constituents and instead towards representing the policy interests of those who have shoveled money into the Congresspersons' reelection campaigns.

These two problems have to be addressed before America can pull itself away from its current trajectory towards economic collapse. But the public must remain aware that the Congress and the Presidency have a selfish motivation in NOT addressing these two problems.

Therefore, the first step to fixing the problems in our political system or even opening a meaningful dialogue between us and the government is that President Ray must resign. Under our Constitution, the Vice President will become the new President. President Ray is so corrupted in vision and so out of sync with what America stands for — both the reach and sanctity of our freedoms and the preeminence of the private sector — that he has neither the outlook nor the public trust to remain in office during this critical time. His disapproval ratings rival those of Nixon. His incompetency rivals that of Biden. His arrogance rivals that of Trump. His facile duplicity rivals that of Obama. Presidential abandonment of America's core values has accelerated unabated through every recent Administration. That sad trend must be reversed if America as we know it is to survive and prosper.

That leaves you, the American people. Only you can provide the fundamental changes that are needed. There comes a time in the life of a nation, when the people must demand changes. That time for America is now.

After reading the paper, CD asked the others, "Well?"

Thomas then said, "Launch it! And I love that it carries your signature, Alex."

"As soon as we're on the plane, let's send it, OK?" Thomas looked from one to the other. Their statement would become part of what would be known as The Second Federalist Papers.

Chapter 79

The reaction in the United States to the latest paper from the clones was immediate and intense. The pundits filled the complete ideological spectrum, but few were willing to argue with Hamilton's logic. Most of the pontificators of the media shied away from any deep discussion of the Second Federalist Papers and instead continued to hedge with the qualification no one knew who the writers in fact were. In true fashion, the media focused on the author of the paper rather than on its content. Hand-writing analysis confirmed again that the signature on the statement was "uncannily similar to the original Hamilton." Liberal media outlets, in keeping with their agendas, gave minimal and skeptical coverage to the Second Federalist Papers, and most discerning Americans relied on BBC or other such news outlets. Many Americans relied on various blogs and opinion outlets, ranging widely from rightist conspiratorial to woke elitism.

The White House was bombarded with requests and challenges for a response, but the Oval Office was uncharacteristically silent.

———

The office telephone of the Director of the CIA chirped, and Director Lucado answered it immediately. She listened, smiled, then hung up and buzzed her trusted Fabian Miles.

When he entered, she said with her first smile in days, "We have them. G2 has located them. They are in the Buckhead section of Atlanta. Our people will be there within minutes."

Miles responded, "Great! Now what happens?"

Without responding, Director Lucado called the President on the special line that had been set up for dealing with the clones affair. After she finished informing the President of the breakthrough, the President replied, "Great work, Joelle. That G2 program must really be something. Once you have those fucking clones, talk to Trentini. He's prepared a special place to keep them. Of course, keep them separated from each other. Great job, Joelle!" the President repeated and broke the connection.

After she had hung up the phone, Lucado grimaced. "What a micromanager," she muttered. She looked over at Miles. "Now we wait. Stay available, Fabian. Once we have them, we'll need to make some special arrangements."

"OK, Madame Director," Miles replied, then added, "Madame Director, what about TT? Do we really want him involved once we have the clones?"

"No way, Fabian. We'll keep them. This is a CIA operation, not a DOJ operation. If they get hold of the clones, they'll want a long investigation, evidence, a trial, due process, and all that bull shit. We absolutely won't go down that road."

"But the President," Fabian responded. "He wants Trentini involved?"

"Oh, TT will be involved all right. Just not right away. Just stay available, Fabian."

"No problem," Fabian replied and started to leave the office.

"Wait here, Fabian. We should hear from Atlanta within minutes. Our problems are about over, and with a little truth serum and a little creative interrogation, we'll find out who they really are and who's really behind them."

Lucado waited impatiently for a report from Atlanta. She expected that the clones would offer virtually no resistance and that she could easily put them in a CIA facility and proceed with the questioning. As she was planning the next steps, another of her special phones beeped. She immediately answered it, "Lucado here." She listened to the brief report from the Chief of Operations in Atlanta.

Director Lucado slammed down the phone and glared over her desk at Fabian Miles. "I'm getting just like Screamer, slamming down phones. This clone shit's causing me to unravel."

"So what's wrong, Madame Director?" Fabian asked.

"They got away. The team raided the address that G2 identified. No one was there, but they'd been there."

"Do we know for sure it was them?" Fabian asked.

"Not until we do the DNA analysis, but why else would people vanish and leave stuff in disarray? Anyway, they're taking DNA samples now.

"The President's going to hit the roof that we lost them."

"Yeah, he will, but he does that routinely anyway," Lucado sighed.

Chapter 80

It was 9 A.M. in Washington, D. C. In the Oval Office, President Ray, increasingly obsessed with the clones issue, had called together his top advisors yet again. A meeting featuring the top brass of the Administration so early in the day was a rarity for this President, but President Ray was now focusing on nothing but the clones. Nothing else mattered. A digital message from CIA Director Lucado had greeted the President at his 7:00 A.M. daily breakfast of sausage and sawmill gravy and three eggs over easy. The message was brief: "Major developments have occurred, and they are not favorable. I need to brief you in person ASAP." There were already rumors circulating through the morning talk shows of another major setback in the search for the clones, and a feeling of doom and desperation had taken root in President Ray. The latest statement from the clones had garnered surprising public support, and even some in the President's own party were treating the statements with respect and contemplation. Thus, the President had given the attendees only an hour's notice for this morning's "urgent" meeting.

As the principals were assembling in the Oval Office, Trentini, attempting to establish himself as a top dog in the Administration, quickly claimed the wing chair closest to the chair the President always took, but TT remained quiet and motionless. Secretary of State Cordero sat expressionless while FBI Director Fogg was consciously trying to project an air of detachment. A stickler for legality, Fogg was one of the President's least favorite people. Ray did not trust Fogg who was attempting to de-weaponize the FBI Director's office after years of abuse and corruption. President Ray resented that he could not control or manipulate Fogg.

Only Lucado among this group knew the devastating news that she was about to reveal. She was banking on her long-time friendship with President Ray to get her through this meeting without a presidential meltdown. As usual the President was keeping everyone waiting long enough to communicate that they were secondary, that he was primary. From the point of view of official position, the stark absence was the Vice President. The relationship between President Ray and Vice President Armstrong had become so caustic that for all practical purposes the Vice President no longer existed as an Administration official. Armstrong maintained to all who would listen that the President's animosity to him stemmed from Armstrong's being a person of high values whereas Ray was, in Armstrong's opinion, an amoral charlatan and a bully.

"What's going on, Joelle?" TT asked. "Do you have something that's going to make Screamer happy?"

"I think the President ought to hear it first," Lucado replied without looking up from her papers.

"Yes, I think I should hear it first." President Ray said as he strode into the room. He had obviously been listening to the conversation. Everyone in the room suspected that he had listening devices in the room just for the convenience of eavesdropping prior to meetings. It fit his pattern of assembling people in the Oval Office and making them wait for his late entrance.

As everyone began to stand, he magnanimously said, "Please sit. I hope everyone's doing well. I am. But I know we're all frustrated with this clones affair. We need some kind of breakthrough in communicating with them. We need to get their confidence, assure them of our good intentions."

Even from such an innocuous sounding introduction, no one in the room could mistake the President's disposition. He was clearly in one of his destructive moods. His demeanor was stiff, his voice was dangerously quiet, and in spite of his words, President Ray was clearly in the grip of stress and gloom.

Lucado tried to break in, "Mr. President, I—-"

"Hold on, Joelle. Let me clarify our policy. We need to work on earning enough of their trust that — "

"My God, Mr. President, will you please let me tell you what has just happened? You need to hear this." Lucado clipped her words and was visibly angry. Everyone in the room gaped at her in shock. They had never heard her like this, and especially toward the President.

The President appeared unable to react, then said, "Yes, I'm sorry, Joelle. I shouldn't have jumped the gun like that. I'm truly sorry. Please proceed." The President's words were apologetic, but his facial expression was stony.

"Mr. President, the short version's that we had the clones in our clutches, and they got away. They were in Atlanta. Our surveillance identified them to be at a certain address. Our people raided that address, and they were no longer there."

"So, someone was at one time there? Were the clones there?" President Ray asked.

"We don't know for sure, but I would say yes."

"Any dead Americans this time, Director Lucado?" There was no mistaking the menace in President Ray's voice.

"No, Mr. President."

"Aha!" the President interrupted. "This was an off-the-books operation. Right, Director Lucado?" the President asked. When the President used titles, his advisors knew to watch out.

"Yes, Mr. President."

"This whole thing reeks of amateurishness, Director Lucado! What makes you so sure that they were the clones? Were they the clones? Were they?" The President's irritation was now mixing with anger. He stared coldly at Joelle Lucado.

Lucado had known John Ray for some years. At one time she had thought he had the potential to be one of the great Presidents. But that estimation of Ray's possible destiny soured as she became more familiar with his inner character. Now, in this Oval Office encounter, she well knew where things were headed, and for the first time since she had been in the Administration, she simply did not care.

The President stood, paced, then turned to face Lucado who remained seated. "Now, let me make sure I understand all of this," he paused, then continued, "this *circumstantial* evidence, Director Lucado. In order to get these clones, these threats to our national security, we have killed an innocent teenager, caused a public massacre in Florida where you lost a lot of your own people, knew the clones were in Florida and missed them, demolished a business establishment in Atlanta killing a bunch of people, knew where the clones were in Atlanta and missed them yet again, and now once again have no idea who they are or where they are? Do I have this right, Director Lucado?" The President's tone had turned derisive.

Lucado could only respond meekly, "Mr. President, we've had setbacks, but the clones obviously have substantial outside help."

Everyone remained completely still. They awaited the explosion.

The President did not disappoint them. "Setbacks!" he shrieked, his fists clenched. "Setbacks! You've bungled this whole fucking thing from the beginning, Director Lucado. Under your watch, we've been made fools of. Under your watch, we've had our people killed. These fucking clones have issued statements mocking this government. Mocking *me*! Well, I won't stand for it. If you can't find them, *Director* Lucado, you're fired! You're fucking fired! I want you out of your office by the end of business today. Do you understand?"

No one in the room moved a muscle. Lucado began to say something but when she looked up again at President Ray, she held back. The President was visibly shaking, his face had turned red, and there was spittle on the corners of his mouth. He whirled around, took two steps, then whirled back and faced Joelle Lucado. "I asked you a question. Do you fucking understand?" The President gripped the back of a nearby wing chair. Everyone else remained frozen and stared at the President. His fingers were white. His hands were shaking. The purple veins in his neck stood out. Then the President clutched his chest. He took two steps, uttered something that sounded like "No!" and grasped the back of the wing chair. Before anyone could react to what was happening, the chair toppled over under the President's death grip, and President John Ray without another sound crumpled to the floor.

<h1 style="text-align:center">PART FOUR</h1>
<h1 style="text-align:center">Chapter 81</h1>

TT sprang out of his chair when President Ray collapsed. "Lucado!" He yelled as he rushed over to the President who was now lying full out on the floor of the Oval Office. "Get security in here, and get a medic!"

Cordero and Trentini knelt beside President Ray. Ray was already showing the still pallor of death. Lucado told the secret service to secure the office and the White House premises, to let no one in or out of the building.

FBI Director Fogg was on his personal cell phone. After several rings, it was answered on the other end. Not waiting for pleasantries, Fogg said, "Mr. Vice President. I'm in the Oval Office with some others. You need to get here as fast as you can. No delay at all. Something has happened to the President. Tell no one, no one at all, Mr. Vice President. The press can't know that we have a situation." He paused, obviously listening to something that Vice President Armstrong was saying. "That works. Make it as fast as you can."

The next thirty minutes were a blur of activity. The White House physician was on the scene in a matter of minutes and quickly ascertained that the President had apparently suffered a massive heart attack. He pronounced the President dead. Everyone quickly agreed that secrecy about what had happened was paramount. No word could leak out until the Vice President was in charge, and he would then call the shots. The Vice President was in the new gymnasium of the Pentagon where he routinely played badminton two mornings a week. This particular morning he was fortunate to be teaming up with Dean Kops, a young American athlete from California whom the Vice

President was sure could carry him to victory in the cutthroat doubles that was played at the Pentagon in spite of the fact that Kops could see out of only one eye.

"He should be here in another 5 or 10 minutes," Fogg announced to no one in particular. "He's taking a chopper."

The White House went into an unannounced news lock down. Though outward appearances were that the day was another usual day in the White House, the tension underneath the pretense was a mixture of fear, panic, anticipation, and lack of focus. Not surprisingly, of those who knew that the President was dead, none seemed emotionally distraught.

Those reporters already in the pressroom had no inkling of what was going on in the Oval Office. The only complication was how to take care of Premier Mi Dung of the People's Republic of China who was supposed to arrive with several aides at the White House at any moment for a personal morning meeting with President Ray. Secretary of State Cordero quickly dispatched several underlings to preside over the serving of an elaborate, time-consuming breakfast to Premier Dung and the showing of a long video in the hopes that the Chinese delegation while greedily consuming the delicacies would also eat up some time.

At that moment two physicians from Georgetown Hospital were ushered into the Oval Office to validate the President's death. They had been brought into the White House through the underground tunnel from the Old Executive Office Building. They quickly examined the President, and then one of them said, "The President is indeed dead." He turned to the resident White House physician, "We can counter-sign whatever needs to be signed." The three physicians quickly made some notations on the documents, and all three then signed, signifying the time and circumstances of death. One of the doctors said, "We'll have to get a coroner in here."

"In due time. Not yet." TT said. He was determined that no word of President Ray's death get out yet.

Secretary Cordero then addressed the Georgetown physicians, "Gentlemen, you understand that you need to stay here in the White House until we get things sorted out and make all of this public, and we ask that you surrender your cell phones, tablets, smart watches, and any communication devices and not communicate with anyone outside the White House in any way."

"Of course," the one doctor replied cordially.

"There is no way I can just wait around," the second doctor said haughtily. "I have patients waiting. I am a doctor, and I need to get back to the hospital."

"Doctor, please help us out, and be reasonable, "Cordero said hopefully.

"There is no way that I can just sit around here and wait. Furthermore —"

Cordero fairly screamed, "Doctor, step into the outer office and wait until you are escorted from the White House. If you do not cooperate, you will be arrested!" Cordero motioned to one of the three military guards who were standing just inside the door. "Sergeant, Take this man to Office 14 and do not let him out until I say it's OK."

"This way, doctor," said the guard.

"And take his cell phone and everything else he has," Cordero yelled. The doctor seemed to be in a state of shock as the military guard led him to Office 14. Office 14, an addition during the Trump years, was a cyber-secure room down the hall from the Oval Office.

Cordero then turned to the remaining doctor and said, "Would you mind checking your cell phones and other electronic communications devices with Secret Service?" He motioned to the two tough looking Secret Service guards standing inside the Oval Office beside the door leading to Phyllis's office. "I am sure your property will be safe with them. Then they will escort you to a conference room where you will be served breakfast if you like."

The physician obediently handed over his cell phone, tablet, and smart watch to the Secret Service guard who then led him from the room. Another Secret Service guard immediately replaced that guard. In this moment of crisis, Secret Service guards seemed to materialize as needed.

The group could hear the thumping of a helicopter landing on the back lawn of the White House. After several minutes, the Vice President, still in his gym clothes, stepped into the Oval Office. The Secretary of State quickly briefed the Vice President on what had transpired.

"My God!" Vice President Armstrong said in a whisper. He stood with his hands at his side and turned back to Cordero.

Before he could say anything, Cordero said, "Mr. Vice President, we need to get you sworn in."

"Yes, of course," Armstrong said weakly.

"Mr. Vice President, I took the liberty of calling the Chief Justice. He is already here and can administer the oath whenever you are ready."

"Bring him in," The Vice President said, his voice stronger now.

The Chief Justice of the United States was ushered into the Oval Office. The official White House photographer had been brought in earlier to record the events in still shots, but video would be used to record the administration of the oath of office to the Vice President.

Cordero took it on himself to position the persons for the best photographic record. Then the Chief Justice administered the presidential oath to the Vice President. The words of the oath are specified in Article II of the Constitution. Armstrong enunciated them distinctly and with conviction:

> "I, Royster Armstrong, do solemnly swear that I will faithfully execute the office of President of the United States, and will to the best of my ability, preserve, protect, and defend the Constitution of the United States."

"Congratulations, Mr. President," The Chief Justice said and without being asked, he strode from the room. No one dared ask him to delay his exit or refrain from contacting anyone about what was happening in the nation's capital. After all, he was the head of a coordinate, perhaps more powerful, branch of government.

"Gentlemen, we have work to do," the new President said in a surprisingly strong voice. "I want a statement readied for release immediately, but first I want to meet with everyone here briefly. Yes, there'll be some policy changes, and, to be honest, you all know that. But there has also got to be continuity. President Ray didn't keep me informed about anything at all. Therefore, I need to get up to speed as quickly as possible on everything. I want briefings this afternoon from everyone on what is happening in your arenas, and I want everyone to be present at every briefing so that we're all on the same page."

The people in the room looked nervously around at each other. President Armstrong continued, "Yes, this afternoon. Basically on the record, verbal executive summaries. No PowerPoint. That can come later. Just get me up to speed so I can make it through the next few days."

"Yes, Mr. President," Cordero said.

TT and the others quickly agreed.

"Good!" the President said. "I'll have a schedule prepared, and we'll start this afternoon at 1 o'clock. Now what was the purpose of this morning's meeting that everyone was called to? Everyone but me, that is," he added with a neutral smile.

For the first time since President Ray's collapse, Lucado spoke up, "The President wanted a briefing on the clones affair." She now chose her words carefully, "Some unsettling things have happened in our search for the clones, and I was briefing the President when he," she paused, then continued. "Crumpled after a temper tantrum."

President Armstrong looked incredulous. "He got that mad?"

"Well, yes, he was angry, but we don't know that that caused the attack," Cordero attempted to smooth over the implications.

TT then said impatiently, "Yes, yes, right, right. Only the physicians can say officially what the cause of death was, but the fact remains that while he was blowing his stack, he apparently also blew an artery and dropped dead. It's about as simple as that."

Lucado struggled to suppress a smile that was threatening to burst forth into laughter.

The new President held up his hand, indicating that the conversation should stop. He turned to Joelle Lucado. "OK, Director Lucado, how about your briefing me on the clones situation right now, and everyone else please stay for this briefing."

"Mr. Vice President, sorry, Mr. President," Cordero interjected, "We 'll need to get a statement out to the public as soon as we can. We can't keep them in the dark. First things first."

The President stared at Cordero who, after hesitating a full five seconds, added, "Sir."

"Thank you, Mr. Cordero. We will, but first I want to have some knowledge about this clones situation. President Ray, as you know, was deliberately keeping me completely out of the loop. " He turned to Lucado, "I want to know everything, Director Lucado."

"I'll be happy to, Mr. President," Lucado said. She was thinking *I guess I'm not fired after all.*

They all nodded in agreement, and the second high-level meeting of that day in the Oval Office began, albeit this one with a different President and a radically different tone from the previous meeting.

Chapter 82

The President's spokeswoman, Diana Holk, stepped into the Oval Office dreading asking President Ray how she should deal with the clones' demand that he resign. She was stunned at seeing not President Ray but Royster Armstrong standing behind the presidential desk. Her shock deepened when she saw who was in the room and that they all wore sober expressions. "What's going on, Mr. Vice President?" She asked softly.

"Sit down, Ms. Holk," President Armstrong gently said. Cordero stood and offered Diana Holk his chair. After she had slowly sat, the new President said, "A few minutes ago, President Ray had a heart attack. He's been pronounced dead by the attending White House physician and by two outside physicians from Georgetown. He was in a meeting with these gentlemen and Director Lucado. I wasn't here."

Diana Holk did not react. After a moment, the President asked, "Are you OK, Diana?"

Holk straightened in the chair. "Yes," she said, and then with surprising force, she continued, "I'll need to draft a statement, sir, and," she held up the clones' latest paper, "I'll need to draft a statement about this." "That is, sir, if you want me to. I don't mean to — "

"Diana, yes, I want you to draft something about President Ray and that I've already taken the oath of office. Now what's this other thing you're talking about?"

Holk handed the copy of the clones' latest paper to President Armstrong. "Mr. Vice President — I mean, Mr. President — the clones have just issued a strong statement. The President did not respond to it. You, all of you," she motioned to the Cabinet members in the room, "need to read it if you haven't already. I'll step out here and make copies for everyone."

"OK, make the copies. Thank you."

Diana Holk quickly left the office and was back in several minutes with copies for everyone even though everyone had already read the statement She then handed out copies of the clones' latest broadside.

"I think we're all up to speed on this statement," the new President said.

Holk responded, "Mr. President, in the Brady Room and in the Media Club, they're clamoring for some reaction from the White House." It was her habit to refer to the White House pressroom as the Brady Room since it had been designated as such to honor James S. Brady, the presidential spokesperson who had been injured in the attempted assassination of President Reagan. Members of the press corps now had two places to call home, the refurbished Brady room and the new, luxurious Media Club. The Media Club had been added by an earlier administration to honor the "world class coverage of the news by *The New York Times*, the planet's premier newspaper," at least that was the accolade used to dedicate the room just one year prior to that newspaper's sliding into its self-induced decline.

The new President, still seated at what had been President Ray's desk, leaned forward on his elbows. "You know? The Brady Room's built over the top of the old White House swimming pool, the pool where, so the joke goes, LBJ used to troll for Jenkins. Well, I think maybe we should get rid of the press room and go back to having a swimming pool. And maybe just do away with that Media Club. It was built just to curry media favor anyway."

No one in the room smiled. "Sorry. I was just trying to add some lightness to this heavy occasion," the President said to no one in particular. "We have to function, gentlemen, and we can't do it if we stay in this mood of shock and depression. We have to be mentally sharper than we've ever been. Immediately we have to release a statement informing the country that President Ray is dead. Diana, can you give me something simple in a matter of minutes?"

"Of course, Mr. President," Diana Holk replied and started to leave the room.

"But no statements of any kind until the members of his family have been told and had time to get out of the public eye in case any of them are currently in vulnerable places. And, Diana," the President called after her. "There'll be another lengthier statement later today on the clones' situation. So just tell the press that we're giving the clones' paper serious attention, but given the death of President Ray, we won't comment further on it anytime soon. But not a word of his death until I've delivered my statement to the nation."

"Serious attention, Mr. President?" Lucado, her eyebrows raised, asked. "Do we want to elevate their statements to something to be taken seriously?"

President Armstrong looked directly at Lucado, held her gaze, and said, "Absolutely, we do, Madame Director. If by some chance they're the real thing, we need to take them seriously." He paused. "And we need to take advantage of them. They may well have insights that we — we non-clones — cannot have. Just think. One of them might actually have the DNA of Thomas Jefferson, might be identical in DNA to Thomas Jefferson. If that's the case, then, yes, we've got to take them seriously and hear what they say. But make no mistake about it. We won't allow them to discredit this government, not during this vulnerable time." He nodded toward Holk, and she left the room.

"OK, gentlemen. A lot needs to be done. Once we've informed the public of the President's death, I'll personally call the major world leaders and assure them that the American government is stable and under control. Douglas, you call the second tier of world leaders, but not until I have addressed the nation."

Secretary of State Douglas Cordero nodded.

President Armstrong continued, "I'll get the SECDEF to monitor for any military activity that might indicate someone trying to take advantage of our domestic situation. And Joelle and Director Fogg, you two need to prepare a full briefing on the national security aspects of the clones affair for me and the rest of us. I want to know everything that there is to know. Let's schedule that for two o'clock today."

"Yes, Mr. President," Fogg and Lucado replied in unison.

President Armstrong nodded, then spoke. "We're all going to be in a period of adjustment. For the next few days, it'll all be about President Ray. While that stuff's going on, the ceremonial stuff, I want all of you to make it a priority to bring me up to speed on everything. Everything. I need to know everything. President Ray shared virtually nothing with me. We can't have a President who knows nothing. Get me up to speed, gentlemen. OK?" He did not wait for an answer. "Joelle, you and Fogg lead off at 2 o'clock. Everyone be ready to add whatever needs to be added. I want us all on the same page, my page, on this clones stuff by the end of the day."

Lucado stood to leave the Oval Office. "One piece of news, Mr. President. Senator Sullivan undoubtedly will hold hearings looking into the death of President Ray."

"She's OK," Armstrong said. "She's about the only one in the Senate I trust."

After Lucado's fleeting frown, they all nodded and voiced support for Royster Armstrong. After they had left the room, President Armstrong opened the desk drawers, aimlessly looked in them, closed them, then walked to the side table, opened those drawers, grunted, closed them, and turned to the sole Secret Service guard still in the room, standing beside the closed door. "What's your name, sir?"

"J. D., sir," the Secret Service guard replied.

"J. D., please do something for me. Please go out there and find me a Bible. It's apparently been quite a few years since the Good Book's been in this office."

"Yes sir," The guard replied and gave the hint of a smile. "Yes sir," he repeated with emphasis and obvious approval.

Chapter 83

A tall man dressed in a cowboy outfit from Stetson down to the boots entered the room where the clones were waiting The tall man took stock of them without a word or a smile. He pulled out his cell phone, punched in a number and said, "They're all here. Is everything ready?" He waited for a reply from the other end of the conversation. "Good. I love you, honey. Fly safely."

He clicked off, turned to CD and said, "Hello gentlemen and lady. My name's T-Bone." T-Bone did not offer to shake hands. "My daughter, Omi, is flying you. She says come on aboard."

"Thank you, sir," CD replied. He looked at the others and raised his eyebrows in a gesture of helplessness. "So we're not going to know your real name?"

"Right. T-Bone is all you need to know. We need to move it on," T-Bone said with a tone of urgency. "I understand that you're naturally worried about whether I'm your government or truly a friend. If I were your government, CD — yes, I know your names — you would be in shackles now — or dead. I suggest you trust me and trust my daughter who's now your ticket to a safer location." The well-informed man's tone was all business.

The group all glanced at each other, and with a discomforting mixture of doubt and reassurance, CD led them out onto the runway which looked like an abandoned, neglected airstrip from decades earlier. "Don't worry about the condition of the airstrip, gentlemen and lady. It's perfectly serviceable. I keep it looking like this so no one else will dare try to land here." T-Bone walked with them to the plane, a gleaming HondaJet.

Still unsure of this man or the pilot, CD figured that if necessary they could overpower the woman pilot and take control of the plane. Olive was thinking similarly that since a woman was flying them, unless there were armed men on board, they were probably in safe hands. She also knew that unless specially configured, the plane they were now boarding had a maximum capacity of only five passengers. Therefore, she reasoned, the only person on the plane was Omi, the pilot referred to by the mysterious T-Bone. Plus if these people planned to capture the clones, they would hardly have needed a sleek, relatively rare HondaJet to do it.

The pilot, Omi, was already in her seat busy with a checklist and hitting various switches and checking dials as she called out, "There're only 5 seats back there. One of you will need to sit up here with me."

The clones all looked at each other with the same thought, but Thomas was the closest to the cockpit and the quickest to respond, "I'll do it. Somebody has to." He turned to the others with a smirk and then took the cockpit seat to the pilot's right.

'Shit," muttered Ben.

"Please no profanity," the pilot said over the intercom. No one could see the smile that she was trying to suppress.

Without looking at Thomas who was also trying not to look at her, she handed him a paper and said, "Read these off to me, please." She studied some dials on her left.

Thomas took the list from her thinking all the while, *she seems familiar. I hope this is not a trap.* He could not see her face until she turned to him.

Thomas's mouth fell open as he jerked back in surprise, his eyes wide. It took him only a few seconds to put it all together. "Abby?"

"Well, Thomas, now I guess no more fake names," said the woman with whom weeks earlier Thomas had traveled across western America. Now that very woman for whom Thomas had on their trip together felt such a strong attraction sat across from him.

He leaned over toward her and asked quietly, "OK, Abby. What's your real name?"

She leaned toward him. "Omi," she whispered. They kissed, much like they had some time ago on another airfield.

The five passengers gawked. "I can't believe that!" Ben exclaimed. "That guy wastes no time!"

When the extended kiss ended, Omi brushed back her hair and said, "Omi Sherman."

Thomas asked, "And that man was your father? Who is he that he has his own private runway?"

"He used to work for the United States government, part of a small intelligence somewhere in the federal government, not the CIA. He's no longer on the official payroll, but he still does some work for them." Then Omi said softly through the intercom, "Fasten your seatbelts, gentlemen and Olive."

"No doubt, we'd be well advised to do that. There could be some cockpit turbulence," Alex said in mock seriousness but real envy as he looked at Thomas and Omi. "And Thomas, keep your hands off the pilot. We want to get there in one piece." They all laughed, but the five passengers still wondered at the relationship of the two in the open cockpit. But at that moment, Thomas slammed shut the cockpit door.

"I think the name 'cockpit' is most appropriate," Ben said. They all laughed.

"I think there must be some history there," Rufus observed with a smile.

"There is" was all that CD said. After all, it was CD who had arranged for Thomas's escape from California.

Chapter 84

The CIA briefing that President Armstrong had demanded began promptly at 2 P M in the Oval Office. Secretary of State Cordero, CIA Director Lucado, Attorney General Trentini, and FBI Director Fogg sat facing the President who sat behind his large executive desk. After an hour and a half had passed, the clones matter had been vetted and discussed thoroughly. Now President Armstrong stood and much like President Ray before him, he paced. Finally he asked, "Do we have any firm idea at all where they are? Not speculation. I'm asking if we have any hard facts about their current location."

Lucado responded, "All we know for certain is that they were in Atlanta a day or so ago. The DNA confirms that. We don't know where they are now. If we want to capture them, we're no closer than we were when this thing first broke."

President Armstrong stopped pacing and faced Lucado, "Why, Director Lucado, do we want to capture them?" When she did not immediately respond, he continued, "Can anyone here tell me why we want to *capture* them?" He emphasized the word 'capture.'

Cordero spoke. "I think, Mr. President, that President Ray instituted a capture-at-all-costs policy, and, therefore, we went down that road. That was the policy. Once the President directed us along that path, we had no choice but to try to carry out that policy."

President Armstrong leaned over the conference table, his hands pressing flat on the table. "There is always a choice, gentlemen. Always! If the policy's wrong, you delay, delay, and delay, and if you can't delay in good conscience, you resign. You never carry out a policy that violates your own estimation of what's right for the nation. Anyway," he straightened up and continued pacing, "That tells me what the policy was. It doesn't tell me why that was the policy."

Lucado answered, "President Ray was convinced that the clones are probably indeed political saboteurs. The Ray policy assumed that possibly they're not clones at all. They're conceivably creations of some bizarre, Soviet-inspired, scheme to create monumental turmoil on our own domestic political scene. Remember, the clones or whatever or whoever they are came out of GeneVision, a company with Soviet ties and maybe even Soviet financing."

"Soviet, Madame Director? Soviet?" The President intoned. He realized that Lucado had reverted to Cold War terminology.

"I mean Russian, Mr. President. "GeneVision has Russian ties. And our people now know that Marina Novokatnaia, the head of GeneVision, fled to Russia after the discovery of the clones. She's now in Moscow. The Russian connection is incontrovertible. That's why President Ray decided that he needed to apprehend the clones. I think he feared that indeed they could conceivably be clones, that the involvement of a genetics company with cloning experiments added to the possibility that they could be clones. This would further the Soviet — the Russian — goal of disrupting our domestic political scene." Lucado briefly seemed like she would stop there, but then she continued. "And I for one, Mr. President, with all respect, sir, I for one think that's the right policy. We don't know if these so-called clones are genuine or if this whole thing's a hoax. If they're Russian-programmed clones, they're dangerous. They could even be some kind of high-tech sleepers. If they're not clones, and this is a gigantic hoax, they're even more dangerous." Several in the room nodded in agreement.

""Programmed?" President Armstrong looked directly at Lucado. "Nobody has said anything about their being programmed. Cloning's one thing. Programming's something else entirely. Anyway, none of that justifies shooting down that plane or killing all those people in Atlanta. Those actions have made the government look bad and moved public sympathy to the clones."

No one responded. The President then said quietly, "There're simply less intrusive and less inflammatory ways of handling the clones." Then the President added, "And bringing them in. I like that terminology better than 'capturing' them."

When still no one in the room spoke, the President, with a tone of finality, continued, "OK, I've heard enough. As of now the policy of capture-at-all costs is no longer the official policy. I don't care where they are, so let's not spend any more resources on trying to find out where they are or trying to capture them. Instead, we need to open a back channel to talk to them and eventually talk to them in person. You people are the top brass in the Executive Branch. You figure out how we can do that. And like I said before, if you think this isn't the right way to go, resign. If you're going to resign, I just ask that you wait until a respectable passage after the funeral and the other observances we'll have for President Ray. And I'll issue only one statement about the clones in the next week and that'll be to the effect that we welcome their suggestions but that we won't respond to statement after statement that they issue. We won't get into a statement duel with them." He paused and looked at his advisors. He felt that Lucado, Cordero, and Trentini probably opposed his ascent to the Presidency and, like President Ray, wanted to capture the clones though they probably did not share President Ray's boundless paranoia or penchant for violence. But their opposition did not matter to Armstrong because he now was President and his word was law.

Cordero then suggested, "How about testing the waters with a tweet to the clones?"

President Armstrong looked taken aback. "Tweeting is no way to make policy and no way to handle the clones issue. Forget tweeting. The Trump fifty-tweets a day presidency, well, you see where it got him. So there will be no tweeting, understood?"

Everyone nodded assent.

"Good," the President said. "If there's nothing else, let's adjourn."

Strangely for this gathering of top government officials, there was no conversation as they all left the room. President Armstrong then realized that he had about ten minutes before his next meeting, this one with other leaders of his party to discuss whom he should nominate as the new Vice President. Ten minutes was all he needed. He buzzed his chief administrative assistant. "Get Mr. Trentini back in here, please."

TT reappeared after several minutes. "TT," the President began, "Since you first visited me at the Vice President's house and informed me of the ruthlessness and no holds barred approach that President Ray was taking in trying to capture — and kill — the clones, I've thought long and hard about what I would do if I were President. Well, now I am President, and I already realize what Ike found out back in the 1950's, that a President really doesn't have all that much power to actually get things done."

"Unless, like Obama and Biden, he's willing to ignore Article Two of the Constitution," TT replied.

President Armstrong nodded in agreement and continued, "Or, TT, like Trump, he's willing to fire everyone who hesitates to toe the line. Well, anyway, the thing I want to get done is to open a dialogue with these clones and I want that dialogue to be face to face. But because we've poisoned the water so bad, killed people in Florida and Atlanta, and as a result lost track of the clones, I doubt that those clones are willing to talk to anyone from Washington. I wouldn't if the government had been trying to kill me. Not for one minute. So the job I want you to do might well-nigh be impossible. I want you to open a back channel to those clones. We've got to talk to them. We've got to find out if they're the real thing. And if they are, then we have to find out if that somehow means that they have special insight because of their DNA and all that. Once we're talking to them face to face, we'll be able to figure out if they intend to disrupt and discredit the government, and if they do — " The President did not finish the sentence. "How 'bout it, TT? Can you do it?"

Without hesitation, Trentini replied, "I'll do everything I can, Mr. President. It'll be difficult, but we'll give it the full shot."

"That's all I ask, TT. Of course, I'll give you any assistance I can."

Trentini then asked, "Mr. President, can I speak frankly?"

"Of course. Please do."

"Mr. President, at some point we'll indeed be face to face with the clones. What if we determined that they're in some way dangerous, that it was a Russian plot, or something like that?"

"What do you mean 'something like that'?"

Trentini said, "What if it's just a power play, Mr. President, because they just don't agree on current policies or that they don't agree on the size of government. Our government is colossal. They, or at least their forefathers — or whatever we call the original framers — could never conceive of a government with the reach, size, and clout that the federal government has today. What if these clones, because of their DNA heritage, want to dismantle our current structure, return to the past?"

"First of all, TT, you seem to be assuming that they're indeed clones of several of our original framers. Second, you seem to be assuming that as such they'll share those framers' views about government, share those views automatically and without realization that in today's world, big government is inevitable, even wise."

"I'm not assuming those things, Mr. President. I guess I'm asking what do we do with the clones if we determine that indeed they're not a positive asset?"

The President then looked at TT long and hard and finally said, "TT, once we have them face to face, we will — how to say it —protect them."

TT looked at the President, searched President Armstrong's face, and then spoke softly, "You mean seize and detain them?"

"Without one second's hesitation, TT." President Armstrong paused for what seemed like ten seconds then said, "So now that you know what I intend to do, are you still with me?"

"Yes, enthusiastically. Mr. President."

"Good, then,' the President stood and held out his hand to TT. "Our official policy's to go face to face with them. If necessary, the covert objective of the policy will be to take them into protective custody. You and I, TT, are the only ones who fully comprehend the strategic objective. Let's keep it that way."

The men shook hands, and Trentini left the room and headed through the South Portico of the White House for his limousine. For the first time, he thought that President Armstrong might even be more devious than the bellicose President Ray. TT had only one contact who might know something about the clones. If that one contact could help find the clones and send them a message, maybe, just maybe, the President would get his dialogue. And get his clones. Armstrong is one smooth operator, TT thought. Keeping his own people in the dark. Talk about Russian duplicity. They don't have anything on Armstrong. Attorney General Trentini got into the rear of his limousine and headed down Constitution Avenue to the Department of Justice.

Chapter 85

The telephone call from Attorney General Trentini was a total surprise. "How are you, TT," T-Bone said in answering the phone.

T-Bone and TT had worked together as fellow cops in Baltimore in their younger years. One night, T-Bone while off-duty happened upon a street thug who was robbing an elderly man in a wheelchair. T-Bone drew his firearm and ordered the thug to the ground. The thug turned, uttered some expletives, and started toward T-Bone. T-Bone's firearm jammed, and the thug then drew his own pistol and ordered T-Bone to the ground. When T-Bone refused, the thug pointed his pistol at T-Bone's midsection and said, "This'll be fucking slow and painful." That's when TT came on the scene and quickly dispatched the thug to wherever street thugs go after meeting the business end of a standard issue Sig Sauer. T-Bone always felt that he owed TT. So did TT.

"I'm fine, T-Bone, and how are you?"

"Doing fine, TT, and I bet you are calling about business, right? I can always tell from your tone of voice."

"Yes, T-Bone. It's about those clones. Now, our people say they apparently were in Atlanta. So, well, you know everything that happens in Atlanta."

"TT, —"

"Let me finish, T-Bone. President Ray was out to capture or maybe even kill those clones. You probably guessed as much. And this was if they really are clones. Anyway, we have a new President now. Royster Armstrong. I've just finished a two-hour meeting with him, and he's drastically changing the official policy. T-Bone, it's a new day in Washington. He's making it very clear that his policy is that he wants a dialogue. He asked me to try to set it up. That's why I'm calling you. I'm not asking you for any information. I'm not asking you if you know anything. I'm just asking that if you can, that you'll get word to them that we want a dialogue, that the new President can be trusted, that things have definitely changed. That's why I called, T-Bone. Your country needs you to pass this message to them if you can."

"Right, if I can. Of course, I don't know anything about them other than what I hear on the news, TT."

"Of course, T-Bone." TT then laughed. "T-Bone, I don't for a minute believe that anything happens down there without your knowing it. The President's new policy's a chance to get things right, to get back on track on this clones issue. And President Ray's history. So we can make a real break with his idiotic policies." TT grimaced in the realization that he was misleading his friend as to the new President's secret objectives. If T-Bone ever concluded that TT had intentionally lied to him so monumentally, well, that would at least be the end of the friendship, maybe even the end of TT. TT was well aware of T-Bone's code of pay-back.

"Yes, to quote Frankfurter, Ray's death proves that there's a god. But I doubt I can help you, TT, but I'll do what I can."

"So how's golf, T-Bone?"

There was a pause. TT thought for a moment that he had gone too far. In code he'd now asked T-Bone for information after promising that he wouldn't. The line remained silent, then finally, T-Bone responded, "I haven't played for a while, TT."

"Thanks, T-Bone. I owe you."

"You do, TT. You do."

They both broke the connection simultaneously. TT leaned back in his office chair and hoped he'd understood what T-Bone was saying. When they had worked together in the past, they'd often had to ask each other how things were without phone tappers completely knowing what message they were passing to each other. T-Bone had just messaged that he thought the clones possibly had been in Atlanta, but he had not volunteered anything further. That was not new news, but it was a verification.

TT leaned back in his chair and replayed the conversation on his phone recorder and thought through the various scenarios. At the same time, T-Bone texted a warning to Omi.

Chapter 86

"So the new President wants a dialogue. Very interesting. Very interesting indeed," CD said. Omi had briefed them on the short text she had received in the cockpit from her father. She had also explained to them that the plan was for them to land at Natchitoches Regional Airport in Louisiana. Her father had an arrangement with that airport and had obtained a covert Administrative Operations clearance for them to proceed and land in Natchitoches without any record being created. Air traffic control had been directed from the Pentagon to give them a green light to Natchitoches and to keep all other air traffic far away from them. Then Omi had turned off the plane's transponder.

"What's this Administrative Operations program I keep hearing about?" Ben asked.

Olive answered. "It's a joint State-Defense Department special operations program. High value captures are taken to black sites, interrogated using whatever methods are required to get the targets to talk, and once the information's extracted the targets are dropped by parachute into Russia, Chechnya, Dagestan, or some other backward, hostile country. That last part of the Administrative Operations program was thought better than turning them over to the Egyptians or somebody like that just for torture. Let somebody else figure out what to do with them. We frankly don't care."

Ben, Thomas, and Alex looked at each other. Finally Thomas spoke. "And that's another example of how this country's lost its bearings. Having black sites at all, never mind whether it's torture or not, and dropping people through the air into the evil empire - none of this reflects the values underlying our system." Thomas Jefferson had a strained, tense look on his face.

"For fucking certain," Ben said through clenched teeth. "I guess some people will argue that in today's world, such ruthlessness is necessary, but necessity's the mother of evil. That lesson's repeated time after time in world history. Until recently, our great country had refused to go down that sorry road."

Alex joined in the condemnation of the American response to political Islam and the terrorist threats emanating from it. "If you look at the founders — us — and what they, we, stand for, though it isn't unanimous, it's undeniable that our constitutional system will fall if it abandons its Christian principles. Black sites, torture, and all that hardly make the Jesus cut."

"For example?" Rufus asked testily.

"For example what?" Alex responded with just as much heat in his voice.

Rufus quickly said, "For example, did any of our framers actually say in words that our system assumed a Christian or godly foundation? That sounds like church propaganda to me."

"Or that it would fail," Olive added. "Stripped of that foundation, our system will fail. That's what they said."

Alex glared at Rufus. "Well to start with President Adams. He wrote, and I can quote him. 'The general principles on which the fathers achieved independence were the general principles of Christianity. I will avow that I then believed, and now believe, that those general principles of Christianity are as eternal and immutable as the existence and attributes of God.'"

Thomas quickly added, "And the first Thomas Jefferson wrote, and I too quote, 'I am a Christian in the only sense in which He wished anyone to be: sincerely attached to His doctrines in preference to all others.'"

"And don't forget the first Benjamin Franklin," Ben said. "'As to Jesus of Nazareth, my opinion of whom you particularly desire, I think the system of morals and His religion as He left them to us, the best the world ever saw or is likely to see.'"

"And my own Alexander Hamilton on his death bed affirmed his strong connection to Jesus Christ," Alex said. "And we can never forget that President John Adams said, ' Our Constitution was made only for a moral and religious people. It is wholly inadequate to the government of any other'. And everyone knows that President Washington was a strong Christian and believed that Christian principles were essential to the proper functioning of government."

Ben added, "There has been a move in this country, usually pushed by those who oppose Christian principles, to claim that most of the framers weren't Christians. Well, these misguided atheists need to go back and check the record."

Thomas took up the argument, "But those people are too closed-minded and agenda-driven to be inconvenienced by the principles of Christianity. There's no way that those people, the anti-Christians, will accept an historical record that threatens their own preconceived views."

"Then if what you all are saying is true, why exactly do those people claim that our nation was indeed not founded on Christian principles and that at best most of the framers were deists?" Rufus asked.

"Because those atheists have their own agendas," Thomas said. "They define any non-orthodox embracing of Jesus Christ to not be Christianity."

Alex picked up Thomas's explanation. "Those atheists and professors who so strongly spout that most of the framers were not Christians define Christianity so narrowly that, for example, few would make the cut today unless they were something like the old Westboro Baptists. And it's extremist, delusional sects like the Westboro people who give the Big C Church a bad name."

"That might be going a little far," Ben chuckled. "Probably those people just don't really understand what Jesus meant when he said if you believe in Him you will not perish but will have everlasting life. Doing a little research threatens the things they choose to believe in. They let their personal, subjective beliefs determine and fuel their nonfaith which is a faith in itself, and it should be the other way around, meaning that their faith should set the boundaries on their beliefs."

"What are you getting at? You are referring to John 3:16, but what do you mean that they do not really understand what that verse means?" Rufus asked.

"Well, the Greek word in John 3:16 is 'pisteuō' and we translate it as 'believe,' but 'pisteuō' really does not mean 'believe' as we use that word in English. Pisteuō in older Greek really does not have a modern English equivalent. The Greek is more along the lines of an active verb of our word 'faith." If you 'faith' in me you will not perish. If you embrace your belief in me to the extent that it automatically manifests itself in your life and in your actions, you won't perish. Belief in John 3:16 isn't just a head thing. You practice in your actions what you assert in your mind. That's what Jesus was talking about in John 3:16.

"So it isn't that you just say,'OK, I believe in Jesus' and then go on doing things that are incompatible with that belief. That would mean that indeed you don't believe in Jesus in the way He was talking about it." Alex looked around at the others, and then added, "Satan *believes* in Jesus, meaning that he believes that Jesus is who He claimed to be. Just mere mental acceptance isn't enough, and just mere mental acceptance dumbs down what Jesus was talking about."

"Fascinating," CD said, "but this isn't a small group doing Bible study. Let's get back to the task at hand."

Ben smiled and said, "CD, sometimes I wonder about you. You can't just casually separate what we were just talking about from what you call the task at hand. Separating a strong concern for what God wants for us and what He seeks in us from what we expect from our government is largely what has gotten our nation into the downhill slide that it's in today. CD, don't think in terms of separation."

Rufus then said firmly, "Enough! We get the point. But you need to understand that the threat today's different in scope and degree from what our founders - your fathers - faced. Today it's a duel between Islam plus an increasing number of anti-Christians on one hand and western civilization on the other. Do you three realize that Islam is the only religion or school of thought of any kind, religious or nonreligious, that wants to dominate and absolutely exterminate everything outside its own belief system? Exterminate. Eliminate completely. Do you three grasp that?" He looked from one to the other. The clones just stared back at Rufus without expression. Rufus continued, "They're the only organized thought system in the world that stones the victims of rape, lets the rapists go free, kills homosexuals just because of their orientation, forces women into subjugation, kills with impunity those who don't agree with them, practices the assassination of persons who disagree with them, condones the outright killing of innocents, including women and children, even beheading children because they have non-Islamic parents. Look at Mohammed himself. He was a thief and a murderer. That is Islam's founding, and you clones need to comprehend that! This is a world-wide crisis." This was the first occasion on which the three young men had seen Rufus grow heated.

Alex likewise was heated. "What you don't understand, my good man, is that there's always a crisis that's claimed to be greater than anything in the past. Those in power primarily use fear — raw, naked fear — to deceive and emotionalize the public. Part of the process is to make you believe that the current threat — today terrorism and climate, yesterday the Soviets, tomorrow who knows — but they make you believe that the threat of the day is the worst ever faced." Alex's voice rose in volume. "It's a crock. It always is. I think you, my friend, have been duped. Fear can be used to justify anything. We've arrived at torture being part of the American way. What next? Murder? Do you just want to murder them now, Rufus? And we become more and more like them. Is that what you want, Rufus?"

Everyone stared at Alex who was now red in the face. Thomas thought it, then CD said it. "Alex, you have the force and heat of argument that your namesake must have had. But let's step back a little."

Rufus interjected, "He's just a kid, CD. He doesn't understand the danger, the evil, that Islam is. He doesn't understand how fear is used to control. Just look at the pandemic frenzy over lockdowns and vaccines. Even to the point of changing the definition of *vaccine* so that the newly created chemical could be touted as the vital cure-all and injections required.

Alex exploded, "Fuck that!" Alex looked fully ready to come to blows. "Is all of Indonesia a threat? Do you want to torture all of them, too?" Alex was practically yelling. "They're Muslims, you know. And let's torture them in some secret black site so the world won't see it because deep down we know what we're doing is despicable."

"Alex, you're so full of shit," Rufus said as he shook his head in disbelief. "I can see how you ended up in a duel."

Thomas jumped from his leather co-pilot's seat and stood beside Alex, "Bullshit to you, Rufus! Your black sites have to stay secret because under our Constitution, the Constitution that I love, you can't do all that shit at home. Our system's built on the idea that the government is inherently untrustworthy and that individuals have a right to liberty unless due process takes that liberty away. Well, those black sites are not due process. In short, Rufus, you and your kind, are totally trashing the values that our country was built on."

Rufus leaped to his feet. His face was only two feet from Thomas's. "Your kind? Your kind? What do you mean by that, clone?" His fists were clenched.

Benjamin Franklin stood, placed a hand on Thomas's shoulder. "Sit down, Thomas. Please." He then looked at Rufus. "Roof, there will be no fighting." Ben's voice had a curious tone of authority and gentility. "We're on the same team. Please, Rufus, go back there and make yourself a drink."

Alex just muttered, "Unbelievable."

Rufus looked at Ben, then glared at Alex and Thomas and without a word walked the few steps to the bar in the rear of the jet, winking at CD and Olive on the way. Thomas went back to the cockpit. Alex sat and just looked out the window. "Fuck it!" he muttered, then more loudly said, "I bet Jesus doesn't take too kindly to secret torture sites."

No one responded.

Olive and CD had watched the whole exchange with some amusement. Alex and Thomas, they knew, were too smart to physically fight Rufus. Rufus could easily handle several trained commandos at once. Taking Alex and Thomas would have taken all of three seconds, and Alex and Thomas also knew that. What they did not know, but what CD and Olive did know, was that Rufus was in total control of himself at all times and never was even close to anything physical. He seemed totally angry, but Olive and CD knew that Roof was Mr. Control and that Mr. Control was trying to discover whether there was fire in the clones' bellies. Rufus had learned that their bellies were blazing.

Olive called out to Rufus, "Roof, make me one, too. Is the show over, or is this just intermission?"

Though his back was to her, Olive could tell that Roof was smiling.

"Fuck him," Alex said loudly.

"Alex, you're too stuck on the F word. I bet they didn't even have that word back in your day," CD laughed.

Before Alex could respond, Ben, still standing, quickly said, "We need to decide about this dialogue with the new President. Somehow we got just slightly off track."

Before anyone could respond, Omi announced in a deliberately sultry voice over the intercom, "No time for drinks. We'll be landing in about 15 minutes. I suggest everyone belt in. And no fighting on approach, please."

"Is air traffic control just letting you fly in, no questions asked?" CD asked.

"We've been in Class Echo, uncontrolled air space, so we don't have to deal with air traffic controllers, and there's no tower here. Plus we have that clearance from State, and there will be no flight strips. Plus, I've been flying VFR."

"VFR?" Thomas said.

"Visual flight rules," Omi replied. "That means we don't have to account to air traffic control, but it also means we don't have their protection from collisions. That's why we've been flying below 18000 feet. Luckily Daddy got us a green light from the State Department so Houston Center is letting us through, no questions asked."

In less than fifteen minutes, the gleaming jet touched down smoothly at Natchitoches Regional Airport, outside of Natchitoches, Louisiana. Though the airport had no control tower, the runway was plenty long for the HondaJet. Omi used only about 2500 feet of the available 5000-foot runway. At the end of the runway an African-American woman wearing a white blouse and a Caribbean style skirt was standing beside a Chevy Suburban van with heavily tinted windows. Omi taxied to the end of the runway and pivoted so that she was facing up the runway, ready to take off should anything unanticipated occur. She kept the jet's engines idling. Omi said, "We wait here, gentlemen and Olive. That lady will telephone me if everything is go. If she calls, she'll take you from here. If she gets back into her car, that means we've got problems, and I'll take off and we'll go to Texas somewhere. We have a backup site ready. Daddy fixed y'all up pretty good."

"Who is your daddy, Omi?" CD asked, even though he knew. He just wanted the clones to understand the heavy hitters who were trying to help them.

"Have you ever heard of the Mercedes Man?" Omi asked, looking directly at CD.

"Your father is the Mercedes Man?" CD asked in mocked wonder.

"One and the same," Omi replied.

"Wow. He's a legend," Rufus joined into the charade as Omi, CD, and Rufus were educating the clones. "In the old days he was one of the most talented arms dealers in the West. He was at one time on a first name basis with Assad and government leaders on both sides, at least, that's the word on the street. Then when Obama came in, the Mercedes Man got dissatisfied and broke his formal ties to Washington. He was always a little weird and unpredictable. He was going to run for the Senate, but was overheard disparaging Italians, and that was the end of any political future he might have been contemplating. He's now something of a renegade, but he can still pull all the strings you can imagine."

"Apparently," Ben said in awe.

They all watched out the window. The woman was on the telephone, but Omi's cell phone had not beeped. They waited and watched as the woman talked animatedly on her cell phone. In the distance several persons were outside a small airport building looking at the HondaJet sitting at the end of the runway. Omi explained, "They've probably never seen this kind of plane before."

All of the gawkers were using binoculars. "That can't be good," CD said. "They'll see everything, and then somebody'll put two and two together."

"Maybe not," Omi said. "You'll get out on the opposite side from them. They won't see you, and they won't know how many of y'all there are. And there's no tail number on this plane."

At that moment, Omi's cell phone beeped. "Omi," she answered. Omi listened then said, "Pull your car to the other side. Get as close as you can." Omi broke the connection and said, "OK, it's a go."

They all started preparing to exit the plane. "Hold on. There's one more thing," Omi said with a smile. "You'll need to put these on." She held out colorful, aggressively Caribbean dresses. "Disguises. Olive, you too, so that you look Caribbean."

"You've got to be kidding," Alex, having recovered from his earlier anger, said with mock seriousness. "Those colors does nothing for me."

"Alex, no color's going to help you," Thomas said.

As they laughed and changed into the loud dresses, Alex had the fleeting thought that what happened to Thomas, his reuniting with Omi, could it happen with him? *Could the woman on the tarmac possibly be Angelina? And how long ago that seems! How much had happened since then!*

Omi and Thomas embraced without a word, both with tears in their eyes. Finally, Thomas uttered in a strained voice, "Will we somehow get together again?"

Omi whispered back, "Thomas, you have a larger destiny. We'll always have the what-might-have-been. But we're on the same side, so who knows? Maybe." They embraced and kissed again. Then Thomas turned, and the fugitives all bounded down the steps and into the waiting Suburban.

The spectators in the distance could only see was what looked like five colorfully clad women getting into the waiting car. As the car doors were slamming shut, the jet dove down the runway in a burst of speed. As she lifted off the tarmac, Omi pushed the jet to its gas-guzzling maximum climb out in order to distract the spectators.

The driver of the Suburban said, "Welcome to Louisiana, My name's Rebekita, and I'm your chauffeur. Buckle in, please," and with those words, Rebekita sped from the airport.

As Rebekita picked up speed, her passengers could see the three spectators running to their own vehicles. CD said, "This doesn't look good. They're obviously coming after us." He turned to Rebekita. "Can you lose them?"

"No problem," she smiled. Alex now knew that indeed this was not Angelina, but whoever she was, she was a speed demon worthy of the Daytona Speedway. The Suburban was already doing over ninety mph.

"Damn," Rebekita said.

CD asked. "So what's your connection to all this?"

"I'm a friend of Omi's. Those two pickups, well, there's no way I can get away from them. I saw them at the airport. They are both built for speed. Hold on!"

With that, Rebekita two-wheeled it into the campus of what CD thought must be a local community or technical college. She veered behind the main building and slid to a stop, knocking over several metal trash cans in the process. There parked in front of her were two Chevy Suburbans exactly like the one they were in.

"Quick!" Rebekita exclaimed. "Split up. One of you boys in each car and one adult in each car. This way maybe they won't capture everyone."

CD hesitated.

"There's no time! Move!" Rebekita said with exasperation. "The Mercedes Man set it up this way as a backup. Didn't he tell you? Anyway, my sisters, Katerina and Jenifur, are driving those cars. They're the best, so move!"

CD turned to the others. "OK, let's do it. You three go to different cars. Olive, Sweetie, we'll split up. Roof, you go with Thomas."

"There's no way I'm splitting up from you, CD," Olive said with determination.

"We really need to get moving," Jenifur yelled from her car.

CD motioned to the clones. "Each one of them needs one of you. We don't have a choice," He quickly kissed Olive. "Olive, you've got to go, too!"

"No way," Olive said emphatically.

"How sweet," Katerina murmured, then yelled loudly from her car, "Let's go! Can y'all move it?"

They all ran to their separate cars, each with its motor already running, ready to exit the campus and flee to who knew where. At that instant, the two black pickups wheeled around the three-story classroom blocking one of the two exits from the parking lot. Two men, clad in black assault suits, jumped from each pickup. CD saw immediately that all four were armed with a favorite for short-range sniper takedowns, the L129A1 designated marksman rifle. The Suburbans tried to reverse out of the parking lot to the one exit still unobstructed. The assassins immediately leveled their rifles and shot out the tires of Rebekita's Suburban which then veered into a bike rack next to the classroom building. Jenifur's and Katarina's Suburbans sped around the academic building and picked up speed down the main exit road from the campus. The sound of the shots echoed through the small campus, and a number of students quickly but cautiously peered around the corner of the building. Others watched from the upper classroom windows overlooking the scene one story below. Alarms and sirens immediately sounded throughout the surrounding buildings, and loudspeakers sounded in the buildings and on the grounds of the campus, "The campus is now in complete lockdown! All students and faculty and staff are required to shelter in place. Stay away from windows, and lock all doors." After a pause of five seconds, the announcement now in its repeat cycle blasted throughout the campus again.

Two of the men jumped back into one of the pickups to head after the two Suburbans that had escaped from the parking lot, but with its tires spinning and the motor roaring the pickup had gone only a few feet when two Natchitoches Parish Sheriff cars, sirens blaring and lights flashing, careened into the parking lot of the normally peaceful campus and blocked the pickup. The brakes of the pickup screeched, but it still crashed into one of the police cars. One of the black-clad men still gripping the sniper rifle jumped out of the pickup and approached the police car. The two Sheriff's deputies were slow to exit their own damaged vehicle. The student onlookers could see that the man wearing black was holding a badge of some type in one hand, showing it to the Louisiana Sheriff deputies. He still held his rifle in the other hand. "Drop that weapon! Now!" The sheriff's deputy yelled.

"We are federal government!" The man yelled back to the deputy. "Look at this badge, officer!"

Students watching from the window above the parking lot saw a second armed, black-clad man run towards the Chevy Suburban that had not escaped. The man's rifle was leveled, and he was clearly not deterred by the presence of the local police. He jerked open the door of the Suburban and pulled Rebekita out and quickly handcuffed her. She kicked the man viciously, and he slammed her against the Suburban. Another man, also wearing all black, joined him, and they pulled from the back seat two women adorned in bright, tropical clothing. One was shoved roughly into the side of the car. The other woman broke free and started to run. The woman being held against the car yelled, "No! Don't run! You can't — " but to the surprise of the students watching the scene play out below them it was a man's voice, not a woman's, that had yelled out. One of the black-clad men quickly overtook Olive and roughly slung her to the ground.

At this moment, a Community College Campus Security three-wheeler sped into the parking lot, and two hefty campus cops, each sporting yellow sunglasses, jumped out. One yelled, "OK, what's going on here? This whole area's now under my command." The armed men and the Natchitoches Parish Sheriff deputies glanced at the campus cops who quickly realized that the scene was way beyond their control. "OK, carry on," one of the campus cops yelled authoritatively.

Before CD could finish warning Ben not to run, the black-clad man calmly aimed his rifle at Ben and fired a single shot. Ben yelled in pain and fell to the ground. CD watched in horror. Ben lay motionless.

The gunman stared at CD and growled, "You're next, bitch, if you cause any trouble at all. Turn around," the gunman ordered.

"Fuck you!" CD yelled, but he did not run. "You won't shoot me with all these students watching. And I wonder how many cell phones are videoing all this. In two minutes, buddy, you'll be on Facebook, YouTube, Instagram, tweeter feed, and every news alert in the country." CD spoke loudly so that the students could distinctly hear him. CD then yelled up to the stunned students, "Tweet this whole thing! We are being kidnapped. Get this online!"

The man now squinted at CD. "Well, you don't sound like a lady to me." The gunman then slammed the revolved into CD's head, but CD did not go down. As blood began to seep from CD's head, the gunman glanced at the windows where he could see dozens of students watching what was happening below. Practically every student held a smart phone, obviously videotaping the entire incident, with many no doubt already uploading the footage onto the various social media of cyberspace. Without changing his expression, the gunman, regaining his calm, aimed his gun at CD and said quietly, "It is your call, tough guy. Turn around and place your hands behind you, or I guarantee this time you won't remain standing." CD noticed the man's accent and phrasing.

CD did not turn around. As he saw the man's finger begin to tighten on the trigger, he muttered, "So much for dialogue," and turned around and held his hands behind him for the inevitable handcuffing. The armed man cautiously approached CD and quickly cuffed him with his arms tightly behind him. Then the man ripped off the upper part of the Caribbean dress that CD was wearing. "Well, what have we here? I do not see no breasts. You do not need no bra, do you?" the gunman said in a mocking voice. He then turned to the gawking students and yelled out, "This person here is a cross dresser. They are all perverts and terrorists that we are to terminate." He spat on the ground in theatrical disgust. In his high volume yelling, the man's accent was more distinct. His word choices were also abnormal. CD now knew that these men were Russians.

One of the black clad men yelled, "I have this one. Let us get out of here!" Pointing to Rebekita, Olive, and CD, he shouted, "Forget them! Let's go!"

CD then looked full face at the windows above and yelled as loudly as he could as he motioned with his head to Ben's motionless body still lying on the pavement, "That's one of the clones! It's Benjamin Franklin! These are Russians, and they're killing him!" The gunman immediately silenced CD with a vicious blow to the side of his head. This time CD fell, unconscious, beside Rebekita and Olive who had been tightly cuffed and thrown to the ground.

The campus cops realized that they were not prepared for such a deadly situation and had quietly retreated into the classroom building.

Ben's captors then picked up Ben who was still unconscious, quickly bound him, and roughly stuffed him into the cab of the pickup. By this time, the leader of the men who had apprehended the clones had convinced the Sheriff's deputies that this was indeed an FBI operation on special detail from Washington to capture a deadly gang of terrorists who had entered the country illegally at the local regional airport. Four local deputies walked with the two gunmen that they had blocked from pursuing the escaping Suburban.

One of the deputies said, "Well, by now it's all over YouTube. You boys probably ought to get on out of town as fast as you can." He then proceeded to move the sheriff's vehicle that had blocked the exit from the parking lot.

The gunman then asked, "Is it possible to confiscate the cell phones of the students or to prevent them from uploading the videos? It is possible, no?"

All four of the local policemen laughed and did not bother to respond. Then one of the local cops said, "You boys ain't from around here, are you? Must be a Yankee accent."

"We come from New Jersey, a special FBI unit," the lead gunman quickly responded. He then addressed his colleagues, "OK, speed please!"

One of the agents jumped into the pickup carrying Ben, and the others piled into the other pickup, and the two pickups noisily sped away from the campus.

The national news would have a field day with this one. There was already a black helicopter with twin turboshaft engines hovering at a very low altitude overhead. The chopper with a TV News logo on the fuselage then began to follow the pickups.

As the deputies headed back to their own vehicles, one commented, "People from New Jersey sure talk funny."

"Government people all talk funny," another deputy replied. "But that ain't no New Jersey accent. My sister lives in New Jersey. She raises little white dogs up there, bless her little heart, and I know New Jersey when I hear it. That ain't New Jersey. I don't know what all it is, but I know what it ain't, and it ain't New Jersey."

Chapter 87

Two miles from the disaster in the college parking lot, Jenifur and Katerina encountered a roadblock fully manned by police. As soon as they pulled up to the roadblock, dozens of plain-clothes agents with firearms drawn approached the two cars. "Everybody out of the cars, one at a time, and lie flat on the ground."

Alex, Thomas, Rufus, Jenifur, and Katerina each complied without talking. Finally after all were prone, face down on the ground, Rufus said, "Humor me, are y'all the good guys or are you with those bastards back at the college."

"I assume that you're somehow the leader here," responded a muscular man standing over Rufus. "How about you telling me who everyone here is."

"Show me some I.D.," Rufus replied.

The man laughed. "You don't seem to appreciate your position, brother. You're all under arrest. You're now my captives. You have a choice. You can either cooperate, or you can choose to do it the hard way."

At that instant, the agent, easily jerked Thomas to his feet. What he said then surprised all of the captives. "OK, which clone are you?"

Thomas looked stunned and after a short pause, he responded, "I'm Joe Smith. I attend college here and happened to be in the parking lot, and they grabbed me. But I've heard about those clones on the news."

The man laughed, and then said, "I'm special agent Pete Garland of the FBI. We'll know all of your identities soon enough." Then he ordered his agents to cuff the captives. Once they were cuffed, they were stuffed into several government vehicles.

As the government vehicles sped down the road, Agent Garland established a telephone link to FBI Director Fogg. "We got two of the clones, Director, but I don't yet know which ones we got. And we've got three other persons. A black man and two beautiful women, and we don't know anything about these three."

Fogg replied, "Great work, Agent Garland. Bring 'em to D.C. I'll get back to you on where to take them. Obviously, don't let anyone see them, and put all your agents in quarantine until we can thoroughly brief them. No word about this at all to anyone understood?"

Garland replied, "Understood, Director."

Chapter 88

In the college parking lot, CD stood weakly. The students were still videoing the actions in the parking lot. CD said sotto voce, "Rebekita, this could get ugly. You look like a student. Get lost."

"Right," Rebekita said quietly and calmly walked to a door of the classroom building. She quickly picked the lock. The door led into a maintenance room. Rebekita quickly found a cleaning person's uniform, ditched her colorful Caribbean clothing, put on the uniform, grabbed a broom and bucket, and walked out unnoticed into the classroom hallway.

While Rebekita was blending into the student population, four black SUV's veered from around the classroom building and slammed to a stop just feet from CD and Olive. One agent jumped from the lead SUV and stepped briskly up to CD flashed an identification card and said, "Agent Gorman, CIA. You two need to come with me. Relax. It's over. You're in good hands now. Whoever those people were, we're certain they were trying to kidnap the clones."

"Not trying," CD said. "They got one."

The agent's alarm was clear. "OK, then we don't have any time to lose. Let's go."

"Let me see that I. D. again if you don't mind," Olive said.

Without hesitation, Agent Gorman showed Olive his identification. Olive scrutinized it carefully. "It's real, CD," she said.

"Give me your own I.D.'s," Gorman said to Olive and CD.

"We aren't carrying any," CD replied.

"I'm not surprised," Agent Gorman remarked.

CD then said, "Agent Gorman, those people who kidnapped the clone were definitely Russians. I recognized their accent."

"How do you know they were Russians?"

CD realized that he would now be revealing his identity, "I used to teach linguistics. I know that accent."

The CIA agent now looked even more alarmed, "Damn!" He exclaimed. "OK, everybody, load up." The agents hustled Olive and CD into one of the government SUV's, Agent Gorman got into a second SUV, and the caravan sped from the parking lot.

Agent Gorman then got through to CIA Director Lucado. "Madame Director, we've got two people. I'm pretty sure it's that Tulane professor that's on our Capture List and his wife. They were both with the clones, and a squad of Russians ambushed them and, the professor and his wife say the Russians -—if they were Russians, we don't know for sure who they were -—actually captured one of the clones. I'm emailing you a full report."

Lucado, stunned, said, 'Take the professor and his wife to Andrews. Find the others!" Lucado felt exhausted but at the same time, exhilarated now that she actually had someone in custody. Lucado was now confident that this breakthrough would enable her to eventually capture the whole bunch.

"We've already started that search. We've got the drones in the sky already, Madame Director."

Lucado broke the connection without another word.

Chapter 89

President Armstrong's meeting with Finnish President Kyllikki Lemminkäinen was wrapping up. President Armstrong was relieved that he had not had to endure the ritual sauna. For years whenever a high Finnish government official would visit the White House, the Finnish delegation would insist on diplomacy in the nude, and unbeknownst to the American public, whoever was President at the time and the Finns would retire to a sauna at the Pentagon. President Armstrong did not like to be nude with strangers at all, but in this case there was no chance that sauna diplomacy would occur. President Lemminkäinen was a woman. Though mixed saunas might be perfectly acceptable in Finland, the American First Lady quickly vetoed the proposed sauna. While the President of Finland was giving her final remarks to conclude the meeting, one of President Armstrong's aides whispered something into Armstrong's ear. Reminiscent of President Bush's controlled, neutral expression on his first being told about the 9/11 attacks while he was in front of an elementary school class, President Armstrong's expression did not change. There was a distinct stirring among the reporters. They had gotten the same message on their electronic devices that the President was now receiving.

When President Lemminkäinen had completed her statement, the President, now looking somewhat preoccupied, stood and said, "President Kakatu and I won't take any questions now. Thank you all very much." He graciously took the arm of the Finnish President who wore an amused expression as the President gently but hurriedly led her from the room. She briskly walked beside the President and whispered to him in perfect English, "Mr. President, my name's not cockatoo. It's Lemminkäinen." Then as she consulted her own state of the art

Nokia, she immediately became well aware of why the President appeared preoccupied during the closing minutes of the meeting.

There was the usual pandemonium and tribal excesses among the press as the two presidents were leaving the room. Several cried out, "Mr. President!" Mr. President!" The CNN correspondent yelled out loudly, "Mr. President, did you know that another clone has been killed?"

As soon as they were safely out of sight of the press, President Armstrong said, "Madame President, it's been my distinct honor to have this time with you, and now if you'll excuse me, a matter has arisen that I must attend to."

"Of course, President Armstrong. You have my best wishes for a successful resolution to the situation. And as you know, we have a special relationship with certain countries. If we can be of service to the United States, you will call."

"Thank you, Madame President." President Armstrong hurried back to the Oval Office where Secretary Cordero and TT were already waiting for him. Both were extraordinarily subdued. TT's face was tight with anger.

The door shut, the President said, "OK, let's have it. What's happening?" He sank into a gray and blue wing chair directly across from the two advisors, his elbows on his knees, his face a mass of worry.

Cordero said, "Mr. President, we don't have any independent knowledge yet. All we know is what the news is saying — "

The President leaped from his chair, grabbed the remote off of his desk, and clicked on two flat screens on the opposite wall.

The FoxNews channel was muted. The CNN announcer was in the midst of her report.

"What we know for sure is that the campus is still in a lock down situation. We know that one person was shot and was seen lying motionless on the paved parking lot. Students and faculty who were in this building that you see on your screen supplied the video that we have. The whole area's been cordoned off by the Louisiana State Police so that we can't get any closer. The students and faculty of this college were watching from the classrooms one story above the parking lot where the shooting occurred so that they had very good vantage points. The videos that we have obtained show one person on the ground who has been shot and two others who're on the ground, apparently unconscious. The person who was shot was then placed into the cab of one of the pickup trucks. At this point we don't know whether it was a kidnapping or whether the persons who were doing the apprehending were in fact undercover law enforcement personnel. One of those persons claimed that they were FBI agents and that the apprehended persons were terrorists. He even shouted out to the onlookers in the classroom windows that the persons they were taking into custody were members of a sex ring. We simply don't know at this time whether they were in fact FBI agents, and we haven't been able to get a statement from the FBI. But they were all wearing black, and that alone raises questions. Now to repeat, and this is what has caught everyone's attention here and is potentially the bigger story, one of the persons who was in handcuffs before he was knocked unconscious by an FBI agent yelled out 'That's one of the clones! It's Benjamin Franklin! The

CIA is killing them!' As soon as he yelled that is when the FBI agent slammed him in the side of the head and apparently knocked him out. The ironic thing here is that that person was dressed as a woman, but the voice was that of a man, and he - I guess it was a he - had had his shirt ripped off and indeed he or she did not look like a woman.

"We don't yet have a clear close-up video of the face of anyone involved. But needless to say, with all the students and faculty members videoing the encounter, there's going to be a wealth of video materials available and probably already is being uploaded onto our own site and social media sites as well. This topic's actually trending as fast as anything I've ever seen on twitter."

The President grabbed the remote and snapped off the television with an angry jerk of his hand. He looked livid. Reminiscent of President Ray, his face was red, his fists clenched. "What the hell has happened, and who did it, and how do we get the definitive version? Damn, this job is a crock! Why did I ever want it?"

"Mr. President, we don't know for sure that the one who was killed was a clone," TT said.

Cordero interjected, "We don't know for sure that he was killed. He could have just been wounded."

The President looked squarely at TT. "Was this an FBI operation, TT, maybe one that went terribly wrong?"

"Absolutely not, Mr. President. I myself sent out orders as soon as our last meeting was over that all FBI searches and surveillance operations were to cease immediately pending further orders from me personally." TT stared hard at the President.

The President held TT's eyes, then said, "I understand, TT, go ahead."

Cordero looked from the President and then to TT. "Am I missing something here?"

Both TT and the President ignored the question.

"The FBI's pretty compliant, Mr. President. In reaction to the years in which the Obama Administration aggressively weaponized the FBI and DOJ, they have been reigned in. Fogg has gotten the FBI back on track. I'm as sure as I can be at this stage that it wasn't an FBI operation."

"But you aren't one hundred percent sure, are you?" It was Cordero who had noticed that TT was uncharacteristically looking down at his hands while he claimed that the FBI was not involved.

'No. Not one hundred percent, but I stand by it. This wasn't an FBI operation."

The President turned to Cordero. "Douglas, do you have anything operational going on in this matter?"

"Not in this country, Mr. President. We do have a surveillance operation going on in Russia. We're watching Novokatnaia among others, but nothing at all in this country."

The President continued methodically. "That leaves Defense and the CIA."

The three remained silent for what seemed like a time of endurance. Finally, the President crossed behind his desk and buzzed the Chief of Staff on the intercom. "Lee, tell Director Lucado and Secretary Shulla that I need to see them in the Oval Office as soon as possible." The President listened to Lee Brown's response, clicked off, and walked back to the wing chair, slumped in it, and moaned, "What the hell's going on? I thought I was

President, but it seems like somebody else is trying to run the show."

The Chief of Staff soon informed the President that Lucado was already on her way to the White House.

TT then said in a surprisingly small voice, "Mr. President, I have to ask this. Was what happened actually one of your private operations?"

President Armstrong snapped, "TT, that's a fucking stupid question! No, absolutely not!"

Cordero stared at TT, then at the President, but said nothing. *Why would TT even think that?* Cordero kept his thoughts to himself.

Chapter 90

Katerina and Thomas rode silently in the backseat of the SUV until eventually Thomas said, "Katerina, who exactly are you? And Rebekita? And Jenifur?"

Katerina answered in a whisper, "Shhhhh. Whisper, Thomas. This car's probably bugged. We're part of a group trying to protect you three."

"Who is *we*?" Thomas whispered back.

"Let's just say that we used to work with that lovely young thing who brought you to Louisiana." Katerina explained. "We all worked in the same unit. Now none of us is in the government, but we sort of got together to help out CD."

"What unit?"

Katerina whispered, "The unit was called the Procurement Project. I think you've heard of it, and we're now trying to keep you clones from getting killed."

"You mean there's an organization that is protecting us?"

Katerina replied, still whispering, "Yes. You need to trust us. From what I've seen you've got some pretty powerful people after you, not just from our own government, but there are others after you too."

"Here's what I know, Thomas," Katerina continued. "When that earthquake happened in California, the head of GeneVision, a Russian lady named Marina Novokatnaia, started acting erratically. CD was on the Board of Directors. The Board was put on a plane to fly off to a secret meeting. It was a trap. CD was tipped off, and he didn't get on the plane. The plane crashed, and everybody on that plane, the entire board, was killed. They were the only ones who would have access to GeneVision's records, that is, if they had wanted access. The crash was obviously intentional. Novokatnaia simply wanted the board out of the way in order to protect the secrecy of what she was up to. That's when CD called some of us who had been together in the Procurement Project to try to find the clones and protect them. We failed to protect George, and now, I hate to say it, it looks like we've lost Ben too."

Thomas looked at Katerina incredulously. "Why the hell didn't y'all fill us in from the very beginning?" He had a hard edge to his voice.

"I don't know. You'll have to ask CD." Katerina then added, "Thomas, not only is the American government trying to capture or even kill you, but it also makes sense that the Russians'll try to capture you also. No doubt, Marina Novokatnaia will flee to Russia. She might already be there. My guess is that she'll want to continue her work on cloning humans, and she'll want to do certain biological and physiological tests on you three. She and the Russians no doubt will be after you. Did you notice those accents back at the college?"

Thomas looked drained. "They killed George. They've killed Ben. That leaves me and Alex. I thought the new President wanted to talk."

"It's a hell of a dialogue," Katerina said quietly.

The SUV slowed to a stop. The captive passengers were all asked to get out of the cars, and when they did they saw that they were at a military airport.

"Y'all are the lucky ones," Agent Gorman said. "We're taking you to Washington, and you'll be safe there. No more violence. No more Russians. You're in good hands." Then he looked at Alex. "You look skeptical, young man. I assure you we're the good guys."

"Whatever," Alex replied.

They all boarded a sleek Bombardier Global 6000, and Agent Gorman immediately separated his captive passengers from each other. The jet was then quickly airborne. The captive passengers remained skeptical but were certain that at least their "hosts" were not Russian.

Chapter 91

Marina Novokatnaia said with assurance, "It continues to unfold exactly as we thought it would, Tovarich." She used the older forms of address among her close friends, all of whom yearned for the days before the change, for the unbridled reach of Soviet control.

"Except that we never counted on President Ray's cooperating so thoroughly," Sergei Verionsky said. As head of Russia's FSB, he wielded all the powers and more of the old KGB. "I always thought it was just a matter of time before he stroked out. He was such a hothead." They laughed.

Marina turned to the other man in the palatial room deep in the Kremlin, "And you, my dear friend, you handled that professor so beautifully."

Afanasii Pakoslav just nodded his bald head. "Yes, Professor Delna's brilliant in his field, but, like most Americans, amazingly predictable and with relatively low intuitive instincts. He's done his job well. Just as we knew he would, he's gathered the clones together all at one place so now it's the extraction that we must focus on." Pakoslav turned to Novokatnaia. "And, Marina, that was brilliant to have me tip him off to not get on that plane. Now he trusts me completely."

Marina smiled, "Yes, well, he kept the clones alive, and you were so right that President Ray's primitive reaction would be to kill them. It's such a shame that they killed Project Seventeen. He was perhaps our best product. He even had the bearing and remoteness that the first George Washington was reputed to have had. But, alas, we still have three others to work with."

"Marina," Pakoslav replied, "You're such an optimist. We won't have anyone to work with if we can't extract them and extract them alive. Our people say that this new President wants them alive, but then he tried to kill them in that village in Louisiana. So something's not right. Either we have incorrect information, or he doesn't control his own people."

The slight eye contact between Verionsky and Novokatnaia did not go unnoticed by Afanasii Pakoslav. Because of the immense power that Verionsky wielded, Pakoslav did not want to engage in a dangerous confrontation, but he was familiar with the devious ways of the FSB chief. Turning to Novokatnaia, Pakoslav raised his eyebrows. "And Marina, what is it that you're not telling me? If I'm to be able to assist in this extraction, you need to be open with me." Even though he was addressing Novokatnaia, the three of them knew that the query was actually for Verionsky.

Marina Novokatnaia glanced at Verionsky who had an amused and smug look on his face. After a long pause, Verionsky stood and said, "Afanasii, you're most perceptive. Yes, we haven't been completely candid with you." Though his tone was amiable and intended to exude honesty, Pakoslav knew that everything about Verionsky was controlled and calculating. "That little action in Louisiana wasn't President Armstrong. He hardly has the balls to do anything like that. He's a weakling. A "wimp" as our friends at the American *Newsweek* magazine label various American Presidents. No, Afanasii, they were our people. The extraction of the clones is already underway. We had a helicopter and a plane waiting, and were it not for incompetence of our own people on the ground, those clones — all of them — would be ours now. But our operatives blew it. That, of course, will be their last operation. They've been recalled to Moscow, and I'll deal with them here. But, anyway, when the time is right, we'll get those clones. They can't stay out of sight forever. And as you say, the professor is predictable. So what we need from you, Afanasii, is your analysis of where he'll take the clones. Once you tell me that, they will be ours!" He balled his fist as if clutching a clone.

Pakoslav realized that he now had to tread very, very carefully. If he gave the wrong prediction of Professor Delna's actions, Verionsky might well deal with him in the same way he apparently planned to deal with the Russian agents who failed to capture the clones. If he gave the right answer and the clones were indeed captured, then his usefulness to Verionsky and Novokatnaia would be at an end. He knew too much for them to allow him to live once they had the clones in hand.

Choosing his words very carefully, Pakoslav said, "Professor Delna is predictable, yes, but when cornered he's not nearly so easy to predict. The times when I've seen him act out of character, out of pattern so to speak, is when he's desperate. The situation for him now has become desperate, so I don't expect him to act consistently with his usual pattern."

"What are you trying to say, Tovarich Pakoslav? That now you suddenly cannot predict for the very person you described as amazingly predictable? I believe those were your words, were they not?" Without waiting for an answer, Verionsky continued, "This is a critical state operation, Tovarich Pakoslav. You are to inform us of your best estimate of what Professor Delna's actions will be at this time and where he'll go. That's your job, Tovarich. Are you up to it?" Verionsky's tone was calm, but his clipped words were spoken with a cold edge.

Afanasii Pakoslav, surprising even himself, spoke plainly. "Tovarich Verionsky, I realize, of course, that this whole affair is critical to the state. That's why I've been helping GeneVision all these years. I'm certain only of one thing as far as the professor's concerned." Pakoslav needed to play his ace, but he knew he had to do it carefully. "Professor Delna will conclude like everyone else that the attack on the clones was an American operation.

No one would ever even speculate that we would mount such an action inside of the United States. No, under these circumstances, I can tell you quite definitively what Professor Delna will do. He'll go underground. He'll go hard underground, Tovarich. There'll be no communication from him at all for some time because he'll feel too threatened by the White House. He'll attempt to secure the clones such that they can't be extracted by anyone. But at some point he'll reach out to someone on the outside for help, and when he does, we'll then have a chance to grab the clones. Until then, forget it. We will know nothing."

"So what exactly is your prediction, Afanasii?" Novokatnaia asked.

"My prediction, Marina, is that he'll be incommunicado for several weeks, maybe longer. Then he'll attempt to communicate with someone he trusts, someone who can get to their President."

Verionsky asked, "And who would that be?"

"Well, it can't be the Mercedes Man. That card has been played, and the American CIA'll be watching him closely from now on. And it can't be that black man, because he's traveling with the professor. And it can't be anyone of his old cronies in the State Department because no doubt they're all being watched also." Pakoslav was bluffing now and was betting his life that neither Verionsky nor Novokatnaia would know whether Professor Delna even had any reliable contacts left in the State Department. One thing Delna had intimated to Pakoslav but that Pakoslav had never told anyone else was that Professor Delna had worked for American intelligence inside the Soviet Union. "I'll have to review our network analysis of Professor Delna before I can hazard a guess about whom he'll contact."

"Very well, Tovarich Pakoslav," Verionsky said quickly. "But I advise you to make it more than a guess. Please do your analysis, and let us meet tomorrow morning and bring this matter to a conclusion."

Pakoslav realized that the conversation was over. He stood. "Very well. I'll do it, Tovarich Director." Pakoslav left the room.

After Pakoslav had left the room, Verionsky turned to Novokatnaia. "What do you think, Marina?"

Novokatnaia knew that the Russian cloning aspirations could not go forward without her, so she had none of the hesitation or fears that Pakoslav had. "I think it'll be impossible to predict what that professor will do. He's now isolated. He has no one to reach out to. He's cut off, and there's no way for us to predict what he'll do, where he'll go, or anything."

"We thought he was isolated before, but he has managed to contact other people. He's managed somehow to keep the clones from the American government, even with all of their surveillance capabilities. To do all of this, this professor is more than meets the eye, Marina."

"But he just had a close call with capture, Tovarich Verionsky. That alone'll cause him to, as the Americans say, put the wagons in a circle."

Verionsky looked confused. "What does that mean?"

"That's a saying they use to describe what the American cowboys in the old days did when the indigenous, savage Indians would attack the train of wagons. They would put the wagons into a circle, sort of like a portable fort," Novokatnaia explained.

"What is a wagon?"

"Think of it as our delejans, Sergei Andreeyovich."

"Oh." Verionsky paused. "So we need someone to get inside that fort?"

"Are you thinking what I'm thinking, FSB Director Verionsky?" Novokatnaia asked very formally.

"I am indeed, Marina," Verionsky replied informally then said with finality, "Pakoslav."

Novokatnaia stood and walked to the door. "Da, Pakoslav," she echoed and left the Kremlin office.

After Novokatnaia had left the office, Verionsky walked over to the ornate credenza, poured himself a glass of cognac, reclined on the plush settee, and smiled. He still had not informed anyone that his own people had already captured one of the clones. He would tell Marina Novokatnaia and Afanasii Pakoslav in due time.

Chapter 92

In the late-night meeting at the White House, Lucado and Shulla finally finished briefing the President about the violence in Louisiana. Shulla's briefing took less than a minute because DOD had no clone-related activities underway. Lucado withheld selective critical facts from her own briefing as her own private agenda was gradually taking shape. She would never reveal that President Ray had wanted her to eliminate Defense Secretary Shulla.

"So your agents are all accounted for, and there's no 'off the books' operation going on? You give your complete, personal assurances, Director Lucado, that all your agents are accounted for and that your people had nothing to do with this whole thing?" President Armstrong's tone was almost accusatory. "Nothing at all, either directly or indirectly, your people or people contracted to you? Do you have people on the ground in Louisiana?"

"We have no one on the ground in Louisiana and we have nothing to do at all with the events in Louisiana, Mr. President. And, sir, I can assure you that we're doing nothing to undermine your policy of trying to contact the clones." Following the recent patterns of so many in government, Lucado had mastered the art of deception to the point of outright lying.

"Same question, Mr. Shulla. What about your people?"

"Mr. President, DOD's not involved at all, directly or indirectly, in the effort to find the clones. We're hands-off on this whole can of worms, Mr. President."

TT was sitting quietly during what had amounted to an interrogation, but now he spoke for the first time in twenty minutes. "Mr. President, we've got a serious problem. Assuming that the CIA didn't do it — "

Lucado cut him off sharply, "Not assuming, TT. CIA didn't do it, period!"

TT, nonplused, continued, "OK, CIA didn't do it. FBI didn't do it. DOD didn't do it. I absolutely had nothing to do with it." TT looked directly at the President, then continued. "As far as we know, there're not any rogue agents out there doing their own thing. And there's no other government operation going on that could account for the violence in Louisiana." TT glanced at the President and then continued. "So the question is, who else has the knowledge and resources to mount this kind of operation?"

President Armstrong said, "There're lots of parties in the private sector that could try something like this. Remember how Ross Perot did his own rescue operations in Iran back in the 80's. There're even extremists in the other party who might try something like this. Someone with the self-importance and money of a Trump could try it."

Cordero was surprised at the President's naiveté. "Not with lethal force, Mr. President. No private entities in our country would do anything like that, at least not inside the country. And the right-wing fringe in the Republican party simply doesn't have the resources or organizational expertise to do anything like that even if they did have the guts. Which they don't. Mr. President, these people were apparently armed with the latest weaponry. They had advance knowledge that the clones would be in Louisiana. In Louisiana of all places. What are the odds? They had fake government identifications. Mr. President, this clearly wasn't a local or private operation. And that leaves only one likely party, Mr. President."

Joelle Lucado's cell phone vibrated. Only one person had the private number that she kept on when she was in the Oval Office. Fabian Miles, and he knew to contact her only in an emergency. With dread, she said, "Gentlemen, I have to take this." Without waiting for their acknowledgments or for the President's permission, Lucado walked as far from the others as she could get in the oval shaped office. "Yes, Fabian, talk to me," she said softly into the phone.

TT started to speak, but President Armstrong held up his hand, obviously wanting to overhear what Lucado might say. She was laconically listening. Finally she said, "How definitive is that?"

After another period of silence, she said, "Do we have people there now?" After another pause, she broke the connection without another word.

Her face ashen, Lucado walked the few steps back to the wing chair she had occupied, but she did not sit down. Instead she gripped the back of the chair, looked from one man to the other, then stepped around the chair and fell heavily into it. With a major effort at self-control but with her voice quivering nevertheless, she said, "Mr. President, we've analyzed the video and audio that we could get from that college campus in Louisiana. The students and faculty recorded a lot of stuff with their cell phones. And we've gone over the surveillance camera footage. Our analysis indicates that the people who tried to get the clones were — " she paused. "They were Russians. The accents were definitively Russian. We even have facial recognition of one of their agents. He's a known Russian agent who was last seen in this country four years ago. It was beyond doubt a Russian operation, Mr. President. And Louisiana state cops on the scene unwittingly let the Russians get away."

There was a stunned silence in the room. Finally the President asked, "How sure are we of that?"

"My people say there's no doubt, Mr. President. None. The facial recog is one hundred percent. We have six relatively clear recordings, and the English is good, but the accents are detectable. We don't have a voice profile analysis of these particular persons. And there're some other physical indicators, things that are distinctive to how Russians handle firearms, pick up people, kinetics, and things like that. But the key thing is that from facial recognition analysis, we've identified one of the kidnappers as a known Russian agent." Lucado withheld from the President that the professor and his wife were now in the clutches of the CIA.

"Russians!" the President hissed. He hesitated, and then seemed to be thinking out loud. "Leaving aside the question of why the CIA's operating within our borders and why it's not the FBI who is handling the aftermath, why would the Russians risk an act of war on our own soil?" President Armstrong had fleeting thoughts of becoming a wartime President, but a war directly with Russia was unthinkable. A proxy war would be quite acceptable, but not a direct clash.

"Mr. President, " TT said, "On the FBI CIA issue — "

"Not now," the President snapped. "That can wait."

TT then said, "Quite right, Mr. President. The information is that the Russians, if that's who they were, carried out an illegal operation on American soil and, using deadly force, captured one of our people."

"Not just one of our people, TT," President Armstrong interrupted. "Maybe one of our clones!"

"There's never before been such an occurrence inside our country, Mr. President," TT pointed out the obvious.

"What jerks!" The President said. "And how can trained police be so incompetent?"

Ignoring the President's question, Cordero asked. "Do we know who they captured?"

Lucado answered, "We know that he was a male, judging from his movements and what the onlookers are saying, not from the dress he was wearing. That must have been some kind of disguise. He was the right age and sex to be one of the clones. We don't know as a fact that he was one of the clones, but we do know that he was shot and kidnapped, and we do know that he fits the parameters of a GeneVision clone."

"Mr. President, we need to lock down all ways of getting out of the country." TT's voice had a sound of urgency. "The Russians are trying to get the clones to Russia so they can continue what GeneVision was doing here in the USA. Those Russian bastards want our framers. Mr. President, what we're facing is a cloning gap!"

The President looked sharply at TT. "TT, this is not *Dr. Strangelove*."

TT responded with a hint of hostility. "Mr. President, don't — " then TT caught himself, "We shouldn't try to smooth it over."

Cordero said, "Might I suggest something more subtle than a lockdown, Mr. President? They'll try to get the person they captured out of the country. There's no doubt on that one, and they're probably already on that track. Let's put our undercover people at the airports and ports on high alert."

DOD Secretary Shulla then said, "Mr. President, I suggest we institute a DRVU over the Mexican border and all coastal areas of the United States."

The President looked confused. "A what?"

"A DRVU is a Drone Enhanced Visual Umbrella, Mr. President," Shulla replied. "It effectively watches every square foot of the border and penetrates the ground up to a depth of over 300 feet."

The President obviously had never heard of this technology. "Wow," was the totality of his response.

Shulla continued "And just because this was in Louisiana, we can't assume that they'll take to the sea or the air from the South. That's too obvious. They could just as easily use a much busier corridor like Tijuana or LAX."

"But speed requires that they make for the Gulf coast or New Orleans," Lucado said. "They know we'll be after them. Mr. President, the CIA has the resources to execute the DRVU. We can handle that operation." Joelle gambled correctly that Shulla still wanted nothing to do with what he had called a "can of worms" and would not object to the CIA's encroaching on what would ordinarily be a DOD operation.

"OK, Joelle, do it," the President ordered quickly. "Institute all those measures and every other measure you can come up with to make sure no one leaves the USA without a thorough check. This is a nationwide search for these Russian agents and their prisoners. And not just from Louisiana, but from every airport and every port and every border crossing of any type. Plus, I don't like the way Homeland Security's been kept in the dark on the whole clones matter, and I intend to bring them in, and this is the right time to do that." The President stood. "As far as dealing with the Russians is concerned, we'll wait on that. Everything at this point has got to be kept as quiet as we can manage. Otherwise, we'll never get this clone back alive."

"Assuming that he's still alive," Cordero added.

TT frowned. "Just one thing, Mr. President. DHS's a disaster of bureaucratic inefficiency and a cesspool of infighting and turf sitting. I think it would be a grave mistake to bring them in at this point." Cordero and Lucado nodded in agreement with TT.

"OK, OK. I'll hold off on that, but at some point, DHS has got to be brought in," the President said. "Keep me informed of absolutely every development."

"Before we leave, Mr. President," Cordero said with a worried tone. "What do we tell the public? We can't tell them the Russians got one of our clones."

"We'll tell the public that it was a professional gang of kidnappers who want to hold the clone for ransom, that we're searching for them with every means we have, and we'll leave it at that so as not to compromise the search. And, for God's sake, we don't say anything about the CIA. And we don't say anything about the Russians." The President said but could not conceal the doubt in his voice.

"Yes sir," they all said in unison and left the Oval Office.

The President paced for several minutes then called TT who by this time was again ensconced in his private limousine. When TT picked up, the President quickly said, "TT, we absolutely must get those clones. We must get that dialogue started. Lucado said in her briefing that two cars escaped from the college scene. Only one person was kidnapped. That means there're two clones out there which the Russians didn't get. Those clones have got to be scared and desperate. The time to get them is now. Put it to them that we're their rescuers, TT."

"Right, Mr. President."

"Get them, TT. Promise them anything. Just get them."

"I will, Mr. President." TT knew he had no way to guarantee success.

The President ended the call. He then intoned to himself through clenched teeth, "If those clones cooperate, no problem. If they cause trouble, it'll be the last fucking thing they do."

Chapter 93

After speeding through the Louisiana countryside for no more than thirty miles, the pickup carrying Ben headed down a dirt road and descended into a deep swamp. Ben had faked his injury on the college campus. He had thought that he could use that ruse to create a diversion or even escape. The shot that the onlookers had thought might have killed him had merely grazed his arm. Once the kidnappers had thrown Ben into the truck, they quickly realized that he was not hurt.

"Did you really think you could fool us that easily?" One of the Russian agents asked in heavily accented English.

"We are not to talk to the clone," the other agent said harshly.

"OK, no problem."

Ben attempted to engage his captors in conversation but to no avail.

After a short, bumpy ride, the pickup pulled into a clearing that had been carved out of the swamp. Ben could see a helicopter waiting, the same chopper with the TV News logo that had hovered over the college campus. He was roughly pulled from the pickup and for the first time, his hands were tightly bound behind him with an electronic cuff, and he was turkey-trotted to the waiting chopper.

Ben's captors now spoke only in Russian, and Ben realized that the chopper was being manned by Russians and that the signage on the fuselage was fake. In the chopper Ben was tied to a seat, and the chopper quickly took to the air but stayed at treetop altitude. After being in the air no more than five minutes, one of the kidnappers roughly administered an injection into Ben's arm, and within seconds, Ben was unconscious.

When Ben woke up, he had no way of knowing how much time had elapsed, but he realized that he was in a tiny, windowless cabin on some kind of small boat. His hands were no longer bound. The door was locked. There was no porthole, and the only furnishings in the room were a mat on the floor and one metal chair. In one corner was a primitive toilet. The inscription on the toilet was in Cyrillic.

"Some way to treat a clone," he muttered. "I guess I'm being treated to free cruise to Moscow." Ben's free cruise would be on a Russian nuclear-powered submarine, which was waiting for him in the Gulf of Mexico.

Chapter 94

Sergei Verionsky was on the fourth hole of the Moscow Country Golf Club in Krylatskoe when his cell phone vibrated. He recognized the Kremlin number and stepped away from the three Russian mafia criminals, referred to in the west as oligarchs, who were his golf partners for the day. When he was out of their hearing range, he answered his phone, "Verionsky. I am listening." He intentionally answered in a terse "I am listening," reminiscent of the Soviet days.

"Sir," the voice said. "We have a special urgent transmission from North America. It is kraenee bezopasnee."

The ultra-secure classification was reserved for only those matters so designated by Verionsky, and currently the clones matter was the only topic eligible for that designation. "I understand. I'll be there in twenty minutes."

Verionsky made a quick exit from the golf course after impressing his partners with the urgency of the call and thus his own importance. In the rear seat of his Dartz Prombron that was speeding to the Kremlin, Verionsky thought to himself, *those mafia thugs. Once we get control of this country we will not need people like that around any longer.* Then he fidgeted nervously, *I hope to God that this is a good report. If there were a God, I'd pray that we got that clone.*

Fourteen minutes later, Verionsky strode into the secure communications office adjacent to his own Kremlin office. Once the door was completely shut and the jamming apparatus was operating, Verionsky said to the attending officer, "What do we have?"

"Tovarich Verionsky, we received a burst transmission from the *Turkov*. I will put it through the decrypter now." The young officer pressed several buttons and a single sheet of paper slid out of the attached printer. Verionsky snatched up the paper and silently read.

From Captain Andrei Kashelkin: We have the young target. He is sedated. It is the Franklin clone. Captain Andrei Kashelkin, *Turkov*.

The Turkov

Verionsky leaned back in the large leather swivel chair. The Russian helicopter had taken the American clone into the Gulf of Mexico and transferred him to the *Turkov*, a nuclear-powered attack submarine of the Victor V class capable of running at a depth of seven hundred meters, possibly more, at forty knots and with a very low noise coefficient. Verionsky was quite confident that the Americans could neither track nor detect this advanced sub and that the clone would soon be in Russian hands.

He pulled out his cell phone, put it on scramble, and dialed Marina Novokatnaia.

"Yes, Sergei," she answered.

"Marina, get out the champagne. We have our boy."

"The operation was successful?" Novokatnaia asked breathlessly.

"Yes, success is ours. It's the Franklin clone."

"Beautiful!" Novokatnaia exclaimed. "And do we have anyone else? We believe that professor, Charles Delna, was escorting the clone. Do we have Dr. Delna? I want him. Sergei, I want to deal with that pompous ass personally."

"No, Marina. Apparently, we have only the boy. And remember, we need the professor to lead us to the other clones."

"Shit," Novokatnaia exclaimed. "I wanted to deal with that ass. He would've enjoyed the Lubyanka."

"He may yet, Marina, but today, let's enjoy what we have. We have our own clone, and he's one of the American heroes of their revolutionary period."

"So we have one clone, they killed one clone, and they have two clones. Yes, this is going to be very interesting, Sergei. Come over to my place, and let's celebrate."

"Good idea," Verionsky replied. "I'll be there in time for dinner. How about a little snack beforehand, Marina?"

"That, too, is a good idea, but I have a big snack in mind." Marina soothed into the cell phone. Of course, the sultry intonation did not make it through the high-tech Russian scramblers.

Chapter 95

Carsten Shulla had been up all night in one of the secure Pentagon Communications Rooms closely monitoring the action in the Gulf of Mexico. When the Russian submarine had jammed the American communications, Shulla had begun to fear the worst and had decided to wake up the President. Though the American drone on the scene had a visual confirmation of the transfer of one person from the helicopter to the submarine, the jamming of all of its systems prevented pictures or any effective action by the drone. Plus the Russians and the Americans knew that the Russian submarine could easily destroy the drone should that become necessary. The situation looked as if it could quickly escalate, but then just as quickly the jamming had stopped, and the *Turkov* had disappeared below the surface of the black waters. Shulla, therefore, held off on waking up the mercurial President. The Russian sub had dived so deeply into that area of the Gulf of Mexico known as the Grand Canyon that not even the deep-penetrating, American submarine tracking systems could find her. With the *Turkov* no longer on the scene, the entire incident had de-escalated and by 4:00 A.M., it had become clear to Shulla that any chance of getting the kidnapped person back had evaporated. In short, Shulla realized that if the missing person were indeed a clone of one of America's constitutional framers, the Russian kidnapping was a national catastrophe and probably an act of war. After delaying for two hours, the gravity of the situation finally convinced Shulla to awaken President Armstrong.

Chapter 96

In the Oval Office, the antique Ingraham Waterbury clock chimed 8 A.M.

"This thing's already consuming my presidency," the sleep-deprived President complained. Shulla had briefed the President in the wee hours of the morning, and now the two were meeting again. "OK, let's get started. Carsten, anything new?"

Shulla looked aged and tired. "Mr. President, here's the executive summary." He handed the President a single sheet of Pentagon embroidered stationery that contained the highlights of what had happened overnight in the Gulf of Mexico. Then Carsten again went over the details for the President. During the briefing, President Armstrong did not say a word, but his tense face initially signaled his impatience but eventually showed alarm.

When Shulla had finished, the President said nothing for a full minute. Then he said darkly, "Carsten, you should have awakened me the instant you knew that a Russian sub was involved in the kidnapping of an American even if no clones had been involved. I can't believe you didn't wake me up immediately. Why didn't you?" The President was barely containing his anger.

"Mr. President, there was nothing you could've done that we weren't already doing. And like you just said, this clone matter is consuming your presidency. I guess I was trying to keep some of that from happening."

"Let me protect myself, Mr. Shulla. You don't ever keep critical information from me on anything. Do you hear me, Carsten?'

"Yes, sir, Mr. President."

The President's tone then lost its accusatory edge, and he asked, "Who else knows that the Russians have kidnapped one of our clones?"

"Mr. President, the media's in full speculation stampede."

"But we don't know for a fact which clone they have," the President said, apparently thinking out loud. "Not that it matters."

"Mr. President, those individuals which the FBI rescued are being flown up here for our people to debrief. Once we've questioned them we should learn more about what happened, which clone it is, and a lot of other stuff. And remember, Mr. President, we believe that the FBI has two of the clones in custody. Fogg has them."

"OK, yes, that's the key thing. We finally have some clones. At least, I think we do. But where's that professor? He seems to be the one who was masterminding the clones escaping our efforts." The President's voice for the first time hinted at satisfaction. "I can understand more and more every day why John — President Ray — was so obsessed with this whole thing. It changes so fast that we can't get a handle on it." The President paused then quickly continued, "Carsten, can you stay here for a while, stay in the Oval Office? I have Cordero in a few minutes, and I want to talk to both of you about something."

"Sure, Mr. President. I'll do whatever you want me to do."

President Armstrong's tone became didactic. "Don't ever - ever - tell a President that, Carsten. Presidents too often want things that they shouldn't get. Remember Obama only had to indirectly hint, he was too clever to directly ask, he only hinted, and those hints triggered repeated abuses at the IRS, the FEC, Justice, you name it. And Trump! He would demand his people to do various things, and if they didn't, he'd just fire them. The result is that he ended up with only second-rate sycophants around him. All the good people had either been fired or quit. This country's so damn infatuated with Presidents. People almost worship the President. They think the President should protect them, lead them, nurture them, give them jobs, give them food, give them money if they don't have the right amount, forgive their loans, protect them from floods and hurricanes and earthquakes, run the economy, prevent riots, cure the sick, find clones, everything. This country has an addiction to the Imperial Presidency. These unrealistic expectations set us presidents up for inevitable failure and lure presidents, me included, into taking risks that we should never even think about taking."

The President's secretary opened the door to the Oval Office. President Armstrong had told his three secretaries and Chief of Staff that they did not need to knock, that they could walk in any time whenever an appointment was supposed to be concluded. "Mr. President, the Secretary of State's here."

President Armstrong did not rise from his seat. "Bring him in, Phyllis. Thank you."

Douglas Cordero entered the room, shook hands with the President, and then registered surprise on seeing Carsten Shulla sitting in the tall wing chair near the coffee table. "Carsten, good to see you," Cordero said. The two men had always had a formal, uneasy relationship. They were two professionals who knew that both were now caught up in something of an historic magnitude that they could not hope to control.

"Gentlemen, I wanted both of you here today to give me some advice. I've got a difficult decision to make." The President looked intently at each man. "I don't know either of you very well, but I've always respected your honesty and your class. Even though you worked for President Ray originally, and I don't have to tell you that I didn't at all respect his honesty, and we all know that he had no class. Anyway, I'm relying on you to give me your frank advice and I'm relying on your integrity that none of this conversation leaves this room. Yes, I know when this is all over, you'll write your books, and I can't control that, but for now, this stays just between the three of us, OK?"

"Yes, Mr. President," both men agreed.

"Douglas, read this." President Armstrong handed Cordero the Executive Summary that Carsten Shulla had prepared.

Cordero read it, looked up, and said, "My God, the Russians! I've heard the media stories this morning, but my God, the Russians have one of our clones! One of our framers of the Constitution! This begins to look like an act of war, Mr. President."

President Armstrong put a hand on Cordero's arm. "Let's not go marching off to war just yet, Douglas. Carsten, fill Douglas in on what happened last night and who is on the way here."

The Secretary of Defense then briefed Douglas Cordero much like he had earlier briefed the President. Once Shulla was finished, Cordero said, "Mr. President, obviously there's a lot we don't know yet. But we have apparently got two of the clones. One President Ray murdered, and the Russians have one. They're all accounted for. I guess there're only four. I hope so. When these clones get here, then we should be able to get a much better feel for everything."

"Right, right," the President said hastily, "but that's not exactly why I wanted you two here. Yes, we'll have to deal with that, but there's another matter. Gentlemen, I don't feel at ease with Joelle Lucado heading CIA. I think there's too much that she's not telling us. She was too much of a willing hatchet man — hatchet woman — for Ray, and I've got no reason to think she'll give our new policy her all. Ray wanted to capture and sequester the clones. He even killed one. My policy's the opposite. I want to bring them in and learn from them." The President manufactured an earnest sound but glanced nervously at his two advisors and continued. "These clones possibly represent one of the greatest political breakthroughs in western history. Just think, a link with our constitutional past! Gentlemen, we must bring them in and have them talk to us. What do they see when they look at our governmental system today, over two hundred years after that system was launched? What insights do they have that we can profit from? Our system's in dire trouble, at least according to some. Some people even talk in terms of restoring America or making America great again, whatever that means. Gentlemen, we must bring them in and team with them. And I don't think I can trust Lucado to help that to happen."

Shulla quickly said, almost impetuously, "And she's just too damn powerful, Mr. President."

"What if they aren't cooperative, the clones, Mr. President, or what if they make unrealistic demands?" Cordero asked.

"Like what?" President Armstrong responded.

"Like that we're doing everything wrong and like we should step down or something," Cordero said. "They'll have public credibility and could undermine the entire governmental structure, your administration. You know, today's governmental structure isn't at all what it was two hundred years ago. The views of these clones may well be obsolete, Mr. President."

The President looked at the two men intently before responding. "If it looks like they would undermine the system or would generate too much public unrest, we'll continue to dialogue with them." The President paused, trying to choose his next words carefully. "But we'll control that dialogue and we'll structure things so that they cannot easily undermine what I want this Administration to accomplish."

Shulla and Cordero glanced at each other. "What does that mean?" Shulla asked.

"I'm not sure exactly what we'll do, but they won't be allowed to just run amok, foment unrest, or anything like that," President Armstrong said. "We'll just have to contain them somehow."

"That's pretty vague, Mr. President. We'll need to develop some contingency plans," Cordero said.

"And I would need to know just what you mean by 'contain them,'" Shulla chimed in.

"OK, OK," said the President with sudden impatience. "But what about Lucado? That's what I want your opinion on."

Cordero looked to Shulla who suddenly showed no willingness to speak. Finally, the President asked, "Carsten, should I fire her?"

After an excessively long period of thoughtful silence, Carsten Shulla responded, "In time, yes, Mr. President. She has the wrong mind set for a dialogue of trust with the clones. But I wouldn't do it until we locate the professor."

Cordero then interjected, "Plus, if there's any hope at all of getting back the clone that the Russians kidnapped, we need Lucado. She's got the best assets in Russia. Getting our clone back from the Russians'll be an intelligence-based operation, not a military operation."

"We hope," President Armstrong interjected.

"Lucado might not be the right mind set for a dialogue of trust," Cordero continued, "but she's the right mindset for clandestine operations. And she knows Russia like no one else we have."

"And that's what we need right now, Mr. President," Shulla added firmly. "You can order her to follow your lead on finding the professor, order her to work with TT, and at the same time, give her a free hand to work on the Russian angle. Mr. President, I share your feelings about Lucado. And we all know that President Ray was probably going to get rid of me pretty soon anyway. What I am saying, Mr. President, is that you can count on me, and when you feel that you need someone to replace me, just say the word, and I'll go quietly."

"Carsten, I want you to stay on. I trust you, and I need you. You're a professional, and you believe very deeply in serving your country first. I'm glad you're my Secretary of Defense."

"Thank you, Mr. President, for your support," Carsten Shulla said solemnly.

The President and Cordero began to rise, but Secretary of Defense Shulla said, "Gentlemen, there's one more thing." The President and Cordero sank back into their chairs.

"Go ahead, Carsten," President Armstrong said.

"You seemed to rule out a military option a few minutes ago. My people are already coming up with a plan for an interdiction of that submarine. I can present that plan to you once we have it. Once we locate the sub, we think we can stop her and get our clone back. But we don't have it all worked out yet exactly how we'll force her to surface and all that."

The President looked alarmed. "That type of military confrontation would almost definitely lead to something bigger. We don't want a confrontation."

"If — *if* — we can avoid it, Mr. President. But they have one of our framers. We simply can't allow that. I don't see that if indeed we can interdict the sub that we have any option but to do it." Cordero said forcefully.

Shulla added, "Mr. President, all we're doing now is coming up with the best plan we can come up with. Once we have the plan, then it's your call, but we have to examine that option," Shulla said.

"When can you have a plan, Carsten?"

Shulla replied, "We can have something preliminary this afternoon, Mr. President. My D and I people are working on it now."

The President looked irritated. "D and I?"

"Sorry, Mr. President. Detect and Intercept."

"Oh, OK. But Carsten, I don't want anything preliminary. This thing is moving fast. You present a plan — a proposal if you have confidence in it — this afternoon at one o'clock, here in the Oval Office. I'll have Phyllis contact everyone to be here."

"Yes, Mr. President," Carsten Shulla responded.

As everyone was again beginning to stand, Cordero raised his hand. "Mr. President, may I come back to something we talked about earlier? Do you care to expand on what you mean by 'contain them' when you said we would somehow contain the clones if they refused to cooperate with us?"

The President quickly responded, "I'll have TT's people take them to the Eagle Rock." The Eagle Rock was the Executive Branch's own secret facility in Alabama. "I can assure you, gentlemen," the President continued, "that if those clones are indeed clones and if they're intend to disrupt the functioning of this government, that will not be tolerated. We'll hold them incommunicado at the Eagle Rock."

Cordero persisted, "OK with the Eagle Rock, Mr. President, but you can't hold them forever. Will you imprison them indefinitely? Silence them somehow?"

President Armstrong, as President Ray had often done, stood, walked to the middle of the three tall windows, and stared out at the White House grounds, then turned to face his two aides. "I'll silence them, yes. If they don't agree to remain silent and have private discussions with us, then, yes, I'll have no choice but to put them under some kind of house arrest. They'll leave me with no choice, gentlemen. In a way, the choice is theirs. But my allegiance is to the stability and security of this nation, not to the clones."

"Then with all due respect, Mr. President, your policy isn't all that different from President Ray's. He wanted to silence them, but he was more like a bull in the china shop about it. You're much smoother and more polished, Mr. President, and I mean that as a complement." Cordero was prepared to say more, but the President cut him off.

"Well, I don't throw things, Mr. Secretary, and I surely don't want to kill the clones."

The three men sat in silence for some moments. Shulla and Cordero now clearly understood what TT had learned the day before, namely that underlying his professed policy of opening a dialogue with the clones, President Armstrong would take strong measures against the clones if their views on the current state of American government or the plans of his own Administration were a threat. Armstrong, like Ray before him, favored an expansive, aggressive government that would provide a myriad of services for the American people. If the clones jeopardized those plans, then the clones would have to be silenced.

The President broke the shared reverie. "And call me Roy, Carsten, Douglas. It's just the three of us in here now. I'd like it if every now and then somebody called me Roy instead of that Mr. President." He emphasized the words.

"I can't do that, Mr. President." Carsten said, looking the President straight in the eye.

"Me neither, Mr. President," Cordero said, smiling. "But thank you."

"Whatever, Mr. Secretary. Just don't call me anything bad behind my back."

The three men laughed, then the President said, "OK, we'll look at the military option this afternoon, and I'll keep Lucado on for now but y'all help me watch my back, OK? I don't trust her."

"Absolutely, Mr. President," Cordero said.

"My pleasure, Roy, I mean, Mr. President," Carsten said, and again they all laughed. It was the last levity the three would have that day.

Chapter 97

Joelle Lucado sat in the back of the nondescript CIA Ford Excursion. Her driver would arrive at the CIA's small, brick safe house on Maryland's Aberdeen Proving Grounds in another fifteen minutes. Lucado wanted to make the trip to the safe house personally to put her "package" as much at ease as possible, so she chose to use ground transportation instead of her usual helicopter. Going by car would give her time to think and would make it easy for her to avoid the press. She was hoping that it could also be done without anyone else in the Administration being aware of her actions, but Lucado was not naive enough to think the President could be kept in the dark for long. The Aberdeen Proving Grounds was the perfect place for the safe house since APG already had tight security, and with the CIA's own added security, this particular safe house was reserved for extraordinary situations.

Ten minutes after going through the MD 22 Harford Gate onto the military base, Lucado's car pulled up in front of a plain, two story house. Lucado opened her own door and started toward the house.

"He's around back." The security guard standing outside the house pointed to the brick walkway leading around the house. Lucado followed the walkway and then entered the rear yard with its magnificent view of the Chesapeake Bay. Perched on a picnic table at the edge of the gently undulating water was the motionless, solitary figure of a man staring out across the water.

Lucado approached him silently but before she could say anything, without turning towards her, the man said, "I was wondering how long it would take for someone in authority to come. Welcome to my prison, Ms. Lucado." He turned to face Lucado.

They both just stared at each other. Finally, Lucado said, "So you're George Washington." It was a statement, not a question.

"And am I such a threat that the head of the CIA herself comes to visit me?"

"Oh, yes. Yes, you are indeed." Lucado gave a fake laugh. "You are indeed," she repeated softly. She slowly circled the clone as if inspecting a being from outer space but with no apparent fear, only curiosity.

Lucado had read the reports on the questioning of this clone that had already taken place. He had given practically no information and was quite ready to endure any amount of pain had his interrogators been inclined in that direction, but Lucado had prohibited anything but hands-off interrogation techniques. She had explicitly prohibited truth serums, sedation of any kind, and any physical means of extracting information. Joelle Lucado extended her hand in a gesture she hoped would reduce the tension. She held her hand extended for an awkward period but then withdrew it when her captive simply ignored it.

"Ms. Lucado, your people have treated me properly, but the isolation's been difficult to say the least. What's happened to my compatriots?"

"Soon enough, you'll know it all. For now, I'm here to bring you up to speed and to give you a warning."

"A warning? It's a miracle that I wasn't on that plane when your government shot it down, so what's left to warn me about?"

Lucado raised one eyebrow. "'Your government?' Don't you think that it's also your government, Mr. Ball?"

"My government wouldn't try to kill me, Ms. Lucado. My government would've tried to rescue me, Ms. Lucado. Are you here to kill me, or are you here to rescue me, Ms. Lucado? If the former, then proceed with the task. If the latter, then that task also beckons you to delay no further."

"You know, Mr. Ball, you even talk like him. And," Lucado paused and eyed him, this time as if he were a meat specimen. "My friend, Jeff Shaara was right in his description of you, or rather your DNA father. Somehow, you do convey nobleness and dignity and also remoteness, Mr. Ball. Or do you prefer Mr. Washington?"

George Washington did not reply.

Lucado broke the ensuing silence. "My warning's that you need to know that there are those in the government who would want to treat you unkindly, maybe drain you of any information they can get, then dispose of you. I'm here to tell you who you can trust, and who you must never trust."

"The word is *whom*, Ms. Lucado, and I know there are those who want me dead. That plane was shot down. I was supposed to be on it. Someone gave the order to shoot it down."

"How do you think it is that you were permitted to bail out at a low altitude over Maryland, Mr. Ball? It's because there are elements in our government who want to help you stay alive. And help you go public, and do it without fear. I'm one of those people, Mr. Washington."

The CIA had anticipated that President Ray would attempt to intercept the GeneVision plane, and with the bribe of over five hundred thousand CIA dollars Lucado had arranged for the GeneVision pilot to fly dangerously low and slow over an abandoned area of Maryland's Eastern Shore. Simultaneously with that maneuver, the CIA activated sophisticated digital radio frequency memory jamming (configured to resemble sun-spot activity) of both the FAA's radar as well as the radar from the Air Force planes dispatched by the White House. This blocked tracking of the GeneVision plane from Potomac TRACON that controls the airspace over that section of Maryland and prevented anyone from detecting that someone had jumped from the plane. Augustine Ball was forcibly jettisoned from the plane, his low altitude chute static-line deployed, and he endured a hard landing in a muddy field a half-mile from the CIA's retrieval team. He was for a short while hidden by a crazy-acting woman and her husband, but after threats from CIA operatives along with their promise of a substantial sum of money, that couple had taken the CIA agents out to their barn and ushered them into a hidden feed room where Augustine Ball was in hiding. The CIA retrieval team quickly took him, and the operation was declared a clean success.

"If you're as well-intentioned as you assert, how do you explain this?" Augustine Ball pulled from his pocket a page torn from a local newspaper. The brief article he held out to Lucado belied Lucado's beneficence:

Longtime residents of Dorchester County, Myrl and Jackson Heaps, were found dead in their two-hundred-year-old farmhouse. Apparently Mr. Heaps shot his wife with a pistol grip shotgun and then turned the gun on himself. The couple had long been known to be despondent over what neighbors identified only as "family matters." The County Coroner has ruled the deaths a murder and a suicide and has said there is no reason to suspect any criminal acts other than what Mr. Heaps himself did. Jackson Heaps served in the U. S. Army as a military policeman for seven years and recently retired from his job as a postal worker in Cambridge. Myrl Heaps ran her own small engine repair business in a building on their farm.

When she finished reading the article, Lucado handed it back to the young clone. "What're you saying, Mr. Ball?"

"Ms. Lucado, you're head of American intelligence. I think you know perfectly well what I'm saying."

"Humor me, Mr. Ball."

"Ms. Lucado, I go by Mr. Washington now. I think that carries more clout and authenticity. Wouldn't you agree?"

Lucado showed some subtle signs of impatience, but her voice remained calm. "It might look like foul play, Mr. Ball, but I assure you that we had nothing to do with it. I'm here to help you, and if you make the tragic mistake of rejecting my help, you will most surely fall into the hands of the same people who shot down that plane."

George Washington said nothing. He turned and just looked forlornly out over the Chesapeake. Finally, Lucado asked, "Well, are you going to cooperate, Mr. Ball?"

"Let's get two things straight, Ms. Lucado. One, you will address me by my proper name. Two, I'll cooperate once you've brought all of us," he paused, then repeated, "All of us clones together. I'm sure your agency can do that." He now turned to face the Director of the CIA. "Right, Ms. Lucado?"

"Mr. Ball — Mr. Washington — "

"Yes?" George Washington faked a smile.

"Mr. Ball, this isn't a negotiating session. I came to offer my protection. You have no idea at all how powerful the interests are in the government who would like to snuff out your life and the lives of the other clones. Yes, I'm head of intelligence and I've done some things that I'm not proud of, but all of it on behalf of my country. But be that as it may, I'm here to offer you protection and assistance. If you reject my offer, I'll have no option but to turn you over to the FBI. You don't want that, Mr. Ball. If you're in your right mind, you'll accept my offer."

"And if I do, what then?"

This was the first break in George Washington's facade that Lucado had searched for. "Then I take you to a safe house and try to find the other surviving clones and get you all together."

"I thought this was a safe house."

"It is," Lucado said. "But I propose to take you to a much more secure facility in Virginia where there aren't so many people around. Here there're too many chances for people to see you, and there is the Chesapeake. We cannot control who might be using high powered binoculars out there, searching for you."

George Washington stared out into the Chesapeake and pondered his options. Though he was outwardly calm, he fully knew that he desperately needed help. He thought through his options as he tapped his fingers nervously. If he were discovered by the right people in their boats, he would be safe. If the government people Lucado referred to found him, he would be finished. After all, they had shot down the plane that he had been thrown out of just days earlier. But it was unthinkable to him that the head of American intelligence would not have been involved in the assault on the GeneVision plane. She had had the farm couple that rescued him killed and then had him brought to this safe house. And obviously, once he was out of the GeneVision plane, they had shot it down anyway, reneging on any deal they'd had with the pilot. Beyond doubt, Lucado's had blood on her hands.

He turned to face Joelle Lucado. "I reject your offer, Ms. Lucado. I'll take my chances here." George knew that he had no bargaining power, but he felt he needed to see Lucado's reaction and her next step. She did not disappoint him.

Lucado keyed her cell phone. "Come and take the detainee to our other station." Lucado watched as four well-built security men were quickly on the scene. George Washington did not resist, and they bound him tightly and placed masking tape over his mouth. As they bodily carried him to a waiting van, Lucado could tell from his eyes that he was smiling, and she knew that she had not won the encounter.

Chapter 98

"Mr. President, we've questioned the black man at length. His name is Rufus Forest. He's some sort of security guard for the professor, and he refuses to talk to anyone. The background shows that he was formerly a street thug then suddenly started his own security company. The money had to come from somewhere. Our guess is that the professor set him up and is his only client. He says he'll talk only with you, sir," TT said. TT and FBI Director Fogg stood opposite the President's desk. The President leaned back in his red, leather executive chair. A wealthy political supporter had given him the oversize chair, and the President had brought it over to the Oval Office from his vice presidential office.

The President looked incredulous. "You mean your people can't get anything out of him, nothing at all? He won't talk at all?"

"Oh, he talks, Mr. President, but he doesn't say anything. He's clever. But more disturbing than that, sir, is that he, well, he doesn't seem like the genuine article," Fogg said.

"Explain," President Armstrong said.

"The way he fields the questions. He talks, but he says nothing of substance. And he's not rattled at all. Just a regular old security guard wouldn't handle it this way. Plus, we can't find out anything about him other than the public record. His tax returns don't give us anything. It all looks so — so —" Fogg searched for the right word.

"Sanitized?" the President asked.

"Yes, sanitized. Deliberately contrived. Basically accurate, but concealing and deceptive," Fogg said.

"I thought we had databases of facial recognition, gait recognition, voice analysis and all that stuff. Have we used all of those means to find out about him?" the President asked.

TT spoke up, "We've done all of that, but there are some CIA databases that we can't access without a presidential directive, and that's our next step. Besides, we know who he is. We just don't know anything worthwhile about him."

"Maybe there's nothing worthwhile to know about him."

"Maybe," TT concurred.

"So if you need some order from me, let's get it done," President Armstrong said and called in his Chief of Staff.

Within ten minutes, the brief order was signed and countersigned by the Attorney General. "Obviously, make this top priority, TT," the President said as TT and Fogg left the Oval Office.

————

Lucado did not resist the presidential order or even protest it, and two hours later, TT reported to the President that the special files held by the CIA showed nothing new or unusual about the security guard or the professor.

Chapter 99

President Armstrong walked alone through the secret tunnel from the White House to the Old Executive Office Building where he entered an unmarked basement room that he had reserved for meetings and encounters for which he wanted complete secrecy not only from the media but also from most of his own staff. The room was equipped with burgundy leather furniture centered around a large oval coffee table. To one side, a mahogany credenza, emblazoned with a golden presidential seal, supported an ornate silver tea service and a platter of Norwegian cloudberry scones. Once he gained access to a government expense account, Royster Armstrong had regularly had the Scandinavian delicacy flown in from Café Picasso in Drammen, Norway. On entering the room, the President saw seated in one of the chairs a relaxed African-American man, attired in a wrinkled Hawaiian aloha shirt and khaki pants. Two Secret Service men stood just inside the door.

"Gentlemen, you can leave us alone," President Armstrong said to the two security men.

"Are you sure, Mr. President? We were told to stay close to this man."

"I'm sure. Thank you."

"We'll be right outside, Mr. President, if you need us."

"Thank you, gentlemen, we'll be fine."

The Secret Service men left the room.

"I guess you're Rufus Forest?" the President said. It was as much a statement as a question.

"I am, Mr. President, and I appreciate your taking time to see me."

The President had already determined to be direct and to the point with his detainee. "Mr. Forest, why is it that we cannot find out anything about you?" The President waited for a response.

"There's not much to know, Mr. President. I was a bad student, but this professor from Tulane pretty much rescued me and set me up in business, and that's about all there is to know. I run a small but successful security business."

"How many client do you have, Mr. Forest?"

"I'm sure you know the answer to that, Mr. President. After all, you have all the governments info on me, including the IRS."

"So how many?"

"One at present."

"That professor, right, Mr. Forest?"

"Yes, he pays well and demands me pretty much around the clock."

The President laughed. "Strange, to say the least, don't you agree, Mr. Forest? A professor with full time security. Most unusual."

Roof did not respond.

The President continued. "I might be delusional here and there, Mr. Forest, but not on this clones stuff. You and the professor were involved in concealing the clones. Well, that didn't work. We've got two of them. So you need to come clean on the professor. What's his background? He obviously has some very unique training. Why does he need you? What'a his interest in the clones? Last chance, Mr. Forest. I'm trying to be civil. I'm trying to let you know that we're on your side, but you're giving me nothing to work with. We have the two clones. They'll talk eventually."

Roof responded, "Mr. President, I hope you can understand that since 2008 this office has not inspired confidence, and in light of everything your dead predecessor did, I really don't feel any motivation at all to cooperate with the United States government until I have some reassurances that I'm not in danger and that my friends aren't in danger."

"The clones, you mean?"

"Anyone, Mr. President. Your predecessor—"

"I am not my predecessor, Professor," President Armstrong snapped. "What my predecessor did is irrelevant. If you don't understand that, then you're the one who is delusional. There's a thousand mile gap between what I want for the clones and what he wanted."

"How do I know that, Mr. President?"

"You're still alive, aren't you?"

"A tricky statement, Mr. President, but you can just snap your fingers, and those two goons out there can haul me off and work me over. So the fact that I'm alive at this moment means nothing."

The President leaned back in his chair and just stared at Rufus. Rufus held the President's gaze. Neither man blinked. Then President Armstrong stood and walked over to the credenza. "Tea, Mr. Forest?"

"Yes, Mr. President, thank you." Rufus surprised the President by accepting his offer. "And how about a scone, Mr. President? Are they for the taking?"

"They are," the President said with a laugh. He brought two cups of steaming tea to the coffee table and then brought two scones with clotted cream and cloudberry preserves.

"One thing about this office, Mr. Security Guard. You eat well. These scones can't be beat. I had them flown in from Norway."

As the two began to work with their tea and scones, the President said, "Mr. Forest, please help me. I have inherited a team that I cannot completely trust. President Ray kept me completely in the dark on this clones issue. I attempted to fight him on it once and he basically banished me from the White House. Then, praise the Lord, he had a heart attack. What I want is to simply talk to the clones, to see if they're willing to have an honest dialogue about the current deplorable state of the American political system and make serious, realistic recommendations of how to fix it. I want first to make sure that they're who they claim to be. That means some kind of DNA analysis. I'm not a scientist, so I don't really know what that entails, but obviously it's a critical prerequisite to determine once and for all that they're the real thing. That should be pretty simple to do. I don't want to do them any harm whatsoever. I don't want to detain them at all. They can go wherever they want to go to, talk to whomever they want to talk to, just like anyone else in America."

From his training, Roof was able to recognize the telltale biological signs of deception as the President spoke. "Just like me, Mr. President? Are you saying that I'm free to just get up and walk out right now?"

Without hesitation, the President responded, "Absolutely. If you want to leave, go ahead. But if you do just walk out, you're putting the clones and the U. S. government into an adversary relationship. That's the very thing I'm trying to change."

"I'll take my chances, Mr. President." Roof stood and walked to the door, half waiting for the President to retract his offer that Rufus could just walk out. The President said nothing.

When Roof opened the door, one of the security men immediately stepped in front of him. "Sir, you'll have to wait —"

"It's OK, " the President said. "We're finished. Escort Mr. Forest out. Use the Metro exit. And no tails."

"Yes, sir, Mr. President." They shut the door behind them and began to lead Roof away, but after going halfway down the long hall, Roof turned, walked back to the conference room, opened the door, and walked back into the room, glanced at the President, turned, and shut the door.

"So can we talk candidly?" President Armstrong raised his eyebrows in anticipation.

"Mr. President, I won't tell you where we've been or how we got to where we got to. I'll tell you about the present situation, as I know it. One clone seems to have been taken at sea by the Russians. I think your people on the scene out in the Gulf of Mexico know more about that than I do. Your FBI got two clones at the same time they got me."

"Which one did the Russians take?"

Roof considered whether he should reveal that information, then replied softly, "Benjamin Franklin."

"We are already doing everything we can to get him back."

"It'll be a national calamity if the Russians take one of our founding fathers into the depths of the Evil Empire. And I might add that it will be the end of your presidency, and this country will plunge into a constitutional nightmare," Rufus warned.

After an intense thirty-minute discussion in which Rufus added no new information, the President and Rufus stood. Then President Armstrong' tone immediately hardened. "Thank you, Mr. Forest, but I'm sure you understand that I cannot let you just go roam the streets, talk to the media, and all that."

Roof was not surprised at all. "I fully expected that, Mr. President."

President Armstrong called in the two security guards. "You know where to take him" was all the President said, and the two guards led Roof from the room.

Chapter 100

The President's meeting in the Cabinet Room with his closest aides was somber as it had been fully one week since the President's secret conversation with Rufus Forest, and the professor had still not been located. This particular meeting was larger than the President's usual clone-related meetings as it included the Joint Chiefs, his chief economic advisor, the National Security Advisor, the liaison with Congress, the President's Press Secretary, the Secretary of the Treasury, the Secretary of Homeland Security, and the all-important presidential pollster.

After covering a number of routine matters, President Armstrong turned to the nomination of a Vice President. Under the twenty-fifth amendment Armstrong was obligated to nominate a new Vice President since that office had been vacated when Vice President Royster Armstrong automatically became President on President Ray's death. The President had considered a short list for over a week, discussed it with his party's leaders, and finally had settled on Roberto Esposito, the junior Senator from Texas. Esposito was Hispanic, dynamic, and in line with the President's political views. The only drawback was that at only 45 years old, Esposito was fairly inexperienced on the national scene and could well emerge as a rival to Armstrong in the next election should the Armstrong presidency plateau. In spite of rumors that the young Senator was in league with organized crime and had illegally used campaign funds for his personal vacations, the discussion among the President's advisors took only several minutes. The President's advisors were generally agreed that the President should be able to name his own person even if that person had questionable connections.

The President's pollster spoke up. "Mr. President, our data indicate that Esposito will help your ticket in those states with greater percentages of Hispanic voters, but he also has high negatives in some key states like Ohio because his home state, Texas, is a right to work state and Esposito has made some statements in favor of that. So my recommendation's to proceed cautiously with this nomination, maybe even give it more time, float some trial balloons to test public reaction. I know that he's arguably qualified, but my job's to alert you to the political and electoral implications of this nomination, and these are potentially serious long-term debits to his being your nominee."

"Duly noted," the President quickly replied. "But I'm nominating him because I think he's the best person for the job, not for what he might bring or might not bring to the ticket in the next election. Let's move on," the President said, abruptly changing the subject. "Carsten, give us the latest on that Russian submarine."

"Still nothing, Mr. President. It's very easy for a submarine of that class to stay hidden, and it can actually stay submerged for months if need be. We're covering every area where it's likely to surface and we're covering every route from open waters to any Russian submarine base. Plus we're still covering every area where they might try to transfer the captive to another ship or even an airplane. But so far, nothing, nothing at all, Mr. President."

Everyone in the room seemed disheartened even though they had already known that the military had not been able to find the Russian submarine.

"Joelle?" President Armstrong did not look up from his notes.

"Nothing, Mr. President. "We have every eye in the sky programmed to recognize any unusual activity of any type in the oceans. Of course, if they work a transfer at night under the cover of clouds, there's nothing we can do about that. But we've turned up nothing."

"I thought we had the capability of penetrating through cloud cover," the President said.

Lucado responded, "Yes, we do have enhanced visual penetration, Mr. President, but only in the daytime. During darkness, we're still limited if there's a cloud cover." Then Lucado added didactically, "That's why I said *at night*."

Though the condescension registered with the President, he gave no sign of it. "Ladies and gentlemen, if there's nothing else, then let's adjourn." The President stood, and everyone else obediently stood in unison. Several of the President's advisors seemed surprised at the extraordinary brevity of the meeting and the cursory attention given to the issue of the Vice Presidential nomination, but they said nothing. As everyone was leaving, the President said, "TT, Carsten, Secretary Cordero, Jonathan, please hang on for a few minutes if you will."

The four had anticipated that the President would want to discuss the clones situation in a more tightly controlled group. The other persons filed out of the room except for Joelle Lucado who stayed behind even though the President had pointedly not asked her to remain after the meeting.

"Yes, Joelle, what can I do for you?" the President asked, still making no eye contact with the CIA Director.

"Mr. President, if you're going to discuss the clones, I think I should be present. After all, the CIA has more information on this issue and has more experience with it than State, Justice, and Defense combined." Lucado waved a dismissive hand towards Cordero, Shulla, Fogg, and Trentini as she spoke.

TT opened his mouth to respond, but the President cut him off. "We're not going to talk about intelligence, Ms. Lucado, unless you have something additional to report." The President waited. When Lucado did not respond, he continued, "In that case, Ms. Lucado, schedule a time today with Phyllis when you can give me a complete briefing. OK?"

"Of course, Mr. President," Joelle Lucado said flatly and quickly left the Cabinet Room.

Not missing a beat, the President said as everyone sat down, "OK, TT, what have we got on that professor?"

TT's tone was energetic but not upbeat as he consulted his notes. "We still have nothing on that idiot professor, nothing at all. He's simply disappeared. What's curious and noteworthy is that a professor in this digital age of pervasive surveillance even knows how to go off the grid. There's no digital trace of him since that incident in Louisiana. He's obviously not only a professor. He's got training from somewhere, and, Mr. President, I hate to say it, but he could be working with Novokatnaia. After all, he wasn't on that plane that took out all her Board of Directors." TT then turned to FBI Director Jonathan Fogg.

"Mr. President, if I may," Fogg said, "Another unusual aspect of the whole thing is that Dr. Delna's wife is also missing. We're pretty certain that she's the other woman in the videos from Louisiana, but we can't be positive about that. But what we can be positive about is that she also has completely disappeared."

President Armstrong concluded, "The bottom line, then, is, he's stalling, waiting for something."

"But for what?" TT asked.

'Maybe he's waiting for the clones to contact him," the President said. "We have two of the clones. We can use them to flush him out."

"Mr. President, I'm going to be very honest," Cordero said. "I don't like how we're bypassing the CIA. They've got the resources and the experience. So, I've got to ask it. What's the problem with Lucado?"

"It's a question of trust, Douglas," President Armstrong said testily.

"But there's no way that your own people, or the FBI, Jonathan," Cordero said nodding to Jonathan Fogg, "can have the resources or the tradecraft to do what the CIA can do."

Jonathan Fogg responded, "Mr. President, at the Bureau, we absolutely do have the resources to look for the professor and his wife as widely as need be, and though we're the proper agency to handle things within the borders of the United States, Dr. Delna and his wife may well be outside our borders, in which case, the CIA indeed has superior resources and reach." Then Fogg added, "Regrettably."

TT joined in, "Moreover, Mr. President, it begins to resemble a plumbers operations when we start doing all this stuff outside the normal channels, bypassing the CIA, using what you call 'your own people.'"

"Plumbers?" President Armstrong asked.

"Nixon, Mr. President," TT replied.

"Of course, of course," the President recovered, holding up both hands in a peace gesture. "Well, I don't want there to be any doubt that we're doing this thing the right way. I'm just not sure that Lucado can be trusted to carry out our policy with all deliberation."

"Mr. President," Cordero said, this time with more force than was typical of him. "There comes a time when you either have to trust her or fire her. But bypassing her is a risky strategy, and it's just a matter of time before she realizes that you're bypassing her."

Shulla joined the fray, "My guess is that she already knows and is just waiting for you to lower the boom."

"Or waiting for you to call her back onto the team is more like it," TT said. "Mr. President, I recommend you remove her as CIA Director, reassign her, and have Fogg here take over the CIA, put someone else in at the FBI, and move forward on the clones issue as fast as we can."

"As fast as we can? What the fuck does that mean?" the President asked impatiently. "We can't move at all until we hear something from that asshole professor. The two clones we still have are unwilling to talk without the professor, and we have no idea where he is."

Cordero looked from one to the other, then said, "I agree with TT, Mr. President. You need to fire Lucado, and get someone in there that you trust one hundred percent."

"I agree," Shulla said.

"Well, gentlemen, I've been waiting for you all to come together on this. I've wanted to get rid of her from day one. But I like TT's idea of reassigning her instead of firing her." The President then showed that he had already thought through the Lucado issue in detail. "I'll meet with her today and reassign her to a new Mideast Unit within DHS. TT, give me three names of people you would be satisfied with to head up the FBI if — and I repeat, if — I move Jonathan over to CIA. I haven't decided on that one yet. But, I do want it all done fast, like within the week. Can we all do that?"

"Yes, we can, Mr. President," Cordero said, presuming to speak for everyone.

"Good, then if there's nothing else, we're finished here." The President stood, and the others quickly stood also. "I'll handle Lucado when I meet with her later today. TT, I want you to be at that meeting, so please check with Phyllis to get the time."

"Yes, Mr. President," TT said.

President Armstrong hoped this decision would open the door to his gaining control over the clones dilemma, and he felt more optimistic than at any time since he had become President. "Gentlemen, I have an appointment with some wealthy PAC people that I have to get to," and with that President Armstrong strode from the Cabinet Room.

Chapter 101

Following his conversation with Cordero and Shulla about what to do with Lucado, President Armstrong had delayed his decision on Lucado's fate, but after two days of no action on the clones front, Armstrong finally decided to fire her or, if she agreed, allow her to resign. He had decided not to transfer her to the Department of Homeland Security but, as he once put it to Cordero, "to get her the hell out of my government." As is typical of Presidents, he had begun to think of the U. S. government as *his* government. The concept that it was the people's government and that he actually, not just theoretically, but actually, worked for the people had long been absent from the corridors of the White House.

CIA Director Lucado was ushered into the Oval Office. The President walked over and with surface cordiality, said, "Please," and motioned Lucado to a straight chair across from the coffee table. The President sat opposite her in a recliner.

As was becoming his modus operandi, the President immediately got to the point. "I wanted to see you today, Ms. Lucado, because I think you and I aren't sufficiently on the same page, and we need to do something to rectify that."

"Mr. President," Lucado began.

The President held up his hand to stop Lucado. "Let me go on, please, Ms. Lucado." President Armstrong's irritation was already apparent. "I want those clones. I want a dialogue. President Ray only wanted to eliminate them. That's no longer the policy. It's imperative that I have people in my government who're one hundred percent on board with my policy of establishing a dialogue. I won't compromise on that." The President paused briefly. "It's my impression that you're not in sympathy with that policy. Am I right about that, Ms. Lucado?"

"Mr. President, am I here this afternoon for you to fire me?"

"Not fire. Rather ask you if you'll resign. And you haven't answered my question. Am I right that you don't agree with my policy of dialogue?"

"Mr. President, my job's to carry out whatever you determine the policy to be and not to follow my own policy preferences."

"Dammit, Lucado, just answer my fucking question!" The President was no longer willing to conceal his anger.

"Mr. President, everything I've done since you took office was in accord with your policy objectives. Plus I've undertaken actions on two fronts to help make a dialogue possible."

"Oh?" The President leaned back and raised his eyebrows. "Go on."

"First, I've deployed every possible human and technological asset we have with the objective of recovering the clone the Russians kidnapped in Louisiana. I've got sufficient contacts in Russia so that I'll know the instant that clone shows up in Russia, and I have the people already in place over there to extract him. These are people whom I've personally cultivated over the years, Mr. President, and they're willing to follow my lead on this." President Armstrong perceived loud and clear Lucado's subtext that she personally controlled those assets and that any hope of getting Benjamin Franklin back rested with her and her alone.

"It's a question of when we have the opening of extracting him, not if. Mr. President, I now have in place teams of human watchers all over Russia who're prepared to snatch the clone at the first opportunity. I've deployed CIA drones to detect any submarines approaching any Russian port and also other non-Russian ports."

"I would expect all of that of the CIA, Ms. Lucado. And second?"

And now Lucado played her ace. "Second, Mr. President. We've learned that the George Washington clone wasn't on board the GeneVision plane that President Ray shot down, and we know precisely where he is. Mr. President, I'll shortly have that clone in hand. And I can deliver him to you."

The President looked totally stunned. "You're telling me the Washington clone is alive?"

"Yes. He's very much alive. I can produce him."

"Can?"

"Yes, can, Mr. President."

The President stood, and as was his habit walked to the window looking out onto the White House lawn and stared out for a full minute. President Armstrong had not missed Lucado's deliberate word choice. He turned to face Lucado. He spoke quietly. "Are you blackmailing me, Joelle?"

"Of course not, Mr. President. I'm just saying that I need to stay in office so that I can assure you that you get this clone that no one else even knows is alive. That'll make for one mighty good dialogue, don't you think, having three clones instead of just two?"

"And if you do not stay in office?"

"In that situation, I would hope that I can turn over this clone to the United States government, but I cannot make any guarantee."

"So what does it take for you to guarantee that you will, and I emphasize the word *will*, turn over the George Washington clone to me?"

"I stay in office and have complete discretion to question the clones."

The President snorted, "No way will you have complete discretion to question them. I can agree that you stay in office.

You agree to turn over the Washington clone to the FBI and not to question him at all."

Lucado did not even take time to ponder the President's offer. "Agreed."

President Armstrong concealed his surprise at Lucado's quick concession. "When do I get my clone?"

"I'll turn him over to Fogg tomorrow morning," Lucado said.

"I want him now. You obviously have him. Turn him over instantly, or the deal is off, and I'll have you arrested."

"Mr. President, that's no way to inaugurate our alliance. You and I are on the same team with the same objectives. It'll take me several hours to get him transported here. And I don't think for a minute that you're going to have the Director of the CIA arrested. What an absurd threat!"

"Where is he, Joelle?"

"He's in a safe house in California," Lucado easily lied.

"I want him here today, Joelle."

"He will be, Mr. President. You have my word."

"Good. Thank you. That'll be all. Please leave."

Lucado left the Oval Office. The President sank back down into the plush recliner and just sat there, drained and exhausted.

Chapter 102

Within two hours President Armstrong had TT, Carsten Shulla, and Jonathan Fogg in the Oval Office. The President played the recording of his conversation with Lucado, then without a word, played it again without interruption.

TT was the first to speak. "That changes lots of things. First, George Washington's alive, and we have no idea how that might electrify things. Second, Lucado's temporarily in the driver's seat because she's in control of our intelligence assets and contacts in the Evil Empire. Even after she turns over the clone, she's still in the driver's seat. Make no mistake about it."

Fogg took up the analysis, "And without her at the helm, she's virtually warning us that those assets will dry up. This is criminal on her part."

"Right," the President said. "Now what about the Washington clone? She'll produce him, and Fogg, you take possession of him. Then what?"

"Then we see what he knows, what his objectives are, how cooperative he might be, and we determine what he thinks of twenty-first century American government."

"And we still have the professor on the loose. What do we do about that?"

TT quickly replied. "We no longer need him. We've got the clones."

After a short silence, President Armstrong agreed. "TT, you are probably right. However, when do find him, we'll detain him and bleed him dry."

"Meaning what, Mr. President," Fogg asked.

"Meaning, Mr. Fogg, that your boys interrogate him, no holds barred."

After about twenty minutes more of conversation, the President stood, signaling that the meeting was over. "OK," he said. "We're arriving at the place where we can have our dialogue and find out whether they're with us or against us. On Lucado, we'll have to figure out some way to get a handle on her contacts in Russia."

TT said what they all knew. "She's personalized that bevy of contacts and our assets in Russia to the point that it's going to be very hard for us to smoothly get control of them."

"It won't be smooth," Fogg said.

"OK, gentlemen, thank you again." The President adjourned the meeting.

The President's aides left the Oval Office as the President once against sank down into his recliner, once again emotionally drained. "Why did I ever want this job?" President Armstrong wondered aloud the question that numerous previous Presidents have asked. Of course, if they were honest, they would already know the answer. The lust for power.

Chapter 103

While the Oval Office conclave was going on, in the CIA's Langley complex, Lucado worked the phones.

"What have you learned from the professor?" Lucado's question was to the head agent at the CIA's facility at Joint Base Andrews, formerly known as Andrews Air Force Base, where CD and Olive were being held incommunicado.

"Nothing of any value, Madame Director. He and his wife refuse to talk about anything substantive to anyone but you. If you authorize enhanced interrogation techniques, I think we can make some headway."

"I'll talk to them first. Then we'll decide when and where to go down that road," Lucado replied. "In the meantime, treat them right."

As she broke the connection, Joelle Lucado smiled. *It's all coming together nicely*, she thought. *I have the Washington clone, and now I have the professor and his wife. Those two will tell me everything they know and then sayonara.*

Chapter 104

To even the expert observer, the CIA hangar at Andrews resembled a functional hangar even down to the jet fuel trappings outside the building, but it was by no means just any old ordinary hangar. The unmarked, unpretentious facility was constructed after 9/11 and housed two state of the art, soundproofed interrogation rooms, several small bedrooms which served as holding rooms or cells, and several offices, all protected against eavesdropping. These rooms had witnessed a number of CIA interrogations, most of them of suspected Muslim extremists or right wing extremists, and for many of those questioned, these rooms had served as way stations to CIA black sites in Eastern Europe, America's own remote gulag. Olive and CD had been deposited in Interrogation Room One.

On entering the interrogation room, Lucado eyed CD coldly. "So you're Professor Charles Delna." She turned to Olive. "And you, my dear, are Olive Delna."

Olive had a fleeting moment of surprise that she kept well hidden. Both she and CD had hoped that the CIA had not discovered Olive's identity.

Lucado continued, as if reading Olive's mind, said. "Oh, yes, we've got a complete file on you, dear. All these years you thought you were off the grid, but you, my dear, were always well lit up on our radar." Lucado's condescending tone was borderline menacing.

Olive's tone was also cold. "That's comforting, my dear. I always knew I could depend on our precious government to look after me."

Lucado turned back to CD. "But you, Professor. You're a little harder to pin down. You're so under the radar that that alone raises all kinds of questions. Care to enlighten?"

"Ms. Lucado. I'm a professor of linguistics at Tulane. That's pretty much it."

"Pretty much," Lucado echoed. "Very well, then professor of linguistics. If you won't voluntarily enlighten me, I have some friends waiting outside whom you'll be more than eager to talk to." Lucado stood and headed to the door. When she reached the door, she turned back to face CD and Olive. "You'll find that my friends aren't nearly as pleasant as I am, professor of linguistics." The door was audibly locked several seconds after Lucado left the room.

"Well, Olive, I guess you've been outed," CD said with a smile.

"Yeah, I guess so. Anyway, why do they think you're anything other than a professor? You've never done anything. I've done it all. They'll just let you go back to the classroom. Me, they'll question and question and question and then they'll fire me without a pension."

Both, of course, knew they were being listened to and watched through the room's two-way mirror as they went through their preplanned script. What they did not know was which of Olive's false biographies the CIA had uncovered and how long it might take them to discover the truth about her and also about CD. They both continued to hope that the CIA was still somehow unaware of the Procurement Project. Though their words were pretense, their shared worry was very real. Both had quickly recognized Lucado as a scheming, devious woman of immense power who would stop at virtually nothing to get control of the clones. Olive and CD now realized that they were nothing more than disposable means to that end.

Outside of the interrogation room, Director Lucado gave directions to six men whom she had specifically instructed to be present at the hangar on this night. Except for Fabian Miles, these men, all clad in black and armed with Glock 33's, were experienced CIA heavies. "Gentlemen, I need to know that I can count on you. The two persons in that room," Lucado said as she motioned to the interrogation room, "are a threat to this nation's security." Lucado and the six men eyed CD and Olive through the two-way mirror.

Lucado continued. "The two perpetrators in that room have repeatedly flaunted federal law and have assisted the clones to remain beyond our grasp. That alone's clearly not in the national interest. For example, I can tell you six what the rest of the world doesn't know. The Russians have captured one of the clones, and that clone is now in Moscow."

"Shit," one of the men muttered.

Lucado did not miss a beat. "The damage from that development's beyond calculation. If the other clones stay on the loose, running wherever they want to, they too will obviously be captured, if not by the Russians, then by the Chinese, the Iranians, whoever. So I've had a choice to make." The men all noticed that Lucado spoke in the past tense. "First, I could have turned these two over to the FBI and the President and let them handle it from there. The danger of that we already know. Politicians can't be trusted to make the tough decisions to protect the national security. Or second, and this is what I have decided and this is why I need you here tonight and need to remind you of your oath of confidentiality and secrecy. Is everyone on board with that?" Lucado pointedly asked the question before she gave them her decision.

Each man knew from past experience to give Lucado a verbal affirmative, which each did without hesitation.

"So here's what we must do." Lucado walked up close to the two-way mirror in which now ironically CD and Olive were both staring into as if they were seeing through the mirror and listening to Lucado. Her face was only inches from theirs. "I want you to take them to Banska Bystrica Four." The reference was to the CIA's facility in Slovakia, four miles outside of the scenic village of Banska Bystrica, where unrestrained by the niceties of American law and the American Constitution, the CIA could routinely use any interrogation techniques deemed productive.

"There they'll be questioned with whatever means are required to get the truth from them. I want all of you except for Mr. Miles — Fabian'll stay at Langley — to remain there until our people on the scene there have completed the job. Agent Byron, I want you to update me at least on a daily basis."

"Yes ma'am," Agent Byron acknowledged sharply. "And once we have gotten everything from them?"

They all waited with anticipation for Lucado's answer. It did not surprise them. "I don't want to ever see them again. Understood?"

Again, Agent Byron answered sharply, "Yes, Ma'am, Madame Director."

"Then we're finished here," Lucado said matter of factly. "Mr. Miles and I'll leave first. Your plane is ready and waiting. Once we're gone, get those two out of the country." Accompanied by an armed security guard, Lucado and Fabian Miles left the room.

Chapter 105

The door to the interrogation room opened, and the five CIA security men walked into the room, ready to bind and gag CD and Olive and put them on the CIA plane for Slovakia. "We can do this the easy way if you cooperate," Agent Byron said to CD and Olive. "We'll put you both into straitjackets, shackles, and handcuffs. We'll hood you and then take you to the plane. Once aboard, we'll take off the straitjackets and the hoods, but you'll be restrained to your seats. If you don't cooperate, we'll leave the straitjackets on. Are we clear?"

"Where're you taking us?" Olive asked.

"On a European vacation," Byron responded nonchalantly. "Will you cooperate?"

Both CD and Olive had decided already that resistance would be futile, that they would have to pick their time carefully because given the skills of most CIA agents and the apparent ruthlessness of Lucado's own people, CD and Olive would probably get only one chance to escape, and that the escape window would be appallingly slim. Stalling for time, CD said, "Look I'm only a professor, and I don't know what all this is about. I want a lawyer."

"Sir, I'm assuming from that that you won't cooperate, and I haven't yet told you in detail what the hard way is if you do not cooperate with us."

"What's the hard way?" CD asked.

'This," and without warning, Byron struck CD hard on the side of the head with a blackjack that he had been carrying in this hand. CD slumped to the floor, unconscious.

Olive screamed and said, "You fucking bastard!" She bent down over CD, cradling his head in her arms. She looked up at

Byron and said through clenched teeth. "You'll pay. I guarantee it."

"How touching. Pay? Not hardly," Byron said, now with a cruel grin on his face. He turned to the other men, "Get her ready for the plane. If she resists, use this." Byron tossed the blackjack, now with CD's blood on it, to one of the men. Byron turned toward the door as the other men grabbed Olive.

Shots suddenly sounded outside the hangar. The men stopped and jerked upright in surprise. The man closest to Olive just stood there, confusion registering on his young face. The other men ran to the door. Two more shots were heard outside of the building. Byron himself stood frozen as the three men rushed past him into the outer room. The man closest to Olive looked towards Byron for clarification of what was happening. Olive, with the lightning fast reflexes that had gotten her a 1A rating in the self-defense training she had undergone as part of the Procurement Project, slammed her knee into the man's crotch. He doubled over in agony as Olive ripped the Glock from the holster in the small of his back. The man rose up in time to receive the solid blow on the side of his head from the Glock. He fell to the floor, not fully unconscious but severely dazed. Byron rushed at Olive who stepped lithely to the side and viciously smashed the Glock into the back of Byron's head as he passed her. It hardly fazed the big man. He turned and started to draw his own gun.

"Do that and you die, you bastard." Olive said, sounding like a female version of Clint Eastwood. Byron moved his hand slowly away from his own pistol. "Now what? Are you going to shoot me?" Byron said as he raised his hand to the huge cut on his bleeding head.

Olive said, "Give me the excuse, bastard. There's nothing I would like better. But in the meantime, face down on the floor, arms overhead."

Several more shots were heard from outside the small building. Byron took a step towards Olive.

"One more step, please take it," Olive said. "Oh, I forgot. I really don't need an excuse." She raised the pistol and pointed it directly at Byron's midsection. "Midsection wounds hurt a lot, they take a long time to kill, and I reserve them for the most despicable people." As Olive began to pull the trigger, Byron yelled as if in pain, fell to the floor, and in one swift, fluid movement swept his leg across Olive's ankles sending her to the concrete floor in a heap. The gun fell from her hand and clattered across the floor.

Byron was on top of her in a flash. He smashed her in the face three times in quick succession. Olive had one hand pinned behind her but with two fingers of her free hand she viciously gouged Byron's eye. He screamed in pain and grabbed at his eyeball which was now grotesquely hanging from its bloody socket by an optic thread. He fumbled but was able to draw his own Glock. "Bitch!" he screamed in rage. With one hand over his useless eye, the trigger finger of his gun hand squeezed at the black trigger of the Glock.

Olive clamped her eyes shut and clenched her fists. She heard the deafening shot ring out and then another and then another. She had expected to feel the jolts and stabbing of the bullets, but she strangely felt no pain. *So this is what death is like? No pain, just....* Suddenly, Byron fell heavily on top of her. Blood flowed from a hole in the side of his head and more profusely from another bullet rip in his neck. Olive pushed the dead man off of her and rolled to her side. She crouched on all fours, and then she saw CD in a half sitting position on the floor holding the gun that had been knocked from Olive's hand.

"CD," Olive cried tears of joy. "I love you." She crawled over to CD. "Next time, please don't play it so close." Then Olive added, "My love."

"How about a thank you?" CD said with a weak smile as he put his arm around his life partner whom he had almost lost.

"Yes, thank you." She embraced him. Then in mock seriousness, Olive drew back. "But I thought you were an expert marksman. Two out of three shots? You must be losing it." Olive managed a weak smile as she teased CD.

"Oh, you mean that third shot?"

"Yes, that would be the one I mean," Olive said.

"That was for him." CD motioned to the man whom Olive had first clubbed with her own pistol. He was lying on the floor with a small pool of blood having drained from the neat hole squarely between his eyes. "He'd drawn his own gun," CD said quietly. "Mistake number one."

"And mistake number two?"

"He was aiming at you."

At that moment, they heard several shots from outside the hangar. CD and Olive peered out of the window to see Lucado and Fabian Miles along with two of their personal security guards pinned down behind a black limousine thirty yards away from Lucado's own car. Across from Lucado and Miles, Olive and CD could see several men who had taken cover behind another car. On the door of that car was the small FBI emblem.

At that moment, Olive and CD heard a voice over a loudspeaker. "Director Lucado, I am FBI Director Jonathan Fogg. I'm acting under orders of President Armstrong to take you into custody. You're being charged with domestic espionage under the American First Defense Act. You and everyone with you are directed to throw down your weapons and come out you're your hands raised." Then there was silence.

CD whispered to Olive, "The FBI is after the CIA?"

"It looks that way. Unreal!"

Lucado turned to Fabian Miles. Both were still crouched behind the black limousine. "Fabian, they're after me, not you. I'll let them take me. You get back to the office and use that Washington clone to trade for me. This whole thing's some kind of high stakes game that the President's playing, and it's going to irreparably damage the nation. When they take me in, you're the only one who can protect the security of the nation. You do that by forcing them to release me, and then together we can try to make things right."

For the first time in his CIA life, Fabian Miles doubted Lucado. "Madame Director, that makes no sense to me. The Washington clone's no threat to the nation, and turning him over to the President cannot possibly be a threat to the nation. And realistically I can't go marching into the White House and bargain for your release. Once they know I've got the Washington clone, I'm dead meat." He paused and stared at Lucado who glared back at him with cold, tired eyes. "Madame Director, with all due respect, I can't do it. Plus, there's no way they're going to let me go."

"Fabian, there're things I haven't told even you. You've got to trust me on this. The President, TT, and the others are trying to turn this nation into a dictatorship, and the clones are the only thing preventing that. That's why I can't let them have the Washington clone. They'll kill those clones fast track. You're the last chance we have, Fabian. Please, Fabian, for your country."

The loudspeaker blasted forth again. "Director Lucado, what is your decision?"

Lucado did not respond. Fabian suddenly stood, tossed his .38 out into the open parking lot, raised his hands, and started out into the open. Lucado stiffened with rage, turned to her security guard. "Shoot him!"

The security guard stared at Lucado, dumbfounded. "You're asking me to shoot our own man in the back? Fuck that. No way."

"That's Fabian Miles," Fogg said softly to his aides. "What the hell is he doing here?" Fogg then activated the loudspeaker again, addressing Fabian Miles who was slowly walking towards the FBI contingent. "Keep your hands raised, Mr. Miles, turn left, and go straight to the black SUV." No one had noticed the black Toyota Land Cruiser with its lights off which had crept into a position on the far side of the CIA hangar.

Lucado and her security guard looked to the left, but the CIA hangar blocked their vision so that they could not see that not only was there an SUV on the scene but that there were also a dozen armor-clad FBI agents. "Shoot him," Lucado hissed at the security guard.

"No way," the guard responded.

Joelle Lucado then reached under her waist length blouse and drew the Steyr L-A1 that she secretly kept on her person. She fired once at Fabian Miles.

He yelled, grabbed his side, and stared at the blood coming through his shirt. "What the fuck?" He had tried to shout but the sound was muted. He sank to his knees.

"Somebody shot him!" Exclaimed Fogg to the aides who were crouched with him behind one of the FBI vehicles.

Lucado then burst forth from her hiding place and advanced on Miles who was lying on the ground, moaning. She raised her small handgun again and took aim at the helpless Miles. He stared up at her. "Director Lucado, what — ?" Before he could finish the sentence two loud shots rang out from the agents hidden beside the CIA hangar. Lucado fell, no more than three feet from Miles. She never saw the agents, fixated as she was on eliminating Fabian Miles.

Fogg stared horror-struck at the scene playing out on the asphalt parking lot in front of him. The Director of the CIA had been shot, but only after she had shot her top aide in cold blood.

Miles, now bleeding profusely and in the early stages of shock, stared at Lucado. Though the FBI sharpshooter had mortally wounded Lucado, she was still moving slightly. Lying on the ground, the life draining from her, she twisted painfully in order to see Fabian's face, only inches from her own. "You could've saved everything, but you're a traitor." Her voice was barely audible, but Miles had known the CIA Director long enough to perceive her hatred. Then he knew what she intended to do.

"No!" he shouted with surprising strength.

Lucado, as her final earthly act, squeezed the trigger of her small handgun with what strength she had left. Being only inches from Miles, she could not miss. The 9mm round entered Miles's left ear and instantly killed him.

A second shot rang out from the FBI sharpshooter, and Lucado's body jerked sideways. Her grip on the Steyr relaxed, and the gun slipped from her fingers. Four agents in flak jackets rushed to her, kicked her handgun aside, and dragged Lucado's lifeless body from the open parking lot back to their concealed position. Not knowing who might be in the hangar or what dangers lurked there, the agents would not expose themselves any longer than required to drag Lucado out of the line of fire. Two agents checked Miles and then rushed back to the safety of their cover.

"Lucado's dead." Director Fogg received the confirmation radio message from the agents who had recovered Lucado's body. "So is Mr. Miles."

"OK," Fogg said to no one in particular. As he turned to the hangar from which shots had sounded earlier, he said, "Now we've got to figure out who or what's in there. Whoever it is, they're armed, too."

Watching the violence in the parking lot outside the secret CIA hangar, CD and Olive were both stunned and relieved. They were free of Lucado and the rogue CIA operation, but clearly the FBI was playing for keeps. The FBI had just killed the Director of the CIA!

"OK, how do we play this? We have about one minute before they're in here." CD was the one asking the question. Usually he could rely on his instincts to guide his actions, but what he and Olive were now facing was bizarre beyond anything they had ever trained for or anticipated. They were fugitives from a government that was plummeting into chaos.

Olive and CD then quickly sketched out their strategy to each other, if it could even be called a strategy.

Olive summarized their predicament. "It's clear that the government is in a meltdown. The FBI Director killing the CIA Director. A new President who says he wants a dialogue but whose people are killing to get their way. One clone dead, one clone in the hands of the Russians, and the other two clones who knows where. And here we are. We've been on the run, and we've got two dead bodies in the other room. CD, I'd say we don't give away anything until we are reunited with Alex and Thomas and Rufus."

"Right. I'm not worried about the dead bodies. The first thing I'm worried about is whether the new President is for us or against us. He says that he wants a dialogue. I say no dialogue until we're all together, the clones and us. No divide and conquer. Plus, we want our own independent outlet to the press. That'll protect us from being hushed up."

"Or disappearing," Olive interjected then asked, "Should we insist on a lawyer?"

"I'd say for the time being, no. We rely on the press to protect us from the government. Lawyers will use the judicial system if it comes to blows, and we know that could be foolish if we want the truth to prevail. The media's a better hope if it's truth that we want."

Olive looked incredulous. "Are you serious? The media? Truth?"

"There're enough media outlets that the truth will be in there somewhere," CD said, then added, "I hope. At least the government won't have a monopoly on what's being said. And remember what the first Hamilton said, that the diversity and multiplicity of interests is the most effective check on governmental power, and that works for the media and truth, too."

"Just keep in mind, CD, that the feds routinely read emails from the press just like everybody else's, and listen in on their phone conversations, too. This is a different time from when Hamilton lived."

"The best journalists already know how to set up outside ways of communicating as well as we do, Olive, so we should be OK."

"Once we've made the initial contacts," Olive reminded CD.

"Right. Once we've set up working arrangements with the right media people."

Director Fogg's voice sounded through the loudspeaker. "This is FBI Director Fogg. All persons in the building are ordered to exit the building. If you're armed, you're ordered to toss your weapons out in front of you as you exit the building. You're ordered to exit the building now with your hands raised."

CD started to the door. "Wait!" Olive said. "You said the first thing you were worried about was the new President. What's the second thing?"

"They can't know of your connection to the Procurement Project. Our story's that you were knocked unconscious and don't know how these two were killed. I killed them. That way, I can spin the story, and we don't have to worry about their getting one version from you and another version from me. OK?"

"That works," Olive said with a smirk. "You're the hero, and I'm the helpless female. The usual macho male bullshit, right, CD?"

"Right." He smiled weakly.

"That'll work for me this one time," Olive said with a smile. She gave CD a quick kiss and said, "Well, here we go." Olive started towards the door.

"One more thing," CD said hurriedly. "Once we're outside, they'll split us up. Stay with the plan. We say nothing of consequence until we're all reunited. That's the bottom line. Stay with it."

"You have one minute to exit the building!" Fogg's voice over the loudspeaker was monotone but emphatic.

Olive walked out of the front door and tossed her weapon aside. She was immediately grabbed by two men and thrown to the ground. She was thoroughly frisked for weapons and for bombs. When the frisking was completed, one of the men said, "OK, ma'am, please stand up and place your hands behind you."

Olive did as she was told. She was immediately cuffed, and the men started to hustle her to a waiting car as CD exited the building, tossed his Glock on the ground, and raised his hands. He then saw how roughly the men were treating Olive and shouted angrily "Hey, you'd better be — " Before he could complete his warning, CD was lifted off his feet and thrown to the ground by two men who, as they had with Olive, thoroughly frisked him. Then CD was jerked back to his feet and tightly cuffed.

One of the agents turned to Fogg who had watched the entire process from just thirty feet away. "He had the one firearm, Director, a Glock. He tossed it out on the ground as directed. He's got nothing else on him, no I.D., nothing."

Fogg now walked up to CD, stood six inches from CD's face, and said coldly, "Whoever you are, you'd better have a fucking mighty good reason for being with our late CIA director. You're in deep shit, to put it so you can understand it."

CD looked surprised, "Late CIA Director?"

Fogg replied, "Yes, late. You will be late too if you don't cooperate fully. First, you're carrying no ID. Maybe you can explain why, and maybe you can enlighten me just who the fuck you are and," Fogg motioned to the hangar, " how you ended up in there."

"Director Fogg," one of Fogg's agents shouted from the door of the hangar. "There're two dead bodies in here,".

Fogg looked squarely at CD. "OK, go ahead. Who the hell are you, and how did you end up here?"

"I am Charles Delna. I'm a professor of linguistics at Tulane University. Somehow, that woman whom you say is the CIA Director thought I was caught up in this clone thing, and she had her goons seize my wife and me. That's about the gist of it, Director Fogg."

CD had decided that he would not reveal his link to the clones unless Fogg already knew CD's role. Fogg did not disappoint CD.

"You might indeed be a professor, but I damn well know you have been harboring those clones, so don't bullshit me. But we'll cover all of that later. Right now, tell me what happened in that building, and tell me how you killed those two men. I guess you're the one who killed them, aren't you?"

"What happened in the building?" CD had a habit of repeating questions in order to give himself a little time to formulate his answer. He paused, looked pensive, then continued. "The CIA Director — "

"Lucado," Fogg interjected.

"Yes, Lucado. Her goons brought us to this building. She showed up and asked us a few questions. Then she said they would take us out of the country, some place in Slovakia, so they could drain every stitch of information out of us without interference from American law." CD added the embellishments, familiar as he was with certain CIA practices since 9/11. "Then dispose of us."

Fogg did not look surprised. "Interesting," he said. "You say her goons brought you to this building. From where?"

CD now had to decide whether he would stonewall Fogg or pretend cooperation. He fully understood that someone was questioning Olive at the same time. "I'm willing to say that they brought us in from outside this area, but until I'm reunited with my wife I won't give any more details?"

Fogg smiled. "And why not, Professor?"

The question surprised CD. He had expected a threat or at least some pressure. "Because my experience with the government in the last few weeks has been so sordid and so arbitrary that I don't trust you or anyone else to deal with me and my wife fairly. So even though you're the Director of the FBI, you've got bigger problems than me right now. You just killed the Director of the CIA. Your government is falling apart, Director

Fogg, and until I'm reunited with my wife and until we have a lawyer I'm not about to talk any further."

CD had deliberately used the magic word 'lawyer.' This word invoked the highest level of legal protections under the old *Miranda* case such that technically Fogg could arguably not question him further. Undoubtedly, Fogg knew this, but under the national security umbrella, Fogg would simply ignore *Miranda*.

Fogg smiled knowingly at CD, paced for several moments, then turned from CD and opened the heavy steel door to the hangar and disappeared inside. After a full five minutes, Fogg came out of the building, stood in the doorway, and just stared at CD. After another minute, he walked over to CD who was still in cuffs. "Professor, I'm not your enemy. I came to this site under the hope that you and the clones would be here. Clearly the clones aren't here, and I don't think for a minute that you're going to tell me where they are." Fogg had gambled that CD did not know that the FBI had already seized the clones.

"That's right, Mr. Fogg."

Fogg did not miss a beat. "My President desperately wants to open a meaningful dialogue with the clones. He's worlds apart from that imbecile Ray. Ray's dead. His policies are dead, Professor Delna. Dead. There absolutely has got to be a dialogue between the President and the clones. You can make that dialogue happen, Professor, but if you're holding out, we'll have no alternative but to think that for some reason you don't want that dialogue and that the clones have something to hide, like maybe this whole clone thing's a giant hoax." Fogg knew that the "clone thing" was not a hoax, but he wanted to keep CD talking.

"Director Fogg, if you want a dialogue, if the President wants one, take me and my wife to him. Together."

Fogg again surprised CD, "No problem. That's what we'll do, but first, tell me what happened inside. Exactly how did you overpower those two men? Exactly how were they killed?"

CD described in detail how the men had knocked Olive unconscious, how he had seized the Glock when the men had gotten careless, had he had disarmed and subsequently killed Lucado's security guards.

When CD had finished describing the events that had transpired inside the hangar, Fogg just stared at CD with an expression of disbelief. Finally he said, "You mean to tell me that you, a mere linguistics professor, from a disabled position, plugged a trained, armed soldier between the eyes? What's your background, Professor? What training do you have?"

"None. None at all. It was a lucky shot. Sure, I've been to the range a few times with friends, but believe me, Director, I was petrified, and it was a lucky shot."

"Well, actually I don't for a minute believe your story, Professor. There's a lot of missing information." With a wave of his hand, Fogg dismissed the topic. "But it doesn't really matter that much how you killed them. I just wonder why you feel you need to cover up the facts about what happened in there." After a pause, Fogg added, "And I'll find out pretty soon. Professor, I have the resources to figure out exactly who you are and what training and background you have. And that in turn, Professor, will tell me a lot about this whole clones matter." Fogg's tone had become totally skeptical. "You could just come clean now, you know. It would save a lot of time, and would even help the clones unless you're lying."

"That's the way it is. We were completely lucky. God apparently wanted us to survive. It's in His plan, and with all due respect, Director Fogg, without His intervention, neither my wife nor I would be alive." CD was aware that Jonathan Fogg was in his own unorthodox way a nondenominational Christian and would not debunk CD's claim of God's protection. CD himself suddenly felt weakened. He had invoked a divine explanation not because he thought it was true, though he did, but for the ulterior motive that it would hopefully deflect or even eliminate further interrogation by Fogg. It might even help get CD and Olive reunited.

Fogg paced again, this time more slowly and with apparent concentration. Finally, he turned away from CD and faced the two agents who had stood by while Fogg was questioning CD. "Agent, turn it off." The FBI agent turned off the video recorder that had caught the entire exchange between Fogg and CD. "Take him and his wife to the Castle." The reference was to the FBI's new, high-tech facility in rural Virginia.

"Together?" the agent queried.

"Sure," Fogg replied. He was relying on the fact that everything Olive and CD said to each other in the van on the way to the Castle would be captured on audio/video and thoroughly dissected. Of course, Olive and CD knew that too.

After CD and Olive were securely ensconced in an unmarked FBI van and en route to the Castle, Fogg said to his contingent, "Get rid of those bodies, clean up this site, and remove any evidence that anyone was ever here. Take Lucado's body to The Shack. We'll figure out what to do there, but there can be no trace that anything happened here. Also, get DNA samples."

With that, Fogg walked slowly to his own car and lowered himself into the rear seat. "Let's go to the White House, Sam."

Chapter 106

President Armstrong's expression was a mixture of shock and disbelief. FBI Director Fogg had finished briefing the President on the events that had occurred at the CIA's secret hangar at Andrews. Attorney General Trentini, Secretary of State Cordero, and Secretary of Defense Shulla sat motionless, waiting to see what the President's response would be to the CIA Director's going rogue, murdering her closest aide, planning on killing the professor and his wife, then herself being gunned down by the FBI Director. Added to those events, the professor and his wife were now in FBI custody.

The President stood, paced around, and then sat down heavily in the ornate, burgundy wing chair that President Ray had brought into the Oval Office. "So now, how do we get control of the CIA? How do we find out how far the corruption reaches into the CIA? And the professor, but now that we've got the two clones, he's not that important. But we need to find out what he knows." The President looked tired and drawn.

TT broke the long silence. "My guess is that the professor and his wife hid the clones from us."

"Exactly," Shulla said. "His role in this whole thing needs some explaining. For one, how could he escape our searches for so long?"

"Is he a Russian spy?" The President asked.

Cordero was instantly disturbed by the President's naïveté. "No way," he said simply.

"How can you be so sure?" President asked.

"Because all this time that he apparently had the clones, he could have taken them to Russia, and he didn't. Second, none of his actions suggest in the slightest that he's colluding with the Russians."

"Maybe you're right. But maybe the Russians want these clones here in the good old USA so they can foment unrest and spread disinformation. This professor and his wife too have surely gotten training from somewhere, and they show up on none of our databases," Fogg said. "Plus, he speaks Russian. We found that out from just a little snooping around at Tulane where he's a professor. But even though there're questions about who he is and what his background is, that's not enough to draw any way out conclusion like he's a Russian agent."

"Whatever. It's enough to leave it as an open question, and that means we regard him as if he's an enemy," the President said. "We can put him and his wife in cold storage. Our issue now's the clones. Now that we have two clones, I really don't care a whole hell of a lot about the professor or his wife. Plus, here's something else that I haven't told any of you yet. I had a face to face with Lucado. She claimed she had the George Washington clone and would produce him today. I don't know where he is. She didn't say. But that means that President Ray in fact maybe didn't murder the Washington clone. If Lucado was telling the truth, that clone's alive, and we have to find him. With her dead, that might be very, very difficult."

The others in the room, looked around at each other. Finally TT spoke. "Mr. President, with all due respect, sir, if we're to advise you well, we have to know all of the facts. I know that there are things Presidents have to hold tight, but, Mr. President — "

"Whatever. You know now," the President snapped.

After an awkward period of silence, Shulla spoke with confidence and vigor. He was determined to contain the internal hemorrhaging of the government. "To find out about the Washington clone, we have to get into Lucado's files, Mr.

President, and I already have people on the way to secure the CIA headquarters."

Everyone in the room stared in disbelief at the Secretary of Defense. "You what?" Cordero exclaimed. "You're having the military occupy the CIA offices? Shulla, you're a total idiot. No one even knows Lucado's dead, and you're making it look like some coup out of a banana republic." Cordero turned to the President. "Mr. President, call him and his dogs off, sir!"

President Armstrong barked, "Mr. Shulla, tell the military to stand down and not to get anywhere near the CIA headquarters. This nation will go into a panic if that happens. That was one of the most ill-conceived, idiotic actions I've ever heard of a government official taking! Ever!"

"Mr. President, the nation will also go into a panic if they find out that the CIA's out of control and that you haven't done anything to control them." TT stood as he talked. "I suggest the FBI quietly secure Director Lucado's offices while you announce to the nation that Director Lucado was killed in an unfortunate shooting accident at an undisclosed CIA practice range."

Cordero responded vehemently, "The press will rip that to shreds. The only way we can handle this is to tell the nation the truth, that the CIA Director had a mental event and that she was gunned down when she murdered her own assistant."

"A mental event? That's the truth?" Shulla's face was turning a light shade of crimson. "That's as much a lie as anything else I've heard."

"OK, just shut up, everybody!" The President exclaimed. "Where's Lucado's body?"

Fogg looked at TT questioningly. Everyone looked at Fogg. Fogg glanced again over at TT. Unnoticed by the others, TT nodded slightly.

Fogg cleared his throat and said weakly, "Mr. President, we eliminated the body and sanitized the site. I felt that would be best in order — "

The President interrupted Fogg, "Mr. Fogg tell me in English what does that mean? Eliminated. Sanitized."

"Mr. President, we incinerated the body and cleaned up the CIA hangar where it all happened so that there would be no forensic evidence."

"You incinerated the body?" The President's jaw dropped. Along with everyone else in the room except for TT, President Armstrong was incredulous. "Why the fuck did you do that?"

"Mr. President, I think I was caught up in the drama of the moment and simply made a bad decision."

"You are fucking right; you made a bad decision!" the President exclaimed. "You're fucking fired, Mr. Fogg! Fired! Now! Get out!" The President was now shouting.

"Mr. President, may I suggest some calm and some time for reflection," Cordero said. His tone was quiet, but his voice still showed the tension of the moment.

"Yes, Mr. President," TT said. "If the nation knows the FBI Director shot the CIA Director and that you then fired the FBI Director, the nation, the markets, will go into a free fall. I suggest we wait. If you want to fire Fogg, that is surely your prerogative, but the timing is important."

"And you can bet your balls that the Russians will take full advantage of it," Cordero interjected.

The President clenched his fists. "OK, Fogg you can stay on, but, TT, I want you to personally handle all this fucking clone stuff, the professor stuff, everything, and Fogg, I don't want you doing anything at all without checking with TT first. Better yet, don't do anything period. Stay out of sight, and no talking to anybody."

"Yes sir," Fogg said.

Everyone was silent. The rapidly unfolding events were exhausting everyone, and they all realized that the feverish pace into which their deliberations had been sucked was impairing the quality of their decisions.

They sat. Finally TT asked in a thin voice, "So how do we find the Washington clone, and how do we secure Lucado's files?"

President Armstrong said, "They are one and the same question. Those files will contain the location of the Washington clone."

"Hopefully," TT said meekly.

"But those files, if we can find the right ones, will be heavily encrypted," Cordero observed.

"OK, for now, we appoint an Acting Director. I want the new director in place at Langley before we announce anything. Then, the first order of business is to find that Washington clone and turn him over to Justice. TT, you'll take it from there."

"Who, Mr. President?" Cordero asked.

"Who, what?" President asked.

"Who do you want as the Acting Director of the CIA?"

"I want Senator Sullivan," the President quickly responded. She has credibility from both sides and will bring some stability and calmness to the whole situation. The Senate will have no problem confirming her."

Caroline Sullivan was a moderate in a party of conservatives. She had been in the Senate for twelve years, and somewhat unusual for that body, she was apparently not in the financial clutches of any outside interests. Her speeches on the Senate floor and in her election campaigns were noteworthy for their Dirksen-like diction and lofty vocabulary. Her career had been scandal-free as was her personal life. Her husband was a well-known, though irritable, sports fisherman and at one time had hosted a relatively unpopular television program dedicated to hunting and fishing.

"That sounds good, Mr. President." TT quickly endorsed the President's choice.

"Sometimes Caroline gets stressed and acts hastily, Mr. President," Cordero observed. "And she has a mean streak," he added. In the past, Senator Sullivan had gone after Secretary Cordero in several oversight hearings, and Cordero apparently had not enjoyed being the target of her incisive questioning.

"She's the one." President Armstrong did not even acknowledge Cordero's remark. "I'll see if I can get hold of her now, and get her on board before we announce anything about Lucado," President Armstrong said. "Hopefully she'll accept."

The President stood. "That's enough for one day, gentlemen. Hell, that's enough for one lifetime! I'll personally try to get hold of Senator Sullivan. TT, keep those clones out of sight. Then tomorrow after I finish with Sullivan at Camp David, I'll go to The Eagle Rock and meet the clones, and I might as well meet with the professor and his wife."

The Eagle Rock was a secret government installation outside Auburn, Alabama. It was under protected airspace so that the in-the-air eyes of the media could not watch the comings and goings. Few outside the top echelons of the Executive Branch knew anything for sure about The Eagle Rock. The official story was that it was a military installation dedicated to some kind of unspecified, specialized training. The media had never been allowed inside The Eagle Rock. In fact, it was a glorified meeting facility and residence where the President could conduct meetings in total secrecy. President George W. Bush had been known to use The Eagle Rock on several occasions. In a break with transition protocol, the Bush Administration had concealed even the existence and function of The Eagle Rock from President Obama whom they considered not trustworthy enough to know about the facility. When in his last month in office, President Bush had become convinced that that assessment was indeed accurate, he made sure that the secrecy of The Eagle Rock was protected, that Obama would hopefully never know anything about it. Obama's transition team had been told that the facility was a low-level training base, one of many scattered throughout the nation. When Obama's second term of office was concluded, in an extraordinary, secret meeting, Bush then briefed Obama's successor, President-elect Trump, on the existence and true purposes of The Eagle Rock. As President, Trump made regular, but undisclosed, use of the facility. Biden knew about it but apparently never used it. President Ray had used the facility several times. President Armstrong himself had never been to The Eagle Rock but felt that now was the time.

"One more thing, Mr. President. If Sullivan accepts, do you want her at The Eagle Rock?" Cordero asked.

"No," President Armstrong responded. "She'll have her hands full at Langley. And rest assured that she'll accept. She'll be the new Director," the President said confidently.

TT looked worried. "Mr. President, do you really want the clones and all these other people all together at the same time, in one meeting? Things could be hard to control with all of them together."

The President stood, "TT, we've got to find out who they are, what they have to say, where they stand on the issues, whether they're a threat to this nation's stability or not."

"And maybe it's not whether they're a threat but whether they can help get this nation back on track," Shulla said.

"Yes and that, too," President Armstrong said without conviction, smiling. "Thank you, gentlemen." They all stood and moved to the door without shaking hands.

The President kept his smile and watched them exit. As soon as they had left the office, he dropped the smile and pressed a button on one of the desk telephones. When his speechwriter answered, President Armstrong said, "Write me a short statement announcing the appointment of Senator Caroline Sullivan as Acting Director of the Central Intelligence Agency. I'll need it tomorrow morning, but I'd like to take it with me to Camp David in an hour or two. Just something short. And prepare a digital authorization for Senator Sullivan to have complete CIA access, and I need that right away."

"I'll have the authorization to you in fifteen minutes, Mr. President. But can I ask, what about Lucado? Is she stepping down?"

"Yes, she's leaving that office, but don't put anything about her in the statement. I'll handle that part myself. And not a word to anyone. Anyone at all." The President placed the phone back in its cradle, smiled, and then buzzed Phyllis and asked her to get Senator Sullivan on the phone.

Chapter 107

As the President readied for his short flight to Camp David, Senator Sullivan was being driven to the White House from her Capitol office in the Hart Building when her cell phone beeped. The incoming call was from her top legal assistant on the Intelligence Committee that she chaired. She closed the partition between her and the front seat to enable complete privacy for the conversation.

"Yes, Jay. What have you got?" Sullivan expected Jay Howie, her top Administrative Investigator, to fill her in on his efforts to investigate whether the NSA was, as rumored, carrying out complete digital surveillance of the Federal Reserve.

"Senator, activate your scrambler before we go on. I'm on scrambler now."

Senator Sullivan pressed the red Encrypt icon on the screen of her high-tech phone. "OK, Jay, I'm on. What's happening?"

"I've just sent you a video from Joint Base Andrews. You need to look at it. I received it from our guy at CNN. He says they'll go live with it as soon as they determine that it's not a hoax."

"Tell me more, Jay." Sullivan was imagining a crash or a secret plane or something along the lines of an unidentified drone.

"Senator, it looks like Director Lucado has been shot and killed."

Before he could continue, Senator Sullivan exclaimed, "Repeat that, Jay." She could not believe what she had heard.

"Joelle Lucado's dead. She was shot, and, Senator, you're not going to believe this. She was shot by Jonathan Fogg! If the video is genuine."

"Fogg?" Sullivan could hardly believe what she was hearing. "What happened? And how did somebody video it? Do we know that it's not a hoax?"

"It looks genuine, Senator. The video's from an anonymous person who saw it happen and videoed it with his phone. The quality's not great, but it's good enough for CNN to air. The phone was apparently one of those late generation androids which can take long range videos if you have the right app."

"OK. OK. Tell me what happened on the video, Jay."

"Someone else got shot, too, but we can't tell who it was. There was never a face forward frame with that other person, but here's the strange part, Senator. It was Lucado who shot the other person from just a few feet away. She had already been shot and was down on the ground but was still alive. She then shot the other person."

"Hold on, Jay." Sullivan's limo was approaching the entrance to the White House grounds. Sullivan pressed the intercom button and said to the driver, "Don't go in, Sean. I need more time. Drive around until I give the word."

"Yes ma'am." Sullivan's driver veered sharply away from the White House gate and headed out towards the Washington Monument.

"Jay, I'm back. Send me the video."

"I just did, Senator. You should have it by now."

"How do we know it was Lucado? How certain are we?"

"Unless it was photo shopped, there's no doubt. None at all. It's a face forward shot, and there's no doubt, Senator. CNN trusts the video. They're saying it's the real thing."

"Anything else?"

"You'll see it on the video. After the shooting, Fogg used a speaker and ordered people inside the hangar to come out, but whoever videoed it, we hear him saying on the video that someone's coming, and he shut it off. Probably he was some serviceman and would get in deep shit if he was videoing stuff on that part of the base."

"OK, Jay, I've got the video now. See what else you can find out. And call Loup at CNN and see if they'll hold off until we can get a handle on things. If he resists, tell him there's more to the story, that he'll be glad if he waits, and tell him that if he won't wait, we'll give Fox the scoop on the next part of the story."

"OK, Senator, good luck over there."

"Thanks. I guess now I know why the President was so insistent that I come over tonight and not wait until tomorrow."

Sullivan snapped on the video that her aide had just sent to her. After watching and re-watching the video of the carnage at Andrews, Sullivan told her driver to return to the White House.

Chapter 108

President Royster Armstrong pulled out all of the stops in making his pitch to Senator Sullivan that she take over the Directorship of the CIA. After the President gave his version of what had happened at Andrews, a version which, though incomplete and avoiding any mention of the clones, was largely consistent with the video that Sullivan had watched, Sullivan asked the one question that Armstrong had hoped she would not think of. "Where is Lucado's body now, and has there been a post-mortem examination?"

The President, usually not at a loss for words, seemed to Sullivan suddenly to turn pale. "Caroline," the President said slowly. "Director Fogg saw that the body was so shot up that he thought it best to order cremation in order to avoid conspiracy theories spinning out of control."

Sullivan could not believe what she was hearing. "Has Lucado's body, in fact, been cremated?"

"Yes, Senator Sullivan, it has. Fogg realizes that it was a bad, very bad decision, but it is what it is."

"Mr. President, that's an understatement. That decision alone will generate conspiracy theories by the dozens. What else are you not telling me? Is all of this in some way related to the clones matter?"

President Armstrong realized that if Sullivan took the position at the CIA, she would find out everything about the clones soon enough, really as soon as she got hold of Lucado's files, but Armstrong intended to triage those files personally as soon as TT had impounded them. And, on the other hand, if Sullivan did not take the CIA post, then she did not need to know anything about the clones matter beyond what she already knew, which was not much. So the President opted to play it close to the vest. "Senator, we don't know yet. We're still trying to figure all that out."

"Give me the latest on the clones, Mr. President." Sullivan's demand was direct. Though Sullivan was too experienced in the ways of Washington to expect the President to be forthcoming, she was curious to see how he would handle the issue.

"We don't know anything else at this point, Senator. It's that simple. We're looking for them, and to be honest, we think we have a good lead on where they are and we're trying to establish a dialogue with them. We're surely not trying to capture them like President Ray was. They're not our enemies."

Sullivan stared intently at the President. President Armstrong did not meet her gaze. He continued, "They represent a fantastic breakthrough in science and an historic opportunity for our government. I'm not going to blow that opportunity, Senator Sullivan, but I'm sure you understand that I really cannot go into detail. Of course, if you become Director of Central Intelligence, then you'll know it all, perhaps more than I know." The President tried to disarm Sullivan with his toothy, broad smile. "So, how about it, Caroline? Will you be this nation's new DCI? The country needs you. We're in an unsettled situation. Not only do we as Americans need your expertise, but we need the stability and credibility you'll bring to that position, to that agency. America needs you like never before. And I need you, Caroline. Can you accept this position? Will you?"

Caroline Sullivan, a speech pathologist, had also developed her long-time interest in facial and body language. Her research reached back to the early groundbreaking work by Paul Ekman on lying, and Sullivan had mastered the art of distinguishing truth from deception. She was sure that the President fully believed in much of what he was saying. But Sullivan was deeply disturbed by her reading of the President's unspoken language that hinted at large omissions and knowing deception. When he had said that they did not know anything more "at this point," Sullivan was virtually certain that he was lying. But Sullivan had no way of knowing in what direction the deception went. Were the clones truly at large? Or were they being held somewhere? Had Lucado detained them before she died? Had she even taken the location of the clones to her grave? Sullivan in her quick mind rapidly cycled through numerous questions and possible answers.

President Armstrong knew Caroline Sullivan well enough to know that along with her immense intellectual abilities, she also had a gigantic curiosity quotient. He had teased her with just enough disinformation and just enough "the nation needs you" verbiage à la LBJ that she would find it difficult to resist the opportunity to get in on the ground floor of the clones issue.

Sullivan's sense of curiosity and her discomfort with ambiguity prevailed. "Mr. President, I'll take the post, and given what happened at Andrews, you need to get out in front and announce the appointment right away."

"Definitely, I'll do that. You'll, of course, be Acting DCI until the Senate approves the appointment, but did you know, Caroline, that the Senate has never not approved a President's DCI appointment?"

"Well, actually, yes, I did know that, Mr. President."

President Armstrong smiled again, this time genuinely. "How about you come up to Camp David first thing tomorrow morning and we announce it then and there?"

"That'll be fine, Mr. President, but I need to get your authorization to go over to Langley right now and get up to speed on everything. There're going to be a lot of questions and conspiracies, and I need to be able to deal with them and put them to bed. And, Mr. President," Senator Sullivan hesitated and looked intensely at the President. "I plan to handle everything truthfully as far as the nation's security will allow it."

"Ah, yes, Caroline, but what is truth?" The President immediately realized the profound biblical indictment of that question and wished he had not uttered it. "I'll have a chopper ready for you tomorrow morning at eight o'clock."

"Thank you, Mr. President, but I still need your authorization to access Lucado's files at Langley."

The President smiled. "No problem." He had already prepared a digital authorization that would give Sullivan access to Lucado's office and files. Sullivan already had all the clearances this required, and the presidential document would take care of any barriers from the CIA's own internal human and digital firewalls. The President walked over to his large desk and picked up the spherical computer drive used for the most secret governmental documents. He handed the drive to Sullivan. "You are good to go, Director Sullivan. Welcome to the team." Though the President had anticipated that Sullivan would accept his offer, he now felt a wave of relief that Sullivan had in fact accepted.

"Thank you, Mr. President." Caroline Sullivan now realized that the President had been pretty certain from the beginning that she would end up accepting the CIA position. She had a worried expression as she briskly walked from the office to her waiting limo. It would be a long night at Langley.

President Armstrong smiled after Sullivan had left the Oval Office. He realized that TT would have already impounded and removed the clones' files from Lucado's offices. Though undoubtedly there were copies of the files elsewhere at the CIA, Sullivan would not be able to find them for a matter of days. Plus the President had other plans for how the clones matter would be handled, and by whom.

Chapter 109

Though it is highly unusual for an announcement of a major executive appointment to be made at Camp David, the relative seclusion and the restricted access to what happens at that secluded outpost made it easier for the Armstrong Administration to limit and at least for now eliminate media questioning of Senator Sullivan. The White House had long ago organized a special press corps credentialed to cover Camp David events and to represent the vast media establishment, and President Armstrong was confident that he could at least temporarily limit the speculation by announcing the appointment of Senator Sullivan in the controlled environs of Camp David. But at the same time, the President was cleverly relying on at least some speculation regarding the killing of Joelle Lucado in order to provide a distraction from his even more important secret meeting with the clones that would be held at The Eagle Rock in short order.

After the President introduced Senator Sullivan to the small Camp David press corps and following Sullivan's own noncommittal remarks accepting the appointment, the President then surprised the journalists covering the event. "Ladies and gentlemen, I'm sure you understand that Senator Sullivan is under a tremendous pressure of time to get up to speed not only on the events surrounding the auto accident which killed Director Lucado, but also she needs to get up to speed as quickly as possible on other events affecting the national security. Therefore, I'm asking that you hold your questions until Senator Sullivan can in the very near future hold a formal press conference open to the larger media establishment. Thank you very much." The President then in a staged gesture of gallantry took Senator Sullivan's elbow and quickly escorted her from the stage. Her grimace from the firmness of the President's grip told any journalists perceptive enough to pick up on it that more was going on than just an announcement, that Sullivan was being muzzled.

Unexpectedly, the usually docile Camp David press corps broke out into indignation and immediate suspicion of the President's motives. Questions were yelled.

"Why was Lucado shot?"

"Does Sullivan know anything about the clones?"

"Why won't you let her answer questions?"

"What are you covering up, Mr. President?"

When a journalist who had been one of the Administration's most unabashed apologists yelled that last question out in a loud voice, the President whirled around with unmistakable anger. "I'm not covering up a single damn thing, Mr. Randall, and I resent the accusation of your question. I'm attempting to provide some calmness and stability during these days when, quite frankly, our nation's having an extremely rough time. And your hysterical accusation is helping the extremists and those who would destabilize our government. I would hope you could be more patriotic, Mr. Randall. Since 2021, divisiveness and acrimony has emanated from the White House. I am trying to change that, but your type of questioning just continues to divide us." With that, President Armstrong realized that he had provided fodder for the always-hungry press corps. "Gentlemen, I apologize for my outburst. I'm under a lot of stress, and I just ask for your patience and understanding," and with that the President hurried from the briefing room to a raucous chorus of questions being shouted by the members of the fourth estate.

When the door to the briefing room was securely shut, the President said to Sullivan, "This way," and led her into his auxiliary office. "Fuck the press! Dammit, they'll do anything to attack me or anyone else in power. It's Trump all over again! Why can't they love me like they loved Biden? Shitheads, all of them," the President exclaimed.

Caroline Sullivan was surprised at the vehemence of the President's castigation of the press. "Mr. President, I'll hold a brief news conference once I get to Langley. Maybe that'll soften them up a little. They're actually pretty easily led, you know."

"Yes, I know, Caroline." The President feigning calmness, continued. "But no press conferences until I give the word, OK?"

Sullivan was again surprised. "What about transparency, Mr. President? And what about the fact that we're still a democracy, and the people have at least some right to hear from their government officials? And what about my independence to seek the truth wherever it is and whatever it is?"

"You work for me now, Senator Sullivan. No press conferences until I give the word. And your mission's not to seek some amorphous, unknowable truth. Your mission is to protect the security of this nation."

Senator Sullivan did not respond.

"Well?" the President asked.

"Very well, Mr. President, but your preventing me from holding a press conference could very well come back to haunt you when they begin to ask why no press conferences in the wake of Lucado's death. I really think I need to meet with the press, if only in some kind of background briefing."

"Senator, it's final!" the President exclaimed in a loud voice, jabbing the air with his hand. "No press conferences, no briefings, none, nada! It's a dangerous situation we're now in, and if you muddy the waters, well, things regarding you could get out of control."

"Mr. President," Sullivan said, looking directly at President Armstrong. "Is that a threat?"

"As Nixon once said, Senator Sullivan, Presidents don't have to threaten." He paused. "Just do your job."

Without another word and thoroughly disheartened, Sullivan left the room and headed for the unmarked CIA helicopter which would take her directly to Langley.

The President watched Sullivan through the window and then turned and walked into the adjoining smaller, secure communications office that housed the most advanced and secure communications equipment available on the planet. The President himself was a hands-on techie and did not use anyone to place secure calls for him. He actually enjoyed playing with the sophisticated equipment. With a smile, he quickly punched in the requisite codes. TT answered on the second beep.

"Hello, Mr. President. The news isn't good, sir. I've got all of the files my people could find, and there's no mention anywhere of the George Washington clone. We've gone through Lucado's computers, everything, her papers, her house, you name it. If Lucado actually had him, he could be anywhere. I could not find out where all the CIA's safe houses are, and no doubt Lucado was using houses that are off the books anyway."

"I expected as much, TT. But you've got the whole FBI at your disposal. Find that fucking clone!" Armstrong, not waiting for TT's response, slammed the End button with the palm of his hand, "Shit!"

The President rushed back to his living quarters and gathered some personal items. After he had alerted two specially selected aides that he was ready to leave, the two aides left for Marine One, the presidential helicopter that would take the two aides to a secluded vacation spot on the Outer Banks of North Carolina where the President liked to visit. One of the aides bore a remarkable resemblance to President Armstrong. The two were indistinguishable from a distance, and from a distance was as close as the media would be able to get to either Marine One or the North Carolina retreat. The press corps would be told that the President was going to North Carolina for a short get-away. Borrowing from some of the world's most infamous dictators, most notably Saddam Hussein, President Armstrong was using a look-alike to distract the world from his real location. President Armstrong left through the rear service door of the kitchen and got into a small, concealed compartment inside the cargo area of a delivery truck marked "Maryland Gourmet Products." The truck featured a large map of Maryland emblazoned on its side panel with a De Colores chicken superimposed on the map. The truck was a gaudy, familiar vehicle to the Camp David establishment, and its screaming garishness on this occasion served to conceal who was hidden inside of it. Maryland Gourmet Products itself even had a public telephone number that went to a special operator at the White House who would be on what was known as "good food" duty until the truck was needed for another special run to Camp David. Because the media would be watching, the truck on this occasion as on every occasion went through all of the regular procedures that all delivery vehicles leaving Camp David endured. The check of the cargo area was quick and cursory, on personal orders from the President himself. Once clear of the gates of Camp David and the media, the President got out of the smaller compartment and lay down on the comfortable foldout couch in the cargo area of the truck for the short ride to the Eastern West Virginia Regional Airport outside Martinsburg, West Virginia, where the President would take an unmarked, new generation Dassault Falcon 8X to The Eagle Rock's airport in Alabama. The exhausted President had just started to drift off to sleep when the truck stopped, and the Secret Service agent who was sharing the cargo area with the President said, "OK, Mr. President, we are at runway 26, and your plane is ready."

The agent opened the cargo door and the ramp leading into the sleek jet was only two short steps from the truck. The President bounded up the up-ramp.

"Welcome aboard, Mr. President," the President's personal flight attendant said.

"Thank you. Nice to see you again." In less than twenty seconds the President was out of sight inside the jet. In another two minutes, the jet was taxiing for takeoff.

Chapter 110

Under the watchful eyes of several FBI guards along with Director Fogg himself, Olive and CD were escorted onto an unmarked plane.

"I hope you can already tell that we earnestly want to cooperate with you and that we earnestly want a dialogue, Professor," Fogg said.

"Have you noticed," CD said as he turned to Olive, "that he never addresses you. He's either a male chauvinist or he's scared of you, my dear."

Olive smiled. "I'm the one who should be scared, don't you think? After all, this government that he's part of has tried several times to kill us. So frankly, I'm skeptical."

The two continued to talk as if Fogg were not even present, though he was in the seat directly across the narrow isle in the small jet. "What guarantees do you think they'll give us when we tell them we won't cooperate in the least unless we have some media people present?" Olive asked CD.

"My guess is that they'll never let the media within a thousand miles of our friends. That would be too dangerous for the government if things don't go their way."

"Don't you think it's little juvenile for you two to pretend that I'm not even here?" Fogg asked. To Olive and CD's surprise, he had no hint of irritation in his voice. "I'm on your side. You've got to believe that. And another thing you need to know. You don't have any other allies in this government. I'm your only ally."

CD turned to Fogg. "And why should we believe you?"

"Here's some stuff that you don't know. The CIA's out of control. Lucado had her own agenda. Even the President didn't know what she was up to. She wanted all of the clones under her control. We don't know what all she was up to or why, but we're pretty sure that she wasn't going to turn over any clones to the President, and a dialogue was the farthest thing from her mind. That's why she was going to hustle you two out of the country."

"But why did you shoot her?" Olive asked pointedly.

Fogg replied, "You saw what was going down. She was armed and she shot her own person. That guy was her top assistant. Obviously she didn't want him talking. For all we know she also had — has — people with orders to execute you two and the clones if anything to happen to her. But we took the chance. She was out of control and had to be contained."

"Contained? Is that the nomenclature for killed?" Olive's tone was skeptical.

Fogg shrugged, "Maybe so, but that's water over the dam. Right now we're going to a secret facility to meet with the President. And by the way, the ones you call your 'friends' will be there too, so you two need to think about what's best for them and better yet, think about what's best for the nation."

CD almost sneered. "The Kennedy thing, Mr. Fogg? We're at the service of the country? We're pawns of the country, a country being run by a corrupt government?"

Olive turned to stare out the small window. "Give me a break," was all that she muttered.

Fogg sighed and stared out his own window.

Olive and CD looked at each other. Now for the first time, they knew that Alex and Thomas and hopefully Rufus were not only alive but in federal custody. Without a word, they stood, walked several rows to the rear of the small passenger compartment where they could whisper without Fogg or the guards hearing them. Even if the plane were bugged, the noise of the rear-mounted engine would render any bugging useless.

Chapter 111

"Where are we?" Rufus asked as the small jet taxied to an unmarked hangar. Agent Gorman glanced at Rufus and smiled but did not answer. Rufus scanned the surroundings for anything that would hint at their location, but there were no signs on any of the buildings. That alone was extraordinary and suggested that they were at some secret government installation. There was even dense growth suspended overhead that effectively shielded the ground from any planes or drones, and when Rufus looked closely he could tell that the growth was artificial.

"Where do you think we are?" Alex asked Rufus.

"I have absolutely no idea, but it's obviously a secret government airport of some type," Rufus responded quietly.

Gorman smiled, "Yes, gentlemen, this is a special government conference base which only the most important people ever get a chance to visit. The President, by inviting you here, is already telling you that he's on your side and that he desperately wants to right the wrongs committed by his predecessor. Please give him that chance."

"It would be a gesture of good will if you would tell us exactly where we are," Thomas said.

"I'll leave that to him," Gorman said as he motioned out the window to the figure walking briskly across the tarmac toward the plane.

The two clones and Rufus were totally surprised to see President Armstrong walking alone toward their jet. "He doesn't even have the Secret Service with him," Alex observed.

"Where we are, he actually doesn't need security, but you can be assured that they're close by," Gorman said.

One of the flight crew opened the door of the jet and lowered the jet-ramp. "Good day, Mr. President," he said.

"Hello, son, "President Armstrong said as he bounded up the steps and entered the small passenger compartment. "Gentlemen, welcome to The Eagle Rock," the President said with a smile. "This is a secret, presidential conference facility. We use it obviously for the most important discussions that we in the Executive Branch ever have. That tells you how much I value our meeting together, and it's some measure of my thanks for your agreeing to come here to meet with me."

"Thank you, Mr. President," Rufus said quietly.

With less respect, Thomas said, "We really didn't have any choice, Mr. Armstrong, so it's not exactly accurate to say that we agreed to come."

President Armstrong did not take the bait. "But you're here. That's what's important, and I do thank you for being here, and I hope our dialogue can begin right away. So to keep things sort of equal, you know who I am. Can you tell me who you are?"

The three quickly responded.

"I am Alexander Hamilton, or at least a later generation of Hamilton."

"Thomas Jefferson."

"Hello again, Mr. President," Rufus said in monotone.

Looking at Alex, the President extended his hand, "I'm truly honored. Truly, Mr. Hamilton. You cannot realize what a spectacular honor this is for me." Alex accepted the President's hand. Turning to Thomas, "And, Mr. Jefferson, I welcome you here and thank you for the honor of meeting you." The President extended his hand, "Mr. Jefferson, this is a hand of friendship." Thomas shook the President's hand.

"And, Mr. Forest, I'm glad to see you again, and I hope we can make more headway than we did before, and I hope you understand that I had no choice but to bring you here."

"Of course, Mr. President." Roof's tone was unmistakably skeptical.

"How about keeping an open mind, Mr. Forest?" The President asked, this time with no perceptible smile.

Rufus was never one to respect authority, especially the authority of a President. "Mr. President, with all respect, for now, let's just say that I'm not here voluntarily and am really not inclined to go into much of anything until I'm reunited with my friends and until you guarantee our safety and future. After all, your government's been pursuing us relentlessly and has even tried to kill us several times. So, Mr. President, I hope you'll understand if I'm reluctant to start spilling my guts to a corrupt government that's proven unworthy of even a scintilla of trust." Rufus's tone was hard, and he held the President's gaze for a full five seconds, but all the while Rufus had a confident, broad smile.

The President looked down briefly then back up at Rufus. "Mr. Woods, I understand where you must be coming from, but I hope you'll just keep an open mind."

Thomas and Alex both snickered. President Armstrong, not comprehending, looked irritated.

Then the President resumed his earlier smile, "Very well, gentlemen. I hope we can earn your trust," the President said contritely. Turning to Gorman, he said, "Mr. Gorman, how about helping our guests get settled in before you return to Washington. My people'll show you where to go." Without another word, President Armstrong turned and exited the plane.

"OK, let's see what kind of quarters they have here," Gorman said, and the four headed down the steps of the jet onto the tarmac. Joined by several of the President's aides, they strode briskly to one of the nearby buildings.

"If we're to get settled in, as the President put it, it looks like we'll be here for a while," Rufus observed.

"I guess it depend on how well we dialogue," Thomas said wryly.

Chapter 112

An hour after being planted in their minimally furnished rooms in what was a spartan residential building, Thomas, Alex, and Rufus gathered in Rufus's room to discuss the amazing events they had shared over the past several days. They were well aware that they were under constant video surveillance.

"Now what?" Alex wondered aloud.

A knock on the door broke the silence that followed the query that Alex had voiced but which all three felt. "It's open," Rufus shouted with college dorm informality.

A young man opened the door. "Gentlemen, if you'll follow me, the President would like to get started."

The trio followed the young man outside the building. The sun was intense as was the humidity. "We're in the south, that's for sure," Rufus said in an effort the get their guide talking. The guide did not acknowledge Rufus's statement.

"Can you at least tell us what state we're in?" Alex asked as they walked briskly toward a plain concrete building.

"The President himself will fill you in completely," the guide responded without looking at any of the three.

They walked another two hundred yards and then entered a plain concrete building sporting a small sign that read "Conference Hall." Once inside, the trappings were no longer austere, but instead were aggressive Scandinavian contemporary. Colorful acrylics lined the walls of the surprisingly large entry lobby, and the indirect lighting was subdued and restful. A green, glass obelisk fountain about five feet high with cascading water down its sides provided a stunning focal point in the very center of the lobby. "I guess the President likes this sort of stuff," Thomas said as he motioned to the fountain and then stared at the paintings.

"He does indeed, gentlemen," the President said as he entered the lobby from a hallway that was partially concealed by a large bronze statue of something resembling an angel holding a machine gun. "This "stuff" as you call it shows both the majesty and also the danger of human potential. Take this Dali," the President said turning towards a large multi-colored painting of a squad of soldiers whose expressions reflected the mire and weariness of battle. The label for the painting read "Why, Man, Why?" The painting was directly in front of Alex, Thomas, and Rufus. They all stared at the disturbing painting. "Anyone who glorifies war has never been at war, or if they have and still persist in glorifying war, their memories have clearly abandoned them. Just take a look at the suffering in those faces." The President paused. "It's very sad that this is so much of human history. Now, look closely at the trees. Up there, to the left, there's Satan, in all the seductive splendor of Evil. Concealed, invisible to the soldiers, smiling — smiling at the plight of the soldiers and indeed at the plight of mankind in general, reveling in the gore and the pain and the suffering and the maiming and the killing. After all, gentlemen," President Armstrong turned to face the clones and Rufus, "this planet that we live on is Satan's turf. Remember that when Satan tempted Jesus and said I'll give you all of this, meaning the earth itself— I'll give you all of this if you'll just bow down to me, what was Jesus's response? Jesus didn't say 'Satan, this isn't yours to give.' He knew that this earth is where Satan can roam freely and distribute his wares of fear, deception and distraction to those who are weak enough or stupid enough or misguided enough to accept them. This painting has all of that in it. That's why it's such a masterpiece, arguably Dali's best. Most paintings done in this medium aren't so full of meaning, but this one is."

The President stood silently, obviously admiring the masterpiece. They all took in the multiple messages from the painting. "Now, let's back off about twenty feet, and we'll see even more clearly Dali's genius," the President said, and they all walked back from the grim painting.

Now, having walked to more than twenty feet across the lobby away from the painting, they turned to face it again. The scene depicted in the painting somehow just from standing farther away from it had transformed into something quite different. The soldiers still showed the pain and the marks of battle, but Satan was no longer smiling. Instead, his expression was one of frustration and fear as he looked upwards towards the clouds. And in the clouds, there was Christ looking down on the scene below. Christ was not smiling but had a tear in his eye, clearly saddened by the sickening scene of man-made suffering below Him.

"Now walk just a little this way," the President said as he took several steps to his left. The three men followed the President. Turning to the painting, he asked, "Now what do you see?"

"Amazing," Thomas said quietly. The gaze of Jesus was now affixed on Satan. Jesus's visage was a mixture of strength, anger, and sadness. Satan's expression was fear and resignation. "Satan knows the end game, and so does Jesus," President Armstrong said quietly. "But Jesus, even though He knows how this whole thing will play out, is still saddened by the present plight of man. Man continues to try to do things independently of God, to do it his own way. Won't we ever learn?" The President sighed. "This painting always touches me and reminds me of why I must do everything I can to protect our nation from the ravages of war, the torn families, the destroyed lives, the destroyed futures." He turned to Alex and Thomas, and his tone subtly turned more serious. "And it reminds me, gentlemen, of why I must do everything I can to protect the stability of this nation. Without stability, we'll essentially disintegrate, and with disintegration will come violence, division, war, you name it. And if that happens, then the hope of America will indeed have been extinguished."

They all continued to stare at the painting. The President continued, "So this painting says that we humans make choices, but we see the impact of our choices only in the limited dimensional space in which we exist, but every choice we make has impact in the spiritual dimensions. The heavens rejoice when we choose good. When we opt for the good, there must be singing, rejoicing, and celebration in heaven." The President paused. "Yes, our choices play out on the battlefield of good and evil, and the heavens grieve and tears are shed by the angels and by Christ himself when we choose evil." President Armstrong turned to his three guests. "That's why, gentlemen, I will allow nothing — nothing, gentlemen — " the President emphasized as he looked directly at the two clones, "to threaten the security and stability of this nation. We're this planet's only dependable force for good, and there's nothing that Evil would rather have than for the United States to be sidelined. And that won't happen on my watch."

There was an awkward silence as Rufus, Alex, and Thomas considered President Armstrong's strong words and his great awareness of the force of Evil — and his distinct message to the clones that they were expendable if they stood in his way.

"OK, let's move along," the President said. "Our conference room's this way." The President then led the trio down another hall and opened a large oak door. "Please," the President said as he held the door for Alex, Thomas, and Rufus.

There were several other persons already in the dark paneled conference room. CD and Olive were seated at the large glass-topped conference table. Across from them were Attorney General Trentini, Secretary of State Douglas Cordero, and the President's new Chief of Staff, Kit Tersense. They all stood. "Folks," the President said, addressing the government officials, "This is Alexander Hamilton, Thomas Jefferson, and Rufus Forest. We all know who Mr. Jefferson and Mr. Hamilton are. I think Mr. Forest must be their security. He hasn't been willing to share his role in this whole thing until they are confident of our intentions. So let's make that happen." The men at the table introduced themselves.

Thomas, Alex, and Rufus hugged Olive and CD. "We knew you must be around somewhere," CD attempted to lighten the mood, but they all realized that the less they said, the better, so no words other than greetings were exchanged at this reunion. They all felt relief to see that the others were still alive, and they all had unanswered questions about what had happened to Ben.

Tersense, Armstrong's Chief of Staff, then said, "Gentlemen, please take these seats." She motioned to three of the five empty seats on the side of the table across from TT and Cordero "But first please serve yourselves. There's pastry, cheeses, venison sausage, other delicacies, coffee, and tea," she said, pointing to the end of the conference room to the credenza loaded with food choices.

"I wonder if the taxpayers who paid for all this eat this well," Rufus said sarcastically to no one in particular.

The room was a strong mix of contemporary furnishings with dark paneled walls. Some paintings, less spectacular than the paintings in the lobby of the building, hung on the walls. An ornate, modern Hadeland Glassverk chandelier hung above the table from the high ceiling. The conference table was elaborately fitted for electronic equipment, but no such equipment was currently in evidence.

Rufus took a seat at one end of the row of empty seats. Both Alex and Thomas helped themselves to an abundance of food from the credenza along with hot tea, brought their take to the table, and spread it out before them. Rufus did his best to suppress a smile. The others at the table pretended not to notice.

"You aren't at the Golden Bow-Wow, Thomas," Rufus whispered. Thomas and Alex ignored Rufus. "Chow time," Alex said loud enough for everyone in the room to hear.

President Armstrong in a move apparently intended to make the clones feel more at home said, "Good idea," and walked to the credenza and took a slice of pastry, some pickled herring, and piled a combination of orange marmalade and brown, Norwegian gjetost on a slice of yeast bread.

Before anyone could say anything, Alex asked in a loud voice, "Where is Ben?"

The President himself answered tersely, "All we know is that the Russians seized him in Louisiana and now we don't know where he is. They took him to a submarine, and frankly, gentlemen, we haven't been able to locate that sub, and if it's already reached Russia, we haven't been able to locate the clone."

"The clone?" Alex said.

"Sorry. Ben," the President responded.

Everyone simply waited for a further response from either Alex or Thomas, and finally Thomas said with an incredulous and accusing tone, "You're telling me that the Russians have Benjamin Franklin? The Russians have one of our nation's founding fathers? Am I hearing this right?"

Everyone looked at the President. He responded quietly without making eye contact with Thomas. "Unfortunately, yes, but we've got assets in Russia, and we're working on it." Then sounding more forceful, "We'll get him back. Make no mistake about that, Mr. Jefferson."

"Yeah" was all that Thomas said as he shook his head, disbelieving.

But Alex was clearly angered. "Of course, none of this would've happened if your government, Mr. Armstrong, hadn't been trying to capture us, if your government hadn't killed George, if your government hadn't killed all those people in Florida, if your government hadn't killed all those people in Atlanta. Mr. Armstrong, you're coming into this meeting with all that bloody baggage, and I for one don't see why we should trust you to do anything for us or for Ben. You people are in it for yourselves, and that's the basic problem underlying the state of your government. It sickens me, Mr. Armstrong."

The President's advisors sat motionless, fearing that the dialogue that President Armstrong sought was already headed to the trash heap. The President looked directly at Alex. "I cannot dispute that, Mr. Hamilton. But all of that was another Administration. All of it," The President emphasized. "President Ray is dead. So are his misguided and immoral policies. That's why I wanted this meeting. So we can gain your trust. So we can show you that we want you to be a part of our attempts to fix our government. I don't know how to put it any more clearly, Mr. Hamilton."

There was a prolonged, awkward silence.

"OK," President Armstrong finally said. "When we find out anything about the clone the Russians have, I'll definitely tell you. So let's move on."

"He has a name. His name is Benjamin Franklin," Thomas said pointedly.

"Of course. I apologize. Ben," the President said without conviction.

Alex and Thomas then laid out in emphatic terms how they thought that contemporary American government had radically departed from the constitutional principles the framers had set forth in 1787. Since Alex and Thomas had already made those views public in their *Second Federalist Papers*, little was new in their presentation to the executive officials present at the table.

President Armstrong, assisted by Cordero and TT, then launched into an eloquent defense of the current practices of centralizing governmental power in the Executive branch at the expense of a sold-out Congress and how the necessities of the war on terror meant a reduced right to privacy. At the end of the long session, it was clear to all that light years separated the clones from the trio of President Armstrong, Secretary of State Douglas Cordero, and the Attorney General Trentini.

When the chasm between the parties reduced everyone to silence, President Armstrong said, "Well, gentlemen, we now know where we all stand. Let's take a break." Without engaging in any pleasantries or small talk, the President and his advisors immediately left the room.

Chapter 113

In a well-hidden CIA safe house in rural Virginia, a steady tone awakened George Washington. He did not recognize it, but he knew it had to emanate from outside the above ground basement suite into which he had been deposited. He tried the French doors, and to his surprise, he found them unlocked. He walked out into a small yard. It could be no more than ten by fifteen, and a high fence, undoubtedly electrified, confined the yard. George cautiously stepped into the yard. He had no idea where he was. All he knew was that it had taken three long hours by van to make the trip from the Chesapeake house where he had earlier met Director Lucado.

George paced the yard, and then heard the tone again. He glanced around, saw nothing, then out of the corner of his eye there was a glistening of light on a small metal object about thirty feet above the fence. A small drone! It hovered, almost motionless, as if it were watching George. Though he did not realize it, he was staring at a third generation SV-500 Nano-Drone.

George just stared at the hovering drone. It became still for a few seconds then slowly circled the yard. Then it again remained still for a few seconds before again circling the yard.

George continued to stare up at the drone and pointed to his face. The drone hovered briefly and then zoomed away out of sight.

George had no idea whether the drone was a government drone or a drone managed by some private individual, but now for the first time George had hope. Yes, as an old movie said, "hope is a dangerous thing" because hope emboldens risk-taking. George smiled. *Somebody knows I am alive. I can now make some plans.*

"What's so funny?" George had not heard the guard approach.

"Nothing, just thinking." George had assigned the name Hulk to this guard since he was built like a cross between a professional wrestler and an oversized wine barrel.

"Well come on inside and get something to eat. We can't starve you."

"What can you tell me about my situation?"

"Not a whole hell of a lot. To be honest with you, we don't know what we're supposed to do with you except that we're supposed to await instructions."

A second guard now walked up. "Yeah, and those instructions are long, long overdue." George had named this guard Baldy for obvious reasons.

The three walked into a small kitchen. "Sit here." Baldy motioned to a chair at the kitchen table and took a chair for himself. Hulk brought a plate of sandwiches to the table.

"How about some TV?" George motioned to the wall-mounted television.

"We have strict orders for no TV, no radio, no texting, no nothing with the outside world."

"You can't be serious," George said in mock irritation.

"Actually," Hulk drawled in a Southern accent, "it wouldn't hurt to get some news."

"OK, but what happens here stays here, OK?" Baldy looked to Hulk for assurance.

"Sure, no problem," Hulk said and switched on the TV. The news channel was in the middle of a broadcast:

> . . . so the situation is clearly grave. Director Sullivan
> has declined to hold a press conference, and the

President has not been seen since this morning when
he appointed Senator Sullivan to run the CIA.

The news scroll at the bottom of the screen informed the
three that CIA Director Lucado had apparently had a stroke
while driving and crashed head-on into a gasoline tanker and
that her body had been incinerated in the resulting inferno.

The three stared at the television in shock and disbelief. "My
God!" Baldy exclaimed.

"She told us that she was personally handling our situation
and to take orders from no one else. So what're we supposed to
do now?" Hulk was clearly worried. They looked at each other
and then both looked at George. "I guess we wait to hear from
her replacement."

"Who are you anyway?" Baldy asked.

George answered, "I guess I'm someone that Lucado had a
personal grudge against because I'm not a spy and I haven't done
anything subversive. I'm not a terrorist. But I'm a concerned
citizen, and I know beyond any doubt whatsoever that detaining
me here's a violation of several of my constitutional rights."

"Yeah, but who the hell are you?" Baldy sounded insistent.

"Forget him. I think we need to call in." Hulk said. "Lucado's
not around and for all we know no one else even knows we're
here or anything about us."

"Or him," Baldy added, motioning to their detainee.

The urgent sounding of an alarm startled the three, and that
was quickly followed by the sound of glass shattering. A delayed
action tear gas grenade rolled across the kitchen floor.

"Shit," Hulk exclaimed. "Get him to the basement," Hulk
ordered.

"No way," Baldy said. "Let's get out of here!"

A loudspeaker blared forth. "This house is completely surrounded. Come out with your hands up. You've got five seconds." Then nothing.

"Fuck! Now what?" Hulk exclaimed.

Both men started coughing and covering their faces. "I can't breathe!" Baldy yelled.

"My eyes!" Hulk yelled.

"I'm getting out of here." Baldy started for the kitchen door.

In the chaos neither had noticed that George had covered his face with a cloth towel and calmly walked from the room and exited the living room door. A muscular young man immediately grabbed him and hustled him to a car just outside the metal fence into which a large entry had been neatly sliced.

As the young man was opening the rear door of the car, George turned and saw Hulk and Baldy spread-eagled on the ground, being roughly cuffed by several armed men. "Go easy on them," George said, motioning to the two guards. "They're just pawns that Lucado was using." He turned to face the young man. "They didn't even know who I am. Do you?"

"I do indeed, Mr. Washington. We took your picture." He held up the picture of George standing in the yard pointing to his own face. The picture was high resolution and somehow showed the facial features that made it unmistakable that indeed this was George Washington. "Mr. Washington, you're now free."

George looked intently at the young man and frowned. "I'll never be free," George said with immense sadness as the two got into the car.

The young woman driving the car, turned and said, "Hello, Mr. Washington. I'm Omi. Mr. Washington, I helped get Thomas out of California, and we've been trying to help CD and Rufus keep y'all out of the clutches of the government."

George just nodded but said nothing.

Omi continued, "I've already met Thomas and Alex, and now I'm privileged to meet you. Mr. Washington, like I said, I work with CD and Olive and Rufus and I'm going to try to take you to them."

"I don't know any CD or Olive or Rufus," George said quietly.

Omi stared at George Washington. "You don't know them?" Omi asked.

"No. Who are they?"

"They're the ones who kept Alex and Thomas out of the government's hands. They're friends, Mr. Washington."

"Alex and Thomas?" George asked. His face portrayed no major emotion, only a question.

"You don't even know about Alex and Thomas? Alexander Hamilton and Thomas Jefferson?" Omi was incredulous.

George's head shot up in amazement. "You mean, I'm not alone? There really are others?"

"Yes, Mr. Washington, there are others," Omi said softly. She paused, realizing the shock it had to be to George to learn that there were other clones of such historic significance. "And you're not alone, but I'll be honest. Right now we don't know where Alex and Thomas are or CD and Rufus and Olive for that matter. But we're making progress. And I think we'll be able to locate them."

"Who are these people?" George asked. "Are they clones, too?"

"No, they aren't clones," Omi replied. "They're just regular people who are part of the team trying to save y'all. Mr. Washington, it's a long story."

"How many of us are there?" George asked.

"There are four. The fourth is Benjamin Franklin, and we don't know where he is."

"Benjamin Franklin!" George exclaimed. "And you don't know where he is?"

When Omi did not immediately answer, George persisted, "Madame, you need to tell me. I need to know the situation. Where is he?"

"OK, Mr. Washington. This is not good. He was seized in Louisiana. We think, no, we're pretty sure, that it was the Russians. They took him out to sea and put him on a Russian sub, and that's the last we know."

George Washington fell silent. For the first time, he knew there were four clones of the founding fathers, and he knew who the four were. And he knew that the Russians had kidnapped one of them.

After an extended silence, George said, "Tell me about this Olive and CD and Rufus."

As they drove, Omi told George about Olive, CD, and Rufus and what had befallen them and the other three clones. Omi omitted any reference to the Procurement Project. When they had finished, George just stared out of the window of the van, saying nothing. Eventually, the van pulled onto a large, private airfield. On its single runway sat a gleaming HondaJet with its two GE engines running.

"That's our transportation, Mr. Washington. The plan's to fly you to a safe location. From there we'll continue to try to locate the others—"

"The others." George echoed.

"Yes. CD, Rufus, Olive, Alex, and Thomas. But until we locate them, there's not much we can do." Omi looked pessimistic.

"Omi," George said, calling her by name for the first time, "why is it that you can't locate them? Is it because they're in hiding, or is it because someone has kidnapped them too?"

Omi answered, "We think that the government has them. Things sort of fell apart after the Russians got involved, after they got Franklin, and we lost track of them. There's a lot of government infighting and turmoil going on now, and our best guess is that Alex and Thomas are in government hands. I don't think they're in any danger, at least not yet."

"Why do you think that?"

"Because, Mr. Washington, of you. You are free, free to talk, free to appear in public, free to use the Internet, free to use Instagram, free to tweet. If anything happens to them you're free to expose it. If they harm Jefferson and Hamilton, the public reaction will be merciless. Things would get violent, — very violent — and the government knows that."

George, as was his style, mulled it over before responding. "OK, we fly to this safe location you have in mind. Then there'll be some changes. First, I'll need to manage things."

"Manage things?" Omi asked.

"Yes, run the show," George responded. "That's apparently why I was born. I don't desire it, but I think it is to be."

Omi had expected as much and simply smiled. This George, just as his father, was a born leader.

They walked quickly to the waiting plane, and within five minutes they were airborne.

Chapter 114

The sparkling Abrau-Durso was flowing freely in the Kremlin as the small assemblage of Russian governmental oligarchs toasted their good fortune of having one of the American clones. The President of Russia himself stepped confidently to the middle of the floor of the expensively restored Amber Room, a resplendent chamber once again referred to as the Eighth Wonder of the World by some architectural specialists.

"My dear comrades and my esteemed honored guest." President Polzinov spoke in heavily accented English for the benefit of the single American in the room. "We are on the precipice of a major era in world history. We are honored to have with us a luminary who harkens to the past glory days of the United States, its commencing period of history before it sank into moral depravity and economic decay."

Polzinov turned to face the individual who was seated in an ornate, but uncomfortable chair of red fir rimmed with amber, gold, and lapis lazuli. Benjamin Franklin continued to stare straight ahead and did not acknowledge the Russian President. A Kremlin aide seated just behind and to the left of Franklin's chair whispered something into Franklin's ear. Franklin's expression remained blank, and he remained completely motionless as everyone in the room stared at him.

After an awkward silence, President Polzinov continued, "Our opportunity, comrades, is to find the path to rapprochement with the United States, and we believe that you, Mr. Franklin, can help bring our two countries together." He looked directly at Benjamin. "So we only ask that you keep an open mind. We agree with what you said in what your media has called *The Second Federalist Gazette*, that the wealthy and rich aristocracy has captured the United State government and that the regular people now have no voice in the affairs of state. We would like to help change that, Mr. Franklin, by giving you complete freedom to talk to the American public without fear of being captured by the American government. It is clear that your government —— actually, Mr. Franklin, it is not your government but is rather an alien collection of self-serving billionaires. Remember how President Trump used to claim that the people would run the government? What pompous and empty words coming from a billionaire! A billionaire! From your estate here in Russia, you will have complete freedom to talk to the real American public and encourage them to take back their government from the wealthy few.

"As you must be acutely aware, that alien government wants at least to silence you and your colleagues. Indeed, Mr. Franklin, they want to completely eliminate all of you. Kill you, Mr. Franklin! Hear me! Did not that alien government indeed kill one of your colleagues by shooting down an unarmed and harmless, private aircraft? That alien government continues its lawless endeavors and now has apparently captured and silenced your other colleagues. We conclude that they have been captured from the simple fact that no one has heard a word from them in weeks. This fact, and I will share something else with you, Mr. Franklin. The American President has sneaked away in the dark of the night to a secret facility that that government calls The Eagle of War. President Armstrong is there right at this very instant that we speak. The American public has been duped to think he is vacationing at his Camp David or at a beach resort. We suspect that your colleagues if they are not dead are at that Eagle of War facility and that the American President is personally participating in attempting, shall we say, to rehabilitate your colleagues. I believe that during the Bush years, the alien government called it enhanced interrogation. We call it torture, and it is abhorrent to all civilized peoples."

Given Russia's ongoing practices, no one in the room dared risk making eye contact with anyone else when Polzinov referred to torture.

The President did not miss a beat. "No one in America knows about the existence of the Eagle of War, and might I add that the name alone causes us great concern, but we have known about it for some years. It is what the media of your country refers to as a black site." President Polzinov turned to the Russians in the room, smiled, and switched briefly to Russian. "We Russians love our black bread. It is a staple of life. But we abhor black sites. They are a blight on life." No one in the room responded in the least to the President's strained attempt to add a degree of levity because they were all aware that the Russia of today had continued the old Soviet practice of arbitrarily torturing and murdering opponents of the regime. Each oligarch had a standby exit plan should he (or she, there were several women in the room) fall out of favor and become candidates for the Black Dolphin or Matrosskaya Tishina, two of Russia's despicable prison dead-ends for the government's targets.

President Polzinov turned back to Benjamin Franklin and switched back to English. "I fully understand, Mr. Franklin, that you may not share my desire to negotiate a rapprochement with the American government because of the circumstances under which we freed you from the alien American government. We had no option but to do what we did, Mr. Franklin. Why? Because the American government is beyond reason, and we are hoping to bring them back to the table of discussions. Quite honestly, Mr. Franklin, we believe that the American government, in the grip of the rich and wealthy aristocracy as it is, is planning on some kind of preemptive isolation of Russia, and we cannot permit that. They tried that during our special military operation in the Ukraine, and it did not work then, and it will not work now. Therefore, Mr. Franklin, much rests on your shoulders. I believe it is no accident that you are here at this particular time."

President Polzinov pointed to the heavens, implicitly invoking a god in which he did not at all believe. "Help us, Mr. Franklin. No, not us. Help your own country and our planet, Mr. Franklin. It was the American President Kennedy who said we must all learn to live together on our one precious planet. So, I offer a toast to Mr. Benjamin Franklin. It is you, Mr. Franklin, who holds in your hands the future of whether indeed we can do what President Kennedy said we must do." President Polzinov lifted his glass of Russian sparkling wine, and all in the room except Benjamin Franklin lifted their glasses in a toast.

Benjamin Franklin had not moved a muscle during the long lecture by the Russian President, and he did not move a muscle now. Everyone in the room remained quiet and perfectly still, waiting for Benjamin Franklin to say something or at least to nod. He did neither.

"He's surely stoic, isn't he?" Verionsky whispered to Marina Novokatnaia.

"We will soon change that," she whispered back. "We'll give him a couple of days. Then we will begin."

Chapter 115

President Armstrong himself opened the afternoon session at The Eagle Rock and immediately addressed Thomas and Alex. "Gentlemen, I think the time's here for you to indicate whether you're willing to moderate some of your views. Your views are from two hundred years ago when the nation was agrarian, isolationist, and thinly populated. That world was feudal, monarchic, and its parts remote from each other, reachable only with great effort and passage of time. In those conditions, the constitutional ideas of splintering power — drastically splintering power," the President emphasized, "and giving the state subdivisions a great deal of power and the idea of a preeminent Congress was a pinnacle of wisdom, and history tells us that those principles escorted that nation through industrialization, urbanization, huge population increases, and at least one world war. But that nation and those old conditions no longer exist. Mr. Jefferson and Mr. Hamilton, the world has changed. With the advent of the Second World War and then on into the dangerous years of the Cold War, and now into the age of Islamic terrorism and Chinese adventurism, things have changed. The demands on government have escalated. The need for rapid action, secrecy, and a united front — the governmental virtues that George Washington praised over two hundred years ago — are indispensable to guaranteeing the security of the nation today, just as they were in his time. Splintered power became a brake and a barrier to coordinated and rapid action by the government. In short, our governmental structure has evolved to accommodate to realities and threats of modern times. Yes, power primarily now resides in the presidency, not the Congress, which incidentally has become a sad national joke because of its timidity, lack of creativity, and preoccupation with just staying in office, and yes, the states have had to surrender a lot of their power, and I might add that they did so quite willingly, all in order that the nation which our constitutional fathers started would not become obsolete but rather would flourish and thrive as a stable beacon of freedom and compassion in a new, often hostile world."

The President stopped his soliloquy and looked from one clone to the other. "Let me emphasize that last point, gentlemen. This nation must remain stable. There are so many citadels of evil in the world today, ranging from Russia itself to the various strains of Islamic terrorism to the Chinese surveillance state, that the civilized world's quite frankly dependent on the United States to carry the banner of freedom and compassion. We have no choice but to remain stable. I've sworn an oath to protect the national security of the nation, and stability's an essential prerequisite to that security. If we falter, the forces of evil will exploit that weakness and spread their grip on the planet. We cannot allow that to happen. We're the undisputed leader, therefore, in the planetary battle of good against evil. Gentlemen, I need your help. If you undermine the structure of government that has been in place now for decades, that'll introduce a spiral of instability that'll in turn threaten not only the United States but also the entire world. So, gentlemen, the time has arrived for you to choose. Which will it be? Embrace where the nation is now and help us move forward or cling to ideas from two hundred years ago and try to take us backward?"

The President realized that he had posed the choices rather starkly, but he decided that he would let it lie as he had articulated it.

CD began, "Mr. President, with all due respect —" but the President cut him off.

"With all due respect, Mr. Delna, I would rather hear from the clones." The President turned to Thomas. "Mr. Jefferson?"

Thomas launched into what sounded to CD like a prepared statement. "Mr. President, Mr. Cordero, Mr. Trentini, and others. We're here under duress. We've committed no crime. We are no threat, neither in terms of clear and present danger nor in terms of creating imminent lawless violence. We clearly are no threat to national security, and we clearly are as patriotic as that term can possibly contain meaning. Therefore, Mr. President, we're being detained here illegally.

"But as opposed to it being illegal for us to be detained here, is it not also unconstitutional?" Thomas looked squarely at the President. "Our detention is a total violation of the fourth amendment protection that prohibits government seizure of a person unless there's particularized probable cause as determined by a member of the judicial branch of government. Bringing us here and detaining us here, for every minute that that detention continues, is a violation of the fourth amendment of the Constitution you're sworn to protect, a violation of various federal laws and also, incidentally, a violation of various international conventions to which the United States government claims allegiance. So, Mr. President, for you to sit there and lecture me about stability and asserting that we must do or say something or refrain from doing or saying something is a non-starter and is a shit-bound abandonment of basic American principles and ideals. The very idea that you don't even know your primary duty would be laughable if it weren't so shameful. You just said, and I quote, 'I have sworn an oath to protect the national security of the nation.' Mr. President, your oath of office is to protect and defend the Constitution of the United States. Here, today, right now, you're in blatant violation of your sworn oath. You're making a complete mockery of the Constitution you swore to protect.

"Mr. President, there's no way in hell that we won't say in public what we think should be said and what the nation needs to hear. The First Amendment, Mr. President, you seem to dismiss. We don't. One of our great Justices of the Supreme Court said that the First Amendment is the indispensable matrix upon which all the other freedoms rest. So hearing you ask us to agree to forfeit our right to talk publicly is an affront to the First Amendment and an affront to your promise to uphold and defend the Constitution."

Cordero and TT squirmed in their seats. They had never heard any President talked to in such direct and indicting terms. The President was not smiling, but neither did he appear angry. "Let's take a short break, gentlemen," President Armstrong said and rose from his chair.

As the others rose from their chairs, Thomas and Alex stayed seated. When the presidential entourage had left the room, Alex said, "I couldn't have said it better, Thomas."

"And if there's no room for compromise, my guess is that we will be detained indefinitely," Rufus said.

"Probably," CD agreed. "Except if they keep us for even a short while, they can never let us go. They will have gotten so deep into the cover-up of the clones that they can never reverse field without national revulsion."

"OK, no more talk here," Rufus said. "This room's surely bugged so that even our whispers are recorded."

The five sat silently, and after another five minutes, the President's aides reentered the room and took their places at the ornate, mahogany conference table.

Secretary of State Cordero spoke first. "The President has been called away, gentlemen, and asked me to convey his condolences on missing the rest of our meeting, but he did ask me to put the question to you one last time. Will you assist him in preserving the stability and security of the nation?"

It was Alex this time. "That question's innocuous, Mr. Cordero. It's sufficiently vague that you and we for that matter can interpret it any way we want to, but since the President in absentia is the one who posed the question, perhaps you'll be so kind as to explicate its terms."

Cordero did not miss a beat. He looked coldly at Alex. "It means that you won't make statements without those statements being cleared by the White House. It means that you'll be working for the President, and like me and Attorney General Trentini, you'll take orders from the President. It's a one team, one voice approach, Mr. Hamilton."

Alex also did not miss a beat. "We reject the proposal completely."

Cordero said, "And you, Thomas."

"It's one team, one voice for us, too, Mr. Cordero. Of course, we reject it completely."

"Then, gentlemen, make yourselves comfortable in your new home. You'll be allowed to remain here for the unforeseeable future." Cordero pressed a button on the electronic console in front of him, and eight military guards entered the room. They were the first military presence that the clones had seen since their arrival at The Eagle Rock.

"It's really quite acceptable, your quarters are," Cordero said. "You'll each have your own quarters. Good day, gentlemen. Please go with your escorts."

"So the President's policy isn't dialogue at all, is it Mr. Cordero? It appears to be isolation and solitary detention." CD remained seated.

"Mr. Delna," Cordero said didactically. "Your phraseology is objectionable."

"Just keep in mind, Mr. Cordero and Mr. Trentini, you're in violation of numerous federal statues and, I am sure, a number of state laws of whatever state we are in, and you'll be held to answer for these crimes," CD said then added with emphasis, "Personally. Don't you realize that the President is using you to do his criminal deeds? You are committing serious crimes, and you'll surely pay for it with heavy prison time when all is said and done. Are you really going to let that President use you like that?"

Cordero leveled his hostile gaze at CD and said with patrician aloofness, "What you don't understand, Mr. Delna, is that if the President takes certain steps to protect the national security, then those steps by definition are not illegal. It's the principle of *raison d'état*, but then I guess you don't know anything about that. Mr. Delna, you're in way, way over your head." Cordero turned to the military guards. "Get them out of here."

The guards placed hands on the shoulders of their charges. The clones, Olive, CD, and Rufus stood and were being escorted out when Alex turned and said darkly, "Gentlemen, you have all just fucked yourselves. When this thing is all done, I'll personally make sure that you — each one of you — do heavy prison time, and it won't be at one of those country club prisons that politicians and their wealthy supporters get to go to." He turned, and with his guards' hands on his arm, walked from the room, followed by Thomas, CD, Rufus, and Olive.

TT turned to Cordero. "Douglas, are you sure we're in the clear on this? I think that clone's right that there're some federal laws that we might be in violation of."

"I thought you were going to charge them with sedition, conspiracy to commit terrorist acts, and a bunch of other things, right, TT?"

"Yeah, yeah, yeah, but, Douglas, charging them and convicting them are two different things."

"Who said that they would ever come to trial?"

"We can't keep them here forever, Douglas." TT was clearly having second thoughts with their entire approach to handling the clones.

"We won't keep them here, TT. We'll move them somewhere much more isolated."

"That reminds me. Where's Sullivan? I thought the Boss said she was going to be here."

"I have no idea," Cordero shrugged. "I guess he changed his mind. Maybe he doesn't trust her."

"I don't like it," TT said flatly.

"TT, you heard the President about how our stability is a prime condition for our ability to lead the fight against international evil. We are in the combat zone against evil, and that requires us to make some compromises which otherwise we would not want to make. Are you on board with that policy or not? I am detecting some wavering, and that worries me."

TT hesitated then said in a muted voice, "Yeah I'm on board, but I think there're serious problems, and I think there're going to be other problems down the road."

"Like what?" Cordero queried.

"Well, to start with, there's that George Washington clone. We don't know where he is or what he knows or even if he's alive, but if he is, well, Douglas, that's a huge problem."

Cordero did not respond until the two were walking from the room several minutes later. "On that Washington problem. My bet's that Lucado terminated him and that we've heard the last of him. If not, then we'll face that when we get there, if we get there. In the meantime, get your FBI on a national search for him, and let's get Senator Sullivan to get a search started if she hasn't already."

"And there's another problem, Douglas."

Cordero said, "Which is?"

"The Franklin clone. The Russians probably have him, and that considerably complicates our holding these five incommunicado."

"Because he could make the existence of these two clones public knowledge?"

"Exactly."

"And there's always Senator Sullivan. She might not go along with keeping the clones incommunicado," TT said flatly.

The two men walked on in silence to the aircraft that would take them back to the hallowed halls of their American government.

Chapter 116

Armed Secret Service escorts took the clones, Rufus, CD, and Olive to separate, small cottages. The cottages were hidden from each other by high walls topped with razor wire. As one of Thomas's two guards opened the door to his cottage, Thomas asked, "How long is this my home?"

"I don't know sir," was the only response he got as the guards left, locking the door behind them.

Thomas walked through the studio style room that he estimated to be about 12 by 15. There was nothing he could use as a weapon, nothing with which he could harm himself, and nothing that gave any indication that this room was anything other than a confinement room. The single chair, single table, and single bed seemed adequate enough but substantially below two stars. The plain bathroom likewise approached primitive but would serve its purposes. At least the toilet was more than a hole in the floor. Thomas examined the two windows that looked out the front of the cottage. Both were thick, shatterproof glass, bounded on both sides by heavy screening made of some material that Thomas could not identify. Thomas continued to walk through the room, examining every inch of wall space. He placed the one chair on top of the table so he could examine the grill in the high ceiling but found nothing of note. From his search, he found no listening or video devices, but he was sure they were there.

CD, Rufus, Olive, and Alex went through the same methodical searches and likewise found nothing.

Nor would any of them ever find evidence of listening or seeing devices during their extended stay at The Eagle Rock.

Chapter 117

After several hours of scouring Lucado's computer files and the physical office itself, Sullivan had found nothing related to the clones. She had engaged the top cyber sleuths in the building to decrypt and deconstruct every computer file Lucado had accessed in the past month, but still there was nothing about the clones. Clearly, Lucado's clones operation was totally off the books or the files had been removed.

Senator Sullivan was a canny politico, and she realized that she could trust no one in the CIA, or at least she did not yet know whom she could conceivably trust. So she had called her old office at the Senate and asked four of her top aides from that office to join her at the CIA. Three had accepted. The fourth declined, citing "personal background" reasons for her decline, but on Sullivan's urging, she had also agreed to assist Sullivan in her new role as Acting Director, at least for a while. Consequently, Sullivan had four people whom she could trust.

Sullivan and her four aides were well into a brainstorming session when the administrative assistant from the outer office entered Sullivan's office and said, "Madame Director, there's a gentleman on the phone who insists that he talk to you. He wouldn't tell me his name, but he says he's an employee of the Agency and that he has "absolutely vital information" — those are his words — that you must have. He gives a code name of "Wrestler," but that name's not in our database anywhere, and he refuses to say anything else. What should I tell him?"

With no hesitation, Sullivan replied, "Put him through." She motioned to her aides to stay seated as she walked to her desk and waited.

When the phone beeped, she answered crisply, "Who are you?"

A husky, male voice responded, "Is this line alpha secure?"

"Yes, it is."

The voice continued, "I'm a black operative whom your predecessor dispatched on a special assignment. It's an assignment that you need to be aware of."

"OK. Tell me. What exactly is your assignment? And what exactly is your name, the name that'll appear in our database?"

"Ms. Sullivan, I won't give you my name until you give me your personal assurances that I won't be prosecuted. I want total immunity. And by the way, don't even try to trace this call. I've got a bypass installed so that it can't be traced."

As if on cue, Sullivan's administrative assistant walked in and mouthed the words, "No trace." Sullivan just nodded.

Sullivan continued, "I don't have the power to grant immunity. Only Justice can do that."

"Then get them to do it."

"I still don't know whether this is a crank call or whether you're for real. Tell me something to keep me from hanging up."

"George is alive, and I can sort of tell you where he is."

Sullivan's shock showed to everyone in the room. Her four aides knew from Sullivan's demeanor that she had received a jolt. Sullivan remained silent for a long while then said, "Are you talking about the one who was shot down in a private jet?"

"Yes, one and the same."

Sullivan again remained silent for a long while. Finally she said, "I'll get that immunity for you. Tell me what you can. You don't have to give me your name, but you've got to give me information I can corroborate."

Hulk then told Senator Sullivan how he and Baldy had detained George Washington and how people not from the government had attacked them in the safe house and taken George Washington.

When Hulk had finished his monologue, Sullivan asked, "And you don't know who those people are? You've never seen them before?"

"No, Ms. Sullivan. They cuffed us and left us, and I'm pretty sure their prints and maybe some DNA are on the metal cuffs. They used the old-fashioned kind. It took a while, but we got out of them."

"So how do you propose to get the cuffs to me — without contaminating the sample? And where are you now, and where's the Washington clone?"

"You leave that to us. OK, gotta go." And with that the line went dead.

Sullivan just stared at the phone. She sat still for a few moments then walked back over to where her dumbfounded aides sat motionless. "OK. Let's figure out what we need to do. The President has ordered me to do nothing, not even hold a press conference. This unidentified man on the phone claims that George Washington indeed wasn't killed when President Ray had that plane shot down. Moreover, he claims that while he was holding George pending further orders from Lucado, some well-armed persons attacked their safe house and took George for themselves. He claims to have prints and maybe DNA. Of course, we don't know who this person is, but it sounds completely legit to me. And we don't know where the clone is."

The phone on the coffee table in front of Sullivan beeped softly. She pressed the green button and listened, then said, "Tell her I'm in a meeting and will get to her in about twenty minutes."

After the connection was severed, Sullivan turned back to her assistants and said, "There's a woman in the lobby who has sent up a message to me that she's willing to talk about George." Sullivan stood, paced across the room, and peered out of the window. "This job surely starts with no let-up." She turned to face her assistants. "I'll have to ask y'all to leave the room. This is for your own protection. You already know more than your clearances allow."

When Sullivan was the only person remaining in the large office, she picked up the phone and said to her Administrative Assistant, "Get that woman escorted up here."

The Administrative Assistant replied, "Ms. Sullivan, may I suggest that you use a basement interview room. It'll be more private, and we usually don't let just anyone up here."

"Fine," Sullivan replied. "Have her taken down there. Since I've never even been to the basement, can you be so kind as to have someone take me down there too?"

"I'll do that myself, Senator Sullivan. And, Senator Sullivan, just remember that down in the basement if you need anything or want anyone to assist you, there's a button under the middle drawer. All you need to do is press it. You'll also have a guard with you."

"OK, thank you, but no guard. Make sure that Operations puts a tracker on this person's car. I'm assuming that we know which car is hers."

"If she drove, Senator."

The two women took an express elevator to the basement where Caroline Sullivan was directed to an interview room. After the elevator doors had shut behind her Administrative Assistant, Sullivan told the guard who was accompanying here, "Please stay in the hall, I'll buzz if I need you." Then Director Sullivan entered the interview room. Before her sat an attractive brunette who stood when Sullivan entered the room.

"OK, you have my attention," Sullivan said in an uncharacteristically clipped tone.

"Ms. Sullivan, my first name's Omi. I'm part of a group of Americans that's trying to make sure that our government doesn't capture or kill the clones. We've already lost one clone to the Russians, all because of the perfidy of the Executive branch. My group'll do whatever it takes to keep the clones alive and free. You apparently have two of the clones in captivity. But we have one clone. We have George Washington, Ms. Sullivan, and he's prepared to go public if he needs to in order to obtain the release of his fellow clones."

Sullivan sighed. "How do I have any idea at all that you're telling me the truth, that someone whom you claim to be George Washington is alive and that you have him?"

"Watch this, Ms. Sullivan. May I?" Omi pulled out a 3D flash drive and motioned to the 3D flash player on a table facing a small screen on the wall.

"Be my guest," Sullivan said flatly.

The video quickly came alive. The face on the video looked remarkably like a young George Washington. "I am George Washington. I'm one of the clones. I'm the clone who was shot out of the sky by President Ray. By a series of miracles I've come into the company of friends who're attempting to protect me from the American government. Thomas Jefferson, Alexander Hamilton, and I would like to enter into a public conversation with the President, but we can't do that while the government illegally holds Thomas and Alexander incommunicado in a secret location. Therefore, here's what must happen. They and all of their friends being held with them must be released without condition. They must be free to go wherever they desire without surveillance. If this doesn't happen, I'll go public. Make no mistake about it. I will go public, and the American public will do what they did once before. They will invoke John Locke, and they will throw off this parasitical government just like an old dog shakes off unwelcome dew. Give my friend, Omi, your answer. Let her depart your facility, also without any surveillance at all. If you fail to comply with my requirements, I'm ready to go to the press and social media immediately."

Sullivan, for the umpteenth time that day, remained surprised and speechless. Finally, she said, "There's no way I can do what he's demanding. I don't even know where those two clones are being held. The President's handling all that personally. Hell, I'm the Director of the CIA, and I don't know shit."

"I'll take that as a 'no deal.' Am I free to go? Omi asked as she stood.

"If you walk out of here, do you realize the situation you will have put in place? Two clones in detention who knows where, one captive in the Evil Empire, and a fourth one that no one who knows where he is but he's practically declaring war on the American government, saying it should be overthrown."

Omi repeated evenly, "Is it a 'no deal,' Ms. Sullivan? Am I free to go?"

Sullivan surprised herself by coldness of own her reply, "Damn straight, woman. It's no deal. Your time is up. Get out."

As Omi was shutting the door behind her, Sullivan pressed a button on the underside of her middle desk drawer. "Make sure the tracker is on her car. If she uses uber or public transportation, follow them." Sullivan walked over to the window and similar to her predecessor, just stared out of the window, frowning. And plotting.

Chapter 118

President Armstrong had actually never left The Eagle Rock. He leaned back in his plush chair and switched off the video transponder on which unbeknownst to Caroline Sullivan he was able to watch everything that happened in the CIA's basement interview room. Sullivan's Administrative Assistant, a longtime ally of Armstrong's, had alerted the President to Sullivan's basement interview with the unknown woman.

"Well, well, well," Armstrong said smugly. "Washington's alive. Sullivan has the gall to be playing me. I have two clones. Polzinov has one."

The President then called TT and Cordero into his Eagle Rock office.

After TT and Cordero were seated, the President said, "I've just learned that Sullivan has the gall to be playing me. I have two clones. Polzinov has one. We cannot let the Russians keep that clone. I've decided that we have no alternative. I'm considering ordering a termination team to take out the Franklin clone." The President implied but did not tell his subordinates that Washington was indeed alive.

Cordero was stunned. "You can't be serious! You can't send assassins inside Russia! And, Mr. President, you can't be serious about killing Benjamin Franklin! That would lead to your impeachment. It would also lead to serious problems with Russia. And it would just be wrong!"

"Not to mention the American public," TT added.

"We can do it without anyone knowing it was us," President Armstrong replied.

"Mr. President, please think again —"

The President snapped, "Mr. Cordero, I've thought of nothing else for days. This clones bullshit has consumed my presidency just like it did Ray's, and enough's enough."

Cordero stood. "So all that bullshit about a dialogue was just that. Bullshit, right, Royster?"

President Armstrong did not reply.

Cordero looked at the Attorney General. "TT?"

TT looked tired and gray. "Let's get back to D.C. and consider this again tomorrow. Will that work, Mr. President?"

Armstrong hesitated, then said, "OK, we can sit on it for now, but, gentlemen, we need to put this clones thing to bed once and for all."

"But what you're thinking about is illegal and unconstitutional," Cordero said.

"When the nation's stability's threatened, as it is now, the Constitution's whatever I say it is. That's the only way we can save the nation from disintegration. I believe in a living Constitution, not a dead Constitution. That's what inherent executive power's all about."

Cordero and TT said nothing.

"But we'll continue tomorrow in Washington," President Armstrong said.

President Armstrong's eyes were stone cold. "Gentlemen, make no mistake about it. It's time to take off the gloves. The time for nice talk is over. These people have no idea what our government's capable of. It's time to show them. If you're not on board with this, you'd better speak up."

With no one wanting to extend the conversation, Cordero and TT left the room for their flight back to the nation's capital. On the way to their plane, TT said quietly, "Douglas, I think he's cracking up."

"I agree, TT. Let's don't talk about it on the plane, but when we get back to D.C., we'll find a place where it's safe to talk."

"We need to get with Sullivan," TT said.

"Absolutely," Cordero replied. "We'll call her when we get to D.C.

———

Once on aboard his own unmarked plane, President Armstrong called CIA Director Sullivan. The President had never used the special phone which was an exclusive link between the President and the Director of the CIA. His objective was that this phone conversation would finally set into motion the end of the whole clones affair.

Sullivan heard the buzz of the dedicated phone on the small credenza behind her desk. With dread of what the conversation might be, she immediately answered, "Yes, Mr. President?"

"Are you alone, Ms. Sullivan?"

"Yes, Mr. President, I am," Sullivan responded.

"As the Director of the CIA, Senator Sullivan," said the President, unintentionally reverting to Sullivan's previous title, "There's one file which you would have no way of knowing about. After this conversation, I'll email you the name of that file and how you can access it. Read it through, and if you have any issues with it, let me know immediately."

"What's this about, Mr. President?" Sullivan knew the only front burner issue to Armstrong was the clones.

"This dedicated line is secure, Ms. Sullivan, but I'd rather you just go through the file first, and then we can talk about it in person, face to face. And, Ms. Sullivan, this matter is just between you and me. No one else, none of your assistants, no one, no exceptions, can know about the existence of this file or its contents. It's Top Secret Omega. Understood?"

Caroline Sullivan hesitated.

"Ms. Sullivan, do I have your word that you won't reveal the existence of this file or any of its contents to anyone else, without exception? Remember your oath of office, Ms. Sullivan, that you'll protect this nation against all enemies, foreign and domestic. That's what this whole thing's about. So, do I have your word?"

"Mr. President, with all due respect, I cannot agree until I know what it is that I'm agreeing to." Then, Caroline Sullivan's entrenched curiosity strangled her sense of caution. "But, Mr. President, I agree with the condition that I'll resign if I find the file that objectionable."

"And that if you resign, that you'll reveal to no one the existence or any of the contents of this file?" Armstrong waited for Sullivan's answer. He knew he was gambling but felt he needed the CIA's resources and assets to succeed in his plot to end the whole clones affair.

"OK, agreed," Caroline Sullivan said against her better judgment.

"I expected nothing less, Ms. Sullivan, than your unwavering loyalty to your country." The President broke the connection and sent the encrypted email to the Director of the CIA.

President Armstrong was no fool, nor was he naïve to Sullivan's ability to torpedo his own plans to get rid of the clones once and for all. *If taking the gloves off means anything,* he thought, *it means being ready to cripple Sullivan. Cordero and TT, too.* Armstrong cradled the phone and punched in another number, one that he had used only once before.

"Yes?" The answer was terse. Using code words, the President said cryptically, "Is it foggy there?"

"Yes, Mr. President, there is a deep fog."

"OK, make sure everything's ready to go with no notice," President Armstrong said.

The voice replied, "For everyone?'

"Yes, everyone," the President answered.

"Roger that" was the reply.

The President immediately broke the connection. He leaned back into his cushioned seat as his plane gained altitude. *Sullivan is the one person who could screw up everything. I've got to control her. Cordero and TT, too. It's a gamble, telling Sullivan what I need to do to save this nation, but it's a gamble I have to take. I need her resources. She might think she can stop me, but if she tries anything, she'll be finished for the rest of her life. The technology we now have. It's unbelievable. No, it's believable, but it can achieve unbelievable results. Deepfake, I love it.*

Soon after President Ray's death, President Armstrong had known all along that he would have to get rid of the clones, assuming that they were really clones, and even if they weren't clones, they would have short life spans. He also knew two other things. One, he would have to conceal his true aims, and two, he would have to create an insurance policy to use in case anyone in the White House tried to stop him. That insurance policy was a deepfake rendition of each one of his close advisors where each admitted that they had consorted with Russia — for some it was China — to have the clones disposed of, but worse, to assassinate both the President and the Vice President. Deepfake technology has advanced to where artificial intelligence can create an image of a person which is completely life-like, facial posture, body language, everything. Without special dissection software, the deepfake rendition is undistinguishable from the actual person on which it is based. Therefore, the President could simply give the media damning videos of Sullivan, TT, Fogg, Shulla, and Cordero. The media would do the rest. The videos that President

Armstrong had commissioned showed each person plotting to assassinate the President and Vice President and also to murder the clones. To make their conspiracy even more reprehensible, they were shown colluding with the Russians. The conversations and admissions on the videos made the conspiracy and the fake collusion despicably real. *If only Schiff, Pelosi, and that crowd had had what I have, they could have nailed that narcissist Trump to the cross. Well, do I ever have a surprise for TT the empty-head, Cordero the arrogant, and Sullivan the prude if they try anything. Anything at all. Part of me hopes that they do try something.*

Chapter 119

As Attorney General Trentini and Secretary of State Cordero were getting seated in their private jet prior to takeoff for Washington, D.C., their pilot walked back to their section of the plane. "Gentlemen, our takeoff's being delayed, but it should be only a short delay. The fuel consumption warning light itself seems to have malfunctioned, but we should have it fixed in a few minutes. It's not at all a safety issue, and we can actually fly without it if we have to, but I think we ought to fix it."

"Not a problem," TT said as he and Cordero settled back for the short wait.

After sitting on the tarmac for about fifteen minutes, the pilot reported that they would take off in a few minutes. TT's phone beeped. He saw that it was Director Sullivan.

"Yes, Caroline? How are you?"

"Not so well, TT, where are you and how quickly can we meet?"

TT heard the urgency in Sullivan's voice and replied, "I'm out of town. I just boarded my plane to come back to D.C. I should be there in a couple of hours."

"TT, something has come up and we need to meet as soon as possible, and it must be absolutely secret. No one can know that we're meeting. It can't be in D.C. We have to meet somewhere out of sight."

The plane began to slowly pull away from the hangar, TT turned to Cordero, "Tell the pilot to hold off. There's something big going on, and I don't know that it is yet."

Cordero looked confused but quickly headed to the cockpit.

"Why does it have to be so secret, Caroline?"

"Trust me, TT. We have to talk about it face to face, not over the phone. Where are you? Let's figure out where we can meet."

"Caroline, have you ever heard of the Eagle Rock?"

"I've heard rumors, but I've never been there. Are you there now?"

"I'm here now. So is Cordero. The President just left to go back to D.C. This is a totally out of sight place for us to meet. I'll send you flight info. It'll take you a little over two hours to get here."

"That works."

Caroline Sullivan then made a quick telephone call to a private aviation company that as a Senator she had used when she wanted to avoid prying eyes. She informed her aides that she was heading to the Pentagon gym to work out and would be gone for the rest of the day. Then she quickly took her limousine to the Pentagon. After Sullivan had arrived at the Pentagon and the limo driver had departed, Sullivan walked thirty yards to a nondescript, late model sedan and got in.

The driver said, "I'm supposed to tell you that the plane'll be ready by the time we get to the field."

A short time later, they arrived at a small airfield in Fairfax County, Virginia. As soon as Director Sullivan boarded the plane, her pilot, Guy Skipper, said, "We're ready to leave, Director."

Sullivan replied, "Sorry I couldn't tell you more about where we're going. I've never been to Eagle Rock and don't know anything about it. Cordero and TT landed there and so did the President, and that's all I know."

"If the landing strip will take their planes, it'll take ours." From other pilots, Guy had learned some time ago that there was an off-the-books landing field in rural Alabama that could accommodate his company's planes.

Chapter 120

Slightly over two hours later, as TT, Cordero, and Sullivan entered one of the Eagle Rock's small conference rooms, TT started to talk, but Sullivan shushed him as she pulled a small electronic device out of her briefcase. She then methodically scanned every surface of the room for electronic devices. When she aimed the laser at the room thermostat, a red light on her device lit up brightly. She paused, examined the thermostat without touching it. Next she stood on the small, round conference table and swept a wide, fan-shaped laser beam methodically across the ceiling. Finally, she got off the table and scanned the table itself and then crawled under the table and continued scanning. TT and Cordero watched.

"Impressive," Cordero whispered.

Crawling out from under the table, she then placed her detector on the conference table and focused a neon green beam on the thermostat from which a signal had been detected. Sullivan then pulled from her briefcase a black box with a row of lights, some buttons, and two dials. She pressed one button, several of the lights glowed, and Sullivan placed the device on the conference table. She then turned to TT and Cordero, "As far as I can determine, that thermostat houses the only listening device in this room, and I've fixed it so that the thermostat mike won't transmit anything but silence. I'm not jamming the signal. They could detect jamming. It'll just be silent. As far as I can tell, there're not any video devices in this room though if there are, we are, of course, already compromised." She motioned to the green laser beam pointed at the thermostat. "This'll cause that particular listening device to hear nothing but silence." She then pointed to the black box. "That's a really cool device. It reconfigures any noise in the room, like talking, into silence. So, we have double protection, and that's as good as we can hope for. I think it's safe for us to talk, certainly safer than outside."

As soon as they had taken seats at the table, TT asked, "OK, Caroline, what's happening?"

Sullivan fired up her laptop. "Just read this. Then let's talk." The screen contained the file that President Armstrong had sent to Caroline.

TT and Cordero both read from the screen and slowly scrolled though the document. As they were reading the document, both TT and Cordero turned ashen. Then TT, exclaimed softly, "My God, Washington's alive!" Then TT stood and paced the floor. Cordero just sat, motionless.

"Obviously we have a crisis," Sullivan said, her voice fairly trembling. "The President's holding two clones right here at The Eagle Rock. Jefferson and Hamilton are here, in one of these buildings."

"I know. They're here, Caroline. We've talked to them. But, Caroline, this's more than a crisis," Cordero grimaced, fists clenched. "It's a fucking national calamity. Who the fuck does he think he is?"

"This document's beyond impeachment. It implicates the President in criminal activity," TT said as he took his seat. "The President actually talked about this just hours ago, just before he headed back to D.C., but now it's at another level. It's now an actual proposal. This isn't just impeachable, it's blatantly criminal, beyond any question. Or it's at least contemplated criminal activity. Maybe he hasn't actually done anything yet," TT ventured, attempting to sound a note of hope. "Let's don't assume anything. Is there any chance, Caroline, that this document's a fake?"

"It came from President Armstrong himself. I had to promise not to talk to anyone about it before he agreed to send it to me.

Obviously to accomplish what he wants to accomplish, he'll have to use the CIA, so he had no choice but to bring me in."

"The people being held here—-" TT started, but Caroline Sullivan gently cut him off.

"I feel like we're jumping around. Let's try to be a little more systematic," Sullivan said.

TT looked excited. "One vitally new thing here is that those people who have been helping the clones are right here at the Eagle Rock. They're being held incommunicado along with the clones. It's a white professor and his wife and an African-American security guy who works with the professor. We at the White House knew such people had to exist, but we didn't know who they were until we got here earlier today. Well, Douglas and I didn't know anything about them, but the President surely did, and he plans to do away with them, too."

"But they're here, so we can talk to them and free them," Cordero said.

"Not so fast on freeing them, Douglas. We'll have to vet them first," Sullivan said.

Cordero stood again. "So, here's what I understand. He plans to get rid of these people that he's holding here at Eagle Rock. He plans to send an assassination team to Moscow, or use one that's already there, to kill the Benjamin Franklin clone. And he believes that the George Washington clone's still alive — and that's news to me — but he doesn't know where he might be, but Armstrong plans on 'rendering his disappearance,' as the document puts it, as soon as he finds him."

"And with no clones around to dispute anything, he can claim, á la Trump, that it was all a big hoax, " TT observed.

"And, Caroline, President Armstrong's strategy's to do all of this as soon as he can because he wants the November election to focus on his policies to socialize the insurance industry, create a national health care system, launch the VAT, accelerate the climate policies, and all that stuff, anything but the clones. His calculation's that America has lost its will and that people actually want more government programs. He's gambling that without the distraction of the clones, Americans will choose security over freedom. Well, Caroline, neither one of us is completely for those policies, at least not in the form currently being considered, but since our party's been taken over by the alternative reality crowd, we thought it better to apply the brakes from the inside rather than be martyrs on the outside." Cordero paused. "And that was probably a mistake."

"Isn't it ironic that the President combines the wokeness of the left with the narcissism and Trumpism of the right? The worst of both parties. Based on primaries, media propaganda, money, pandering and image rather than policies, the party system as now functioning is ironically toxic to democracy."

TT seemed prepared to launch into an oral dissertation on the recent decay of the American party system and its failure to put forward its best, or at least competent, nominees, but before he could continue, Caroline cut him off. "Let's stay on topic, gentlemen. We need a plan. I've been thinking about this all the way down on the plane, what to do. The people he's holding here, I can move them to a CIA safe house. As far as Benjamin Franklin's concerned, the Russians have him under pretty close guard so he should be safe from any non-CIA team that the President might try to put together. I doubt that the President has put anything in motion so far. That's why he brought me in. He would never ever have risked bringing me in unless he needed CIA resources. That leaves George Washington. Here's what you don't know. I had a visitor recently at my office who claimed she was part of the group helping the clones stay hidden. She claimed that they have the Washington clone and that if the

Administration doesn't release the other clones, he'll go public. She actually had a video of Washington. I'm sorry to say that I rejected her offer because at that time I didn't know that we had the other clones or where they were or anything. And I don't know how to contact her."

"So, the Washington clone's actually alive!" Cordero's said in amazement. "I wonder how. Ray actually shot down his plane. Anyway, we've got to figure out how to contact him."

"Caroline, why the hell did you reject her offer?" TT was incredulous.

"That was a mistake. I admit that. She demanded that I free the clones, and, like I just said, TT, at that time I had no idea where the clones were. Then she basically broke off the conversation. But, yes, in retrospect it was a mistake."

"The people Armstrong's holding here should know how to contact the Washington clone," TT said.

"We can hope," Cordero interjected.

"So, we'll talk to them and then hustle them to a safe location. Our time's probably limited. Armstrong's inevitably going to find out that we're meeting here without his knowledge, and he'll surely know what we're talking about." Caroline looked worried. "Let's meet these clones now and then get them out of here quickly."

TT ordered the Eagle Rock security to bring the detainees to the conference room. As the detainees walked into the room, they registered no surprise, but CD took note of the new player in the continuing drama. "Senator Sullivan, what brings you here? Have you joined the President's scheme to bury the clones, the very replicas of our founding fathers? You know you'll never get away with it."

Sullivan responded with no animosity. "Let's do some introductions first. Then I intend to bring everyone up to speed."

"OK," CD replied. "I'm Charles Delna. I'm a professor from Tulane, and I have been trying to protect the clones from our benevolent government." CD's sarcasm was unmistakable.

"I'm Olive Delna. I'm Dr. Delna's wife."

"Interesting," Sullivan commented softly.

"I'm Rufus Forest. I work with CD and have for many years."

"CD?" Caroline asked.

"Charles Delna. Dr. Delna. Him" Roof pointed to CD.

"In what capacity, Mr. Forest, do you work for him?" Sullivan waited for Roof's answer.

"I thought this was just introductions, Senator. Let's just leave it at that until you, as you say, bring everyone up to speed," Rufus said with a tone of finality.

"Very well," Sullivan replied and turned to Thomas. "And you must be one of the clones."

"I'm Thomas Jefferson." Thomas added nothing else.

"That leaves me," Alex said. "I'm Alexander Hamilton. There're two others who're missing. Benjamin Franklin who was apparently kidnapped by the Russians and George Washington whom President Ray murdered. Yes, we're clones. We were cloned from those eminent founding fathers, the very ones whom many in this country have been trashing, canceling, and destroying statues."

"Now that we've all been introduced, what is your connection, Senator?" CD asked.

"As you know, Mr. Delna, Joelle Lucado was killed at Andrews. The President's appointed me as Acting Director of the CIA. So, I'm here in that capacity. Here's the short version of what's underway. The President has a plan to dispose of all of you. Secretary Cordero, Attorney General Trentini, and I'll try to keep that from happening."

Sullivan then laid out the President's plan to assassinate Franklin and Washington. When she indicated that Washington was alive, they all registered shock. "Fantastic!" Alex exclaimed. "Where is he? You're the CIA. Surely you know where he is or you can find him."

"A lady visited my office who claimed she had the Washington clone." Sullivan looked directly at Thomas. "That lady must be one of y'all. We want you to contact her, and then we can get the Washington clone to a safe location."

"It sounds like he's in a safe location right now if you can't find him," Olive said.

"Fair enough," Sullivan replied. "But we want to get him involved in stopping the President's plan."

"And get him involved in healing our nation," Thomas added. "Healing our nation's our purpose. This nation has lost its bearings and is abandoning its divine mission. The division, the focus on identities, the hatred, the lying, the Godlessness, the deception, the self-aggrandizement, the creation and self-maintenance of an elite, political plutocracy, the refusal to work with anyone of opposing views, right wing extremism, the regarding of the American people as deplorable and weak of judgment, these are the exact things that were anathema to this nation's forefathers. They're anathema to us, too. It's our purpose to help the nation get back on track. Anything short of that, we reject. Anything short of that, then these evil afflictions will continue, and this nation will accelerate the decline which is already underway. But, Senator, that decline's reversible, but clearly not for long."

Ignoring Thomas's litany of the nation's alleged afflictions, Sullivan asked, "Can you contact the people who're protecting George Washington?"

CD responded quickly, "Will you then bring him here, to detain him with us? Do you seriously think we would betray him so that the President's plan can go forward?"

"What do you want, Mr. Delna?" Sullivan was clearly exasperated.

"I want to know that we can trust you, that you're not just part of this murderous plan."

Cordero said, "That's a tall order, Mr. Delna. I don't know what we can do to put you at ease about the future, what we *will* do that down the road."

"By the way," Alex interjected. "He's actually *Dr.* Delna."

"Whatever," Cordero responded impatiently. "How about one step at a time? We put y'all in a safe place, we find the George Washington clone, get him to a safe place, and then TT and I'll confront the President. Once confronted, he'll have to resign."

"Somehow, we'll have to contact the lady who came to my office, and I don't have any contact info. We tried to track her, but she was quite competent in evading us," Caroline admitted.

"Do we even have her name?" CD asked.

Caroline replied, "The name she used was Omi. She only gave me her first name, and that name's probably a fake."

"Omi!" Thomas exclaimed. "That was Omi. What did she look like?"

CD touched Thomas's arm and looked at the CIA director, "We might — might — be able to contact her. Let's leave it at that."

Sullivan said knowingly, "OK, thank you. Let's hope you can contact them. And we're aiming at getting Armstrong out of office, and the Washington clone can be instrumental in making that happen."

"That sounds good," TT said. "There's no way in hell he can stay in office once this stuff hits the fan."

"We'll have to have guarantees, nonreversible guarantees, or no George Washington," Thomas said flatly.

Sullivan looked exasperated. "We've known about the President's plan only for a few hours. He's got the power to get things started as we sit here talking, and he might've already done so. Time's of the essence, gentlemen. I don't know of any way that we can give you perfect assurances of the fact that we oppose the President's plan and we want the clones to be able to speak freely and all that."

Olive looked skeptical. "'And all that'? What does that mean, Senator Sullivan?"

"It means none of you'll be detained. None of you'll be under surveillance, at least no more than anyone else is our surveillance-rich country. None of you'll be censored by the government. You'll all be as free as anyone else in the country," Director Sullivan said.

"And as Attorney General, I can put that in writing as an official document, if you want it," TT added.

"Here's what we can do," Olive took the lead. "You allow us, all of us, to go to a place of our choosing. The location, only we'll know. You won't. You confront the President. We'll want a video of that confrontation. The President resigns. Then, and only then will we bring in George Washington."

"I have no problem with any of that," Caroline responded, "but I don't think we'll be able to video our meeting with the President. For all kinds of reasons, that won't be possible."

"Give me some of those reasons," CD said.

Cordero also felt that the video-taping idea was a non-starter. "For starters, the Oval Office is equipped to detect and disable any such devices. Second, the President won't permit any recording or video of any type other than what he himself authorizes. And obviously he'll never allow any video or audio capture of anything -—anything at all -—dealing with his plan to murder the clones."

TT added, "The President has an automatic, voice-activated audio recording of everything that happens in the Oval Office. That much I know. Now where those recordings are stored and how to access them I don't know. But after we confront the President, he'll immediately destroy any recording of that meeting. He's pretty smart. I'm sure he disables the system before any discussions about the clones."

"Not if we place his office under guard," Cordero said.

Sullivan waved her hand dismissively, "We'll have no coup, gentlemen. They tried that with Trump, and then he tried it with Biden. There'll be no coup shit here. My guess is that Armstrong's Chief of Staff processes and stores the audio files, so if we need to we can bring her in after we meet with the President and get the audio files from her."

"How about this," Thomas suggested. "You get a video admission from him on the plan itself and a commitment from him to resign immediately?"

"Why would he ever agree to that, Mr. Jefferson?" Cordero responded. "He's a fighter, and he's clever. He'll never agree to a video. He might agree to resign but my bet's that he'll never confess to the plan and will at least go through the motions of resisting the suggestion that he resign."

"He might agree if that's what it takes for him to avoid criminal charges and spending the rest of his life in prison," TT said.

"So, let him off the hook?" Alex's disappointment was obvious.

Sullivan responded, "I like TT's idea. Remember, our purpose is to get George Washington involved and then to start the nation's healing process."

"So, we let him off the hook?" Alex repeated.

Olive placed her hand on Alex's arm. "Alex, history will punish him more than any of us can imagine. Traitors sometimes avoid legal punishment, but they never escape history's condemnation. Alex, he'll get his due. But Senator Sullivan's right. Our focus has to be the nation, not what ultimately happens to Armstrong. His fate will happen. In a sense it already has. We're seeing the plot unfold in the present time, but there's One who has already seen the whole production, and He'll see justice done. I hope we all know that."

Sullivan added, "He's in control. We must just try to be attuned to His will."

"OK, so, let's deal with exactly what steps to take, what to do next," Thomas said.

"Not so fast," Rufus spoke for the first time. "What about Benjamin Franklin? What's the plan to protect him from some American assassination attempt? What's the plan to rescue him from the Russians?"

Sullivan said. "We have some limited resources in Russia, and we can try to rescue the Franklin clone, but—-"

Alex raised his voice as he interrupted Sullivan. "There's something about this whole conversation that needs to be stopped. He's not the Franklin clone. He's Benjamin Franklin. Benjamin Franklin. Ms. Sullivan, you have little or no understanding of who we are and how we think and how we perceive. For all practical and biological purposes, he *is* Benjamin Franklin." Alex pointed to Thomas. "This guy *is* Thomas Jefferson. I suggest we never use the descriptor "clones" anymore. It's not degrading, but it *is* diminishing."

Director Sullivan had a fleeting inclination to resist what Alex was suggesting, but before Sullivan could say anything, Olive validated what Alex had said. "Director Sullivan, Alex is right. I've been around these two gentlemen and Benjamin Franklin also long enough to say with no doubt that they're the real thing. They even talk like their biological fathers."

"Except they us contractions," CD, ever the linguist, interjected.

"Whatever. Thank you, my dear," Olive said with a knowing smile. "Their thoughts, from what I know about our founding fathers, seem to be the same. I now know that their political, economic, and moral principles are practically identical to the founding fathers from which they spring. We can introduce them to people who haven't met them as clones, and that might do no harm, but we shouldn't use that as their core identity because that dilutes and misses just who they are. Director Sullivan, they're the real thing. I think with time you'll come to realize that."

"Very persuasive, Ms. Delna. Very convincing," Sullivan replied. "Fine, I won't be using that word to describe our friends. TT? Douglas? OK?"

"I agree," TT said.

Absolutely," Cordero said.

"So, what do you propose about Benjamin Franklin, Senator Sullivan?" Alex opened both of his palms on top of the table. "Is there really any hope to rescue him? You didn't sound very hopeful a moment ago."

Sullivan frowned. "We have very limited options in Russia to get someone of his stature out. Honestly, Mr. Hamilton, I don't know if we can do it. As you know, I'm new at this job. I'll have to go through exactly who we have in Russia and what access they might have to Franklin. So far, the Russians have revealed nothing. We know they have Franklin, but other than that we don't know anything. Where he is, what kind of security they have around him, what they have done so far, what their plans are. We just don't know. Our people in Moscow know nothing. They have not seen Franklin. They have heard nothing."

Sullivan then turned and stared intently at CD. After a lengthy pause, she asked, "What're your resources in Russia, Dr. Delna? To have so successfully evaded government surveillance and capture for so long, you must have some skills and connections. To have facilitated the clones — sorry, our friends — staying free of the government for so long, perhaps you have people over there who can help with Franklin. It's certainly quite a coincidence that you also speak Russian." The CIA Director had no actual knowledge about CD and had never heard of the Procurement Project, but she did have a gut feel about him.

Sullivan then turned to Olive. "And I do not for a minute doubt that you have skills and contacts in this area also. Am I right, Ms. Delna?"

Olive did not reply.

Sullivan shifted in her seat and stared at CD. CD remained silent for a time. Everyone sensed that something was going on between Sullivan and CD. Finally, CD responded succinctly, "If there's anything I can do, of course, I will."

"Perfect," Sullivan said. "So, you can both contact Washington, the clone, not the city, and also inquire about Franklin. All of you will be allowed to go to a place of your own choosing when you leave here, and that'll be right after this meeting." Sullivan motioned to Cordero and TT and continued. "We three will confront the President. Once we've confronted him, we'll all decide on the next step. Are we all agreed on this?"

Everyone nodded.

"Verbally, please. There can be no hesitation and no reservations." Sullivan said.

Each person verbally agreed to the plan of action that Sullivan had outlined.

"Good," Caroline said as she pulled a cell phone from her briefcase and handed it to CD. "This is a burner phone. It's completely clean and cannot be traced. You can make whatever calls you need to make to leave this place. Let's all leave this facility as quickly as possible, OK?"

Everyone agreed.

Then CD added, "Director Sullivan, how about your plane taking all of us with you to D.C., and we'll make our own arrangements from there?"

"CD, that sounds too risky to me," Thomas said. "We could just be walking right into a trap."

Before CD could reply, Roof said, "It's OK, Thomas. It's no more a trap there than if we tried to go from here on our own. If we had a plane and took it from here, we'd be tracked through every ATC center between here and wherever we went. If we get our own ground transportation from D.C., we'll at least have a chance of not being tracked."

"I give you my word," Caroline said. "We won't track you."

Roof replied with detectable irritation. "Director, we've got no choice but to trust you, but you and I both know that the President and others in the Administration independent of you have state of the art tracking capabilities. It's the President who worries me. With all due respect, Director Sullivan, my guess is that the President tracked and surveilled you before he ever asked you to be the director of the CIA."

"I doubt that," Director Sullivan replied. "He had no reason to watch me."

Roof just chuckled.

CD thought, *I hope she's really not that naïve.*

Chapter 121

During the flight to Washington aboard Sullivan's jet, CD made one call. He fully suspected that the burner phone that Sullivan had given him was compromised, so the one call he made was to the Mercedes Man who in turn arranged for Omi to meet CD at Martin State Airport, nine miles east of Baltimore, Maryland.

When they were beginning their descent to land at Andrews, CD moved up several rows and took the seat beside Caroline Sullivan. "Director Sullivan, please ask your pilot to divert to MTN. We'll deplane there."

Sullivan did not act surprised. "I thought you might want to avoid Andrews, Dr. Delna."

CD replied, "CD, please, Madame Director. We might be seeing a lot of each other in the next weeks."

Sullivan did not relax her formality. "Perhaps, Dr. Delna. Anyway, what's MTN?"

"It's an airport outside Baltimore. We'll get our ground transportation there. And, Director Sullivan, I'd prefer to go with you to inform the pilot. Obviously I don't want you making any arrangements regarding what happens to us once we're on the ground. My guess is that you already have some arrangements in place.

Sullivan showed fleeting irritation before replying, "Not a problem. Let's do it now. My pilot is Guy Skipper, and you can trust him too."

The two walked to the cockpit and directed the pilot to divert to Martin State Airport. CD then told the pilot, "When you taxi, we need to get off as close to the Air National Guard area as possible."

Guy replied, "OK, I've landed at MTN before. The ANG's on the right side near the end of the runway. We should be on the ground in twenty minutes."

CD and Sullivan returned to their seats, then CD moved to the seat beside Roof. "Roof," he whispered. "Omi's meeting us at Martin. We should be OK from there."

"Hopefully, " was Roof's laconic response. Then Rufus informed Jefferson and Hamilton that Omi would be meeting them with ground transportation.

Jefferson just smiled. Hamilton remarked, "You're getting all the breaks, Thomas," he said.

"Hardly," Thomas replied.

"I bet," was all that Alex said in reply.

The jet soon landed at Martin State Airport and taxied down the runway. On reaching the end of the runway, the jet stopped and pivoted. "The ANG facility's straight ahead," Guy said over the intercom. "It's directly ahead of you when you get off the airstair."

As CD rose from his seat, Director Sullivan said quietly, "Dr. Delna, President Armstrong's capable of anything. I don't know where you're going, but don't come out of hiding until I tell you personally it's ok. The words I'll use are 'Get your ass to DC.' Any other words, stay hidden and protect yourselves. If everything's a go, you should respond, 'Please don't talk about my anatomy.' If I use any other words, it'll mean something has happened and it's not safe for you to emerge."

"Sounds good," CD said.

Without another word, CD, Olive, Rufus, Jefferson, and Hamilton walked down the jet steps. Omi walked briskly up to them. Smiling especially at Jefferson, she said, "It's good to see everyone. Follow me."

Sullivan watched Omi lead them away from the plane. *She's the same one I spoke to at Langley. I hope our people are ready to tail them.* Sullivan had anticipated a last-minute change of destinations and had arranged for surveillance at several smaller nearby airports. Martin was one of them, and Sullivan's people on the ground were ready to tail the clones. She felt it was critical to get control of the entire situation as quickly as possible and counted on them to lead her to Washington.

Omi led everyone across the ANG runway and through a number of idle jets. They walked directly into a parking lot where several black SUV's were parked. Omi stopped before approaching any of the cars and said, "Let's wait here."

"Why wait? Rufus said.

Omi replied, "I'm waiting to see what that CIA jet does." She motioned to Sullivan's plane which was still sitting on the runway. "Your director obviously wants to watch us, so let's her see what we're doing. I'm sure her people are here somewhere, but I haven't been able to spot them. This way, everyone." Omi led them to the three SUV's parked together in the lot. "Everyone get in a car. Split up. We need to use all three cars."

Hamilton balked. "This's walking right into a trap. She's obviously got glasses on us, and you say she has her people here."

Jefferson joined Hamilton, "There's no chance in hell that she's not having the CIA tail us."

"Trust me, gentlemen. Get in, please," Omi said impatiently.

Jefferson and Hamilton looked at CD. "CD?" they both said together.

Rufus replied before CD had a chance. "Omi knows what she's doing. Let's go." Roof bounded over to one of the cars and got into the back seat. Everyone else headed to a car. Each of the cars pulled away from the parking lot. After a short delay, several other cars also left a nearby lot and headed in the same direction.

"OK, get us to Andrews," Sullivan said through her intercom to the pilot The jet immediately started taxiing for takeoff.

"Good thinking, Caroline," TT said with assurance. "I think we might be getting to the end game now."

"We'll soon have everyone but Franklin. That's the only problem we have left," Cordero said.

Sullivan frowned, "Don't be so naïve, Mr. Secretary. We still have to deal with Armstrong, and he won't go easily. And then there's Novokatnaia."

While Sullivan's jet was taking off, instead of departing Martin, Omi's three SUV's pulled into a sheltered area behind a row of dumpsters outside the main ANG building. "Everybody out. As fast as you can, get in that dumpster." There was a dumpster directly beside the three cars. It's side door was conveniently open. As everyone was getting out and scrambling into the dumpster, two younger white men, one African American man, and an older white couple got into the SUV's.

"Very swift, Omi," Jefferson said. "Look-alikes."

The decoy cars exited the ANG parking lot and quickly entered Interstate 95 North. Two featureless sedans and one older pickup truck discretely followed the three decoy cars.

"This way," Omi said and motioned everyone out of the dumpster to a small, nondescript sedan.

"Garbage trucks, now dumpsters. This whole thing smells," Thomas said. No one laughed.

"So, where're they going?" CD asked.

"The decoys? They'll take a circuitous route to a notorious stripper bar in Cherry Hill, New Jersey. Between here and there, each of the decoys will be left off, some at rest stops, some at other places." Omi smiled. "When the cars arrive in Cherry Hill, the decoys will be long gone. The CIA, if they're still on the trail, will end up in a stripper bar. All at taxpayer expense."

"Where're we going, and where's George?" Hamilton asked as they were squeezing into Omi's car.

Everyone crowded into Omi's sedan. "I hope this isn't going to be a long ride. This car wasn't made for six people," Olive said.

"Where's George?" Hamilton repeated.

Omi did not reply. She drove out of the ANG facility, across the airport runway and pulled up in front of an old twin-engine turboprop which appeared to have seen it best days long, long ago. "We'll have a short flight across the bay to Easton, Maryland."

Jefferson gazed at the plane. "Omi, will this thing even make it across the bay?"

"Yeah, like, maybe one of the Wright brothers flew it," Hamilton added.

"It's nowhere near as old as you think. We gave it a make-over to make it look old so it won't attract much attention. It's actually only about 10 years old, and, yes, my friend, it should make it across the water."

"OK, one more time. Where the hell is George?" Hamilton was clearly frustrated that Omi had not answered that question.

"Mr. Hamilton, we have placed George Washington in another, secure location. We thought it would be a mistake to have all three of you at the same place in case this location gets compromised. You'll get to be with George in a few days. So please be patient. Everyone, please be patient."

In less than thirty minutes, they had landed in Easton, Maryland. Two cars were waiting for them at the small airport and forty-five minutes later, they pulled up in front of a white, frame house bordering the Chesapeake Bay.

Chapter 122

President Armstrong's Chief of Staff, Kit Tersense, entered the Oval Office. "Mr. President, Secretary Cordero says he, Attorney General Trentini, and Acting Director Sullivan need to see you, and he says it's urgent. Should I give them a time slot?"

Warning bells rang in President Armstrong's mind. "My schedule's pretty jammed today, Kit," he said with feigned calmness. "Find out what he wants. I'm sure it's about the clones."

Kit Tersense replied, "Mr. President, he was emphatic that they must see you today, and I did ask him what it concerned, and he said it was for you only."

"Dammit to hell, OK. Block out fifteen minutes for them, not a minute more." A feeling of dread was beginning to metastasize somewhere deep inside Armstrong's psyche. As the Chief of Staff left his office, Armstrong started pacing. *If Sullivan has told those other two anything at all, that's the end of her. I'll teach that bitch what government power's all about. I won't have some fucking clones created in a lab standing in my way.*

President Armstrong kept to his schedule for the rest of the morning and maintained a convincing façade of calmness. He concealed his anxiety well and even seemed uncharacteristically jovial when talking to the delegation from nation's largest climate change lobby. It used to be the Citizens Opposed to Global Warming, but for propagandistic purposes, they had changed their name to Citizens for Saving the Planet (CSP). He promised the CSP the huge tax increases needed to finance the imposition of California's rigid environmental standards onto the entire nation. He joked to the lobbyists, "Don't worry about taxes. We'll chalk it up to the deficit just like Obama, Trump, and Biden, and all the rest of 'em." This was followed by nods of approval and laughter. Elation ruled the room in response to the President's commitment to the environmentalists' ambitious goal for the nation which they accurately referred to a Californianization. They ultimately hoped to put every state on a state-specific power grid, knowing that not only would that increase utility efficiency but also would allow the government to control household electrical usage.

After a solitary lunch of roasted octopus in Santorini sauce over green salad, a wary President admitted Cordero, TT, and Sullivan into the Oval Office. Armstrong immediately set an impatient tone, no longer making an effort to camouflage his tension. "Ok, Secretary Cordero," he said formally. "You wanted this meeting. What's so urgent? I have a full plate this afternoon." The President stood beside the presidential desk.

The three presidential aides took seats.

With no hesitation, Cordero replied, "Mr. President, it wasn't just me who wanted this meeting. It's the three of us. I'll get right to it."

"Good," Armstrong snapped. "Get to it."

"Mr. President, Director Sullivan's informed us of your plans for the Washington clone and the Franklin clone, that you plan on eliminating them both. Plus, you apparently plan on eliminating the other two clones. Needless to say, this also means you'll have to get rid of everyone who's been helping the clones stay free." Cordero paused.

Before Cordero could continue, TT said, "And, Mr. President, if you fail to get rid of even one person, including each one of us, who knows about your plot, you'll not only be impeached and convicted in the Senate, but you'll also spend the rest of your life in disgrace and in prison."

The President turned red and just stared at Caroline Sullivan. Sullivan held his stare. "Well, fuck you, Sullivan." Armstrong hissed between clenched teeth. "You're fired."

"Then you'll have to fire us, too," TT quickly responded. "You can fire everybody in your fucking cabinet, Mr. President, but this genie's not going back in the bottle."

The President slowly walked behind his large desk. He then said with conviction, "Are you three blind? Remember the antifa and Black Lives Matter riots and the looting of 2020? You remember, those disgraceful breaches of law that no one in our party even criticized. Remember the Trump people storming Congress in 2021 — With his approval, I might add — and how the Republicans rallied around that pathetic, unbalanced man? Well, if we allow those clones to stir up the public, the riots they'll start will make 2020 and 2021 look like child's play. Those clone freaks are lab relics from another era. Their structures and procedures were spectacular for two hundred years ago, I admit, but today they're a recipe for disaster, and I won't let the nation go down that destructive path. That's what the election of 2020 was all about, and I can't comprehend that you three don't see that? That election said that this nation must move beyond those antiquated principles that our obsolete Constitution has saddled us with. Government today needs to be much more active. We are the government, and we must help our people. That Constitution is a dinosaur in the throes of death in the digital age." The President then continued to berate the very idea of allowing the clones to go public, arguing that it was inherently destructive, that the public could not withstand the conflict and widespread violence that would be triggered.

There was a knock at the door, and Kit Tersense stood in the doorway. "Mr. President, your next appointment, the Speaker of the House, is here."

"Kit, tell her she'll have to wait, that some urgent matters have come up. And, Kit, please clear the rest of my afternoon."

The Chief of Staff looked very surprised at the President's order. "Cancel all the appointments, Mr. President?"

"Yes, yes, yes, Kit! That'll be all!" Armstrong's agitation was intensifying. He continued to stand behind his desk as the Chief of Staff left the room. Armstrong then glared at his three advisors. "There's no way I'll stand by as those clones unleash violence, discord, and revolt in this country, and if you three cannot help me with this clones problem, then all three of you are fired." Armstrong glared at his three advisors, then focused malevolently on Sullivan.

"Are you sure you want to go that way, Mr. President?" Sullivan spoke with an even tone. "Your 'obsolete constitution' as you call it, allows you to fire all of us, and you can do that if you want to and we'll gladly go, but I guarantee you that all of this'll become public the second you fire us. I'll make sure of that. And if you fire us, the press'll go wild."

"There have been multiple firings before, Ms. Sullivan. My God, Trump fired hundreds of people. And remember this. Each one of you has signed a binding agreement with criminal penalties not to divulge anything that has been classified, and I've had everything involving the clones classified. It's watertight. But let me repeat those two key words. Criminal penalties. So, bottom line, you can't talk to the press or anyone else or you go to prison." Armstrong for the first time radiated confidence.

TT stood, "Mr. President, you don't really think we'd be sent to prison for exposing your criminal conspiracy, do you? Anyway, we three have discussed it, and we're all totally willing to go to prison if that's what it takes to stop your attempts to eliminate the clones."

"Are you sure, TT? Those penalties are substantial and mandatory, and the standard of guilt isn't the usual criminal standard of beyond a reasonable doubt. The law provides for a much lower standard in this legislation." Armstrong looked smug.

"Mr. President, I drafted those laws. I'm quite aware of the penalties."

Cordero held up his hand, "Those are extraneous details, Mr. President," Cordero interjected. 'The only solution's that you resign the presidency."

Before Cordero could continue, Armstrong said forcefully, "And if I don't?"

TT responded, "If you don't, we'll lay it all out to the public, and the Vice President will invoke the Twenty-fifth Amendment, and you'll immediately be removed from office, the House will impeach, the Senate will convict, you'll be tried for conspiracy to commit murder and treason in federal court, you'll go to prison, and you'll go down right alongside history's other despicable dictators."

"And, Mr. Trentini," Armstrong said, but without conviction. "That'll take months if not years. The energy'll go out of it, and I'll win. You're a lawyer. You know there's no evidence of a conspiracy, and you know this doesn't fit the definition of treason. Oh, and that document that our resident bitch shared with you? There's no record of it anywhere. Yours is the only copy. It's a fake. And by the way, embedded in it are proofs that it's a fake, so that if you think that's evidence against me, think again. It'll show that you three conspired against me."

TT, Cordero, and Sullivan exchanged worried expressions.

"You're screwed. Now get out of my office," Armstrong said confidently.

"Mr. Armstrong," TT replied, choosing to ignore the President's claim that the document they were relying on was fake. "Remember, the House can impeach without even looking at the evidence. That's the Trump precedent. They can do it in one day. And with what you've done, the Senate trial'll take no time. Mr. President, you'll have no defenders. Not one. You can save the nation a lot of misery if you resign. Remember how Trump refused to resign? That just prolonged the hatred, the vitriol, the arrogance against the deplorables, and the violence. His refusal to resign energized his opponents, fed their hatred, and injured the nation. No good came out of his refusal to resign, surely no national good. The only people served by his stubbornness were us Democrats. It extended the life of the one we loved to hate. He single handedly united our party for one of the few times ever and without him, we could never have gotten Biden elected, and we would never have taken Congress. We can thank Trump for that. Once Trump ceased being our uniting, common enemy, our party imploded. Anyway, Mr. President, you can save the nation a lot of misery if you just have the decency to resign. Or you can go down with Trump as a power-hungry, self-centered destroyer."

"Fuck you, TT. You too Sullivan. You too, Cordero." Armstrong snarled.

Sullivan stood, "I think we're finished here. Mr. President, if you don't resign today, we're going public today."

In a sudden change of tone, Armstrong sounded as if he were surrendering to fate. "OK. I'll resign." He said nothing else. He suddenly began to cry.

Sullivan, Cordero, and TT were shocked. They each saw the President as mentally falling apart. "When, Mr. President?" TT demanded.

"Tomorrow morning," President Armstrong said through the tears.

"Mr. President, don't try to do anything stupid," Cordero said coldly. "We have the clones now so they're out of your reach. And I'll call Moscow myself and tell them to heighten the security around the Franklin clone. So, we'll give you until tomorrow morning."

"Now, get out of my office," the President sobbed weakly.

The three sat for several seconds, then TT and Cordero stood. Sullivan nervously fidgeted with the cushion where she sat. Finally she stood, and without a word, the three left the Oval Office.

After the three had left the Oval Office, Armstrong immediately stopped the crying. *Thank you, Dramatics 101. Crying at will. Is it a developed skill? A natural talent? Whatever, it worked. Those idiots will rue the day they fucked with me.*

As soon as President Armstrong was informed that the three were completely off White House property, he opened the bottom drawer of his tidy desk and lifted out a small metal box. He turned the combination on the box and pulled out an unlisted, untraceable cell phone and punched in a number. It was only the third time in his life that he had called that number.

"Yes," was the answer on the other end.

"Is it foggy there?" The President's voice was taunt.

"Yes, Mr. President, there is a deep fog."

"Release the video on Sullivan. Only that bitch, not anyone else yet."

"Roger that."

"You're absolutely positive that the video will work?"

"You've seen it, Mr. President. It's perfect."

"OK, run it." The President killed the connection..

Now we'll see what that arrogant bitch does. The FBI will slam her so fast she'll wish she'd never been born. She knows where that Washington clone is, and we'll sweat it out of her before we get rid of her. TT and Cordero will turn on her to save their own skins, then they'll disappear, too. Then America can be all that she's meant to be. The President for the first time could taste the sweet revenge of victory.

Chapter 123

CD read the encrypted message from Pakoslav. He smiled and announced, "Everybody, come in here. I've got news on Benjamin."

The others quickly came into the dining room. "What's the news, CD?" Olive asked.

"Benjamin's on the way home. I just got this from a friend of mine in Moscow. Here's what he said. 'The one you want is coming home to you. I got him a passport with a fake name. I'll give you that name in another message, the flight number, too. Once they discover that he's gone, the fan will hit the shit. I think that's the American expression. Your young one's a trade delegate and will arrive tomorrow. My friend, we cannot communicate further. It's no longer safe. Our lady friend over here is being given an unlimited budget and state-of-the-art facilities to do here what was done in your country. Truly, this is beyond a brave new world that we're already plunging into. As I said when we were last together, you'll always be my friend. Thank you for everything. I await my fate here.'"

CD continued, "And I've just received the flight info and his assumed name."

Everyone gave whoops of joy and celebration, everyone except CD who remained silent. Olive reached out and took CD's hand as they walked into the dining room. "Honey, he's a good man. Is there any chance that they'll know he's the one who did it?"

"Probably." CD's eyes betrayed his sadness. "In their system, with the surveillance they have, the paranoias and suspicions that pervade everything over there, and the blanket of evil that covers everything in the Kremlin, I have no idea how Pako got Benjamin out, but if he can do that, maybe he can get himself out. I hope so. Oh, my God, I hope so, but I'm scared that he just bought a one-way ticket to the gulag. Or worse."

"We've got problems. Real problems," Roof called out in a booming voice from the living room. Everyone walked in to see CIA Director Sullivan on television. The screen showed her behind a desk talking to someone off screen. ". . . so with this plan we can get rid of Armstrong. He should never have been President anyway. And we can get rid of that sorry Vice President at the same time. It'll look like an accident. That'll be easy to arrange. I have friends in Russia who have given me the details of how to do it and have already given me the materials to use."

The off-screen voice said, "That's perfect Director Sullivan. And the clones? How do we get rid of them?"

"We'll simply round them up. I now know where they are. I'll have them arrested, taken offshore, and there they'll either disappear or meet with an unfortunate accident. I've got the resources to do all this. And once the President, his VP, and the clones are out of the way, then we can put in place the type of government this country has been begging for for some decades now."

That was the end of the Sullivan video. The news anchor then came on screen. "That bombshell interview clearly shows CIA Director Sullivan plotting two assassinations and also plotting to dispose of those persons we know as the clones. The President's already issued a statement denouncing Sullivan and ordered her to be placed in FBI custody. The President himself, we understand, is now in an undisclosed location. We turn to our panel now to explain the best we can what happens now. This is truly the most shocking development in this town since Aaron Burr shot Alexander Hamilton."

Everyone looked at Alex who just smiled grimly, "Looks like she's planning a repeat of history."

Rufus put the television on silent. No one spoke. Finally, Alex broke the silence. "Mighty shit," he said. "Now just when we were about to make some progress and expose the President, we're right back where we started. And I trusted her!"

"We all did," Thomas said grimly.

"We're even worse off than we've ever been. She has a general idea where we are and she's right. She has the resources to find us now that the search area's so small. This whole time she's been laying a trap for us, and we've walked right into it. Gentlemen, I'm sorry. I feel like this is on me, and I've failed you." CD paused. "And I've basically signed your death warrants just the way I've caused Pako's death. This is such shit!"

"OK, one thing at a time. Benjamin arrives in three hours at BWI on Boutique Air," Olive said. "That our immediate problem. How to safely get him. And even if Sullivan gets us, we have to keep her from getting him."

"What the hell is Boutique Air?" Alex asked.

"It's a small domestic carrier," CD said. "I checked the Internet. Somehow we have to meet him. I'll do it, and everyone else stay here. Since Sullivan has betrayed us, we can't risk more than one of us going out in public."

"And we need to figure out whether we should stay here or try to get out of the area," Alex said. "Hopefully they think we're somewhere between here and New Jersey."

"I'm the one to meet Ben." Olive said. "I'll wear a hijab and a headscarf, cover my face and hair, add some weight, and I don't think anyone can possibly know who I am. And they surely can't do anything because I'll be protected by the shield of political correctness. All I need to do is go to Joanne's and buy some material. I can fold and splice it to work."

CD looked worried. "What about iris recognition?"

"I've got IAC's."

"Huh?" Thomas interrupted. "IA what's?"

Olive continued, "IAC's. Iris alteration contacts. They'll change the identification characteristics of my own irises. The CIA can bioscan all they want to, but these irises won't be in any database."

"How come you just happen to have extra iris lenses?" Thomas asked.

Rufus smiled. "Don't even ask, son. There's still a lot about that lady that you got no idea about."

CD looked worried. Olive again reached for his hand, "Honey, that's the only way," she said. "None of y'all can go. Any of y'all will be instantly recognized if there's surveillance out there. And we can't risk it. And that's that. I'm going."

"I think —" CD started, but Olive cut him off.

"Honey, remember. I've been there. It's just like Krasnoznamensk. I've got this." She squeezed CD's hand and they exchanged knowing glances. "I'll be ok."

After a long pause, CD resigned. "OK, Sweetie. I just don't want to lose you."

"You won't," Olive replied softly and headed for the door. "Now, I'm off to Joanne's."

After Olive had left, CD sighed, "I'm so glad I didn't have to go to Joanne's."

Everyone laughed.

"Talk about torture!" Rufus exclaimed.

Chapter 124

In her conservative hijab and headscarf, Olive waited among the passengers in the crowded baggage area as the Air Boutique luggage was offloaded onto the baggage carousel which was already jammed with baggage from a large flight of a major airline. As she was pretending to be watching the luggage carousel, she had spotted Ben quickly even though he had made an effort to disguise himself with a wig, a beard, and some obviously artificial weight. But what was the coup de victoire of Ben's disguise was an aggressive skin condition which adorned the otherwise handsome young man. The blotchy skin screamed for dermatological intervention and served to keep other persons at a distance. The ruse also helped Ben remain hidden in plain sight.

Olive watched Ben as he waited for his luggage. She also watched two casually dressed men standing to one side. The men were watching the people at the baggage carousel more intently than they were watching luggage. Olive instantly knew that they were undercover government agents. As Ben drifted towards another area around the baggage carousel, the men seemed to take no notice of him. They actually seemed to be watching another young man who physically looked surprisingly like an undisguised Ben. Olive watched with amusement as the two agents approach the young man. There followed a short conversation which quickly grew animated. One agent took the young man's elbow and began to force him to walk towards an airport exit. At that moment a man wearing a shirt emblazoned with the words *Fusegu Dojo Sensei* entered the baggage area. As he watched the government agent forcing the young man to the exit, Sensei yelled, "Drake, what's going on?"

The young man being held by the government agent yelled back, "This dickhead claims I'm a clone! He's trying to kidnap me."

Sensei yelled back with raw authority, "Drake! You know what to do. Do it! Imasugu!"

Then, unexpected violence erupted as Drake broke free of the agent's grasp, yelled "Fuck you!" but instead of fleeing, with three karate chops and one kick to the midsection, he floored the agent. The agent quickly struggled to his feet and growled, "Big mistake!" and pulled a pistol.

Sensei yelled, "Yes, big, big mistake!" He flew through the air and with a flying butterfly kick sent the pistol clattering to the floor and with a vicious, second kick put the man on the floor for the second time within twenty seconds. The second government agent wisely just stood motionless.

Pandemonium broke out as everyone turned to watch the melee. Olive seized the moment and quickly approached Ben who had pulled a small suitcase from the carousel. "Ben, I'm Olive. Let's get out of here."

"Olive, I figured that was you. I knew you'd be in some kind of disguise. I guess there's no way they're going to give you any trouble in that disguise. Political correctness and all that shit."

"OK, fine," Olive interrupted. "Let's move. Don't hurry, but keep moving. Just follow me, not too close. Stay behind me."

As Olive and Ben were making their exit from the airport terminal, a crowd was gathering to watch the altercation as the government agent who was still standing had now drawn his firearm and was pointing it at both of the karate men. That was yet another mistake. With stunning speed, Sensei disarmed the agent and after two swift roundhouse kicks and a spinning straight kick, the second agent joined his colleague on the floor. At that instant, a well-suited older man with an impressive pigtail walked up. As Olive and Ben walked past the crowd toward the exit, Olive smiled as she heard the following exchange. "Drake, what happened?" the older man asked.

"These goons claimed they had a warrant for my arrest, that I was one of the clones!"

"Did you have a chance to tell them who you are?"

"They wouldn't listen."

"Well, well, well," the older gentleman said to the two agents who were stiffly getting to their feet. "Looks like you two boys are in some trouble. My client here whom you've just tried to kidnap is our newest attorney. I'm the chief of the Washington, D.C., office, and as you know, we at the ACLU will jump on most any kind of case that makes the news." With smugness, he continued. "I think your assault and your little attempt to kidnap my friend here qualifies for a good case and some good headlines. Armed kidnapping, various firearms violations, and all that. You'd have probably gotten away with it except that Drake here is also the number one student at Fusegu Dojo. That's one of the nation's leading dojos. But from what I just saw, you probably don't know what a dojo is. Oh, and by the way, this guy," he pointed to Sensei, "is the sensei of Fusegu Dojo, and I bet you now have some idea what that means. Anyway, I've just called the local police."

Olive allowed Ben to catch up to her. "Ben, I'd love to stay here and see how this plays out, but I think we can read about it in tomorrow's papers. Let's go."

Olive and Ben headed to Olive's car which was parked on the second level of the parking deck directly across from the terminal building. As they crossed the street to the parking deck, four Baltimore County police cars skidded to stops directly in front of the terminal.

Chapter 125

Everyone at the clones' sanctuary noisily celebrated Ben's arrival, but the atmosphere quickly returned to somber in light of Sullivan's betrayal. They again watched the video of Sullivan revealing her plot to overthrow the government.

"I had no idea that she was so devious," CD said.

"She sure had me fooled," Thomas said. "I even confided in her on the plane."

"Let me see that video again," Ben said. "But this time, forget the tv. I want to see it just on the computer."

As Ben watched the video on a laptop, everyone else watched Ben.

"I need to download an app, so just hold on, everyone," Ben said.

"What are you doing, Ben? Thomas asked.

"Just hang on a few minutes, Thomas," Ben said as he pulled up the Tor browser and initiated a download.

"What's the app?" Thomas asked.

"DFID," Ben replied as he started the installation of the new app. "You can get it through a source on the dark web. It'll give us an analysis of this video. I think the video might be a fake." Ben paused, then said to himself, "OK, here's hoping."

"I thought you didn't use the dark web," Rufus said.

"Basically I don't, but every now and then, it's useful," Ben responded.

Ben ran the app and a series of diagnostic images depicting the deconstruction of the Sullivan video moved across the computer screen. Ben froze the analysis several times, then when the analysis was completed, Ben leaned back and said, "This video's a fake. Sullivan never said any of that shit."

"Explain," Alex said academically.

"Somebody, probably the President's people, used what's known as deep fake technology. That technology can take existing images of a person and existing statements and fabricate completely new sentences and images, complete with body language, facial expressions, inflections, everything. The human eye can't tell what's deep fake and what isn't. I played with deep fake some at St. John, but I had no idea that the technology had advanced so far. That Sullivan video is pretty good. The app I used dissected the video, and it's definitely a fake. No doubt at all."

"How do you know all of this, Ben?" Thomas asked.

"You forget who I am, Thomas?" Ben asked, and they all laughed.

"Amazing," CD exclaimed. "Ben, would anyone else know, could anyone else tell that that was a fake Sullivan, that she didn't say any of that stuff?"

"Not unless they have software that'll deconstruct the video, but first they'd have to suspect that it's deep fake. The app is called DFID. That stands for deep fake identification, and, yeah, the CIA surely has all the technology, but none of it's officially out there in the public. It took me beaucoup hours of searching to find this particular app the first time, and even then I had to rely on some friends I have who know the dark web a hell of a lot better than I do."

"So how do we exonerate Sullivan before they ship her offshore?" Rufus asked.

No one spoke until finally Olive suggested, "Why not give the complete diagnosis to the press, the entire running screen that we just looked at?"

"Use a virtual computer to put it all out there so that the entire public, not just the press, has it all. It worked before. It's not traceable," Rufus added.

"I like it," Thomas said. "Let's do it, and the sooner the better."

"Chem ranshe, tem luchshe," Ben intoned.

"What? Huh?" Everyone said at once.

"That's Russian for 'the sooner, the better,'" Ben said. "I heard that expression a lot in Russia. I asked what it meant. They told me. They wanted me to come over to their side the sooner the better."

"Ben, you're the tech genius. Is a virtual computer the way to go?"

"That's debatable, and I can't say. Beginning in 2021, the government relaxed all pretense of not monitoring all computer activity in heavily populated areas and in areas where anti-administration ideas are widespread, and that policy's continued, even intensified. Where we are right now isn't densely populated, so maybe it's safe to do it here."

"And maybe it's not," Thomas said. "And once they know for sure that we're in this area, we're toast. I say we can't chance it from around here."

Alex looked worried. "Ben, can the government pinpoint exactly where a computer upload comes from?"

"Picture a neural net, like a digital, invisible fishing net, but hundreds of square miles across. It's moved and coordinated by drones which communicate with various government facilities, like military, CIA, FBI, the Secret Service, you name it. So, because they're using drones, the net's completely mobile."

"Mobile on short notice?" Thomas asked.

"Yeah, instantly movable," Ben answered.

"Is this net invisible? Is there any way for us to know whether this geographic area is being monitored?" CD asked.

"The net itself's invisible since it's digital. Is there any way we can detect whether they're monitoring this area? Not that

I know of," Ben said. "Unless you want to go outside and see if you see any drones. But these drones are dedicated for this particular purpose, meaning that they make almost no noise and are super-small, plus the government has even begun to deploy stealth drones. Bottom line? No, there's no way that I know of that we can figure out if this geographic area's being monitored. And remember Atlanta. They apparently have some way to pinpoint uploads in addition to the digital net."

"Shit." Thomas said. "Then how do we upload to the virtual computer without telling them where we are?"

Pessimism began to creep into the room until Olive broke the silence. "Gentlemen, it's simple. We simply drive back to BWI. Stop at the departures level. One of us unloads luggage like he's catching a plane. The other uploads to the virtual computer from inside the car. The upload'll take only seconds, then we leave. BWI has powerful, free Internet. If the government detects an upload, we'll be long gone before they can do anything. If they're still monitoring the airport, they'll be watching the arrivals section, maybe even the departures section, but surely not people unloading luggage."

"And we won't have to worry about the government showing up while we're there," Ben announced. "I've got a surprise for y'all. I looked at the software by which the virtual computer appears. I modified that software so that it can be activated at some future time. You no longer have to be physically present to activate the virtual computer. You actually launch the virtual computer into a sleep state. In a sleep state, it can't be detected, at least I think it can't be detected. Not completely sure. Its instructions are to go live at a set time, make the post, then poof! It ceases to exist. It was really a pretty simple fix, and I'm surprised that I hadn't thought of this before."

Everyone just stared at Ben. Finally, Thomas broke the silence. "I'll never again forget who you are, Benjamin Franklin."

"Yeah," Alex said. "You were more than just the nation's first Postmaster General."

Everyone laughed. "Maybe once we all get free, Ben can fix the Post Office," CD remarked.

"Oh, yes," Ben replied. "That was under the old Continental Congress, before the U S of A actually came into existence. But enough about my illustrious history. Let's focus."

"OK, y'all," Thomas said. "There's something I haven't told anyone. Anyone except Sullivan."

"Oh shit," Olive said, in one of the few times anyone had heard her use coarse language. "What have you done?"

"Olive, it's good. Everybody just calm down. You know I mentioned that I'd confided in Sullivan on the plane? I had a minute on the flight back with Sullivan and I slipped her a micro-device that records conversations. It's called a Jukebox Four. Actually, Benjamin, you gave it to me in Louisiana. Ben took a CIA device, Jukebox Three, changed some things, made it smaller, added a sub micro-transmitter, and most important, he made it so that it can't be detected with any detection methods that we know about. Ben called it Jukebox Four because it improved on the CIA's Jukebox Three, right, Ben?"

"Yeah, and there're several other things about Jukebox Four. First, it —"

Ben was starting to elaborate on the device when Thomas interrupted him, "It will —"

"Somebody land the plane!" Alex yelled.

"Yeah, right," Thomas said. "Sorry. The Jukebox Four's smaller than a green pea. It's small enough for Sullivan to put somewhere in the Oval Office. That's why I gave it to her. Not only will it record but it'll transmit those conversations. So, if she deploys it, then whoever it transmits to will have a lot of the President's conversations, and then people will know what the score is."

"Any conversations the President had with anyone will be recorded and transmitted?" CD asked, then continued. "So, if Armstrong threatened her or anything, there must be evidence of it out there if this device worked the way it's supposed to."

"Right," Ben said. "It can transmit any number of files. Each file will contain about ten minutes of run-time. The device does not retain any files. It records, transmit, and deletes, records, transmits, deletes, on and on."

"But we don't know if she deployed it," Rufus said. "We don't even know if she was in the Oval Office. I would think he's got that office swept pretty often, so even if she planted the bug, he would find it within the day. At least, that's my guess."

"One thing I was going to tell y'all, but Alex was yelling to land the plane, is that the transmissions are burst transmissions that take less than a second, including the deleting of the file, and except for when it's transmitting, the device is sleep and undetectable. The only other time it can conceivably be detected is when it's recording. It'll only be recording if there's an active conversation and probably there's no conversation going on until after, not during, a detection sweep," Ben said. "No guarantees, but the chances are stacked against its being detected by a routine sweep."

"So, if there were any conversations exonerating Sullivan or showing Armstrong's plot to kill all of us, they were hopefully transmitted somewhere. Probably to Sullivan herself, in which case when they seized her, they probably seized that evidence also," Olive said.

"I hope she was smart enough to have the transmissions sent to other people, not just her," Alex said.

"The President's an asshole. I hope she put that bug in his ass," Thomas said.

"I wonder what Sullivan would think of that transmission," Ben said, and they all laughed.

After they had regained their composure, Thomas said, "OK, I think we're getting back in the driver's seat. Let's get that video uploaded."

They quickly discussed and refined the plan to launch the virtual computer from the street in front of the BWI terminal. Then it was decided that Olive and CD, disguised, would make the trip to BWI and upload the video to the virtual computer. Within a couple of hours, Ben, Thomas, and Alex had put together the complete DFID analysis exposing the President's duplicity in attempting to frame Sullivan with deep fake technology, and CD and Olive left for BWI.

Chapter 126

"Douglas, we've got to meet," TT's voice was frantic.

"No names!" Cordero exclaimed. "I'm already where no one can find me. Are you using a burner?"

"Of course," TT replied. Both men were using cell phones which they were confident could not be traced. "Caroline must have put that bug in Armstrong's office. Did you receive the transmission?"

"I did," Cordero said. "Armstrong's playing for keeps. Sullivan's been arrested. So, what do we do now?" Cordero sounded desperate.

"Just stay calm. First, let's make sure we have the same transmission. What does yours say?" TT asked.

"It's just a strange telephone conversation where the President asks the person on the other end of the call whether it's foggy there. Then he says release the video on Sullivan."

"And then he says not to release a video on anyone else. That's got to mean that he has a video on us, too." TT continued. "OK, we've got the same transmission. Armstrong's somehow manufactured this video of Sullivan plotting a government overthrow. We now know from the recording that that video's not authentic. So, here's what we've got. A recording of Armstrong ordering someone to release a video of Sullivan. I know certain journalists that we can rely on. I say we give it to them," TT said, still trying to calm Cordero.

"That's risky. You're right, he's obviously got videos on you and me, too." Cordero's voice still sounded close to panic. "How the hell did he make these videos? And how do we use this recording of Armstrong's framing Sullivan without exposing ourselves? Once we email it to your journalists, Armstrong's people will know where we are. And who's behind this? Who's Armstrong using?"

"I have no idea, but listen, I think I can manage getting this transmission into the right hands. Sit tight and leave it to me. OK?" TT waited for Cordero's agreement.

"OK," Cordero said, relieved that TT was handling matters.

Chapter 127

National pandemonium erupted when the clones' video analysis exposed the Sullivan video as a fraud. The clones' video swamped the Internet, and every television news channel immediately broadcast it. Social media exploded to the degree that a number of major servers were overloaded. Channels, streaming platforms, and other live media assembled experts as quickly as they could to discuss deep fake and to discuss the diagnostic video the clones had posted. Media from around the world referred to the unfolding events as "The Unraveling of America," "The End of America's Democratic Experiment," "America Finished," "America's Return to Authoritarianism," "Armstrong — The New Nixon?," and "The Collapse of Sanity."

Within an hour of the clones' video becoming public, even CSPAN had created a special panel discussion featuring a well-known criminal lawyer and a cyber security expert:

Moderator: [After briefly describing what deep fake is]: How can we be sure that the clones', alleged clones, video itself is not deep fake?

Cyber Expert: The alleged clones aren't the only ones who have the means to analyze a video to discern whether it's genuine or whether it's deep fake. Apps are available for that purpose and, to be sure, our intelligence services also have the best deep fake technology in the world. Presumably we'll hear from them.

Moderator: We have in fact submitted both videos, the original Sullivan video and also the clones' video analyzing the Sullivan video, to an independent lab for their analysis. But let me continue. All of this raises a very troubling question. Did the CIA know that the Sullivan video was a fake, or did other agencies of the government know?

Cyber Expert: Good question. We don't know that yet. Caroline Sullivan's head of the CIA, so I doubt the CIA had anything to do with it. If by chance some other agency or agencies knew or were part of it, then we have a conspiracy that'll dwarf any scandal that this country has ever had. Somebody created the fake video about Sullivan, and the President may well have colluded with whoever it was.

Lawyer: If the President was knowingly involved, that's definitely criminal conspiracy.

Moderator: We're looking at impeachment?

Lawyer: I would say we're looking at least at impeachment and, if he's involved, the crime of the century. Clearly, if the President was involved, he's finished. Then the question is, can we constitutionally and legally get him out of office quickly enough before he does something else unthinkable, like get us into a war or have someone killed.

Moderator: Is there any way other than impeachment proceedings to stop the President? What about the twenty-fifth amendment?

Lawyer: The twenty-fifth amendment on paper should work. We've never used it before, at least not like this, but if the Vice President and a majority of the Cabinet declare the President is, in the words of the amendment unable to discharge the powers and duties of his office, then Armstrong can be removed.

Moderator: What does it mean, 'unable'?

Lawyer: I think it would mean whatever the Vice President and the Cabinet want it to mean.

Moderator: Can the President be arrested?

Lawyer: In my view, if the evidence is incontrovertible, he can be arrested even before the twenty-fifth amendment is invoked. Why not?

Cyber Expert: Let's don't stampede here. We don't know for a fact that the President was involved. I'm not a lawyer, but this video, the Sullivan video, could have been created and disseminated entirely without the President's knowledge. He could be completely innocent of any wrongdoing. This could be an elaborate plot propelling us to a conclusion about President Armstrong that's wholly unwarranted and false. After all, he does have enemies. He obviously couldn't create a deep fake video himself, and we don't currently have any smoking gun connecting him with the Sullivan video.

Moderator: So even if he's in some way involved, he stays in office until we have a smoking gun?

Lawyer: Right. No smoking gun, he remains President.

[Pause]

Moderator [Reading a paper just handed her]: I have just been told by our producer that the video which was apparently uploaded onto social media by the clones is indeed not a fake. That video, I repeat, is not a fake. This is from the non-government, independent lab which we have asked to analyze both videos. For viewers, that lab is Quinn Videographical Labs, LLC, located in Oregon. To repeat, the clones' video has not been tampered with and is not a fake. That video is genuine. That video analysis, that is, the clones' video, is an analysis of the earlier Sullivan video in which someone who appeared to be CIA Director Caroline Sullivan was digitally modified and plotting insurrection against the American government. This might sound confusing since we have two videos so let me try to make it clearer for our viewers. Video number one is the Sullivan video in which someone who appears to be CIA Director Caroline Sullivan is plotting insurrection against the American government. Video number two's the clones' video which seems to prove that video one, the Sullivan video is fraudulent. Our independent lab verifies that the clones' video is genuine. This, the clones' video, presents a technical analysis of video number one and concludes that video number one, the Sullivan video, is a fake, that Sullivan never said the things depicted in that video. We don't yet have an independent analysis of the Sullivan video. We do have the clones' analysis, but we're awaiting an independent appraisal of the video in which Sullivan is presented as plotting against the government.

Lawyer: We know that the CIA among its many triumphs at the same time has a sordid history of human rights abuses, like the LSD experiments of the 1950's all the way up to its use of black sites during the Bush Administration to their validation of the documents which they knew were fraudulent in the Trump-Russia collusion mess, not to mentions the CIA's continuing illegal surveillance of American citizens within our own borders. Therefore, we shouldn't be surprised if that agency is up to its eyeballs in the current cesspool.

Cyber Expert: But I have to doubt that the CIA's part of this. After all, Caroline Sullivan is head of the CIA.

Lawyer: But remember that she's so new in that position that things can be happening there that she knows nothing about yet.

[Pause]

Moderator [gripping her earpiece]: And now I have it from our independent lab, the Quinn Lab, that the original video of CIA Director Sullivan conspiring to assassinate the President and overthrow the government of the United States is a fake. To repeat, that video purporting to show CIA Director Caroline Sullivan conspiring to overthrow the American government is a fake. [The moderator is handed a paper from offscreen and refers to that paper.] By a technology known as deep fake, the Sullivan video is a hoax. Therefore, our outside, nongovernment lab validates the analysis of the clones' video, that the video purporting to show CIA Director Caroline Sullivan plotting against the government is a fake. In view of these two analyses, CSPAN will not show the Sullivan video again. Though we don't have incontrovertible proof of the origin of the fake Sullivan video, the White House has released no statement regarding it. They have surely had time to do so. This stunning turn of events, to say the least, is damning evidence implying a scandal and corruption beyond anything in the history of this country, but just who's behind the scandal, we don't know yet.

Chapter 128

TT's contact at one of the major cable channels arranged for TT to be on a remote, undisclosed set to reveal the contents of the office recording of the President's mysterious telephone conversation.

"Mr. Attorney General, are you ready to go on air?" the anchorman asked.

"I am, Mr. Harvey. Let's get it done," TT said. TT, normally robust looking and fit, now looked drawn and grim.

The anchor then gave the signal to the broadcast team to break into the current program, which was, of course, a panel discussion of the deep fake story.

The camera focused in on the anchorman and TT.

Anchor: We are interrupting the program you're currently watching to bring you additional major news concerning the American presidency. As you already know, if you've been watching our coverage of the current political storm now raging throughout the nation, what's now being referred to as the Sullivan video has been labeled by outside experts as a technological hoax, a fake. That video presents a computer-generated Sullivan that's so life-like that it required a sophisticated, highly technical analysis to discern that it's indeed a fake. Therefore, Director Sullivan never said the things that that video claimed. And secondly, a video submitted by the clones and somehow posted widely on social media gives a technical analysis which also exposes the Sullivan video as a fake, and it was actually the clones' video which first revealed that the Sullivan video was fraudulent. I have with me the Attorney General, Mr. Anthony Trentini. The Attorney General's here to add another element to this sad chapter of our nation's history in which we find ourselves. Let me say at the outset that we're at an undisclosed location because there's sufficient reason to think that the Attorney General himself could be in some danger. Our network has agreed with the Attorney General that we'll disclose neither his location nor other facts concerning what he's about to tell us. Attorney General Trentini has come into possession of an audio recording apparently made in the Oval Office of a brief telephone conversation which apparently the President had with an unidentified party. The recording is only twenty-two seconds long. The recording does not capture whoever's on the other end of the conversation, so we have only one side of the conversation. Until now, there has been no direct link between President Armstrong and the fraudulent Sullivan video. This audio recording addresses that link between the President and the Sullivan video. We'll now play that recording."

A transcript on the screen accompanied the recording:

"Is it foggy there?"

[A Pause]

"Release the video on Sullivan. Only that bitch, not anyone else yet."

[A Pause]

"You're absolutely positive that the video will work?"

[A Pause]

"OK, run it."

Anchorman: We are going to run that recording again.

[Recording runs a second time.]
At the conclusion of the second playing of the recording, TT and the anchorman just stared at each other for a few seconds. Then the anchorman resumed the interview.

Anchor: How can we be sure that this recording's authentic? And how was it made?

TT: A voice analysis, which we haven't yet had a chance to do, can confirm that what we heard is the President's voice. I think we can all recognize his distinctive voice. And to your second question, I don't know how it was made. I suspect that Director Sullivan planted a device in the Oval Office. Director Sullivan, Secretary Cordero, and I met with the President in the Oval Office and confronted him concerning his plan to eliminate the clones, so my guess is that Director Sullivan planted the bug sometime during that meeting. She runs the CIA. She surely has access to state-of-the-art bugging equipment which can be surreptitiously planted even while in the presence of other people. She probably realized that the President has gone off the rails and that some surveillance was a wise course of action.

Anchor: Off the rails? Are you actually saying that the President of the United States is unstable and is himself a threat to the nation?

TT [after a significant pause]: Yes, regrettably yes, Mr. Harvey. His plan, his plot, is to eliminate all of the clones and everyone who has helped them remain out of Armstrong's clutches. Mr. Harvey, there's a lot that you and I haven't gone into. For example, at a secret location, Director Sullivan, Secretary Cordero and I met, and Director Sullivan shared a written, presidential document with us in which the President outlined his plans. Director Sullivan explained to us that President Armstrong had sworn her to secrecy when he gave her that document, and I might add, that when the three of us met with the President in the Oval Office and confronted him, the President threatened us with criminal action and lengthy jail time if we divulge anything about his plans. OK, back to the meeting which Sullivan, Cordero, and I had at the secret government facility—-

Anchorman: Before you go further, Mr. Attorney General, can you tell us something about this facility. Where is it? What's its purpose? What's its name?

TT: No, Mr. Harvey, I'm not going to go into that.

Anchorman: Why not? That would just add credibility to what you're telling us.

TT: Mr. Harvey, I'm here to share the audio recording with you that you just played twice on the air. I won't go into tangential stuff. But I can tell you a little about what transpired at that facility if you want me to.

Anchorman: I understand, Mr. Trentini. Please go ahead.

TT: We discovered that the clones were being held incommunicado at that very same installation. We met with them. Mr. Harvey, we all -—me, Secretary Cordero, and Director Sullivan -—concluded that they are genuinely, authentically, clones of Thomas Jefferson and Alexander Hamilton. We didn't meet the Benjamin Franklin clone. He is apparently being held by the Russians. I have no idea how that happened, but they somehow got hold of him. The President planned to send a kill squad to Moscow to eliminate the Franklin clone. We know that there's a George Washington clone, but I haven't met him and don't know where he is. Mr. Harvey, as I mentioned, the three of us met with the President in the Oval Office, and in light of his plot, the President's own plot in his own words, we asked him to resign and spare the nation a nightmare. His effort to discredit Director Sullivan with this fake video is his answer.

Anchor: Have you been threatened, Mr. Secretary?

TT: No, I haven't, other than as I mentioned, he threatened us with criminal action if we revealed his plans. Other than that, no, I haven't been threatened, but I'm sure that he'll come after me and Secretary Cordero just as he's trying to eliminate Director Sullivan.

Anchor: I want it to be clear, Mr. Attorney General. You're saying definitively that the Franklin clone is a captive of the Russians?"

TT: The President's document says so. Yes.

Anchor: And you're saying that the Washington clone is alive?

TT: The document says he is. Yes.

Anchor: Do you know where he is, whether he's in government custody, or whether he's in hiding somewhere?

TT: I don't know where he is. I'm hoping that at some point in the near future, he'll come forth. We need him.

Anchor: This document in which the President outlined his plans to eliminate the clones. Can you describe that document? For example, does it bear the President's signature? I have a hard time comprehending why he would commit such a plan to writing.

TT: It's a digital document. I saw it in an encrypted email from the President to Director Sullivan. Director Sullivan has it. I've read the document, and so has Secretary Cordero.

Anchor: Why would the President put such a plan into writing?

TT: Good question, Mr. Harvey. Ask him. I personally think it indicates his mental instability.

Anchor: For the record, our producer has asked the White House for a statement, but we don't have a statement yet. A final question, Mr. Trentini. What do you plan to do with this information?

TT: I'm doing it right now. It's now public knowledge. Thank you for letting me bring this information to the public.

Anchor: Thank you, Mr. Attorney General.

It took only seconds for the national firestorm to burst into full blaze.

Chapter 129

As soon as the Sullivan video surfaced, FBI Director Jonathan Fogg had quickly assembled an eight-person team of the FBI's most experienced and least tainted agents and policymakers to discuss whether the FBI should intervene in the current situation and, if so, how. Once the Sullivan video was shown to be a fake and with the revelation that the President was directly linked to the video, the FBI team felt a new urgency to contain the damage that President Armstrong could inflict on the nation. With assistance from the news channel which had just broadcast TT's interview, TT joined that meeting from the remote location.

Once his link to the meeting was established, TT said, "Director Fogg, you're the Director of the FBI. The FBI, in spite of the abuses of recent years, is reestablishing itself as a reliable and patriotic, rule-of-law institution. However, we're in a situation in which there're no laws to rule us. We've got to be guided by principles of right and wrong and do what's required to protect our nation's democracy. Within constitutional boundaries, we must do what's in the national interest to rid ourselves of the greatest abuse of power ever —ever — in this country. Indeed, it dwarfs Watergate. It dwarfs what Trump did to trigger his second impeachment. So, Mr. Fogg, what does your team recommend?"

"Mr. Attorney General, there are no judicial precedents indicating that we cannot arrest a sitting President, and there are no precedents indicating that we can. Therefore, we're guided by the fundamental principle that as a rule-of-law agency, when we observe deliberate actions by anyone which beyond a reasonable doubt amount to an insurrection and also constitute criminal conspiracy, we feel duty-bound to arrest. We could wait for the twenty-fifth amendment processes; however, even if the Vice President and the Cabinet declared the President disabled, there's a likelihood that the President would contest the action or deliberately not comply. During that time elapse, he could do substantial damage to the nation and even commit criminal acts not only against the Franklin and Washington clones but also against anyone else whom he perceives as standing in his way. Mr. Attorney General, we recommend that we go to the White House immediately and arrest the President."

TT, without hesitation agreed. "I totally concur, Mr. Fogg. And once you have him what then?"

"We'll secure him in a hotel under very close guard and let the judicial processes take place or the twenty-fifth amendment or whatever. Our immediate job's to stop the national hemorrhaging and prevent the President from doing irreparable damage to the nation. If he's off the rails as you described it in your television interview, Mr. Attorney General, he could even get us into a war or do something disastrous. We can't stand by and let that happen."

"We're on the same page, Mr. Fogg. I authorize the arrest and will send you a document right now and will memorialize it at the appropriate places. How long before you'll have him in custody, do you think?"

"Assuming that the secret service will let us into the White House, I would say thirty minutes to one hour."

"Their oath is to the Constitution, not to the President," TT replied. "They'll let you in with the proper document which I'm transmitting to you now. Plus, I'll get a warrant from the same judge we always use for short notice stuff. That should take only a few minutes. I'll have the judge email it to you so you can receive it on the way to the White House. Same thing with my DOJ Order."

"Thank you, TT."

Chapter 130

As developments and speculations swirled throughout the nation, the White House finally issued the following statement:

> The President will give a live address to the nation at 7:30 P.M. He intends for his statement to resolve the issues and to expose the falsehoods that have been spreading through the media. The President implores all of America not to be deceived by persons pretending to have the nation's interests at heart. The President is convinced that the high-tech trial and conviction of him and his presidency that has already taken place is a dangerous conspiracy to undermine his Administration, and he asks all Americans to await his statement with an open mind and an open heart.

Widespread skepticism greeted the White House's announcement. It was already widely anticipated that President Armstrong would resign. He gave only one hour's notice for his upcoming statement, and this caused a mad scramble by the nation's major news organizations to cram into the Oval Office. The President chose the Oval Office for his statement rather than the Media Club, even though the Oval Office was smaller. Every news person with any kind of credentials descended on the White House. When 7:30 P.M. arrived and the cameras were set up, the President was still not in the Oval Office. The reporters grew restless and a number began shouting that the President was probably not even in the White House, that he might well have fled the country.

President Armstrong walked slowly into the room. Few had seen him enter the room as everyone was watching the door of his private entrance, the door known as the "President's Door." But on this night, contrary to regular practice, the President entered from the outer office, the reception area through which almost all visitors entered the Oval Office. The President turned back towards the door and slowly shut it. His actions seemed to be in slow motion, labored, and deliberate, like he was a man about to break. A hush fell over the journalists and anchors as the President made his way to his desk. Ordinarily, the President would greet newspersons whom he favored, but tonight he seemed detached and greeted no one, nor did he make eye contact with anyone. Even through the television lens, viewers saw a President that they had never seen before. He looked smaller than before, withered, beaten down, and at the same time angry, as if in the grip of his own demons from within.

One perceptive newswoman could be heard whispering to a colleague, "What's wrong with him? He looks drugged."

"Or almost dead," another muttered.

"Shhhhhhh," was the response from a number of persons as everyone closely watched the President.

The President circled behind his orderly desk and then sat heavily. There were no miniature flags on the desk, no pictures, no mementoes of past encounters, only a few papers.

"Ladies and gentlemen and my fellow Americans," the unsmiling President began, his speaking cadence uncharacteristically slow. "I have strived to lead this country into a new world where we could not only revitalize America, provide programs to make everyone's lives better, and to bring proper medical care, material success, and opportunity to everyone. I have also done what I could do to tackle the difficult problem of climate change. And I have tried to streamline our economy so that we can compete with the Chinese and other emerging economies. I anticipated resistance from the other party, and though their resistance has been duplicitous and dirty, that seems to be the way the Washington game is played, at least by my Republican opponents. But on top of all of that, a private company run by a Russian agent has perpetrated the greatest hoax in the history of science. She has pretended to clone humans, and not just humans, but some of our nation's founding fathers. Well, I am here to tell you that that is all a hoax. She, Marina Novokatnaia, has fled to Russia. That shows her true colors. Those co-called clones have hounded my every effort. They are a devious creation of the other party, with the assistance of this Russian agent, designed to destroy my Administration, and given their corrupt and despicable use of new technology, I have to admit they have succeeded. And I might add, they have succeeded largely because you, members of the press, consistent with your pattern ever since 2016, have filled the airwaves and social media with innuendo, spite, vitriol, and hate. I've invited you here tonight because as the leaders of our nation's media, you do deserve the chance to be in on the ground floor of how this issue will be resolved. You've earned the right to be here tonight. I wanted you here tonight, with me in this Oval Office.

"Tonight, I will move this whole issue to a resolution. We've witnessed a sorry chapter written by men and women who despise the America I was trying to move us towards -—an America where the government is your friend, not your enemy. A government which gives, not one which just takes away. A government which sponsors programs and opportunities that enable every American to thrive, not just to survive. A government that promotes equity, not enmity. The America which my opponents are forcing on you, my fellow Americans, is an anachronism. It is one of racism, limited opportunity, semi-fascism, and dog-eat-dog. I don't want to live in that America, and you shouldn't be forced to live in that America either."

Several perceptive newspersons glanced nervously at each other as the President said these words. One muttered, "What the fuck is he up to?" Several persons near the back of the room moved to the door from which the President had entered.

Tension in the room mounted as the President opened the top, middle drawer of his ornate desk. One prominent tv anchorwoman attempting to exit the Oval Office loudly exclaimed, "The door is locked!"

Two men rushed to the door. They jerked on the doorknob, but the reinforced door would not yield. One man shouted, "What the hell—!"

The cameramen zoomed in on the President as he stood and held a small black object in his hand, his thumb on the red button. Without a word, President Armstrong smiled and pressed the button. The horrific explosion was immediate and devastating.

For the first time in American history, a mass murder had occurred in the nation's capital. Subsequent analysis would show that everyone in the room was killed instantly. The forensics would reveal that the explosive agent was bis-oxadiazole, an experimental explosive twice as powerful as TNT, recently developed by the American military. It would never be learned where, when, or from whom President Armstrong had procured that material. Nor would it ever be learned whom Armstrong conspired with to produce the Sullivan video.

Chapter 131

The clones, as so many in the nation, had watched in horror as the President's suicide and simultaneous murder of all those assembled in the Oval Office was telecast live until the instant when the transmission was severed by the explosion. The national response was immediate on all fronts. Vice President Esposito at that moment was fortuitously at the Supreme Court where a reception for newly appointed federal judges was scheduled for later that evening, and he was sworn in immediately by the Chief Justice. Then from the Court's own meager media facilities, Esposito immediately went on national television to reassure the nation that the injured machinery of the American government would function without interruption. Then President Esposito publicly committed to eliminate in totality Armstrong's plot against the clones and against members of the Executive branch and to welcome the clones into what he called "a healing relationship of trust and counsel."

CIA Director Sullivan had never actually been arrested. She had secreted herself in a CIA safe house in Georgetown as soon as the video attempting to frame her had surfaced. She quickly established communications with the clones, and one day later, Benjamin Franklin, Thomas Jefferson, Alexander Hamilton, CD, Olive, and Rufus were assembled along with top members of the Esposito Administration in the Cabinet Room in the White House.

President Esposito started the meeting. "I want your prayers, God's guidance and your own guidance, your wisdom, and your counsel every step of the way as we try to restore those American values which have been desecrated and abandoned over the past months and years. This presidency, indeed, the nation's mission, is now about a National Restoration. Can I count on you?"

Everyone readily and noisily agreed. At that moment, the door opened and a tall, broad shouldered man with an intensely serious look walked into the room.

President Esposito stood. "Welcome, Mr. Washington. The Secret Service alerted me that you were in the building." Esposito quickly moved to shake Mr. Washington's hand, then withdrew his hand. "No, that won't do," the President said, and then he and George Washington hugged. The sincerity of their embrace was obvious to all in the room.

"Remarkable!" CD whispered.

"Beyond," was all Olive could say in her whispered reply.

"That's him," Thomas whispered to Alex and Ben. The expressions that all three had were almost worshipful.

"Yes," Benjamin Franklin whispered back. "Now, finally, we can begin."

Alex, Thomas, and Ben were still stunned to actually see in person their colleague whom they knew existed but had never laid eyes on before and had at one time even thought was dead. Restrained no longer, Ben, Alex, and Thomas leaped from their chairs and surrounded and hugged George Washington. The room erupted in applause. The tears flowed, and not only from the clones.

Everyone in the room instinctively stood and grew completely quiet as George Washington walked to the empty chair at the far end of the conference table and said to the assemblage, "Mr. President. We're all here to serve our nation and to help with the National Restoration. I am at your service."

"As I heard Lady Olive whisper just a moment ago, what we must do is beyond history, my friends." Then Washington said with force. "Let's begin."

Olive leaned over and whispered to CD, "The fathers have returned." CD, too emotional to say anything, just squeezed her hand and smiled.

President Esposito's gaze slowly rounded the table and from one person to the next, he made eye contact with each. Finally, he focused intently on George Washington, smiled, and announced with reverence, "Our thank you's go to the Holy Spirit." The new President paused, then said forcefully, "Yes, let's begin. America awaits us."

"Oh, and by the way," George Washington said with a broad smile. "I do not, repeat, do not, have wooden teeth." Everyone in the room laughed.

THE END